Blackburn

TOURISM AND GENDER
Embodiment, Sensuality and Experience

This book is dedicated to
James Mahony (1938–2006)
Elsie Davies and Grace Morgan
Tina Ateljevic
Sue Harris

TOURISM AND GENDER
Embodiment, Sensuality and Experience

Edited by

Annette Pritchard

The Welsh Centre for Tourism Research
University of Wales Institute, Cardiff, UK

Nigel Morgan

The Welsh Centre for Tourism Research
University of Wales Institute, Cardiff, UK

Irena Ateljevic

Wageningen University
Wageningen, The Netherlands

and

Candice Harris

Auckland University of Technology
Auckland, New Zealand

CABI is a trading name of CAB International

CABI Head Office
Nosworthy Way
Wallingford
Oxfordshire OX10 8DE
UK

CABI North American Office
875 Massachusetts Avenue
7th Floor
Cambridge, MA 02139
USA

Tel: +44 (0)1491 832111
Fax: +44 (0)1491 833508
E-mail: cabi@cabi.org
Website: www.cabi.org

Tel: +1 617 395 4056
Fax: +1 617 354 6875
E-mail: cabi-nao@cabi.org

A catalogue record for this book is available from the British Library, London, UK.

Library of Congress Cataloging-in-Publication Data

Tourism and gender : embodiment, sensuality, and experience/edited by Annette Pritchard ... [et al.].
      p. cm.
   Includes bibliographical references and index.
   ISBN 978-1-84593-271-8 (alk. paper)
   1. Tourism -- Psychological aspects. 2. Tourists -- Sexual behavior. 3. Tourists -- Attitudes. 4. Gender identity. I. Pritchard, Annette. II. Title.
   G155.A1T5893482 2007
   306.4´819--dc22

2007004442

ISBN-13: 978 1 84593 271 8

Typeset by SPi, Pondicherry, India.
Printed and bound in the UK by Biddles Ltd, King's Lynn.

Contents

Contributors

Martine Abramovici is a PhD candidate in tourism in the Faculty of Business at Auckland University of Technology. Martine's PhD focuses on Italian women and tanning, revealing the body to be a focal point in understanding Italian contemporary society. Her research interests include postmodern consumer society and identity, sociocultural issues, gender issues, the body and embodiment and critical approaches to research.

Irena Ateljevic received her doctoral degree in human geography in 1998 at the University of Auckland, New Zealand. She is currently positioned within the Socio-Spatial Analysis Group at Wageningen University, the Netherlands, and is interested in the cultural complexities of gender, class, age and ethnicity in the production and consumption of tourist spaces and experiences, and how their intersection reproduces power relations of injustice and inequality.

Fabrice Desmarais is a Lecturer in the Department of Management Communication at the University of Waikato, New Zealand. His main area of interest is advertising, in particular how it connects with culture and other areas of study such as sports and tourism.

Sermin Elmas received her Master's and doctoral degrees in Sociology from the Middle East Technical University, Ankara, Turkey. She started to work as a full-time instructor in the School of Applied Technology and Management, Bilkent University, Ankara, in 1991. She teaches tourism sociology, organizational behaviour, social psychology and ethics in the hospitality industry, and has published on tourism sociology and women's studies.

Nashwa Samir El-Sherif Ibrahim lectures in the Faculty of Tourism and Hotels in Helwan University in Egypt. She studied for her PhD in the Welsh School of Hospitality, Tourism and Leisure Management at the University of Wales Institute, Cardiff. Her research interests include gender, human rights and human resources issues in tourism management.

Simone Fullagar is an interdisciplinary sociologist with a post-structuralist interest in questions about leisure, tourism and well-being. She has published widely on narratives of travel and leisure, youth suicide prevention and women's recovery from depression. She is a Senior Lecturer within the Department of Tourism, Leisure, Hotel and Sport Management, in conjunction with the Centre for Work, Leisure and Community Research, Griffith University, Australia.

Huimin Gu is Professor and Deputy Dean of the School of Tourism Management at Beijing International Studies University and an Honoured Professor of the Beijing Tourism Bureau. She has studied in Australia and was a Visiting Scholar at the Hilton Conrad College, University of Houston, while she obtained her doctoral degree from the Renmin University of China Business School. In addition to translations, she has published five books including *Traces of Home: The Development of Dragon Hotel* (with Chen Guorao, 2002) and *Tourism Marketing* (2002). She is currently working with Chris Ryan on a Chinese version of *Researching Tourist Satisfaction*, initially published by Routledge in 1995.

Derek Hall is a partner of Seabank Associates and a Visiting Professor at HAMK University of Applied Sciences, Finland. He lives in Scotland and has long-standing research and publication interests in tourism and gender issues, tourism and regional development in socialist and post-socialist societies, and in transport policy.

Kevin Hannam is Professor and Head of Tourism at the University of Sunderland, UK. He has published widely on a range of tourism matters and is currently editing a book on backpacker tourism. He is the co-editor of the journal *Mobilities*.

Candice Harris is a Senior Lecturer in Management in the Faculty of Business at Auckland University of Technology, Auckland, New Zealand. Her PhD obtained from Victoria University focused on New Zealand women as business travellers. Her research interests include gender and diversity issues in tourism and management, human resource management, and qualitative and critical approaches to research.

Eleri Jones was Head of the Welsh School of Hospitality, Tourism and Leisure Management, which is now part of Cardiff School of Management at the University of Wales Institute, Cardiff. Her research interests focus on issues relating to sustainability and destination development with a focus on human resourcing issues, especially management and leadership issues. She leads a portfolio of European and other projects and is involved in the supervision of a number of international MPhil and PhD research degree candidates.

Fiona Jordan is with the School of Geography and Environmental Management at the University of the West of England, Bristol, UK. Her research centres on the ways in which leisure and holiday spaces and places are represented and consumed. Her doctoral study focused on the experiences of women travelling alone and this, together with explorations of the representation of tourism in popular cultural forms such as women's and men's lifestyle magazines, has formed the basis of her recent publications.

Dan Knox is a Senior Lecturer in Tourism at the University of Sunderland, UK. He has research interests in critical tourism theory, embodiment and practice, popular cultures, everyday lives and the relations between national heritage and identity.

Nigel Morgan is a Professor of Tourism Studies at the Cardiff School of Management's Welsh Centre for Tourism Research at the University of Wales Institute, Cardiff. He has published widely on the sociocultural dimensions of tourism and destination marketing, including several books and numerous research papers and book chapters.

Chaim Noy is an independent scholar, presently teaching at the Departments of Communication, Sociology and Anthropology at the Hebrew University of Jerusalem. His recent publications include *A Narrative Community: Voices of Israeli Backpackers* (Wayne State University Press, 2007) and *Israeli Backpackers: From Tourism to a Rite of Passage* (SUNY Press, 2005; co-edited with Erik Cohen).

Yaniv Poria is located in the Department of Hotel and Tourism Management, Ben Gurion University of the Negev, Be'er sheva, Israel. His main research interest is the management of heritage in tourism and he also writes on gay and lesbian tourist experiences.

Annette Pritchard is a Reader and Director of the Cardiff School of Management's Welsh Centre for Tourism Research at the University of Wales Institute, Cardiff. She has published eight books and numerous research papers on the relationships between tourism, representation and social structures, experiences and identities.

Greg Ringer is an Adjunct Professor in the Department of Planning, Public Policy and Management in the University of Oregon. Greg lectures on international tourism planning and women's studies at the University of Oregon, and serves as Visiting Professor at universities in Africa, Eurasia, Latin and North America, and the Pacific. He is also principal consultant for DrGreg & Friends, a non-profit tourism cooperative which promotes sustainable community development and gender equality through travel.

Chris Ryan is a Professor of Tourism at The University of Waikato Management School, Hamilton, New Zealand. He is the editor of the journal *Tourism Management*, and a Fellow of the International Academy for the Study of Tourism. His books include *The Tourism Experience* (Continuum, 2002) and *Recreational Tourism: Demand and Impacts* (Channel View, 2003). He gained a doctoral degree at the Aston University Business School, UK. He has published over 80 refereed journal articles and undertaken various reports for governmental bodies.

Diane Sedgley is a Senior Lecturer in the Cardiff School of Management's Welsh Centre for Tourism Research at the University of Wales Institute, Cardiff. Her research interests focus on the experiences of minority groups in tourism and leisure. She has published on lesbian and gay tourism and leisure, and is currently involved in research which seeks to understand older women's leisure and tourism experiences.

Jennie Small is a Senior Lecturer in the School of Leisure, Sport and Tourism at the University of Technology, Sydney. Her specific research interest is tourist behaviour in terms of gender, age, disability (mobility and vision impairment) and embodiment. More generally, she is interested in a Critical Tourism approach to tourist behaviour.

Anu Valtonen works as Marketing Professor at the Faculty of Business and Tourism at the University of Lapland, Rovaniemi, Finland. Her major research interests relate to consumer studies, consumer culture, leisure studies and culture theories and methodologies. She is a researcher at the *Tourism as Work* project.

Jeanne van Eeden is an Associate Professor in the Department of Visual Arts, University of Pretoria, South Africa. She is particularly interested in the role of the entertainment and leisure economy in postcolonial South African visual culture and is the co-editor of the book *South African Visual Culture* (Van Schaik, 2005).

Soile Veijola is a sociologist and works at the University of Lapland, Rovaniemi, Finland, as Professor of cultural studies of tourism. Her earlier publications include feminist critiques of theorizing on tourism (mostly co-authored with Eeva Jokinen) and analyses of mixed social orders in sports and society. She is currently leading an interdisciplinary research project entitled *Tourism as Work*.

Erica Wilson is a Lecturer in the School of Tourism and Hospitality Management at Southern Cross University in Lismore, Northern New South Wales. Her PhD from Griffith University focused on the solo travel experiences of Australian women, particularly the constraints they face and how these are negotiated. Her research interests lie with gender and tourism, the tourist experience, leisure constraints and negotiation, and qualitative research methodologies.

Foreword

The editors of this volume, Annette Pritchard, Nigel Morgan, Irena Ateljevic and Candice Harris are on the forefront of a re-energized focus on gender emanating from the critical turn now shaking up tourism's various academies. This collection of essays presents a dynamic project for Tourism Studies, continuing a challenge to us all to think within and outside of our own bodies, be they corporal and/or institutional, about the critical importance of gender equity in our daily world. As these essays demonstrate, gender does indeed matter. For the past decade or so, global feminist scholarship has encouraged us to approach our work in terms of 'intersectionality'. This most cumbersome of words has at its core a reminder that we are complex beings of many identities, limitations, resources, influences, positions and perceptions, studying equally complex situations located in multiple truths. The parsing of these truths as we build knowledge in Tourism Studies takes us back time and again to the diverse facts that shape our ontologies and methods of research, as well as our motivations to challenge the injustices we find along the way.

Being an old 'second waver' feminist myself who has believed in the primacy of gender relative to many other loci of inequalities including race, class, ethnicity, age, nationality, sexuality, ability, etc., the challenge of the 'third wave' to think only through intersections of these categories has caught me out in epistemological crisis, holding on to my ideas about patriarchy. Postmodernism's denial of structural inequalities adds another layer of questions we should address. A good map for negotiating these topographies can be found in reflexive embodiment theory, as we see in both the Editors' Introduction and many of the ensuing chapters. The volume's authors represent a range of nationalities from academies more or less like the ones in the UK and the USA discussed in the Introduction. Their locations are yet another difference we should be sensitive to while we build a truly cosmopolitan scholarship. As the next generation of tourism scholars moves into the Critical Studies arena of feminist analysis we are beginning to see their full-scale ethnographies and complex research projects. What are the concrete or glass ceilings and walls that they will encounter in their scholarship and how will they challenge them? This book leads the way.

Margaret Byrne Swain

Acknowledgements

No book is ever the result of four people's efforts and this book is certainly no exception. We would like to thank all our contributing authors for agreeing to be part of this project and then for cheerfully meeting our deadlines and for graciously allowing us to edit their hard work. We would also like to express our gratitude to our editorial and support team at CABI for their patience and guidance throughout the project. We are particularly grateful to Marlies van Hal whose hard work on the manuscript helped to make this book a reality: we could not have done it without you Marlies. We also owe a special debt of gratitude to two pioneers of gender research in tourism studies who have offered tremendous encouragement to our efforts: Margaret Swain (who also generously agreed to write a foreword to the collection) and Derek Hall (who as one of our original proposal reviewers and as a contributor has supported us throughout). Finally, the four of us owe so much to so many wonderful and supportive people – our families, our friends and our colleagues and students (past and present) - that to attempt to name you here would be an invidious task. Please forgive us and accept our simple thank you for inspiring and supporting us in this and all our efforts.

Annette Pritchard
Cardiff, Wales

Nigel Morgan
Cardiff, Wales

Irena Ateljevic
Wageningen, The Netherlands

Candice Harris
Auckland, New Zealand

20 December 2006

List of Tables

List of Figures

1 Editors' Introduction: Tourism, Gender, Embodiment and Experience

ANNETTE PRITCHARD, NIGEL MORGAN, IRENA ATELJEVIC AND CANDICE HARRIS

Introduction

Why do issues of gender, sexuality and embodiment matter in tourism? Before addressing this question and turning our attention to the implications of gender and embodiment for the tourism industry and its stakeholders, we first need to consider today's gendered world and our own gendered academic collectives so that we may better understand the power dynamics and discourses which shape tourism theory and practice. For some contemporary commentators, academic and activist discussions about gender are 'so last century', a debate out of place in today's post-modern world where relativity, fluidity and imagination have replaced universality, fixity and objectivity, where identities are conceived as performances – mutable, represented, relative and constructed. In such a world the structural inequalities suggested by 'gender' carry little weight, and concerns about the existence and consequences of social differences based on genders are seen to be 'politically old fashioned (as well as clearly detrimental to one's career, both inside and outside academia)' (Oakley, 2006, p. 19). Neither is gender 'sexy' for the woman on the street, and feminism is now so stereotyped and questioned (Chesler, 1997) that almost three-quarters of British women say that they are not feminists (available at: www.womankind.org.uk). It seems as though before we have really begun to unpick the complexities and implications of gender (and certainly before many research fields – including tourism – have engaged with the nuances of masculinities), Western societies have already become bored by issues of femininities, masculinities and genders. Yet, quite clearly, whatever our social or geographic location, whilst our experiences of (dis)empowerment and (in)equalities may vary, none of us live in equal societies and it is a worrying reality that not one country has yet managed to eliminate the gender gap (World Economic Forum, 2005).

In fact, some 40 years after the emergence of the western feminist movement, women everywhere remain severely disadvantaged compared to men across all social criteria and classifications. The statistics are truly shocking: the leading cause of injury and death for women worldwide is domestic violence; one in every three women is beaten, coerced into sex or abused in some other way (available at: www. amnesty.org.uk), and almost twice as many women as men are without adequate food, water, sanitation, health care or education (0.7 billion). In fact, global poverty has a woman's face: whilst 1.2 billion people live in poverty, three-quarters of the world's poorest people – those living in extreme poverty on less than US$1 a day – are women (Booth-Blair, 2005). Two-thirds of all illiterate adults are women and worldwide almost twice as many girls (85 million) as boys are denied schooling; in Chad fewer than 5% of girls go to school, whilst in Afghanistan the reinvigorated Taliban has burnt schools and beheaded teachers offering education to girls (Sengupta, 2006). Without comparable education provision, women continue to be denied access to well-paid formal-sector jobs and advanced opportunities, so that today's figure of almost two-thirds of unpaid family workers being female is unlikely to improve in the near future.

At the beginning of the 21st century then, female workers are still ghettoized across all countries, cultures and occupations; in the UK part-time female employees earn 42% less than their male counterparts, whilst in Japan full-time female workers earn just 51% of their male counterparts' wages (World Economic Forum, 2005). Moreover, in the EU women make up only 3% of major company chief executives, and in Australia only 12% of executive managers in the ASX 200 (Australian Stock Exchange) are women, whilst just six ASX 200 companies (3%) have female CEOs (World Economic Forum, 2005; Australian Government, 2006). For every ten men in executive suites in the world, there is one woman, a ratio that has changed little since the term 'glass ceiling' was first coined two decades ago – so much for its disappearance (*The Economist*, 2005). Women who are in managerial positions 'often need to make a painful choice between a successful career and family' (World Economic Forum, 2005, p. 4), and a recent study in the USA found that almost half of high-earning women had no children compared to less than a fifth of men (Hewlett, 2002). In 2005 women held 15% of all Fortune 500 board seats, which at the current pace of change means that it could take 70 years for women to reach parity with men on corporate boards (Catalyst, 2006a). For women of colour, the figures are even more deplorable and for them, a 'concrete ceiling' means that of the corporate officers in the Fortune 500 only 0.9% are African-American women, 0.4% Asian women and 0.3% Latinas (Catalyst, 2006b).

Such gender inequality is found not only in the business but also the political world, where 85% of the world's parliamentary seats are held by men (Inter-Parliamentary Union, May 2004) and women lead only 12 of the UN's 191 member countries. Indeed, women are under-represented in every sovereign legislature: in Arab countries only 8% of MPs are female and in the USA the picture is only marginally better as 14% of seats in the Congress are held by women. Shockingly, if women's representation in the US Congress continues to grow at its present rate, it will take a further 250 years to achieve a gender balance (Liswood, 2005). It is not surprising that, in this context, the UN has warned that millions of women across the globe are being denied effective representation because of the low numbers of female politicians, judges and employers (*The Independent*, 2006). Yet, in spite of such statistics, gender studies consistently fail to excite the imagination of the media, the general public or the wider social science academy. Indeed, in a recent exploration of the changing face of gender studies, Oakley (2006, p. 19) comments: 'Theorising *patriarchy* is a minority interest, regarded with mistrust as tainted with the politics of feminism, while the biases in our knowledge due to the politics of *masculinism* go largely unnoticed.'

Gender and the Social Science Academy

If our genders impact on both women and men, academia is no different and these gendered power dynamics and discourses also have implications for the ideological underpinnings which shape knowledge production in the wider social sciences and in tourism studies and management in particular. Whilst detailed information is not available for academies in all parts of the world, the research which does exist indicates that the glass ceiling remains firmly intact in our own sector for women seeking to move onto professorial grades; thus, for example, studies suggest that sex discrimination accounts for almost a quarter of the pay gap between men and women in British higher education. A further dimension to this worldwide inequality are 'glass walls', which have created 'women's ghettos' in the humanities, health sciences and education, with the disciplines of English and nursing being particularly ghettoized in this way (Conely, 2005). In such fields women are largely competing with each other to crack the glass ceiling and thus can run the risk of undermining many initiatives that can advance women's careers, such as mentoring and networking.

Regardless of whether a subject is perceived to be 'male' or 'female', women continue to be under-represented at its higher levels in countries like the UK (Rodgers, 2006), whilst in the USA women are grappling with a tenure system which actively discourages them from pursuing academic careers since its requirements make it hard for women to have children and to succeed. Research here demonstrates that female academics in the USA are increasingly avoiding having children and that female doctoral graduates are leaving to pursue careers in the more family-friendly private sector (Marcus, 2006). This 'maternal wall' brings female academics' careers to such a shuddering halt that men comprise over 60% of faculty at US degree-granting institutions – half of whom have tenure, compared to just over a third of women (Phillips and Garner, 2006). Whilst a small number of pioneering universities concerned with the absence of women in promoted posts (in countries such as New Zealand) are proactively establishing mentoring networks to help female academics compete, the upper echelons of higher education remain a male-dominated environment worldwide. Thus, Rosemary Deem recently described changes in British universities as 'glacial in respect of gender in academic posts' (quoted in Phillips and Garner, 2006, p. 19), with surveys reporting that fewer than 5% of female staff are professors compared to 16% of male staff, with men making up 86% of all UK professors. Clearly, in spite of over 30 years of UK sex discrimination legislation, 'there are few signs that female academics are achieving parity with men' (Wojtas, 2006, p. 9).

It emerges, therefore, that structural gender inequalities remain depressingly intact in the world's higher education academies. Significantly for the codification of social science knowledge (Spender, 1981), such inequalities exert an influence far beyond employment and promotion opportunities. A recent study reported in College and Research Libraries (Hakanson in Shepherd, 2006) suggests that male academics are less likely to cite work by their female colleagues in their own research papers. The study was conducted in the gender-balanced field of library and information sciences, yet it found that in papers authored by male academics 70% of citations related to the work of other men whereas, by comparison, female academics cited men and women in equal numbers. Similarly, Aitchison's study (2001) of tourism and leisure journals found that those journals with editorial boards dominated by men published a higher proportion of papers with male authors. Such scholarship highlights the wider phenomenon of gender discrimination in academic research, something which as yet has received very little attention from the academy. It seems opportune then, in our introduction to this collection of essays on gender and tourism, to briefly shine a light into the gloomy corners of the tourism academy and enter its dark Foucauldian world of discourse and power.

Gender and the Tourism Academy

It has been suggested that the study of tourism in all its aspects has the potential to fully embrace some of the new learnings which are reshaping approaches to academic teaching, learning, research and writing, and that its interdisciplinarity makes it particularly well placed to contribute to contemporary epistemological and ontological debates within the social sciences (Ateljevic *et al.*, 2007). However, one of the challenges for critical, interpretive tourism research is not only to confront the gendered nature of tourism experiences and discourses but also to dispute and deconstruct the dominant (masculinist) political and cultural discourses which shape and condition our academic lives and the lives of those with whom we co-create tourism knowledge. There has been a notable reluctance amongst the wider tourism community to unpick the politics of tourism research networks and a particular reticence to critique and problematize the roles of its academic gatekeepers and their influence on the production of tourism knowledge (for some exceptions, see Hall, 2004; Page, 2005). Responding to this challenge, work elsewhere demonstrates how key agents of academic communication in tourism (such as editorial boards and learned societies) remain largely white male clubs, dominated by masculinist research traditions and approaches (see Swain, 2004; Pritchard and Morgan, 2007). It will come as no surprise to readers of this collection then that in tourism (as in all academic fields) 'the very act of naming has been until now the prerogative of males' (Crotty, 1998, pp. 181–182). Indeed, tourism's scholarship continues to be largely rooted in the tenets of a rarely articulated or questioned masculinist scholarship governed by supposedly value-free principles of empiricism, quantification, neutrality, objectivity and distance. In this, the powerful myth which surrounds the dispassionate investigator

> [f]unctions . . . to bolster the epistemic authority of the currently dominant groups, composed largely of white men, and to discredit the observations and claims of the currently subordinate groups, including . . . many people of color and women. The more forcefully and vehemently the latter groups express their observations and claims, the more emotional they appear and so the more easily they are discredited.
> (Jaggar, 1989, p. 142)

Our field of tourism research remains dominated by such technically useful imperatives and by the 'scientific-positivistic paradigm' (Xiao and Smith, 2006, p. 503). Worryingly, studies suggest that tourism doctoral theses produced in the UK and Ireland display little evidence of 'critical' thinking (Botterill *et al.*, 2003), whilst quite recently a survey of 377 North American tourism doctoral dissertations was able to classify only one as women's studies (Meyer-Arendt and Justice, 2002). Although there has recently been a mini-burst of activity in the USA (see Brennan, 2004; Ghodsee, 2005), in such a climate, it is not surprising that issues of gender are seen to be contentious and therefore avoided in favour of 'easier', more academically accepted topics that can be more comfortably accommodated within the business schools where many tourism collectives are located (Ateljevic *et al.*, 2005).

Yet, in spite of the hostile environment encountered by academics interested in gender issues, researchers are responding to calls for tourism scholars to adopt a more critical lens and to confront issues of political representation, cultural commodification, hegemony and globalization. Arguably, the extent to which any social science field engages with gender-oriented research can be a measure of its ontological and epistemological maturity, and a number of scholars have described five key points or moments in the development of gender research (e.g. Eagly and Wood, 1991; Norris and Wall, 1994; Swain, 1995; Stewart and McDermott, 2004): women are invisible and subsumed into a male norm; women are recognized as 'other'; differences between men and women are mapped; women-oriented and/or feminist research approaches emerge; and researchers recognize that gender is one of a number of human status characteristics which affects individuals' experiences and social identities (others include age, class, ethnicity, race and dis/ability).

The development of gender research in tourism enquiry is a complex tale and the key protagonists in the story have been largely (but not exclusively) women (see, e.g. Kinnaird and Hall, 1996). Although two seminal collections of work foregrounding gender appeared over a decade ago (Kinnaird and Hall, 1994; Swain, 1995), it remains true that feminist tourism research does not exist in the same way as its sister field, feminist leisure studies (see Aitchison, 2001 and Pritchard, 2004 for reviews of extant leisure and tourism gender research). However, a sizeable body of work does exist encompassing feminist empiricism (such as tourism employment research); standpoint feminism (exploring tourism, capital and globalization); and post-structural feminism (exploring the role of language and imagery in creating, maintaining and reproducing power) (see Aitchison, 2005 for a more detailed review). Such scholarship has highlighted that although women dominate tourism employment, their situation mirrors that in other sectors, with significant horizontal and vertical gender segregation. Horizontally, women and men typically have different occupations and most women are employed in jobs which reflect their traditional domestic roles; they are typically employed as receptionists, waitresses, cleaners, maids, babysitters and travel agency sales people. Vertically, women are squeezed out of directorships and senior posts, particularly in larger organizations and remain concentrated in lower-level occupations with few opportunities for upward mobility (although recent occupational statistics indicate that women's presence in middle and upper management is growing in some developed countries) (Pritchard, 2005).

Encouragingly, despite the often hostile contemporary environment for gender-oriented and feminist tourism scholarship, such work is being continued by the next generation of researchers and doctoral studies located in what could be described as fourth-moment gender research including those of Harris (2002), Wilson (2004), Jordan (2004) and Ibrahim (2004). However, 'mainstream' tourism research has yet to move beyond the first two moments and much tourism research still occludes female voices and experiences. Gender, feminist and queer studies have largely failed to make an impression on the collective consciousness of the tourism academy and some tourism scholars even dismiss the need for further focus on gender, suggesting that it has already been 'done and dusted'. At the same time, the nascent feminist tourism studies collective that has emerged is also under threat from forces such as postmodernism which Aitchison (2005, p. 207) warns are fracturing 'the coherence of gender and tourism as a sub-discipline . . . [and risk] aborting rather than nurturing the embryonic project of advancing feminist and gender tourism studies'.

Essays on Gender, Tourism and Embodiment

This current collection attempts to continue the gender-focused work which has sought to rupture and destabilize some of the prevailing orthodoxies and rather cosy comfortableness of much tourism enquiry. At a time when gender research is frequently characterized as old-fashioned and irrelevant in the wake of postmodernism and post-feminism, there is a pressing need to restate the case for its place in tourism scholarship, some 30 years after the earliest work. Gender-focused and feminist-oriented investigation in tourism studies presents the individual researcher with a series of personal, political and intellectual confrontations. For many of the contributors here, their research and writing has involved personally and professionally challenging journeys and encounters, often undertaking gender-focused or methodologically 'risky' work in largely positivist academic environments which dismiss the academic credibility of gender research and women's studies and distain researcher positionality and voice.

Yet, over a decade after the first coherent collections of work were published, gender tourism studies more than ever need to embrace approaches which explore the material, the symbolic, the social and the cultural in order to understand how they operate as 'both a site and process of construction, legitimation, reproduction *and* reworking of gender relations' (Aitchison, 2005, p. 22). To date the objects of tourism gender research have almost exclusively been women (rather than women and *men*) and research has largely focused on employment patterns and sex tourism, whilst too little work has focused on women's experiences as consumers rather than producers of tourism. In assembling this volume we were conscious of the need to address these gaps as well as to combine theoretical critique with sociocultural analysis; the material with the symbolic; the body and embodiment; and tourism sites and processes of gender relations.

Until very recently 'the body' has been a silent or indeed an absent entity in tourism research, reflecting its masculinist, disembodied research traditions. But as more and more reflexive and embodied research(ers) have engaged with tourism scholarship we have begun to see a shift and work has foregrounded and conceptualized sensuousness and embodiment (e.g. Veijola and Jokinen, 1994; Johnston, 2000; Franklin, 2003; Cartier and Lew, 2005), performativity (e.g. Edensor, 1998; Desmond, 1999), the senses (e.g. Dann and Jacobsen, 2002) and materialities and mobilities (e.g. Hannam *et al.*, 2006). Indeed, it could be said that one of the central pillars of the 'new' tourism research (Tribe, 2005) exemplified by these (and other) scholars is that of 'embodiment'. As Osborne (2002, p. 51) has written: 'Like subjectivity, the body is the real, the immediate, the experienced, and in a sense one has to stand outside it to understand it, which makes theoretical thinking difficult.' As a result, he continues, 'the term "embodiment" is used to describe the way in which the bodily bases of individuals' actions and interactions are socially structured: that is embodiment as a social as well as natural process'.

Irena Ateljevic and Derek Hall (Chapter 9, this volume) map the main theoretical concerns of this embodiment turn in tourism as the acknowledgement of our sensuous awareness in the experience of place and the performance of tourism; recognition of a context of representation in which culture is inscribed and with it power and ideology given spatial reference: identification of the body as our means of encountering the world as discursive experience; foregrounding of subjectivities and identities; and emphasis on a reflexive situating of critical perspectives. Such recognition of the body and embodiment in tourism enquiry is long overdue as both have been the subject of much recent theoretical debate about the personal and the physical precipitated by feminism, Foucault and queer theory. Today, the body is no longer seen as an unproblematic natural, biological entity external to the mind but rather as a complexly constructed object of social discourses. Thus, it is no longer seen as 'a particularly sexual or sexed body; instead it is seen as an indeterminate potentiality' (Osborne, 2002, p. 51) inscribed with gender-specific meanings 'that reflect the social, cultural, economic and political milieu of its experience' (Wearing, 1996, p. 80).

Together with this reconceptualization of the body and rethinking of the fluidity of genders and sexualities has come a concerted challenge to the apparent neutrality of disembodied constructions of social scientific knowledge (Denzin and Lincoln, 2005). Whilst many social science fields now embrace the embodied and voiced researcher, this is a battle which has only recently been joined in tourism studies following a seminal article by Veijola and Jokinen (1994). Despite the work of these (and other) scholars, our field remains in the thrall of gatekeepers who privilege the 'scientific realist' style (see Phillimore and Goodson, 2004). This style holds that it is necessary to distance the researcher physically, psychologically and ideologically from his or her subject, and minimize the self, 'viewing it as a contaminant, transcending it, denying it, protecting its vulnerability' (Kreiger, 1991, p. 29). By contrast, those of us who would champion the project of embodiment acknowledge the impossibility of separating ourselves from the context that informs our (value-laden) analysis and privileges us with our social position of authoring and the concomitant authority to be able to speak (see Westwood *et al.*, 2006). Such calls for 'a place for powerful, personal authorship' (Holliday, 2002, p. 128) have clear feminist influences (Swain, 2004) and emanate from the fracturing of the naturalist, post-positivist tradition, recognizing a researcher's positionality (in terms of race, gender, age, class and sexuality) as a resource rather than a problem.

The bodyspaces explored in this volume investigate how we and society construct narratives of the self and others as tourists, travellers and employees (Veijola and Valtonen, Chapter 2; Fullagar, Chapter 3; Ateljevic and Hall, Chapter 9; Ringer, Chapter 13; Elmas, Chapter 19); how discourses of desire, sensuality and sexuality permeate the tourism experience and its marketing (Jordan, Chapter 6); how tourism maps sensual topographies of land and skin shaped by colonial imaginaries (Pritchard and Morgan, Chapter 10; van Eeden, Chapter 11); 'how bodies are sites of *psychical corporeality*' (Grosz, 1994, p. 22, original italics) through which narratives of femininity and masculinity and sensual materiality are inscribed and experienced (Noy, Chapter 4; Small, Chapter 5; Abramovici, Chapter 7; Desmarais, Chapter 12; Knox and Hannam, Chapter 16); and finally how travel and tourism offers opportunities for empowerment, resistance and the carnivalesque (Harris and Wilson, Chapter 14; Ibrahim *et al.*, Chapter 18; Pritchard *et al.*, Chapter 17; Poria, Chapter 15; Ryan and Gu, Chapter 8). At this point it is important to note that whilst we had initially considered using themes to compartmentalize these chapters, as the essays evolved it became increasingly clear that such editorially imposed categories were having the unintended consequence of undermining the inter/cross/transdisciplinary nature of the project and were creating artificial intellectual boundaries. Although the above descriptions of the individual essays are one way of outlining their contributions, we could equally say that they discuss masculinities, femininities, sexualities, or positionalities, embodiments, sensualities and experiences. Thus, the volume is presented as a set of essays and we leave it to the reader to make his or her own connections across the chapters.

These contributions reflect the revival of interest amongst some groups of tourism scholars in issues of gender (see Hall *et al.*, 2003) (although it has to be said that the overwhelming majority of 'mainstream' tourism researchers still equate gender with studies of women's experiences and studies of masculinities are few and far between). Yet, there is still much that needs to be done both to gain credibility (and quality funding) for gender-focused studies of tourism and to challenge the glass ceilings, glass walls and glass borders which continue to structure societies. Those of us interested in gender have so far evolved into a 'critical mass' by 'sticking together' on the margins of tourism scholarship. Indeed, this volume could be described as a collection which foregrounds marginal voices and experiences since its contributors are drawn from diverse cultures and locations (which include Australia, China, Croatia, Egypt, Finland, Israel, Italy, New Zealand, South Africa, Turkey, the UK and the USA) and range from doctoral candidates to established professors. We hope that this collection will further galvanize our own and others' efforts to build a coherent sub-discipline and a recognized role for gender tourism studies in the wider tourism academy – and move us from the margins to the centre of tourism investigations. In gaining such recognition, we hope that a heightened awareness of gender issues will also throw light on the lives of the millions of adults and children who experience the darker sides of tourism and who pay a heavy price to support the world's largest industry (see tourismconcern.org.uk and the World Tourism Organization's Global Code of Ethics).

Thus we have returned to the opening question of our introduction: why do issues of gender, sexuality and embodiment matter in tourism? Globally the tourism industry is one of the most important arenas for both women and men and its economic significance cannot be underestimated. But, whilst it employs over 200 million people worldwide, it is a disproportionately important employment sector for women as there has been a steady increase in their employment in tourism at a global level, largely driven by growth in developing countries (Shah, 2000). Moreover, its size, rapid growth and diverse, dynamic and flexible nature mean that it is ideally placed to empower and advance women and it has done so in many countries and contexts. Women can find a voice and independence through their involvement in tourism activities – by becoming part of decision-making processes and carving out new roles in their families, homes, communities and within local power structures (see UNED, 1999; ODI, 2000). The tourism industry thus potentially offers opportunities for a global revolution in the economic, social and political condition of women. Yet, at the same time, it can be a force for ghettoization, oppression and inequality – shoring up exploitative practices, objectifying indigenous women and female employees as part of the tourism 'package' (ILO, 2003) and perpetuating hetero-masculinist discourses which merge the feminine and the exotic (Mackie, 2000) – and tourism researchers have a key role to play in challenging and critiquing such gender stereotypes and traditional engendered roles.

Such gendered, sexed and racialized power dynamics and discourses affirm existing imbalanced human and international relations and thus constrain and limit the life chances and opportunities of millions of women and men. As tourism academics we have an obligation to challenge injustices and inequalities whether in tourism's material or symbolic domains. This is a project which is not solely the concern of women for 'patriarchy and sexism are not fetters worn by women only; they severely limit human possibilities for males as well' (Crotty, 1998, p. 162). If we are to bring back the balance (in ourselves, our communities and our world), the way is not to replace one 'archy' (patriarchy) with another (matriarchy) but to move from either/or to embrace both/and thinking: it is about reuniting the head, heart and body. Here we return to the importance of embodiment because if we want to achieve this paradigm shift and promote a society informed by reciprocity, interdependence and respect, we have to become the change that we seek: we have to embody the politics of love and balance (Fonda, 2004). We hope that you as readers will find inspiration and insight in this volume and become committed to this project, perhaps by taking on and doing gender-oriented, feminist, pro-woman or embodied tourism research or simply by thinking about and practising ethical tourism. Please read, enjoy and reflect.

References

Aitchison, C. (2001) Gender and leisure research: the codification of knowledge. *Leisure Sciences* 23, 1–19.

Aitchison, C. (2005) Feminist and gender perspectives in tourism studies: the socio-cultural nexus of critical and cultural theories. *Tourist Studies* 5(3), 207–224.

Ateljevic, I., Harris, C., Wilson, E. and Collins, F. (2005) Getting 'entangled': reflexivity and the 'critical turn' in tourism studies. *Tourism Recreation Research* 30(2), 9–21.

Ateljevic, I., Morgan, N. and Pritchard, A. (2007) Editors' introduction: promoting an academy of hope in tourism enquiry. In: Ateljevic, I., Pritchard, A. and Morgan, N. (eds) *The Critical Turn in Tourism: Innovative Methodologies*. Elsevier, Oxford, pp. 1–8.

Australian Government Equal Opportunity for Women in the Workplace Agency (2006) Australia's boardrooms closed to women. Available at: http://www.eowa.

gov.au/Information_Centres/Media_ Centre/Media_Releases/2006_Census.asp

Booth-Blair, C. (2005) Women's empowerment: measuring the global gender gap, speech to the Special Meeting of Women Ministers of Culture, Women's Voices and Cultural Understanding, 29–30 August, Reykjavik.

Botterill, D., Gale, T. and Haven, C. (2003) A survey of doctoral theses accepted by universities in the UK and Ireland for studies related to tourism 1990–1999. *Tourist Studies* 2, 283–311.

Brennan, D. (2004) *What's Love Got to Do With It? Transnational Desires and Sex Tourism in the Dominican Republic*. Duke University Press, Durham, North Carolina.

Cartier, C. and Lew, A.A. (eds) (2005) *Seductions of Place: Geographical Perspectives on Globalization and Touristed Landscapes*. Routledge, London.

Catalyst (2006a) 2005 Catalyst census of women board directors of the Fortune 500 shows 10-year trend of slow progress and persistent challenges. Available at: http://www. catalyst.org/pressroom/press_releases/3_ 29_06%20-%20WBD%20release.pdf

Catalyst (2006b) 'Blending in' vs. 'sticking together': women of color use differing strategies for informal networking. Catalyst study finds. Available at: http://www. catalyst.org/pressroom/press_releases/5_ 31_06%20-%20WoC%20Networks.pdf

Chesler, P. (1997) *Letters to a Young Feminist*. Four Walls Eight Windows, New York.

Conely, V.M. (2005) Career paths for women faculty: evidence from NZOPF: 99. *New Directions for Higher Education* 130(Summer), 25–39.

Crotty, M. (1998) *The Foundation of Social Research: Meaning and Perspective in the Research Process*. Sage, London.

Dann, G.M.S. and Jacobsen, J.K.S. (2002) Leading the tourist by the nose. In: Dann, G.M.S. (ed.) *The Tourist as a Metaphor of the Social World*. CAB International, Wallingford, UK, pp. 209–236.

Denzin, N.K. and Lincoln, Y.S. (eds) (2005) *The Sage Handbook of Qualitative Research 3rd Edition*, Sage, London.

Desmond, J.C. (1999) *Staging Tourism: Bodies on Display from Waikiki to Sea World*. The University of Chicago Press, Chicago, Illinois.

Eagly, A.H. and Wood, W. (1991) Explaining sex differences in social behavior: a meta-analytic perspective. *Personality and Social Psychology Bulletin* 17(3), 306–315.

Edensor, T. (1998) *Tourists at the Taj: Performance and Meaning at a Symbolic Site*. Routledge, London.

Fonda, J. (2004) The new feminism: reuniting the head, the heart and the body, speech to the 3rd Women and Power Conference, 10–13 September, New York. Available at: http:// www.feminist.com/resources/artspeech/ womenandpower.html

Franklin, A. (2003) *Tourism: An Introduction*. Sage, London.

Ghodsee, K. (2005) *The Red Riviera: Gender, Tourism and Postsocialism on the Black Sea*. Duke University Press, Durham, North Carolina.

Grosz, E. (1994) *Volatile Bodies: Toward a Corporeal Feminism*. Allen & Unwin, St Leonards, Australia.

Hakanson, M. quoted in Shepherd, J. (2006) Women's work gets male attention. *The Times Higher Education Supplement*, 11 August, 4.

Hall, C.M. (2004) Reflexivity and tourism research: situating myself and/with others. In: Phillimore, J. and Goodson, L. (eds) *Qualitative Research in Tourism: Ontologies, Epistemologies and Methodologies*. Routledge, London, pp. 137–155.

Hall, D., Swain, M.B. and Kinnaird, V. (2003) Tourism and gender: an evolving agenda. *Tourism Recreation Research* 28(2), 7–11.

Hannam, K., Sheller, M. and Urry, J. (2006) Editorial: mobilities, immobilities and moorings. *Mobilities* 1(1), 1–22.

Harris, C. (2002) Women and power: a study of New Zealand women business travellers. Unpublished PhD thesis, Victoria University, Wellington, New Zealand.

Hewlett, S.A. (2002) Executive women and the myth of having it all. *Harvard Business Review*, April.

Holliday, A. (2002) *Doing and Writing Qualitative Research*. Sage, London.

Ibrahim, N. (2004) Women's employment in Egyptian travel agencies and factors influencing their career development. Unpublished PhD thesis, University of Wales Institute, Cardiff, UK.

ILO (International Labour Office) (2003) *Violence at Work in Hotels, Catering and Tourism*. ILO, Geneva.

Inter-Parliamentary Union May 2004, quoted in Liswood, L. (2005) Speech to the Special Meeting of Women Ministers of Culture, Women's Voices and Cultural Understanding, 29–30 August, Reykjavik.

Jaggar, A. (1989) Love and knowledge: emotion and feminist epistemology. In: Garry, A. and Pearsall, M. (eds) *Women, Knowledge and Reality: Explorations in Feminist Philosophy*. Unwin Hyman, Boston, Massachusetts, pp. 129–155.

Johnston, L. (2000) (Other) bodies and tourism studies. *Annals of Tourism Research* 28(1), 180–201.

Jordan, F. (2004) Gendered discourses of tourism: the experiences of mid-life women travelling solo. Unpublished PhD thesis, University of Gloucestershire, Gloucestershire, UK.

Kinnaird, V. and Hall, D. (1994) *Tourism: A Gender Analysis*. Wiley, Chichester, UK.

Kinnaird, V. and Hall, D. (1996) Understanding tourism processes: a gender-aware framework. *Tourism Management* 17(2), 95–102.

Kreiger, S. (1991) *Social Science and the Self: Personal Essays on an Art Form*. Rutgers University Press, New Brunswick, New Jersey.

Liswood, L. (2005) Speech to the Special Meeting of Women Ministers of Culture, Women's Voices and Cultural Understanding, 29–30 August, Reykjavik.

Mackie, V. (2000) The metropolitan gaze: travellers, bodies and spaces. *Intersections* 4, 1–13.

Marcus, J. (2006) Is US tenure track fertile for change? *The Times Higher Education Supplement*, 2 November, 11.

Meyer-Arendt, K. and Justice, C. (2002) Tourism as the subject of North American doctoral dissertations 1987–2000. *Annals of Tourism Research* 29(4), 1171–1174.

Norris, J. and Wall, G. (1994) Gender and tourism. *Progress in Tourism Recreation and Hospitality Management* 6, 57–78.

Oakley, A. (2006) Feminism isn't ready to be swept under the carpet. *The Times Higher Education Supplement*, 3 March, 18–19.

ODI (Overseas Development Institute) (2000) Pro-poor tourism: putting poverty at the heart of the tourism agenda. No. 51, March 2000. Available at: www.odi.org.uk/nrp/51.htm

Osborne, R. (2002) *Megawords: 200 Terms You Really Need to Know*. Sage, London.

Page, S. (2005) Academic ranking exercises: do they achieve anything meaningful? A personal view. *Tourism Management* 26(5), 633–666.

Phillimore, J. and Goodson, L. (eds) (2004) *Qualitative Research in Tourism: Ontologies, Espistemologies and Methodologies*. Routledge, London.

Phillips, S. and Garner, M. (2006) Where 'hello baby' doesn't mean 'bye bye' tenure. *The Times Higher Education Supplement*, 3 March, 18–19.

Pritchard, A. (2004) Gender and sexuality in tourism research. In: Lew, A., Hall, C.M. and Williams, A. (eds) *A Tourism Companion*. Blackwell, Oxford, pp. 316–326.

Pritchard, A. (2005) Tourism, gender and cultures of globalisation. Speech to the Special Meeting of Women Ministers of Culture, Women's Voices and Cultural Understanding, 29–30 August, Reykjavik.

Pritchard, A. and Morgan, N. (2007) Decentring tourism's intellectual universe or traversing the dialectics between change and tradition. In: Ateljevic, I., Pritchard, A. and Morgan, N. (eds) *The Critical Turn in Tourism: Innovative Methodologies*. Elsevier, Oxford, pp. 11–28.

Rodgers, M. (2006) Bias blamed for pay gap. *The Times Higher Education Supplement*, 15 September, 56.

Sengupta, K. (2006) In the shadow of the Taliban. *The Independent*, 8 March, 22–23.

Shah, K. (2000) Tourism, the poor and other stakeholders: Asian experiences. Overseas

Development Institute Fair-Trade in Tourism Paper, ODI, London.

Spender, D. (ed.) (1981) *Men's Studies Modified: The Impact of Feminism on the Academic Disciplines*. Pergamon, Oxford.

Stewart, A.J. and McDermott, C. (2004) Gender in psychology. *Annual Review of Psychology* 55, 519–544.

Swain, M.B. (1995) Gender in tourism. *Annals of Tourism Research* 22(2), 247–266.

Swain, M.B. (2004) (Dis)embodied experience and power dynamics in tourism research. In: Phillimore, J. and Goodson, L. (eds) *Qualitative Research in Tourism*. Routledge, London, pp. 102–118.

The Economist (2005) Special Report, 25 July.

The Independent (2006) This is your life (if you're a woman). 8 March.

Tribe, J. (2005) New tourism research. *Tourism Recreation Research* 30(2), 5–8.

UNED (United Nations Environment and Development) UK Committee (1999) *Gender and Tourism: Women's Employment and Participation in Tourism*. UNED-UK, London.

Veijola, S. and Jokinen, E. (1994) The body in tourism. *Theory, Culture and Society* 11, 125–151.

Wearing, B. (1996) *Gender: The Pain and Pleasures of Difference*. Longman, Melbourne.

Westwood, S., Morgan, N. and Pritchard, A. (2006) Situation, participation and reflexivity in tourism research: furthering interpretative approaches to tourism enquiry. *Tourism Recreation Research* 31(2), 33–44.

Wilson, E. (2004) A journey of her own? The impact of constraints on women's solo travel. Unpublished PhD dissertation, Griffith University, Queensland, Australia.

Wojtas, O. (2006) Leg up from new-girl network. *The Times Higher Education Supplement*, 9 November, 9.

World Economic Forum (2005) Women's empowerment: measuring the global gender gap, World Economic Forum, Geneva. Available at: www.womankind.org.uk

Xiao, H. and Smith, S. (2006) The making of tourism research: insights from a social sciences journal. *Annals of Tourism Research* 33(2), 490–507.

2 The Body in Tourism Industry

SOILE VEIJOLA AND ANU VALTONEN

Departures

I am a serious traveller. Every summer I go to an academic conference, hence I am on my way to one now: 'Global Knowledge in a Widening World', arranged in the Bahamas. In the security control, my wired bra sets off the alarm and the explanation is found only after an inspection in the back room, which I receive in a dignified silence, being a cosmopolitan. This is the world we are − and have to be − travelling in today. We need to abandon ourselves inside out to the mercy of the carrier and, as its representatives, to unknown officials checking upon us, in body and baggage. A speedy transfer to the next queue, to the aircraft itself, whereby I, among others, hurry in as if it were a game of musical chairs, and the last one is left standing. My seat is an aisle seat in a set of three, a few rows ahead of the curtains separating business-class seats from the economy class. My black Samsonite (Pro DLX, if you need to know) is as tricky as ever to lift and squeeze into the overhead locker. It is too high up over my head, and the odd number of elbows bustling on the level of my temples does not make the task any easier.

After getting up and retracting my belly twice for persons seated next to me, and giving a menacing look at the fellow behind me − who, in his fear of flying, is unconsciously kicking the seat in front of him, my seat, that is − I am finally able to settle down. I have already seen my seat while making my reservation on the Internet. There was a computer animation of a pair of their 'new lie-flat seats', and I was asked to 'rotate the seat by dragging it with your mouse'. I did not have the time or interest to start turning my flying seat in the middle of a busy working day, and so I entered the reservations straight away. I did, however, notice that the space between the seats was increased 'from the current 127 cm/50 in. to 160 cm/63 in.' and that I was promised 'privacy for rest and work'. Now this is something: 'Passengers can stretch out and lie flat − even if they are 2 m/6 ft 7 in. tall.'[1] At that point I had wondered whether the seat would even recognize me, with my 50 kg and 1.5 m of height.

When trying to get comfortable in my seat, I realize that there is a problem. My feet do not reach the floor. This will make sitting not only unpleasant but, as far as I know, also unhealthy. The in-flight brochure advises me to move my ankles and stretch my legs from time to time, in order to prevent potential damage. I hope I can trust that it will. To be on the safe side, I am wearing support socks, as I always do these days on long flights.

We are kindly asked to fasten our seat belts. The emblem of speed and mobility is finally ready for take-off. One of the flight attendants smiles at my general direction when she passes us by on her way to the front, and to her straight-backed seat facing us.

* * *

I woke up at four in the afternoon, as always when on this shift. The previous night was, likewise, spent awake on the way here. At the hotel the make-up, getting dressed and getting packed took the usual 2 hours, even though I skipped the routine with the curler. Upon arrival at the airport I realized that my periods had started. That meant one more errand to run, before gliding through the airport to the gate, casually browsing the time on the numerous clocks on the way rather than my wrist watch, keeping up the appearance of a total but relaxed concentration on my upcoming duties in service. Luckily, my gate is not at the farthest end of the airport, so I am only slightly out of breath when I reach it.

All seats are not sold. That suits me fine. The business-class compartment is full, however, which should suit the carrier. People are adjusting themselves to the new seats there, sorting out their things meant for work and rest into different pockets and shaped surfaces. I give a hand here and there, smiling and checking up on everything. There are no children travelling in business class, which saves me – unlike my colleagues who have spent their 'best years' on route flights and have been transferred to charter flights – from dealing with dripping diapers and used breast covers. No extra smile muscle needs to be strained for that.

* * *

It is late and the flight attendants are dimming the lights. I am tired but cannot fall asleep. This is what I hate the most. I look awful after a bad night's sleep, and there is the presentation looming in the near future, in front of my most critical colleagues. Did I remember to take my anti-shadow lotion with me? Should I take a cognac? I'd better not. I put my blinders on and try to fall asleep.

Oh, no. I forgot to remind my colleague about the new deadline. I should do it the first thing in the morning. All right now, inhale, exhale, think of something not work-related. But what if she e-mails them the wrong appendix, not the latest one? I put a reminder on my mobile. Well, well, the only other woman travelling on this side of the curtain seems to be wearing a smarter dress than I am. Evidently she is sacrificing comfort for appearance. At least for the next few hours, I smirk; after the trip she is bound to be quite wrinkled.

I wonder how they are doing back home. I must call the school and tell them I can arrange the school trip to the zoo after all. Who is snoring here? The sound reminds me of my ex. How he is doing now, I wonder. Divorced again? For whom is this seat designed anyway . . . a giraffe? And the blanket is too thin; I shiver. Relax, relax. Oh, yes.

Oh, no. I have to go to the toilet. 'Excuse me, I am sorry to wake you up. I am terribly sorry. Yes, thanks a bunch.'

* * *

Nearly all passengers are asleep. Well, there is always a woman who wakes up the whole row because she needs to go the toilet as soon as everyone else has fallen asleep, and one of them pops up just now: apologizing left and right, dropping items on other people's laps on her way. 'Yes, that's my tampon, thank you' sort of thing. I wonder how she is going to manage with a beauty box of that size in the tiny plane toilet.

Looking at the rows of men in suits sleeping side by side, I cannot help thinking how *cosy* it looks: with shoes off, ties loosened, heads tilted sideways, the dim night light shimmering on the relaxed foreheads, the steady hum of the aircraft's engine working in the background. It is like a home inhabited by men only. And yes, a few women, too – like this one who now returns from the toilet, fussing around her seat while putting her colossal night-gear away.

They sleep, but I am awake. I need to be available if someone should need me.

After a few hours, the passengers are woken up by the voice of the captain. He fills everyone on facts about the altitude, location and weather – technical matters about the world outside the aeroplane. We, the cabin crew, for our part, have been telling the passengers how to behave as regards to safety and what to expect for personal services. We know that it is our job to convey feelings of comfort, care and welcome. For instance, I have deliberately cut off the sharp tone in my voice and always speak to clients in a pleasant voice. Indeed, I have learnt to speak with a smile on my face in such an automated fashion that once, when I returned home and got bombarded by my five-year-old son with questions about the whereabouts of various toys, I turned to him with the same smile and he cut me short by saying: 'Mom, you are not working now. You do not need to show me your gums.'[2]

I guess the task of the captain is, likewise, to produce positive feelings but in a different way. There is never any audible smile in his voice. His voice is strong, alert, positive and careless – not in a reckless or indifferent way of course, but it is invincible and untouched by the eventual personal worries and fears of individual passengers (to get there as quick as we can, for instance, for there is a lovesick person in the plane). Sorting the latter out is our business, that of the cabin crew.

It is time to collect the breakfast trays. Luckily, my armpits have finally dried.

The Body in Tourism Industry

This chapter deals with commercial and business environments meant for *addressing, serving and governing the bodies* of tourists and their servers. It focuses on the physical, social and embodied environments in tourism and travel industries – as part of the wider business-scape of the mobilized global economy. Rather than speaking in abstract terms of 'the body', our aim is to unravel the actual *techniques, performances and 'bodyscapes'* that the travelling and working bodies in tourism are subjected to and subjects of (e.g. Molz, 2006). Moreover, the social and material environment of tourism business is read as a set of spatial and social inscriptions of *the ideal* or *normal body*: one that is formed and sized in a pre-ascribed way to fit the space and the cultural and symbolic place of the service. The third aim of the chapter is to contribute to the blossoming 'embodiment turn' in both social sciences and tourism studies beyond mere lip-service – even if, in this case, lips will literally be discussed through the act of smiling. Needless to say, the bodies of the tourists have been forcefully introduced to tourism studies earlier, and are currently a subject of increased academic interest – as this volume indicates. However, there is a disciplinary field that, we believe, still needs to be alerted to the significance of corporeality: that of business studies. Sustainable practices with respect to embodied realities of the hospitality industries would have a far-reaching effect on the empirical world in which we all travel and work.

In contemporary business-driven environments – from hamburger chains to even universities – an increasing attention has been devoted to the spheres where today's commodities (services as *experiences*) are being produced and consumed simultaneously. Following Bitner (1992), we call these spaces *service-scapes*. In her view, the processes, acts and performances of serving a customer take place in a complex physical and social environment, which, when properly designed, produces satisfied customers and long-term loyalty – in other words, profit. The concept of a service-scape has indeed broadened our understanding of the particularities of service encounters and of their management. However, originating from a profit-oriented business research paradigm, it offers a limited understanding of the complex cultural and social arrangements of the spaces in question (cf. Sherry, 1998). Nor does it provide us with tools with which to critically explore the ways in which meanings are produced in various sites and spaces for tourism business.

In critical social theory and women's studies, for their part, the prominent research paradigm for service work has for some time now been that of *emotional labour*, as thematized by Hochschild (1983):

> The flight attendant does physical labour when she pushes heavy metal carts through the aisles, and she does mental work when she prepares for and actually organises emergency landings and evacuations. But in the course of doing this physical and mental labour, she is also doing something more, something I define as *emotional labour*.
> (Hochschild, 1983, pp. 6–7, italics in the original)

By emotional labour, Hochschild (1983, pp. 5–6) refers to the products 'in which the emotional style of offering the service is part of the service itself, in a way that loving or hating wallpaper is not part of producing wallpaper'. Emotional labour is hence connected to work performances by 'the management of feeling' that helps to create 'publicly observable facial and bodily display'; the aim of the latter is to create emotional states both in others and in self. A paradigmatic example of this kind of 'learning to labour' emotionally is the training of flight attendants.

In other words, by emotional work, we are talking about a *skill* that is being sold for a wage (Hochschild, 1983, p. 7). The importance of the skill of smiling is expressed by the policy of the US airlines in the 1970s: '[U]se them until their smiles wear out and then get another bunch' (Kerfoot and Korczynski, 2005, p. 390). In today's precarious working life (see, e.g. Sennett, 1998; Beck, 2000; Holvas and Vähämäki, 2005), the importance of smiling, and showing *a will to please*, has hardly diminished (see Hochschild, 1983, pp. 127–128).

Emotional labour captures important aspects of the working conditions particularly of women who, in the rigidly gender-segregated labour market of leisure industries (Sinclair, 1997; Roberts, 2004; Brandth and Haugen, 2005; Kerfoot and Korczynski, 2005), are kept in charge of maintaining a pleasant ambience around various social as well as intimate activities. In all service-work, especially those promising positive *personal experiences*, customer satisfaction has to be guaranteed; if not, the business is over. Tourism and travel provide paradigmatic examples of this kind of a 'servient economy'. The intensity of 'personal experiences' inevitably escalates through competition and the cumulating effect of the 'been there, done that' attitude (see, e.g. Pine and Gilmore, 1999). Paradoxically, this particular industry also provides a paradigmatic example of the ways in which 'personal experiences' are created and conditioned through more or less standardized or customized business processes. In its effort to make profit, the tourism industry has to decide whether to offer standardized or customized services – the airline travel represents the former. Accordingly, in this view, the best (read: the most productive) customer is the one who meets and follows the profit-driven standards. Deviations become problems (see, e.g. Zeithaml *et al.*, 2006).

Simultaneously, tourism and travel provide seriously consequential conditions of work for more and more people today (see, e.g. Sinclair, 1997; Ehrenreich and Hochschild, 2002; Gmelch, 2003; Roberts, 2004; M. Haanpää *et al.*, University of Lapland, The Academy of Finland, Finland, 2005, unpublished data). Yet there is too little interaction between the previous two approaches, managing service-scapes on the one hand and understanding the price of emotional labour on the other – perhaps due to the different interests of knowledge embedded in them. Hiring and empowering women as low-paid workers are not necessarily one and the same thing.

Another impetus for our project is the pressing need for understanding *gender* and *gendered labour* in the context of tourism by means of recent theory rather than a manifestation of 'natural functions' allocated to women and men. Accordingly, the research task can be specified as follows: How are the *satisfied and satisfying working bodies* produced in a typical tourism and travel-related servicescape, that of an air flight? Both are required for a successful production and consumption of a personal experience. In order to answer the question, we shall unravel the ways in which *gender* is displayed and deployed in the embodied, spatial and temporal 'arrangements between the sexes' (Goffman, 1977) – in an aeroplane. We shall first discuss the server's performances and then move on to the customer's, concentrating on *the smile*, *the seat* and *the sleep*, as sites and techniques of embodied performances of gender. In conclusion, we shall replay our findings with regard to a sustainable future for interdisciplinary tourism studies.

Serving Like a Woman

Gender at work in tourism

As Joan Acker has stated, jobs are not gender-neutral but are created as occupations suitable for either men or women (quoted in Forseth, 2005, p. 443). A psychiatrist who was consulted in the 1970s to support the discriminatory practices of a US airline company contended that male passengers 'would generally feel more masculine and thus more at ease in the presence of a young, female attendant' (Kerfoot and Korczynski, 2005, pp. 390–391). Today, any experienced flight traveller can see a 'sustained sorting process' (Goffman, 1977, p. 303) whereby men still make up the majority as business-class passengers and women, in their turn, form the majority in cabin crews – even if there are some women also among the former and men among the latter these days. All in all, the spatial and social arrangement, with men seated and women bending to serve, has not significantly wavered. Instead of despondently admonishing the sexual division of labour in tourism, we shall opt for a more complex understanding of the concept of gender and discuss the *qualities*, rather than quantities, of the working bodies of the air hostesses. In these terms the questions would read: What are the *corporeal terms of doing gender* at hospitality-work? How do femininity and masculinity configure in contemporary service-work as company assets, workplace resources and, finally, skills?

Nevertheless, we cannot ignore the empirical fact that, in terms of division of labour, air hostessing is a characteristic part of the gender-segregated and sex-based labour market of tourism and hospitality industries. In this sector of working life, as well as in many others, women tend to form the majority of low-paid, temporal and seasonal jobs. Their labour is composed of the three Cs of catering, cleaning and caring (Toynbee, 2003). It appears to be women's job to take care of other people's bodily and emotional needs.

Statistics of gender division of labour do not, however, summon the lived situation or lived experience of doing the so-called women's work. Indeed, for the purpose at hand, we shall combine the culturally and societally structured *situation of women* with the *agency* – an individual's capacity for action – of women living in that very situation. In the words of McNay (2004, p. 177), 'structural forces only reveal themselves in the lived reality of social relations'. For this task, Young (1990) has provided us with a thematization of the lived-in situation of a woman in *patriarchy*. Patriarchy is a social system in which men, as heads of domestic households, rule the society, and a symbolic order that gives priority to social relations, power struggles and descent between men (Veijola and Jokinen, 2001, pp. 92–93, 236–237). A 'typical situation' of women in patriarchy can be described, for instance, in terms of *modalities of feminine spatiality*, extracted 'the wrong way' from the phenomenological account of Maurice Merleau-Ponty. The latter states that there is a 'world for a subject just insofar as the body has capacities by which it can approach, grasp, and appropriate its surroundings in the direction of its intentions' (Young, 1990, p. 148). In other words, for the phenomenological body to exist, transcend and enact its intentions, it cannot exist as an *object*.

As for a woman, in the situation conditioned by sexist and patriarchal society in which she grows up *as a girl*, the very opposite is true: her body is immobilized in space rather than the *source* of space through the intentional movement of the agent. Perhaps the most important aspect of the lived experience in a typical woman's situation in patriarchy is that of being *looked at* and *acted upon* as an object, rather than being the one who sees and acts on the world herself and thereby constitutes it (Young, 1990). In her treatise, Young illuminates the agency created by active engagement, orientation, coordination and involvement of 'the whole body in gross movement' by its opposite, a 'disengagement', revealed by the commonly known and, in the West, widely understood phrase 'throwing like a girl'. Even Mauss (1935/1968, pp. 76–77) relied on this 'common understanding' in his articulation: '[E]veryone knows that a woman's throwing, of a stone, for example, is not just weak but always different from that of a man: in a vertical instead of a horizontal plane.'

In airline hospitalities, the lack of lateral, forceful motility seems to be fully appreciated: miniature meals and wine bottles are not thrown with all physical might of the body, from one end of the plane to another, at passengers; rather, objects are 'tinkered' with only one body part closest to the object. Meanwhile, the performers are aware of being objects of the gaze and intentions of others while they work. Last but not least, they do not demand much space: when sitting, standing or walking. This means, among other things, more space to be priced and sold to customers.

The modalities of feminine mobility in a typical woman's situation in patriarchy are, in short, appropriated and maintained by tourism work at large, from aircraft to hotels and girlie bars – in all those sites where women are expected to be accommodated and immobilized as well as accommodating and adapting to the moves of others (cf. Gibson, 2003, p. 373). But let us not leave the matter at this rather gloomy and structured situation. There is another way of looking at the corporeal terms of service-work, one that depicts gender as a *changing* instead of an ahistorical concept and lived experience.

In this line of theorizing, gender is analysed as an *act*, 'tenuously constituted in time and instituted in an exterior space through a stylised repetition of acts', as Butler puts it (1990, pp. 140–141). Thereby, it is a habituated performance – related to the concept of *habitus* elaborated by Bourdieu (1990), a system of durable, transposable dispositions that mediates individual actions and social structures (e.g. Adkins and Skeggs, 2004; Jokinen, 2005). 'Habitus is actualised by the "feel for the game", a practical knowledge learnt by and sedimented into the body, but beyond explicit articulation' (Veijola and Jokinen, 2005). It is history and biography embodied, just like gender is for most women and men who have a 'feel for the game' as either one or the other.

According to Adkins (2005), when we see gender as an act and performance we acknowledge it as *work*: as flexible and fluid, performative in character; as a property that can be disentangled and abstracted from a person – instead of being an inherent property through authorship, biology or origin. Gender is more or less a result of interaction and thereby of its reception, *its effect on its audience* (Adkins, 2005). The skill of femininity is, in the context of service work by a cabin crew, a *relational* skill: it can only be accomplished through a partner or respondent in discourse. The power of a smile can only be co-produced with the client; it requires a satisfied customer. Nor is it merely a dyadic relationship between a worker and a client but a *triad*: 'With the entry of customers in the labour process, workers have to juggle the interests of managers and customers' (Forseth, 2005, pp. 441–442). To further complicate the issue, these triadic relationships in themselves include a wide variety of culturally shaped relationships, for example those with a baby or with an adult businessman – with different as well as similar aspects of affiliation.

Theories of gender as a mobile and movable performance have been actively used in studies of working life where, for instance, femininity as a work performance requires mastering social, emotional and aesthetic skills. Compare this, say,

with the technical skills of building or repairing non-living artefacts, which are
traditionally conceived of as masculine traits. The former is useful in creating an
amiable social atmosphere for consumption, bonding or making business in the
many spheres of leisure and cultural industries, at the forefront of new cultural
economy (e.g. du Gay and Pryke, 2003). Femininity has now become *a workplace resource,* required from *all* workers (Lovell, 2000; Gray, 2003; Adkins, 2005).
Moreover, the 'scrambling' of characteristics usually associated with *either* females
or males is boosted in today's team spirit building events: new mixes of traits are
considered important for the success and growth of corporations (Martin, 1994,
p. 208, quoted in Adkins, 2005, p. 120). However, as Adkins (2005, p. 120) astutely
notes, even if gender has now 'become detached from the person and is a mobile
object' it is mostly men who are economically credited for gender flexibility. For
women workers, performances of femininity (emotional, aesthetic and social skills)
are mostly defined as naturally occurring features and functions, to the advantage
of the customer or the employer. They are not considered worthy of recognition
or promotion; nor are women's performances of masculinity always received with
approval (Adkins, 2001, 2005).

The job of the air hostess finely catches many characteristics and requirements
of flexibility in today's working life. She needs to provide both atmosphere and services for the bodies in need, while displaying cold nerves and the ability to give clear
instructions in a situation of emergency in the air. She needs the ability to 'multitask'
in distress.[3] Then again, can we really call her performance a mobile one? Given
the solid division of labour and chores, the sex-based prerequisites of appearance
for the job of an air attendant and the modalities of feminine spatiality so highly
appreciated and appropriated at service-work, one could ask whether gender really
is a mobile performance for women who work for the airline companies. Is it up
to her agency to play the field 'as a woman', or is her field merely a narrow strip
that offers little option? 'For [airline companies] a "professional" flight attendant is
one who has completely accepted the rules of standardization' (Hochschild, 1983,
p. 103). Standardized performances of femininity are often restrictions on individual
agency when it comes to women, even if they can be used for self-expression in drag
shows or as personal assets of a social host on an incentive trip, if one is a man.

Smiling bodies

In the standardized and feminized social figure of an air hostess, the lines of class
and gender fall neatly within one another (e.g. Skeggs, 2004). Working-class women
serve business-class men. She embodies the *attributes* (of friendliness), *skills* (to serve)
and *capacities* (to nurture) of a work performance of femininity. She manages her
work performance as a pointedly feminine accomplishment that, paradoxically,
can be externalized from her as an effect on, and experience of, an audience who
act as the final judges of her working skills. The latter has, needless to say, always
been the case in sexuality-based jobs and social positions (as a wife, a concubine or
a prostituted woman or man).

It bears to note that smile, upon which the performance of femininity at work
depends, is not only a *visual* image. Smile is an *attribute of the entire convinced and convincing body* that relates to another person; it is an embodied display and an act of

amiable hospitality; it lingers in voice, gestures and bodily positions, not only on the lips. It creates the required audience-experience. 'For the flight attendant, the smiles are part of her work, a part that requires her to coordinate self and feeling so that the work seems to be effortless' (Hochschild, 1983, p. 8). The mission is completed when a client feels content like a well-served guest or a well-nourished child. One could say that a smiling body is a *well-trained body* – just like a convincing body of a *soldier* is. Both are given a competence in 'rhetorics of the body' (Foucault, 1977, p. 135). By way of comparison:

> By the late eighteenth century, the soldier has become something that can be made; out of a formless clay, an inapt body, the machine required can be constructed; posture is gradually corrected; a calculated constraint runs slowly through each part of the body, mastering it, making it pliable, ready at all times, turning silently into the automatism of habit; in short, one has 'got rid of the peasant' and given him 'the air of a soldier' (ordinance of 20 March 1764).
>
> (From *Docile Bodies*, in Foucault, 1977, p. 135)

Mauss (1935/1968, p. 75) named the latter as *techniques* of the body, referring to an action which is *effective*, *traditional* and *transmitted* from one generation to another. The air hostess, just as a soldier, combines the 'skill, presence of mind and habit' (Mauss, 1935/1968, p. 78) required for a gender-related competence.

A smiling body is far from a *crying body* – yearning to be consoled and cared for. Equally, it is a far cry from a *laughing body*. Smiling and laughing at a customer are two very different actions (as we can witness in the film *Unforgiven*, directed by Clint Eastwood in 1992). A smiling body is also the opposite of the notion of the *winning body* – the convincing willpower and assertiveness that is connected to the overbearing mobility of the entire body usually linked to a soldier's, a fighter's or a competing athlete's body – in short, a masculine body (Young, 1990; Veijola, 2004). In semiotic terms, the modal relation of *being obliged to want to please* (a smiling body) is in opposition to the *prohibition to want to please* (a winning body); these two cannot, again in semiotic terms, be present simultaneously. The smiling body can be the winning body only in a beauty contest, a line of prostitutes and in the game of love. Not surprisingly, this is how the relations between women working on scenes of interaction in hospitality industries are commonly arranged and displayed (Veijola, 1997, 2004, pp. 112–113).

To sum up the previous discussions, let us return to the notion of *femininity as a skill*. If the skill of hosting customers is constrained by the modality of *being obliged to want* to please, and the means for that are a standardization of form, size, looks, attire, attitude and bodily comportment, not to mention proper age and gender, there is really not much extensional and intentional space left for the embodied female subject to invent for the encounter with the client. Moreover, if her competence is judged by its audience effect and nothing else, the personal properties of her agency are truly separate from herself. She does not 'own' her skills or virtues; nor can these lead to a career, a promotion or mastery of her field.

Her subject position can be outlined with the help of the *artisan*. For both, cumulated experience is, after years of practising, sedimented into the body and realized without conscious attention. But only for the artisan, the resulting skill is also readily acknowledged when services are charged for (Adkins, 2005). The work of an air hostess, for its part, is treated as *deskilled and disentangled labour of hostessing*.

quantitative, homogenous, and serially produced and displayed. Indeed, at its crud-
est, the exploitation of women's work in tourism means reducing it to a display and
embodiment of sexual function and its potential realization for a fee – not a human
resource by means of feminine virtues (Veijola and Jokinen, 2005).

Femininity, in this perspective, is not a skill but a quantified feminine quality. It
runs out eventually, along with the individual person's experience in age. 'Smile-lines'
are not seen as 'the accumulated evidence of personal character but as an occupational hazard, an undesirable sign of age incurred in the line of duty on a job that
devalues age' (Hochschild, 1983, p. 127). Both the 'smile war' (Hochschild, 1983, pp.
127–128) and 'smile factories' (Van Maanen, 1991) of the hospitality and experience
industries lose their 'loyal soldiers' on purpose and replace them with new ones who
are again trained to be happy around people.[4] The air attendants and other hostesses
of cultural and leisure industries, whether workers in girlie bars or VIP lounges of international sports events, are efficiently and serially present, displaying feminine qualities
in exchange for (minimum or no) wage. The feudal economy is still alive. Maids (and
hired men) yield to the slightest wishes of customers and employers for their survival.

Sitting like a Customer

My seat

Let us now approach the issue of working bodies in the air from the other end
of the service situation. The social position and embodied postures we discuss in
this section are those of the *customer*. In marketing terms, *customer satisfaction* is the
cornerstone of the entire business thought (Fisk *et al.*, 1993; Vargo and Lusch,
2004). Even if 'airline experience' and service satisfaction involve several encounters between customer and company – from making the reservation to the 'wash
and brush up' facility at the other end (Westwood *et al.*, 2000, p. 357) – we shall
focus here on the embodied encounters that take place during the flight.

The main activity expected from the customers is *sitting*. How can sitting be a satisfying experience for a customer? In other words, how is the working body of a customer
– after all, this is a business flight we are talking about – constructed spatially and tempo-
rally? To make the task a more challenging one, let us not imagine the experience of the
same model passenger which the airline companies use in their marketing and design
– that of a tall (more room for the feet, remember?) businessman – but instead a different embodied experience, that of *a travelling businesswoman*. With her help, we are able to
depict the work and techniques required from the customers if they want to be satisfied,
without falling into the trap of mere reproduction of some more marketing talk.

First, with a travelling businesswoman in mind, we need to acknowledge the prob-
ability that she has started her working day a long time earlier than her fellow male
travellers, given that, statistically, women still bear the main responsibility of the domestic household even in the West. She has usually taken care of the morning routines as
well as made special arrangements due to her absence. It has also taken her (in average)
a longer time to gain a decent appearance for the public eye, i.e. to perform herself as
a woman, and also to pack up a wider assortment of dress and outfit than men usually
need to do for business meetings. Her luggage is, in other words, heavier.

How does she experience the spatial service of the aircraft when sitting down in her seat? Let us choose two aspects of the satisfying sitting experience for a closer inspection: *body size* and *sleeping*. Neither of the two has received the attention they deserve in tourism and marketing literature, even if they are linked to customer satisfaction in more realistic terms than standardized computer modelling ever is.

By having paid a certain sum of money, the travelling businesswoman obtains the right to an exclusive but temporary use and occupation of a seat that she can call 'my seat' during the flight (Lovelock and Gummesson, 2004). However, even if the seat is 'hers', it is not designed for 'her body', but according to a body that meets certain standards of weight and height. Rather surprisingly, it is *weight* that has gained attention in the literature on embodiment at the expense of *height* (Valtonen, 2004b) – even if it is also through height that we are afforded particular relations with the social and material world. By *affordance* we mean both objective and subjective objects and surfaces that are both part of the environment and part of the organism (Gibson, 1979; Ingold, 2000; Macnaghten and Urry, 2001). 'Affordances stem from the reciprocity between the environment and the organism and derive . . . from how people are kinaesthetically active within their world.' They do not cause behaviour or action but constrain, enhance or resist it. Active, vital, corporeal and mobile beings are, in short, afforded various possibilities in different environments (Macnaghten and Urry, 2001, p. 9).

In an environment like an airplane, embodied passengers are afforded certain ranges of being and doing based on a prevailing sociocultural understanding of a 'proper' body. In practice, therefore, when trying to make themselves comfortable the travellers are engaged in a laborious process of accommodating their bodies to the environment: using recommended or less recommended body techniques, such as stretching their legs or using cushions – in relation to space that has been strictly standardized prior to their arrival. Perhaps they also try to accommodate to social standards of height by using high heels or platforms. The airline industry guides this work by advertising 'room for legs' on their websites; they try to attend to the special wishes of *tall* passengers – who generally are men. (If a woman is exceptionally tall, she might find the extra space for her feet pleasant but find other sources of discomfort instead, with men having to look up at her and not often liking it.) Perhaps we should not be surprised: a recent report informs us that tall people earn more money. For instance, a study conducted by Persico *et al.* (2004) shows that for white men in the USA, a 1.8% increase in wages accompanies every additional inch of height. Heineck (2005), for his part, found out that for a height up to 195 cm there is a wage premium associated with stature for male workers from former West Germany of about 4% for each additional standard deviation increment in height.

Sitting and either relaxing or preparing for a business meeting with legs hanging in the air and elbows raised above heart level while using the elbow rests may prove unsatisfying for a travelling businesswoman. But how does someone in her position experience the need to get some rest in the plane? What happens when she tries to go to *sleep*? The Western arrangement of sleeping relates to the overall individualization process in which and through which sleep has been civilized (Elias, 1992). In the Middle Ages, people used to sleep anywhere when they got tired and the physical space for sleeping was frequently shared with others. Gradually, sleep has been privatized and today the bedroom – or hotel room – has become one of the most private and intimate areas of human life: you either sleep alone or with someone you know well. A dormant body is not visible to strangers and a sleeping person enjoys a particular cultural respect: he or she is not to be disturbed.

'Sleeping with someone' obviously refers to sexual and/or marital relations but it is also a sign of *trust* in a rather profound way. When going to sleep, one needs to feel ontologically *safe* (see, e.g. Veijola, 2006, pp. 90–91). Falling asleep and waking up are carefully prepared for, no matter where and when they take place. When falling asleep, one enters an entirely different world, a world of dreams, a world that is out of control, and even associated with death. It is no wonder that most of the rituals practised before falling asleep aim to ensure safety. For instance, we close the curtains and lock the doors so that no one can see us or, even worse, enter the place where we sleep (Valtonen, 2004a).

During a night flight, all this is unsettled. In this kind of a dormitory, perfect strangers 'sleep together'. But how can you trust fellow passengers you have never met and will never meet again? The task of making dormant bodies safe is allocated to the air hostess. She is awake while others sleep, like a mother. Moreover, while in everyday life dormant bodies are arranged behind the scenes of public and social life, in the aircraft they are visibly present. Fellow passengers may *see* you sleeping; they might see and hear you snore open-mouthed and talk in your sleep. Also, the company employee, the air attendant, sees customers asleep, which is quite an extraordinary situation for a service encounter. Amazingly enough, the latter has been left unexplored by mainstream research on service-scapes. Likewise, researchers alerted to issues of embodiment have so far focused on events that take place during the waking hours.

Sleeping well in an aeroplane is, in short, quite a challenge, and it is even more so for women. When studying women's perceptions of airline services, Westwood *et al.* (2000) found out that women were particularly concerned about 'the proximity of men and women in business class cabins on long haul flights, especially on overnight flights' and 'the majority felt very uncomfortable with the notion of sleeping next to a stranger: "Sometimes, travelling by myself, I really don't like travelling a long distance next to a man I don't know – I don't like sleeping and waking up next to a strange man"' (Westwood *et al.*, 2000, p. 357).

Yet the very challenge of sleeping well has gained new weight in the current fast-paced society. Recent studies report a steady increase of sleeping disorders (e.g. Leadbeater, 2004) that are commonly related to the busy lifestyle and the conditions of new work with its extended and flexible hours of emotional and knowledge-intensive work that is hard to turn off in the mind after office hours (Valtonen, 2004a; Moisander and Valtonen, 2005; Nowtony, 1994). There is also increasing need for face-to-face encounters in the global business world, despite the development of information and communication technology (Urry, 2002). Regular travelling between continents and through different time zones upsets the internal clocks of business people.

One of the problems of sleeping in the air is that a lack of sound, regular sleep becomes visible on the body. A sleepless traveller not only feels tired but also looks tired. Popular media and the marketing branch remind women, particularly, of the close relation between sleep and beauty – and productivity. As a bed manufacturer puts it: '[A]fter a good night's sleep one is fresh for the following day's challenges at work.' Or even more succinctly: '[A] career woman needs more sleep' (*Gloria* magazine, 2003). The market also provides a huge range of night-time skincare products that enable one to benefit fully from the 'beauty sleep' as well as products that help to disguise the traces of sleepless nights (Valtonen, 2005). This is needed since, in the prevailing business culture, one should present oneself as charged with energy and vitality, 'looking good and feeling great', and thereby a worthy person (e.g. Featherstone, 1991, p. 183). A tired body is not a productive body but a soon-to-be-fired body.

All in all, a travelling businesswoman wants service like everyone else – she too is a paying customer. Oftentimes she does not get it. 'Generally, women appeared more likely to feel out of place within the aeroplane', state Westwood *et al.* (2000, p. 359), and continue: 'they perceived men as receiving better and more preferential treatment from the airline staff: "Men do receive better service . . . the front line people are often women, they are programmed to receive requests from men."' All in all, 'men were much more satisfied with the airline experience than businesswomen' whereas 'women were very conscious of reinforcing their status', for instance by dressing 'to look the part' of a business traveller. In other words, maintaining a convincing body takes more effort from them than from men. Women do not think even meals are designed for them: 'Men are very happy to eat a full meal and have four or five courses . . . I think certainly in terms of dinner menus they are geared up towards men's tastes, in terms of serving port and cognac' (Westwood *et al.*, 2000, pp. 358–360).

In sum, the sizing of space, the level of attention and the ways in which the special needs of upholding a conservative feminine appearance are met by the corporation do not necessarily satisfy a travelling businesswoman.

Empty gestures

What we are dealing with here is something more complicated than merely a management issue or an unfortunate dismissal of an important target group in marketing – women. Indeed, we could build upon the previous discussions on the institution of providing and receiving hospitality in the air as follows: the presence of a travelling businesswoman in the cabin makes the patriarchal ideology of business travelling – and making business in general – manifest by breaching its taken-for-granted surface, the sustained patriarchal arrangements between the sexes (Goffman, 1977, p. 302).

Patriarchal social order is arranged socially and materially into various institutionalized and increasingly commercialized spaces where women are *not interpellated* (Althusser, 1969/1994) to be subjects in their own right – as customers and citizens, as proper 'players of the field'. Following Žižek (1997), one could say that the patriarchal ideology is *materialized* and *externalized* in the spatial and temporal arrangements of both social space and the embodied agents acting in it. In the air traffic, for instance, areas such as business lounges are designed and decorated for customers, but only men regard them as 'oases'; women find them uninviting, intimidating and masculine spaces (Westwood *et al.*, 2000, p. 361). For instance,

> there is no doubt that a woman will take longer to prepare herself to get off the flight if she is going straight to a meeting so [you need] to be able to have a proper wash and not be hassled by people knocking at the door, or feeling that you are holding someone up.
> (Westwood *et al.*, 2000, p. 358)

The universal invitation to 'travel with us' made by the carrier is – with regard to women – *an empty gesture*. It is not meant to be taken literally. Instead, throughout the visual images of marketing, the sizing of the space and the rituals of politeness that construct the service behaviour, this very ideology is being manifested, materialized and maintained by means of social action and spatial arrangements – but as one tailored to *fit the size, form and needs of a male body*. Or, rather, they aim to match a series of collective male bodies, against the background of performances of femininity in the service personnel (see Žižek, 1997, pp. 27–30).

The gesture that takes the visible and material form of a *seat* is empty as well: it does not accept a person of a woman's size, but dismisses her, like the Sorting Hat at Hogwarts in J.K. Rowling's *Harry Potter*. The smiling gesture is emptied as well. When a travelling businesswoman, who is borrowing the subject position of a man built into the service-scape of a patriarchal society, expects to be served by another woman – as if she were a universal passenger – the *inherent ambivalence and contradiction of the arrangement between, and within, the sexes* is inescapably revealed and discharged (Žižek, 1997). There are no societally significant meanings or codes of desire attached to women serving other women, except for the cases of a sadomasochist lesbian relationship, the power relations between a mistress of the house and her maid in a patriarchal household, or the mother–daughter bond. (Incidentally, the only airlines that *did* please the women interviewed in the study cited above were Far Eastern or Asian ones.) For the modern and emancipated flight attendants, none of these options is usually viable.

As for men, there is something ambivalent in a situation where women serve their slightest whims and, simultaneously, have command over their bodies. Men are forced to adopt, even if temporarily, a feminine modality of spatiality (Young, 1990): being enclosed, confined and under surveillance in space, nailed in their seats which are – now – not only a territory of one's own but also a prison. Travelling in the air, in short, *feminizes men's lived experience of mobility*. No wonder, then, that the outmost attentiveness and subservience of the controlling agents, the cabin crew, is needed for men to be able to handle the situation of 'citing feminine bodily existence' in patriarchal culture.

Ironically, while the working bodies of the travelling businesswomen are 'faded' in the airline service-scape, the same might some day be true with regard to the hostessing bodies of the cabin crew as well. Having extensively appropriated the image and presence of the young female body in marketing, front desk service jobs, and in creating visual and sexual amenities, the global business-scape may perhaps eventually get rid of women's bodies completely – in order to intensify corporative efficiency, i.e. the bodies will stay, but living women disappear. Namely, as a study by Gustavsson (2005) demonstrates, technological developments on artificial intelligence have enabled corporations to 'hire' virtual employees for interacting with their online customers on the Internet. The number of virtual assistants continues to grow, and most of them are human-like and female. Following the cultural imagination of the creators of these images, 'the male virtual assistants . . . are simply pictures of typical men in business environments whereas, in the visualisation of women, even those who "are strictly business", show cleavage, smile, wave and wink' (Gustavsson, 2005, p. 414). In her prediction: '[W]e will most likely see many more of these female, photo-unreal characters that lack any personality beyond their appearance and which constitute the new, perfect service employee: young, devoted, cheap and always accessible' (Gustavsson, 2005, p. 416).

When thinking of the recent developments between gender and new labour, we could anticipate that femininity, having become a workplace resource, will ultimately be disentangled completely from living women and be virtualized, designed and perfected into an 'embodied presence' that is no longer dependent upon the life cycle or passage of time in human life; nor will it be related to age and experience (of a lifetime or of yesterday). There will be no more need for a restroom or a seat for the flight attendants during the take-off and landing. Instead, we will have 'someone' who is awake, available and smiling 24 hours a day, for millions of customers simultaneously. Her body is not only the playmate (as in the pornography industry) of the imaginary, solitary collectivity of men but also the workmate of other women, who hereby finally lose the possibility of creating a *symbolic social order between women*, something different from the relations of the maid and the mistress of the patriarchal household.

Arrivals

I am a serious researcher. My job is to work at the office at my university and to step out of it every once in a while to be internationally networked and mobile. It is recommendable, I am told, to visit all kinds of conferences, even those of other disciplines. It is nice to return home from them, though. (I hope this queue does not take too long, my feet are killing me and I need to buy both perfume and candies on the way.)

What was I talking about in the conference in the Bahamas? I wanted to explore *the material and social body-to-body relations* – as opposed to face-to-face encounters more common in cultural analyses and business studies of tourism. I felt we need to know more about the ways in which gender is being *systematized and materialized* into a service-scape where work performances meet customer performances. I also wanted to see the sociology of tourism meet marketing and consumer research on common grounds. Namely, I knew from personal experience that a touristic service-scape, as well as an academic enterprise at its best, is a matter of facilitating and appropriating *encounters*, rather than separate perspectives and postures. I wanted these two to build *interdisciplinary cultural studies of tourism* together, a field where 'sustainable practices' are not merely empty gestures but based on independent research and the reconciliation of multiple knowledge interests (e.g. Ateljevic *et al.*, 2007).

I started by introducing accounts from the perspectives of both the traveller and the service worker. I then explained how patriarchy arranges and modalizes individuals on the basis of their gender in certain ways, and how the notion of gender as a contingent habit makes it possible to see gender as institutionalized – and here minutely standardized – performance that refers to the possibilities of action for subjects rather than to 'natural' inclinations or functions. What I wanted the audience to think through is this: all of this takes place through and within embodied existence.

Since most of the audience was in tourism studies and represented various schools of thought, I closed by referring to the worn-out phrase of the four S's of tourism: sand, sun, sea and sex. (Boring, isn't it? Just how many papers have dwelled on it?) But I replaced it with another set of S's: smiling, sincerity, serendipity and sexuality. With the help of these concepts (see, e.g. Taylor, 2001; Hom, 2004), one could perhaps start to get serious about the ways in which the 'meeting grounds of difference' (e.g. MacCannell, 1992) are managed in this world, where culture and economy have been married for good and there is no divorce in sight. Hospitality servers are among those who enable the global mobile economy and profit the multinational corporations; their smiles and affections are integral to the working of the new economy.

Tourism studies loses its connection to lived social realities if its spokesmen keep on fixing their gaze on a model consumer based on a *homo economicus* – and this was the only power point slide I showed:

> *Homo economicus* is a male person . . . sometimes a giant incorporating the whole of society or the world. . . . He is a quintessential stranger; he has no family or friends, no personal history; his emotions are not like ours; we don't understand his language, still less his purposes. . . . We model our questions about ourselves on the idea we have of him. . . . In spite of his elegant foreign name, he is selfish and unmannered, brutish as Caliban, naïve as Man Friday. . . . Judging from the bad press he receives, we actually dislike him a lot and cannot believe anyone could really be so greedy and selfish. He is logical, but even that is unattractive. His shadow stretches across our thoughts so effectively that we even use his language for criticizing him.
>
> (Douglas and Nay, 1998, p. 23)

Mary Douglas and Steven Nay help us realize that the figure we meet seated and served in the cabin or in marketing and company policies is the same figure that runs the airline business. You can find the same figure again within the academic marketing research community whose main aim is to produce knowledge that benefits the needs of, again, the very same figure, as several critical scholars have demonstrated (e.g. Hirschman, 1993; Firat, 2001; Moisander, 2007; Moisander and Valtonen, 2006). The human figure whose satisfaction seems to be the core aim of the entire business-scape is a universal traveller born within a man's body.

(Oh, bugger. It is my eyelash curlers that set off the alarm this time.)

Acknowledgements

We wish to thank Jennie Germann Molz for her encouragement, insight and collegial critique of this chapter at its final stage. Thanks are owed also to Eeva Jokinen, Johanna Moisander, Seija Tuulentie and Jarno Valkonen for commenting on earlier drafts thoughtfully and critically, and to the Academy of Finland for financing it as part of the Tourism as Work project at the University of Lapland.

Endnotes

[1] 'Finnair is the first airline in the Nordic countries to introduce lie-flat seats in its intercontinental fleet – so a Business Class flight is now even more comfortable than ever. The new seats will be installed between December 2005 and April 2006. With the

lie-flat seats, the space between seats will increase from the current 127 cm/50 in. to 160 cm/63 in. – the most comfortable seat in its class. The new seats provide more privacy for rest and work. Passengers can stretch out and lie flat – even if they are 2 metres/6 foot 7 in. tall. Another benefit of the seat is that the back doesn't tilt back into the space of the next passenger. Instead, it adjusts using an electric control into positions for work and rest, inside the passenger's own personal space. In addition to the angle of the seatback, the seat height and the lumbar supports can also be adjusted. There is storage space for laptop computers and magazines, and privacy is further increased by the small dividing walls between the seats. There are several adjustment options in the personal reading lamps. There is an individual electric outlet in the seat for laptop computers. Satellite phones are available for the use of passengers' (available at: http://www.finnair.fi/filecontent/fi/seat/eng/).

[2] A short story from real life, shared with us by Kaarina Kantele (April 2006, personal communication).

[3] See Felicity Hoffman in *Desperate Housewives* seizing the moment in a job interview: 'Watch me multitask' – consulting a future boss while changing diapers.

[4] 'The smile war has its veterans and its lore. I was told repeatedly, and with great relish, the story of one smile-fighter's victory, which goes like this. A young businessman said to a flight attendant, "Why aren't you smiling?" She put her tray back on the food cart, looked him in the eye, and said, "I'll tell you what. You smile first, then I'll smile." The business man smiled at her. "Good," she replied. "Now freeze, and hold that for fifteen hours." Then she walked away. In one stroke, the heroine not only asserted a personal right to her facial expressions but also reversed the roles in the company script by placing the mask on a member of the audience. She challenged the company's right to imply, in its advertising, that passengers have a right to her smile. This passenger, of course, got more: an expression of her genuine feeling' (Hochschild, 1983, pp. 127–128).

References

Adkins, L. (2001) Cultural feminization: money, sex and power for women. *Signs* 26, 669–695.

Adkins, L. (2005) The new economy, property and personhood. *TCS* 2005 22(1), 111–130.

Adkins, L. and Skeggs, B. (eds) (2004) *Feminism after Bourdieu*. Blackwell Publishing, Oxford.

Althusser, L. (1969/1994) Ideology and ideological state apparatus. In Žižek, S. (ed.) *Mapping Ideology*. Verso, London, pp. 100–140.

Ateljevic, I., Morgan, N. and Pritchard, A. (eds) (2007) *Critical Turn in Tourism Studies: Innovative Methodologies*. Elsevier, Oxford.

Beck, U. (2000) *The Brave New World of Work* (trans. P. Camellier). Polity, London.

Bitner, M.J. (1992) Servicescapes: the impact of physical surroundings on customers and employees. *Journal of Marketing* 56(April), 57–71.

Bourdieu, P. (1990) *The Logic of Practice*. Stanford University Press, Stanford, California.

Brandth, B. and Haugen, M. (2005) Doing rural masculinity – from logging to outfield tourism. *Journal of Gender Studies* 14(1), 13–22.

Butler, J. (1990) *Gender Trouble, Feminism and the Subversion of Identity*. Routledge, New York.

Douglas, M. and Nay, S. (1998) *Missing Persons: A Critique of the Social Sciences*. University of California Press, Berkeley, California.

du Gay, P. and Pryke, M. (eds) (2003) *Cultural Economy*. Sage, London.

Ehrenreich, B. and Hochschild, A. (eds) (2002) *Global Woman: Nannies, Maids and Sex Workers in the New Economy*. Granta Books, London.

Elias, N. (1992) *Time: An Essay*. Blackwell, Oxford.

Featherstone, M. (1991) The body in consumer culture. In: Featherstone, M., Hepworth, M.

and Turner, B.S. (eds) *The Body. Social Process and Cultural Theory*. Sage, London, pp. 170–196.

Firat, A.F. (2001) Consumer research for (the benefit of) consumers. *Journal of Research for Consumers* 1.

Fisk, R., Stephen, P., Brown, W. and Bitner, M.J. (1993) Tracking the evolution of the services marketing literature. *Journal of Retailing* 69(Spring), 61–103.

Forseth, U. (2005) Gender matters? Exploring how gender is negotiated in service encounters. *Gender, Work and Organization* 12(5), 440–478.

Foucault, M. (1977) *Discipline and Punish: The Birth of the Prison*. Vintage Books, New York.

Gloria magazine (2003) Good sleep for career women. *Sanoma Magazines*, November 2003, Finland.

Gibson, J.J. (1979) *The Ecological Approach to Visual Perception*. Houghton Mifflin, Boston, Massachusetts.

Gibson, S. (2003) Accommodating strangers: British Hospitality and the Asylum Hotel debate. *Journal for Cultural Research* 7(4), 367–386.

Gmelch, G. (2003) *Behind the Smile: The Working Lives of Caribbean Tourism*. Indiana University Press, Bloomington, Indiana.

Goffman, E. (1977) The arrangements between the sexes. *Theory and Society* 1977(4), 301–331.

Gray, A. (2003) Enterprising femininity: new modes of work and subjectivity. *European Journal of Cultural Studies* 6(4), 489–506.

Gustavsson, E. (2005) Virtual servants: stereotyping female front-office employees on the Internet. *Gender, Work and Organization* 12(5), 400–419.

Heineck, G. (2005) Up in the skies? The relationship between body height and earnings in West Germany. *Labour* 19(3), 469–489.

Hirschman, E. (1993) Ideology in consumer research, 1980 and 1990: a marxist and feminist critique. *Journal of Consumer Research* 19(March), 537–555.

Hochschild, A. (1983) *The Managed Heart: Commercialization of Human Feeling*. California University Press, Berkeley, California.

Holvas, J. and Vähämäki, J. (2005) *Odotustila. Pamfletti uudesta työstä*. Teos, Helsinki.

Hom, C.S. (2004) The tourist moment. *Annals of Tourism Research* 31(1), 61–77.

Ingold, T. (2000) *The Perception of the Environment: Essays on Livelihood, Dwelling and Skill*. Routledge, London.

Jokinen, E. (2005) *Aikuisten arki*. Gaudeamus, Helsinki. [The Everyday Life of the Adults]

Kerfoot, D. and Korczynski, M. (2005) Editorial. Gender and service: new directions for the study of 'Front-Line' service work. *Gender, Work and Organization* 12(5), 387–399.

Leadbeater, C. (2004) Dream on: sleep in the 24/7 society. A Demos Report.

Lovell, T. (2000) Thinking feminism with and against Bourdieu. *Feminist Theory* 1(1), 11–32.

Lovelock, C. and Gummesson, E. (2004) Whiter services marketing? In search of a new paradigm and fresh perspectives. *Journal of Service Research* 7(1), 20–41.

MacCannell, D. (1992) *Empty Meeting Grounds: The Tourist Papers*. Routledge, London.

Macnaghten, P. and Urry, J. (2001) Bodies of nature: introduction. In Macnaghten, P. and Urry, J. (eds) *Bodies of Nature*. Sage, London, pp. 1–11.

McNay, L. (2004) Agency and experience: gender as a lived relation. In: Adkins, L. and Skeggs, B. (eds) *Feminism after Bourdieu*. Blackwell, Oxford, pp. 175–190.

Martin, E. (1994) *Flexible Bodies: Tracking Immunity on American Culture: From the Days of Polio to the Age of AIDS*. Beacon, Boston, Massachusetts.

Mauss, M. (1935/1968) Techniques of the body. *Economy and Society* 2(1), 70–85.

Moisander, J. (2001) *Representation of Green Consumerism: A Constructionist Critique*. Dissertation. Helsinki School of Economics and Business Administration. Acta Universitatis Oeconomicae Helsingiensis, Series A-185.

Moisander, J. and Valtonen, A. (2005) Busy professionals: a cultural approach to time. In: Casedy, D. (ed.) *Proceedings of the International Conference in Search of Time*. ISIDA, Palermo, Italy, pp. 23–30.

Moisander, J. and Valtonen, A. (2006) *Qualitative Marketing Research: A Cultural Approach*. Sage, London.

Molz, J.G. (2006) Cosmopolitan bodies: fit to travel and travelling to fit. *Body and Society* 12(3), 1–21.

Nowtony, H. (1994) Time. *The Modern and Postmodern Experience*. Polity Press, UK.

Persico, N., Posteleweite, A. and Silverman, D. (2004) The effect of adolescent experience on labor market outcomes: the case of height. *Journal of Political Economy* 112(5), 1019–1053.

Pine, J.B. and Gilmore, J.H. (1999) *The Experience Economy: Work is Theatre and Every Business is a Stage*. Harvard Business School Press, Boston, Massachusetts.

Roberts, K. (2004) *The Leisure Industries*. Palgrave Macmillan, New York.

Sennett, R. (1998) *The Corrosion of Character: The Personal Consequences of Work in the New Capitalism*. Norton, New York.

Sherry, J.F., Jr (ed.) (1998) *Servicescapes: The Content of Place in Contemporary Markets*. NTC/Contemporary Publishing Company, Chicago, Illinois.

Sinclair, T. (ed.) (1997) *Gender, Work and Tourism*. Routledge, London.

Skeggs, B. (2004) *Class, Self, Culture*. Routledge, London.

Taylor, J.P. (2001) Authenticity and sincerity in tourism. *Annals of Tourism Research* 28(1), 7–26.

Toynbee, P. (2003) *Hard Work: Life in Low-Pay Britain*. Bloomsbury, London.

Urry, J. (2002) Mobility and proximity. *Sociology* 36(2), 255–274.

Valtonen, A. (2004a) Rethinking free time: a study on boundaries, disorders, and symbolic goods. Dissertation. *Helsinki School of Economics. Series A:236*. HeSe Print, Helsinki.

Valtonen, A. (2004b) *You Should Wear High-Heels: An Autoethnograhpic Account of Gendered Body Height Ideals*. Paper presented at the 7th ACR Conference on Gender, Marketing and Consumer Behavior, Madison, Wisconsin, 24–27 June 2004.

Valtonen, A. (2005) Sleep: leisure pleasure manufactured in the market. In Shove, E. and Pantzar, M. (eds) *Manufacturing Leisure: Innovations in Happiness, Well-being and Fun*. National Consumer Research Center, Helsinki, pp. 20–33.

Van Maanen, J. (1991) The smile factory: work at Disneyland. In: Frost, P.J., Moore, L.F., Louis, M.R., Lundberg, C.C. and Martin, J. (eds) *Reframing Organizational Culture*. Sage, Thousand Oaks, California, pp. 58–76.

Vargo, S.L. and Lusch, R.F. (2004) Evolving to a new dominant logic for marketing. *Journal of Marketing* 68(January), 1–17.

Veijola, S. (1997) Luku, suku ja sosiaalinen. Taipuuko varsinainen sosiaalinen myös naissuvun mukaan? *Naistutkimus/Kvinnoforskning*, April, 2–29. [Number, gender and the social: can the proper social be conjugated in the feminine gender as well?]

Veijola, S. (2004) Pelaajan ruumis. Sekapeli modaalisena sopimuksena. In: Jokinen, E., Kaskisaari, M. and Husso, M. (eds) *Ruumis töihin. Käsite ja käytäntö*. Vastapaino, Tampere, pp. 99–124. [The Body of the Player: Mixed Team Play as a Modal Contract]

Veijola, S. (2006) Heimat tourism in the countryside: paradoxical sojourns to self and place. In: Minca, C. and Oakes, T. (eds) *Travels in Paradox: Remapping Tourism*. Rowman & Littlefield, New York, pp. 77–95.

Veijola, S. and Jokinen, E. (2001) *Voiko naista rakastaa? Avion ja eron karuselli*. WSOY, Helsinki. [Can Woman Be Loved? The Carousel of Marriage and Divorce]

Veijola, S. and Jokinen, E. (2005) Hostessing, gender and work. A paper presented at the 37th International World Conference of IIS, Special session on Hostesses of the World: Gender, Power and Sex, Stockholm, Sweden, 5–9 July 2005.

Westwood, S., Pritchard, A. and Morgan, N.J. (2000) Gender-blind marketing: businesswomen's perceptions of airline services. *Tourism Management* 21, 353–362.

Young, I.M. (1990) Throwing like a girl: a phenomenology of feminine bodily comportment, motility, and spatiality. In: Young, I.M. (ed.) *Throwing Like a Girl and Other Essays in Feminist Philosophy and Social Theory*. Indiana University Press, Bloomington, Indiana, pp. 141–159.

Zeithaml, V.A., Bitner, M.J. and Gremler, D.D. (2006) *Services Marketing: Integrating Customer Focus Across the Firm*, 4th edn. McGraw-Hill, Irwin, Boston, Massachusetts.

Žižek, S. (1997) *The Plague of Fantasies*. Verso, London.

3 Ambivalent Journeys: Writing Travel as the Feminist Stranger in *Desert Places*

SIMONE FULLAGAR

[T]here are new kinds of nomads, not people who are at home everywhere, but who are at home nowhere. I was one of them.

(Robyn Davidson, 1996, p. 5)

[W]e do not know how to designate the peculiar unity of this position other than by saying that it is composed of certain measures of nearness and distance. Although some quantities of them characterise all relationships a *special* proportion and reciprocal tension produce the particular, formal relation to the 'stranger'.

(Georg Simmel, 1950, p. 408)

Introduction

Davidson became a famous international figure in the 1970s when she first travelled with several camels across the outback in Australia. The journey was sponsored by the *National Geographic* and later published as the book *Tracks* (Davidson, 1980). The lone figure of a woman desiring closeness to the otherness of nature and indigenous cultures – to paraphrase Simmel – is the feminist stranger, an emergent figure in Western travel writing (Pratt, 1995). Her traversal and writing of the desert country contested the masculine myths of conquest and mastery that historically inhabit the white Australian landscape and identity (Schaffer, 1988; Davidson, 1989). Yet, Davidson cannot escape her own whiteness as a Western woman and while she travels through a desire to encounter otherness, these journeys are characterized by profound ambivalence. In one particular book, *Desert Places* (1996), Davidson travels with the Rabari people of Gujarat in north-western India on a year-long migratory cycle that traces ancient nomadic paths threatened by changing farming practices. Throughout this piece of travel writing there is an ambivalent desire to overcome a contemporary experience of disconnection – an estrangement between self and world, self and other. Always the stranger, she moves with a sense of not 'being at home' anywhere. Yet, travel becomes a search, a journey towards a place in which she might belong for a while – the elsewhere of a Western subject's imagining. She says, having left India, 'I "live" in England but whenever I'm there for too long I find myself longing for that other place, those other people, and I return to India' (1996, p. 275).

Drawing upon Hegel's (1977[1807]) theory of desire and insights from cultural theory we can deconstruct, or read, the travel narrative as a text through which to examine the ambivalent relation between the western subject's identity and an idealized otherness (see also Van den Abbeele, 1992). Within contemporary literature on travel and tourism there has been a curious lack of theory that attempts to unravel the complex formation of our desires to know otherness. Hegel's work informs much post-structuralist and feminist theory that takes up the question of how we understand the social and psychical nature of desire as it mediates our knowledge of self-identity and otherness (Game, 1991). This chapter engages with several key theorists within this post-structuralist trajectory in order to develop a means of analysing the *universal* journey of selfhood written through the *singular* travel narratives of the western feminine subject Robyn Davidson. In this way Davidson's narrative is irreducible to either register and is not simply positioned as a liberatory tale of the feminist traveller's freedom to move. Narratives of travel have recently become the focus of textual analysis that seeks to undo the opposition between the real and the fictional, emphasizing instead the ways in which our experiences of otherness are always mediated by language, myth and culture (Pratt, 1995; Duncan and Gregory, 1999; Fullagar, 2002).

Desert Places is written through a sense of longing to belong elsewhere, a fascination with, and at times horror at, the otherness of India. The French feminist Julie Kristeva's (1982, 1991) notion of abjection is particularly useful in thinking further about ambivalent nature of journeys into different cultures (Lechte, 1990). The trope of ambivalence has been the subject of recent post-colonial theory that seeks to consider the nature of communication and empathic relations between self and other. As Ang (1996) says: 'It is important to examine these ambivalent moments because they have significant consequences for the prospect of our capability to be "living with difference"' (pp. 41–42). While Ang speaks specifically of multiculturalism, she flags a broader post-colonial concern with exploring the ethical relations bound up with identity and belonging. This raises questions about the way in which otherness is constituted through travel as an intersubjective encounter. For example, what does the ambivalent relation between Davidson and India suggest about the ways in which the traveller can know the difference and communicate with the other? Through Kristeva's (1982, 1991) work I explore the possibility of an intersubjective relation that is both near and far, as a mode of *being with* others.

The Ambivalent Stranger

> I felt more at home here, more in love with life than I ever had in England. Whatever I thought about India, I would find myself, a minute later, thinking the exact opposite with equal conviction. Not for a moment did it allow relief from the discomforts of paradox. Not for a moment did it allow indifference.
>
> (Davidson, 1996, p. 203)

India figures in Davidson's narrative as an object of her empathy or love, and then, as she suggests above, it becomes the object of her loathing. She feels on the one hand 'more at home' in this foreign place, yet she remains always estranged, not quite comfortably settled. The India of her imagination allows her no peace; she is constantly moving between extreme emotions in a state of ambivalence. Volatile moments of hate, rage and anxiety erupt repeatedly throughout her journey with the Rabari, disturbing her bounded and controlled sense of self. Davidson says: 'The words, "I hate India" did not fit with the person I thought I was' (1996, p. 175). There is also a repeated reference to her inability to communicate through the Rabari language and she becomes 'suspended in a vast loneliness'. Ambivalence has a disturbing effect on the self, dislocating the traveller from the place of self-certainty. The other fails to act as a mirror which would secure identity; instead there is a disturbing encounter with the subject's own projection of difference. A cultural strangeness which, in disrupting the inside/outside, self/other boundary, inaugurates what Kristeva (1982, p. 14) terms a narcissistic crisis – the abjection of self. Before we explore the nature of this abject state, let us consider the complexity of Davidson's ambivalent identification with India, and specifically the Rabari.

The sensual images of desert landscapes seduce Davidson, and in turn her reader, into a complex romance with India. She says: 'A squiggle of smoke, a figure in billowing robes, a camel and a bed silhouetted themselves against the horizon. To the east a moon squeezed into the sky; behind me the sun dissolved in the Arabian Sea. This is where I wanted to be. These were the people I wanted to live with' (1996, p. 83). This romanticized otherness exerts a powerful hold over Davidson, generating a fantasy of finding the ideal Rabari community who will accept (and thus love) her as the stranger. When Davidson eventually finds the 'right' Rabari group, she describes the initial relation through the metaphor of kin-like connection. She says:

> Despite the fact that it was impossible to sleep that night – coughing, bleating, gurgling, barking, snoring, sweating, slapping anopheles mosquitoes – I was for the first time, excited by what I was doing. Whatever the discomforts of dang life, here one could breathe. Here would be continuity, friendships. The women were up before first light and called me over for tea.
>
> (Davidson, 1996, p. 77)

Davidson desires to close the distance between self and other through the rhetorical use of 'real experience' in the representation of travel. It is a formulation of truth premised on a notion of empathy as living as the other does. She says: 'At least through the discomforts of my own body, through the exhaustion, illness and rage, I had an idea of how people really lived' (1996, p. 272). It is a desire for empathy, or nearness, which would allow her inside. This insideness would signify the loss of her outsideness, her difference as the stranger. This suggests a longing to be accepted into an unmediated relation with the other where they would become one, where she would become other. Yet, Davidson has moments of doubt about the absolute nature of this knowledge: 'but even if I had been able to speak his language, how much of Phagu's [Rabari elder] world would I have comprehended? Real travel would be able to see the world, even for an instant, with another's eyes' (1996, p. 152).

Davidson's empathy is structured by a desire for acceptance into a community of selves premised on a particular kind of intersubjective relation, or love, that is figured through an imagined oneness. The love of the other is premised on a Judeo-Christian ideal of brotherly love as sameness: to love the other as oneself. The ambivalence in Davidson's narrative reveals the failure of such a notion of empathy as the basis of intersubjective relations, as it implies a form of cultural narcissism. The desire to know difference in cultural narcissism positions the other as an exotic commodity within an economy of sameness (you are different from me; my culture is the marker of a human norm). Judeo-Christian discourse abstracts differences between cultures, turning them into aberrations that can be overcome in the quest for a universal humanness. All differences are treated as the same under the authority of God, making it very difficult to love or know the other as other, as irreducibly different from oneself. Kristeva (1991, p. 192) argues that such an appeal to human sameness relies on a debt to paternal and divine authority. Such notions of brotherly love or fraternity require a suspension of difference through an appeal to a universal sameness in the eyes of God: 'all men' (1991, p. 84).

Ambivalence is an unthinkable position within such a theological tradition, for one must love the other absolutely, and without question as to the nature of the distinction which separates self from others. As Derrida says: 'One becomes a brother, in Christianity, one is worthy of the eternal father, only by loving one's enemies as one's neighbours or as oneself' (1997, p. 285). The virtue inherent in such models of friendship, or fraternity, is implicated in an economy of exchange, whereby the 'gift' of friendship procures the subject's own identity (or salvation). Empathy within such an economy of exchange is the means (as a desiring relation) by which the subject comes to know the other through a dissymmetry, as useful to oneself. Difference and contradictory emotions are something to be suppressed, rather than understood. Ambivalence then, is what an empathetic relation is supposed to overcome in the gesture of reconciling felt differences.

Freud (1963[1930]) contests such assumptions, and his contention lies with the historical failure of universal appeals to love, which he argues are connected to the prevalence of a death drive in destructive relations between individuals and nations. He raises the challenge of thinking love and hate together, and of rethinking the opposition in which hate comes to subsume love in a destructive hierarchical relation. In Freud's terms, this relation informs the struggle of life and death instincts, and cannot be wished away through an idealized notion of empathic love. He says that the ideal of brotherly love is impossible to fulfil as it denies the force of the unconscious: 'such an enormous inflation of love can only lower its value, not get rid of the difficulty' (1963[1930], p. 80). Extending this notion, Derrida suggests that the difficulty or ambivalence in self/other relations is connected with envy as the jealous desire for self-certainty. He says: 'Love would be the attempt to leap beyond this envy. And the aggression whereby *we make an enemy*, whereby we make ourselves our own enemy, is only a reaction. It hides and reveals, at one and the same time, our vulnerability' (1997, p. 281, original italics). The vulnerability of self, the dependence on the other for friendship, is revealed through the destabilizing effect of ambivalence felt in empathic relations with the other.

Freud and Kristeva suggest that the ideal of loving the other as oneself is untenable because of the phenomenon of primary narcissism in which the other will always be implicated in the self's projections and infantile dramas. Empathy implies that one can know the other by becoming the other momentarily, via the projection of self. To love the other as oneself is to exacerbate this narcissistic tendency, rather than encourage ways of knowing the other as other in its alterity (and the limits of that knowledge). In light of Freud's observations on the dynamic of love and hate, I argue that the opposite of love is not necessarily hate, but rather indifference (an absence of desire or emotion). Davidson is profoundly caught up in an ambivalent relation with India because of the impossibility of feeling indifferent towards the other. She is subsumed by the desire to move closer to the other, and this in turn becomes a demand upon the other to obey her Western logic. The question is, then, how is one to negotiate the distance between self and other in order to maintain a respect for, and understanding of, difference?

From empathy to abjection

Davidson's fantasy of travelling with a nomadic community is an attempt to enact two seemingly opposite desires: the stability of feeling at home, as connectedness, and the freedom of movement, as autonomy. But India, it seems, will not remain the stable object of such desires, eluding her grasp and revoking her longing to belong: 'but India, how would I ever learn to decipher it, to be at home in it?' (1996, p. 164). Being 'at home' is associated with a mutual love, a feeling of oneness in which communicative relations are somehow transparent. The Rabari culture and language, however, is an otherness she is unable to decipher. There exists a linguistic and cultural distance that cannot be overcome by her identification with, and love of, this imagined otherness. Post-colonial theorist Homi Bhabha (1991, p. 162) argues that cultural difference is not simply given, but in such circumstances the distinction is produced through a transference which constitutes the other. This is never simply a fixing of an alterity which would mirror back a selfsame identity. Rather, through the relations of love or hate there is an emotional intensification which also provokes movement within the self.

Kristeva says that it is in relations which are characterized by a profound ambivalence that the desire for selfsameness is disturbed, inaugurating what she calls a 'narcissistic crisis' (1982, p. 15). She takes Freud's notion of primary narcissism further in relation to the experience of ambivalence, suggesting how the ego is always uncertain, fragile and threatened. In Davidson's narrative there are three particular instances in which her ambivalent relation to India becomes the undoing of identity and empathy for the other. I argue that Davidson's experience of profound ambivalence inaugurates a narcissistic crisis because of the nature of her desire to belong, to overcome difference and be one with the other.

Repetitions of estrangement

Through her projections Davidson is caught in a repetition of estrangement, the imagined community she desires to feel at home in is transfigured through fear and hostility. The urgency of her wish to become nearer to the other fuels a growing frustration with the communicative distance that maintains her 'outsideness'. Fear subsumes her love for the other, fragmenting the fantasy of feeling one with the Rabari community. She says:

> When I woke each morning it was to dread. I must face them. I must sit and eat with them. Sometimes they smiled at me or laughed but I could not read their faces. They had no inkling what torture it was to be unable to speak, unable to order the world in any way, exposed and wretched in a place where even the sky was strange.
>
> (Davidson, 1996, p. 136)

The uncanny strangeness of the other haunts her narrative, and this anxiety appears through metaphors of engulfment, 'going under' in a sea of incomprehension (Freud, 1985). The Rabari otherness refuses to be held still, or to be domesticated by Davidson's 'desire to grasp the strange' (Kristeva, 1991, p. 180). Kristeva suggests that it is not mere rivalry (as she associates it with the Oedipus complex) which is the source of ambivalence, but a more archaic relation with the maternal. The subject's first relation with the m/other is that which regulates identity through an economy of narcissism (Kristeva, 1982, p. 63). The fusional nature of self/mother relations generates boundary difficulties for the subject who negotiates duel desires for connection and autonomy. These difficulties involve working out where the self and its desires end and the other's begin. It is the process of differentiation in which the emotions of love and hate are intertwined. Kristeva, speaking of this earliest desire, says it is, 'a narcissism laden with hostility and which does not yet know its limits. For we are dealing with imprecise boundaries in that place, at that moment, where pain is born out of an excess of fondness and a hate that, refusing to admit the satisfaction it also provides, is projected towards an other' (1982, p. 60).

The first example I want to explore exemplifies this narcissistic tendency to project hatred onto the loved other, as Davidson's relationship with the Rabari shifts from an idealized communalism to an uneasy and precarious alliance. As her sense of isolation and loneliness grows on the journey with the Rabari, there is a change in the intersubjective relationship. She says: 'What had begun as goodwill was atrophying for want of language to nourish it' (1996, p. 134). Davidson reiterates that her sense of a widening communicative gap between herself and the Rabari produces a profound instability, in which the other becomes the object of hate. This dissolution of self highlights the relation between speaking and identity, suggesting that language works to structure the affective dimension of intersubjective relations rather than being a transparent means of communication. Davidson goes on to say: 'The desire to talk was like some fantastic hunger; they were my torturers, keeping the food just beyond reach' (1996, p. 137). Her longing to speak English is described as homesickness, a desire for the familiar, as she no longer recognizes the other as kin.

Freud describes such experiences in terms of the persecution complex. He says: 'They (the paranoid), too, cannot regard anything in other people as indifferent, and they too, take up minute indications with which these other, unknown people present them, and use them in their "delusions of reference". The meaning of their delusions of reference is that they expect from all strangers something like love' (quoted in Bhabha, 1991, p. 93). We see in Davidson's narrative a nostalgic desire to experience oneself whole again in a communal relation with the other. For Stewart (1984) such narrative longing is a nostalgic reiteration of an origin

story concerning separation from the maternal, the mother tongue in this case.
It is perpetual desire for reunion with one's origins, as the origin place comes to
figure as stability amidst the crisis of self. For Davidson this is a fantasy of belonging within an ideal home as a place of transparent communication, where all the
subject's needs are understood and met by the m/other.

The abject self

Davidson's second narcissistic crisis is produced through her extreme ambivalence
not only towards the Rabari but towards India itself. India is conjured metonymically
through an abstraction of Davidson's horror: the poverty, waste, exploitation – as
they unsettle her fantasy of community. She speaks of a vulnerable moment in which
she cannot escape the other's curious look: an ironic reversal of the touristic gaze:

> I wanted to be left alone. That was all. I walked around the town looking for a den
> to crawl into. I was followed by men who hissed and giggled. I found a stone and sat
> on it. A crowd gathered. I put my head into my hands and absented myself mentally.
> A few moments later I looked up and there, not a foot from my face, was a row of
> men's crotches. Above the crotches was a row of eyes looking at me in that dead
> way. A choking sensation filled my throat, burst behind my eyes. I began hurrying
> through the streets thinking I hate India, I hate India, I hate India.
>
> (Davidson, 1996, p. 174)

This desire to escape the other's gaze leads to Davidson's feeling of revulsion about the
street slums, undernourished children and stench of rotting waste. The gaze is objectifying and masculine, it works to disperse the boundaries of her self as an autonomous
white woman. No longer is it her expelling India's otherness but rather, as Kristeva
says, that 'I am expelled' (1982, p. 4). Davidson encounters the abject within life as a
profound sense of loss, of disconnection, with the desired other. She wonders where
she is and why she is there at all, decentred by a stare which 'strips her of her humanity'. The other is no longer the benevolent source of community she once imagined.
The eye of power is no longer her own, and she hates 'India' for pushing her empathy
into despair and rage at her own profound dislocation. Kristeva makes an important
observation of such experiences: 'It is thus not lack of cleanliness or health that causes
abjection but what disturbs identity, system, order. What does not respect borders,
positions, rules. The in between, the ambiguous, the composite' (1982, p. 4).

Kristeva argues that the abject is not simply a definable object; rather it is what is
radically excluded and draws the self to a place where meaning collapses (1982, p. 2).
Abjection is a feeling evoked by the unconscious whose contents manifest in symbolic
practices without necessarily being integrated into conscious judgement (Kristeva,
1982, p. 7). Kristeva argues that abjection requires thinking beyond Freud's notion
of the unconscious as radically separate from consciousness. The abject is something
'excluded' from consciousness, yet not enough to secure a differentiation between
subject and object. Abjection, then, is something that emerges in between the self and
its own otherness, and manifests in the ambiguous opposition of inside/outside.

Davidson encounters this sense of otherness, which attracts and repels at once
but nevertheless has hold of her; she cannot remain indifferent. Kristeva argues that

abjection 'preserves what existed in the archaism of pre-objectal relationship, in the immemorial violence with which a body becomes separated from another body in order to be' (1982, p. 10). It reveals the inaugural loss which laid the foundations of being, the basis of desire and the phenomenon of exclusion (1982, p. 5). Abjection is connected to the state of fusion with the maternal body, prior to the formation of 'I' through identification; as such it is a 'precondition of narcissism' (1982, p. 12). Abjection, then, is implicit in the formation of identity and its undoing. Unable to identify or grasp the abject, Davidson projects onto India her 'violent mourning for an "object" that has always already been lost' (Kristeva, 1982, p. 15). The other constantly slips through her own projections to reveal a disturbing strangeness, a difference she cannot accommodate within herself. Davidson cannot bridge the gap between self and other; she remains within the ambivalent bind of the narcissistic self steeped in a sense of lack.

When discussing the lack that motivates desire, Kristeva argues that the object of this desire is irretrievable, and while nostalgic, it nevertheless points towards the conditions of desire itself as always based upon an absent otherness. The denial of loss in separation, Kristeva argues, may generate a fear of being autonomous and alone, rather than a Hegelian sense of mastery. At the basis of abjection there is a fear of aloneness or, perhaps more significantly, of loneliness felt in the failure of communicative relations. Davidson speaks of this fear of being alone in her desire to become closer to the other:

> How comforting it must be to pass through life's storms always with the support of the group infusing every action and every thought with one voice extending from the time of one's ancestor's down through the generations, saying, 'It's all right. We are all here. There is no such thing as alone.'
>
> (Davidson, 1996, p. 133)

Davidson's sense of abjection is heightened by the realization that the other eludes her, that it is irretrievable. Yet, unable to let the fantasy go, she is caught in a ceaseless to and fro movement of love and hate; a limbo of restless motion. The more she strives to be nearer the other, the further her identification pushes her away. For it is an identification premised on a wish for sameness, to belong to 'one voice', as she says above. This profound ambivalence towards India is the effect of an encounter with her own split subjectivity, her own abjection: the silence which breaches her communicative relation with the other. A gap or breach within discourse, as the absence against which meaning emerges, is an incompleteness which reveals the impossible fantasy of wholeness and the projections of perfect harmony with others.

There is a third moment in the journey in which Davidson's narcissism is mirrored back, provoking a crisis of identity. Davidson realizes the impossibility of her all-consuming passion for the other; she acknowledges her own profound strangeness and, in turn, the other's alterity. Towards the end of her journey, Davidson observes another woman walking conspicuously through the marketplace: 'I had realised then, with an unpleasant little shock, that no matter how deep my identification with this country went, I would always be seen as alien' (1996, p. 219). Such moments work to displace Davidson's narrative intention of representing the other's reality through writing her experience of nearness, uncontaminated by her own outsideness.

Davidson repeatedly questions the nature of her desire throughout her journey. She asks: 'Where am I? Why am I doing this?' (1996, pp. 102, 141). Finding that she can't give up, and being driven to arrive at the meaning of her journey, she speaks of unconscious forces which move her to know: 'Always I'd been driven by a compulsion to make contact with the world, to be as aware of my life as I could be, to wrestle meaning out of event – and that compulsion lay at the heart of everything I did' (1996, p. 124). There are numerous references to this 'Protestant' drivenness and inferences to the guilt that she feels in failing her goal. The journey is relentlessly hard, lonely and at times meaningless, but she says: 'I had to keep going. I had to. But keeping going had no meaning' (1996, p. 265). 'There was a deeper motive for the prolonging of self punishment; the quest for meaning, of which, so far, this curious journey had remained void' (1996, p. 182). Such metaphors suggest that Davidson's journey is structured by a redemptive longing which moves her to endure a near-dissolution of self in the quest for the truth of self mirrored in the other.

Redemptive longing

Davidson's story is a redemption narrative in which travel figures as a practice of atonement, a working of the self, driven by the desire to save (through writing) the other, and in doing so, to earn her own salvation. Matthews (1968, p. 56) identifies the religious metaphor of the 'hard journey' as it exists within the literature of the West. He cites Dante's pilgrim, undertaking a rite of passage through fear and sin, in which travel figures as a movement of purification. The journey is driven by a dream of blissful reunion with God, a fantasy of recovering lost innocence and the discovery of a transcendental truth (Matthews, 1968, p. 65). Through similar metaphors, Davidson's journey becomes a means of expiating a sense of guilt associated with the difference that separates self and other. Davidson uses metaphors of heaviness – the weight of guilt – to describe her self: 'one carries oneself like a heavy old suitcase wherever one goes' (1996, p. 102). So she must escape her original home in order to feel at home elsewhere, to pursue the fantasy of arriving at the plenitude of oneness again. If we pursue the notion of travel as atonement further, we discover that atonement is a wish for reconciliation, derived from a notion of at-one-ment (Hastings *et al.*, 1924, p. 71).

Davidson's abjection is an effect of being unable to communicate or put into (the other's) words her experience of the journey. In conceptualizing abjection as an alterity which provokes the movement of self, Kristeva asks: '[I]s it not that which characterises writing?' Davidson's metaphors of coming 'adrift' or 'going under' beneath an 'incomprehensible ocean' of difference are an attempt to grasp the unsignifiable. Kristeva argues, in a reading of Joyce, that it is the word which discloses the abject, and at the same time it is the word which purifies the self from the abject (1982, p. 23). It is not until she returns home and is writing the travel narrative retrospectively that the word is able to purify the abject. Writing figures as the means of salvation, a redemption earned through an economy of words, which attempt to give order to the frightening sense of abjection which haunts her travels. The abject shatters the earlier romantic image of belonging within the

Rabari group, and generates a profound sense of failure. She asks: 'For a long time now I could not see how to write about my experiences. They were nothing but a series of disconnected events without a shape, without meaning. I had passed through India as a knife does through ice and it had closed behind me at every step. How does one write about failure?' (1996, p. 275). It could be argued that one writes about failure through a desire for catharsis and the reconciliation of ambivalent emotions.

Through writing, Davidson attempts a reconciliation within the self and concludes her redemptive narrative with reference to the hardship she has endured as the means of becoming nearer to the other. In this way, the difficult 'reality' of the journey stands in opposition to her initial 'romanticism', of which it ultimately becomes a part. She speaks of this empathic experience of the other's reality: 'At least this had truth in it. At least, through the discomforts of my own body, through the exhaustion and illness and rage, I had an idea of how people really lived' (1996, p. 272). For Davidson this notion of authenticity is construed as an immediate truth which is stripped bare of projection and imagination. I would argue that it is itself produced through a fantasy of redemption where the suffering of the body is equated with the acquisition of the truth of the other as it mirrors the self. Understanding between self and other, or empathy, in this Judeo-Christian narrative is premised solely on a negative relation. Pain in this instance is the signifier of the cost, of earning self-certainty in an economy ordered by a desire for presence. Davidson does not get rid of her romantic narrative; rather it becomes a story in which she is positioned ambivalently as the anti-heroine who struggles but fails to acquire knowledge of the other, and thus her own self-certainty.

Davidson's wish to travel exists in a complex relation to her desire to write, to represent the truth of her experience of how the other lives. Her projections of the other are implicated in the economic demands of writing travel for Western consumption, which stem from the fantasy of knowing the other as a mirror of self. Kristeva (1982, p. 34) refers to such a desire to know everything as epistemophilic: as a wish to know what seems to be lacking in oneself. Davidson's failure to secure this knowledge can be read as a narrative in which cultural difference eludes fixing as the object of Western desire. Her story, then, foregrounds a problematic about how we understand the effects of our fleeting encounters with other cultures and the displacement of Western modes of knowing.

The being with of laughter

> [O]ne never laughs alone, one laughs at oneself through the other or, better yet, at oneself *as* other. . . . We laugh not only at the other, but also with the other, *as* others do, all together reunited in one laughter.
>
> (Borch-Jacobsen, 1998, pp. 162–163, original italics)

In this section I examine the fleeting moments of connection Davidson experiences with the Rabari as examples which counter abjection, and reinscribe the cultural relation through a different communication or knowing. As Borch-Jacobsen says in the quotation above, laughter is the means whereby we break from our selfsameness in the paradox of recognizing ourselves in the other. We are different, yet something about our shared humanness joins us in the recognition of our commonality. Laughter shatters the subject's preoccupation with self and hence cultural narcissism. While Davidson's sense of failure dominates her narrative, it is evidence of how a structure of desire premised on cultural narcissism also fails. However, *Desert Places* is not a singular narrative; there are certain moments that offer the reader a glimmer of what a different relation might mean. A relation which is not free of ambivalence, but which recognizes the paradoxical nature of intersubjective relation premised on differentiation and communication. Laughter is a means of unsettling the oppositions of self and other steeped-in emotions such as hatred, as well as the longing to belong premised on a narcissistic love of the other. Such moments enable us to glimpse a mode of 'being with' others, which stands in contrast to Davidson's earlier form of empathy.

Davidson speaks in a different tone of the nature of this communicative gap between self and other. There is a desire which stretches between self and other, as a labile connection unable to be forced or consciously determined but emerges through an openness to difference. There is a tone of humility in Davidson's narrative, a recognition of the other's power to move the self, which stands in contrast to an arrogance underlying her aggressive outbursts. She says: 'What is it, this force of attraction, that leaps across every barrier that humans have been able to construct? In situations like this, when you are receptive to the point of rawness, you become acutely aware of it' (1996, p. 123).

An intersubjective relation emerges to counter the abjection that Davidson has remained engulfed in, yet it is equally difficult to represent. Davidson speaks of the way the Rabari extended themselves towards her, breaking into the blackness of her self-absorption:

> The goodwill in particular kinds of smiles, the ability to extend themselves for others without any expectation of gratitude: these aspects of their humanity had the power to haul me back out of the pit. I would find myself chuckling with them, almost against my will, until affection returned like fresh air behind a storm.
>
> (Davidson, 1996, p. 150)

The abject, which provoked Davidson's writing, is contained within the narrative order of events; we feel it bordering all that she can say, even those moments of laughter. Yet, it is humour which counters the negativity of abjection and shifts Davidson's projections from hate to affection, allowing another understanding of difference. As she says: 'It was for this, their use of laugher as a survival tactic, that I most admired them' (1996, p. 151). Kristeva argues that laughing is 'a way of placing or displacing abjection' (1982, p. 8). For it is a flash of connection across the abyss, a significance generated not necessarily through language but the sharing of a comic interpretation of life from different, but coinciding, positions.

Kristeva (1982, p. 141) speaks of the 'necessity of going through abjection', of facing the void – our own abyss in order that we may find ways of being separate and thus able to live in relation with others. This is a very different sense of endurance to Davidson's Protestant drivenness, which is in effect a repetition of hardship rather than a moving through. Cixous (1991, p. 124) also speaks of the passage of descent into one's own otherness, as that to which Christianity ascribes the negative connotation of 'hell'. Such a movement through this abject place, Cixous argues, involves the crossing of borders which separate and connect the self with others. It is these separations and non-separations which are at the basis of all our archaic and poetic experiences (Cixous, 1991, p. 124). To traverse the abject is to potentially refigure the boundaries which constitute the narcissistic self, shifting the conditions through which desire emerges. Abjection serves to expose the destructive narcissism in which the other is called upon to fill the subject's own lack. This lack is implicated in a horror at the self's fundamental separateness, as it is marked in Davidson's narrative by the other's difference.

Kristeva and Cixous suggest that in order to live in relation to others' difference, the subjects must also be able to live in relation to themselves, to their own strangeness. This is an inner region which remains unmapped and irreconcilable, as it is premised on ambivalent desires: for autonomy and separateness as well as belonging and connection. The passage through abjection is then not one of mastery, as Davidson discovered that the self inevitably fails in the desire to grasp otherness and secure self-certainty. It is instead a movement in which otherness passes through the self, transforming the very boundaries which define the intersubjective relation.

Derrida (1998, p. 107) argues through his reading of French philosopher and surrealist Georges Bataille that laughter bursts the boundaries of meaning, disrupting a Hegelian economy of desire premised on an abstract negativity (see Botting and Wilson, 1998). Bataille (1988) says laughter is contagious, a profoundly social experience. Laughter is not negative because it exceeds dialectics; it is absent in Hegel's economy of life aimed at conservation and the accumulation of knowledge. He argues that '"communication" cannot take place from one full and intact being to another: it requires beings who have put the being within themselves *at stake*, have placed it at the limit of death, of nothingness' (quoted in Derrida, 1998, p. 115, original italics). The question of communication raised by Bataille opens up the possibility of moving in relation to difference through a respect for alterity, and not just in the quest for recognition as that informs the Hegelian desire to belong.

Kristeva argues that a denial of one's own inner strangeness leads to the disavowal of external difference because in confronting that which is foreign or strange to the self we experience the possibility, or not, of *'being an other'* (1991, p. 13). We experience a moment of recognition or negation in our relation with the other's cultural difference, potentially producing a more positive desire. As Kristeva says: 'It is not simply – humanistically – a matter of our being able to accept the other, but of *being in his place*, and this means to imagine and make oneself other for oneself' (1991, p. 13). Implicit in this call for new understandings of cultural relations is a different notion of empathy. In Davidson's situation empathy, as a movement towards the other, is also connected to guilt about the distance between. Empathy in this sense figures as the emotional bridge between self and other, yet as I have argued its formulation within the Judeo-Christian tradition is profoundly problematic in terms of recognizing otherness.

There are moments when Davidson is able to experience 'being with' the other, through a sense of connection different from a Judeo-Christian notion of empathy, for it implies not a standing in the place of the other, but remaining the stranger who shares a sense of human connection while allowing the other's uniqueness. It is a sense of 'being with' others which allows the space of difference to be experienced as a mutual strangeness, a strangeness which, while always far from the self, also has within it a sense of nearness or commonality. As Simmel says: '[T]o be a stranger is naturally a very positive relation, it is a specific form of interaction' (1950, p. 403). The positive moment here is a reference to the formation of friendship as a mode of negotiating between self and other. It is, as Stephen Muecke observes, the beginning moment of something different:

> Something new begins when the answer the local gives is not forced into a universal language of rationality in order to have an understanding determined by this interrogator from a more powerful place. Something new begins if such interrogators have to invest something of their subjectivity, if they have to negotiate, change, and learn to belong.
>
> (Muecke, 1997, p. 184)

However, such a relation is glimpsed only in moments when the striving for nearness ceases; in the recognition of alterity there is a different knowledge generated. In Kristeva's words, such connection occurs when 'meeting balances wandering', where there is a mutual recognition of difference in rituals of sharing, in the 'cosmopolitanism of a moment' (1991, p. 11). Such a moment can be observed in laughter where we identify ourselves with the other. Yet, the nature of this 'being with' creates a third term or in-between self and other, which exceeds both. Borch-Jacobsen speaks of the way this relation 'gathers us together around our own loss, our own death. All of which, obviously, cannot take place unless we let ourselves go, unless *we ourselves* burst out in laughter' (1998, p. 150, original italics). There is, in the moment of experiencing difference, one's own and the other's, a shared sense of the absurdity of life lived in proximity to death and loss. Laughter works to alleviate the tension implicit in the subject's ambivalent holding onto life, meaning and identity as somehow fixed and masterable. To laugh is to lose the serious investment in oneself, through engaging in a moment of lightness with the other.

Kristeva argues that to move beyond cultural narcissism, difference must be the starting point, for the stranger is within me, hence we are all strangers to ourselves. Otherness is framed not in terms of self as centre and other as different but same; nor is it a matter of difference as simply relative in a universal sense. Rather, the strange is something other and we always negotiate through its specificity, for it always signifies the 'improper' part of ourselves, our own split subjectivity. Kristeva suggests: 'It is through unravelling transference – the major dynamics of otherness, of love/hatred for the other, I become reconciled with my own otherness-foreignness, that I play on it and live by it . . . as a journey into the strangeness of the other and of oneself, toward an ethics of respect for the irreconcilable' (1991, p. 182). Perhaps it is through the ironic distance of laughter that a relation of near and far may be glimpsed, as it displaces the tendency towards cultural narcissism and hence the intensification of ambivalent projections. To laugh at oneself is to break the binds of abjection that work to fix the self within an identity that privileges sameness through an idealization of difference.

Conclusion

Marked by the ceaseless movement between a love for, and hate of, India's otherness, *Desert Places* is a disturbing travel narrative. The violence of Davidson's reaction to India, at times frightening in its narcissistic repetition, unsettles the confessional tone which invites the reader's identification. It is a compelling story because of the constant ambivalence produced through a particular desire to intimately know the other; to be so near as to belong to one voice. Yet, Davidson finds, in the absence of the mediating work of a shared language, anxiety and misunderstanding erupt in her everyday encounters into what Kristeva (1982) calls a 'narcissistic crisis'. Haunted by a profound sense of disconnection and loneliness, she experiences a state of abjection arising out of an ambivalent wish to belong. As a violent mourning for the other who remains ever afar, the journey is one long struggle to reconcile the emotions of a fascinated love for, and a loathing of, difference. In her desire to belong to, to become intimately part of, the Rabari culture, Davidson remains irreconcilably the stranger. Through the other she encounters the strangeness of her self, its conflictual and contradictory impulses.

Within the failing of Davidson's nostalgic desire to become one with the Rabari and thus secure her own acceptance through belonging, she importantly identifies the irreducible difference of each culture. A difference that refuses to be reified, or held still, just as it cannot be dissolved or wished away. While the theme of ambivalence is dominant in Davidson's story, there are also experiences which counter the narrative of estrangement and disconnection. These are particular instances of connection between herself and the Rabari, which in Simmel's (1950, p. 407) words involves a relation of 'near and far at once'. These moments stand in contrast to ambivalence as a movement between near *and* far, where difference is negated in a desire for an absolute proximity or empathic knowledge of the other. This sense of nearness is premised on a narcissistic desire for the same. Moments of stillness emerge unexpectedly, through relinquishing the desire to possess knowledge of the other. It suggests a mode of 'being with' others as a form of knowing as communicating, negotiating, accepting the other on their own terms. Within Davidson's narrative these moments generate an alternative trajectory of belonging, a story of a desire for otherness which starts, as Kristeva (1982) says, from the recognition that we are always strangers to ourselves.

References

Ang, I. (1996) Ambivalence and the 'Asian' woman in Australian multiculturalism. *Feminist Review* 52, 36–49.

Bataille, G. (1988) *Inner Experience*. State University of New York, New York.

Bhabha, H. (1991) *The Location of Culture*. Polity Press, London.

Borch-Jacobsen, M. (1998) The laughter of being (trans. T. Thomas). In: Botting, F. and Wilson, S. (eds) *Bataille: A Critical Reader*. Blackwell, Oxford.

Botting, F. and Wilson, S. (eds) (1998) *Bataille: A Critical Reader*. Blackwell, Oxford.

Cixous, H. (1991) *The School of Roots: Three Steps on the Ladder of Writing* (trans. S. Cornell and S. Sellers). Columbia University Press, New York.

Davidson, R. (1980) *Tracks*. Cape, London.

Davidson, R. (1989) *Travelling Light*. Imprint, Sydney.

Davidson, R. (1996) *Desert Places*. Viking, London.

Derrida, J. (1997) *The Politics of Friendship* (trans. G. Colins). Verso, London.

Derrida, J. (1998) From restricted to general economy: a Hegelianism without reserve (trans. A. Bass). In: Botting, F. and Wilson, S. (eds) *Bataille: A Critical Reader*. Blackwell, Oxford.

Duncan, J. and Gregory, D. (eds) (1999) *Writes of Passage: Reading Travel Writing*. Routledge, London.

Freud, S. (1963[1930]) *Civilisation and Its Discontents* (trans. J. Riviere). Hogarth Press, London.

Freud, S. (1985[1919]) *The Uncanny in Art and Literature*. Pelican Freud Library. Penguin, Harmondsworth, 14.

Fullagar, S. (2002) Narratives of travel: Desire and the movement of feminine subjectivity. *Leisure Studies* 21(1), 57–74.

Game, A. (1991) *Undoing the Social: Towards a Deconstructive Sociology*. Open University Press, Milton Keynes.

Hastings, J. *et al.* (eds) (1924) *The Dictionary of the Bible*. T & T Clarke, Edinburgh, UK.

Hegel, G. (1977[1807]) *Phenomenology of Spirit* (trans. A.V. Miller). Clarendon Press, Oxford.

Kristeva, J. (1982) *The Powers of Horror: An Essay on Abjection* (trans. L. Roudiez). Columbia University Press, New York.

Kristeva, J. (1991) *Strangers to Ourselves* (trans. L. Roudiez). Harvester Wheatsheaf, Hertfordshire, UK.

Lechte, J. (1990) *Julia Kristeva*. Routledge, London.

Matthews, H. (1968) *The Hard Journey: The Myth of Man's Rebirth*. Chatto & Windus, London.

Muecke, S. (1997) *No Road: Bitumen All the Way*. Freemantle Arts Centre Press, Western Australia.

Pratt, M. (1995) *Imperial Eyes: Travel Writing and Transculturation*. Routledge, London.

Schaffer, K. (1988) *Women and the Bush: Forces of Desire in the Australian Cultural Tradition*. Cambridge University Press, Sydney.

Simmel, G. (1950) The Stranger. In: Wolf, K. (ed.) *The Sociology of Georg Simmel*. Free Press, New York.

Stewart, S. (1984) *On Longing: Narratives of the Miniature, the Gigantic, the Souvenir, the Collection*. Johns Hopkins University Press, Baltimore, Maryland.

Van den Abbeele, G. (1992) *Travel as Metaphor: From Montagaine to Rousseau*. University of Minnesota Press, Minneapolis, Minnesota.

4 Travelling for Masculinity: The Construction of Bodies/Spaces in Israeli Backpackers' Narratives

CHAIM NOY

> By means of this familiarity with the divine act of creation, the Western traveler became himself creative and divine, or at least legendary and heroic.
>
> (Green, 1993, p. 52)

Introduction

Gendered bodies and narratives play various roles and assume various meanings within the myriad cultures of modern tourism. The symbolic richness of contemporary tourist cultures, as well as the spaces, practices and experiences that they embody, suggest that in the broadest sense of the term, tourism amounts to a heightened arena of consumption and production (performance) of gendered identities. In this chapter I explore narratives of hegemonic masculinity, as these are represented in, and socially constructed through, travel narratives Israeli backpackers tell. This chapter is also inspired by phenomenological sensitivities and seeks to reveal the personal experiences of men and to elaborate upon the telling and sharing of these experiences. In this context, narratives of personal experience supply both a representation and an evocation of different types of masculine identifications. They illustrate various tactics of resistance, improvisation and subversion that are employed with regard to normative discourses.

Addressing Israeli youth backpackers in particular affords an examination of the conflation of local and global cultural gender themes. Images of masculinity that are common in the backpackers' home society and culture ('local') are fused during the trip with representations of hegemonic masculinity in international tourism ('global'). In the narratives of the backpackers who were interviewed for this study, these images mostly reside in one sociocultural site or space: the backpacker's body. This body is at the centre of the chapter.

Locally, it is important to note that among secular Jewish Israeli middle-class youths, embarking on an extended backpacking trip soon after their discharge from obligatory military service is a time-honoured, widespread social custom. On an individual level, the backpacking trip, which is inspired by romantic images and narratives, amounts to a formative, highly meaningful period. On a societal-cultural level, the backpacking trip has come to assume a form of a collective and normative rite of passage (Noy and Cohen, 2005b). The duration of the lengthy travel amounts to an experientially heightened time, wherein backpacker ideology and symbolic system have a major and enduring impact on the youths who engage in backpacking (Sorensen, 2003; Welk, 2004). The many and intense interactions and relationships, typical of backpackers, and the symbolic order of the trip, amount to the heightened sociocultural backdrop against which the drama of the youths' gender identity is fervently negotiated and consolidated (Noy, 2004b). Globally, 'backpacker ideology' is heavily implicated by images and discourses of gender, which in turn it perpetuates. To begin with, by merely undertaking tourism the youths partake in a notoriously conservative ideology-ridden endeavour, described by Aitchison (2001, p. 133) as the 'world's most sex-role stereotyped industry'. Moreover, backpackers are distinctly romanticist tourists (Urry, 1990, pp. 45–47). By the very definition of the type of trip they choose to undertake, in which they adventurously explore and seek 'exotic' and 'authentic' experiences and destinations (that are located in the 'Third World' or in the 'periphery belt'), the backpackers assume a symbolic image. At the very core of the community's ideal an image of a traveller – a valorized male hero – is to be found. A hero who is the male protagonist of what is arguably the West's most powerful and influential genre – the patriarchal travel narrative.

The narratives backpackers relay indicate how a neocolonialist and quasi-militaristic practice emerges, wherein strenuous and risky activities play an important role. These activities amount to a 'must' on the backpacker checklist, without which the cultural capital endowed in the lengthy and arduous trip cannot be consumed. These activities are perceived by the backpackers as a meaningful physical challenge – a challenge which, if overcome successfully, endows manly identity. Furthermore, these activities are performed and mediated by the backpackers' bodies, travelling in and across natural outdoor ('virgin', 'untouched') spaces. In and through recounting their experiences a meaningful relationship is woven between embodied practices and spaces. While the participation in adventurous and risky activities carries manly hues in general (regardless of the backpackers' cultural background: see Elsrud, 2001), in this chapter I wish to focus on masculine-endowing experiences in light of an Israeli travel culture, illustrating how contemporary backpacking amounts in fact to an additional chapter in the national occupation with/of bodies and spaces.

The chapter commences with an interdisciplinary theoretical review of three bodies of literature, in an attempt to contextualize the backpackers' travel narratives and the gender experiences of which they tell. The first considers the body as a metonymic site wherein patriarchic cultural norms are being implicated and inscribed in individual bodies. This section builds on celebrated works of feminists and sociologists who reintroduced the corporeal human body into mainstream thought in the social science. From being censored in the past the body is presently perceived as a metonymic sociocultural site. Oftentimes it is through the body, and through its movements, sensations and representations, that we can learn most clearly about the sociocultural matrixes of power and meaning that surround the person.

The second field concerns the interrelations between engendered bodies and engendered spaces. This section illustrates the socially constructed qualities that bodies and spaces share ('bodies as spaces/spaces as bodies'), as well as the spaces wherein hegemonic masculine discourses are worked on and in men's bodies. Inspired by romantic-idealic ideologies, spaces are conceptualized by tourists as feminine destinations. Both geographically and symbolically spaces are places to be dominated by and absorbed in. Excerpts from backpackers' narratives evince how the romanticist male hero encounters nature, and perhaps more importantly how he returns from this encounter transformed.

The third body of literature addresses the consequences of the unique sociocultural role backpacking assumes in Israeli youth culture. This 'local' aspect suggests a surprising socio-historical context against which contemporary backpacking, and the depths of the cultural experiences it endows, can be comprehended. Following the theoretical introduction, excerpts from male backpackers' travel narratives are interpreted. The backpackers' words and experiences allow a 'experience-near' study of men's lived experience, as these emerge in a masculine-institutional setting (i.e. tourism). The narratives also show how the narrators wholeheartedly embody and perpetuate pressing hegemonic images or, alternatively, how they subvert and resist them. They illustrate the masculine norm by which the young men have to conform, and how symbolic and narrative resources are employed in order to achieve a sought-after social status in the backpacker community.

Masculine Bodies/Masculine Spaces

> Good travel (heroic, educational, scientific, adventurous, ennobling) is something men (should) do.
>
> (Clifford, 1992, p. 105)

The body as a metonymic site of social and cultural norms

During the last two decades the body was the subject of a vast corpus of literature in both social sciences and humanities, occupying the forefront of a paradigmatic shift. Inspired by the works of Douglas (1966) and Foucault and Gordon (1980), feminist thought illustrated the myriad ways by which women's bodies have been suppressed and policed by institutional chauvinist ideologies and discourses. Butler (1993), Grosz (1994), Martin (2001) and many others supplied a detailed account of the ways by which patriarchal discourses – the medical, the militaristic, the religious and the national, to mention but a few – monopolized and manipulated women's bodies, controlling and suppressing it. Moreover, they showed how women's bodies, as well as the bodies of other suppressed groups, were actively absented from emancipating discourse.

Concurrently, sociological thought too yielded vast innovative literature, deconstructing and reconstructing the body as a crucial social site. Bourdieu (1977), and later Csordas (1990) and Featherstone *et al.* (1991), to mention but a few, have plucked the human body out of its previous (ideologically) naturalized state, suggesting that in modern and late-modern (consumer) societies, the body is the embodiment of dynamic social processes; of ceaseless sociocultural pressures and manipulations. In both its biological corporeality and social existence, the body is neither 'complete' nor 'whole' anymore; rather, it is 'unfinished', 'uncompleted' (Bourdieu, 1977; Csordas, 1990; Turner, 1996). This state of the body accounts for the reason it is continuously susceptible to social, institutional and ideological influences. As Frank (1991) observes, social institutions – from national movements and social classes to hospitals and backpacking trips – offer the body goals and aims that tie it to social and institutional discourses which grant it identity and sociocultural capital. By means of the body, and of the goals and tasks it is required to accomplish, the social system defines the ideal body, and with it the preferred bodywork or the bodily 'recipe'.

Similar to more traditional disciplines in the social sciences, the subject in and of tourism research traditionally lacked a body. This absence deprived the tourist of agency (MacCannell, 2001), referring to her or him as the *object,* rather than the *subject,* of tourism research. This absence marked 'a conceptual blind spot' (Grosz, 1994, p. 3) and obscured the mechanisms and the discourses through which tourists are institutionally disciplined. As Veijola and Jokinen (1994) observed: '[T]he tourist has lacked a body because the analyses have tended to concentrate on the gaze and/or structures and dynamics of waged labor societies' (p. 149).

Alongside additional theoretical schools, feminist and feminist-inspired thought initiated a radical change in the direction of repairing this enduring schism. 'Instead of seeing the body as distinct from the mind', and thus 'tied to a fixed essence or reduced to naturalistic explanations', Johnson (1989, cited in Johnston, 2001, p. 183) promotes that the body 'can be viewed as the primary object of social production and inscription'. While emancipatory notions of this type are also applicable to the study of men – indeed, my view is that men's studies are pro/post feminist ('a significant outgrowth of feminist studies and an ally': Kimmel, 2002, p. ix) – it is interesting to note that poignant feminist insights and observations are commonly reserved to the research of women and their bodies.

Empirical explorations of contemporaneous male bodies (particularly heterosexual males) by and large occupy two sociocultural sites in which, and in relations to which, hegemonic images of masculinity are intensively and influentially shaped: war (institutionalized by the military) and the emblematic ethos of the warrior, on the one hand (Connell, 1995; Mosse, 1996, pp. 107–132), and competitive (capitalist) sports and the manly ethos of the sport superstar, on the other (Messner, 1995; Kimmel, 1996, pp. 117–155; Kimmel and Messner, 2004). While elaboration on these institutions and on the heroic images they promote in the West since antiquity lies beyond the scope of this chapter, it is worthwhile noting the unique interrelations between bodies and particular spaces where hegemonic male bodies and identities are constructed ('forged'). These spaces are physical and at the same time function also as sociocultural arenas, wherein the male body ritualistically assumes valorized symbolic capital. The bodies of the warrior and of the sportstar are *constructed and shaped in particular spaces*, to which they are *intimately interrelated*: the warrior acquires his military skills through training in military zones and later embodies the heroic image in battle*fields*. The body of the sportsman wins its prestigious status in well-demarcated spaces too, such as soccer and football stadiums or basketball arenas, wherein the body's performances are publicly observed and evaluated.

Engendering spaces: the place of/the work on the manly body

A third archetypical image of hegemonic masculinity, which will be at the centre of our discussion, is embodied in the ideal of the traveller or adventurer. The traveller's body is an ideal masculine body, one that is founded on powerful romanticist and colonialist discourses of movement, expansion and exploration. At the core of these discourses we find a manly hero who operates in an eventful scene, which is abundant with risks and dangers (Green, 1993; Campbell, 2004; Rank, 2004). Travel is an ideal context within which eventfulness can be encountered, and where spaces that are constructed and perceived as 'authentic' and 'exotic' can endow the male body with esteemed qualities. By their definition, these spaces lie beyond the known and the familiar, beyond the urban and the everyday (*terra incognita*). They are the destinations whereto the explorer travels in order to face the Other – in the form of nature or peoples – to conquer and dominate it.

Critical conceptualizations of engendered spaces were largely promoted by geographical and cartographical feminists. In these disciplines feminist works strived to expose and undo the masculine monopoly of certain spaces and certain types of knowledge that pertain to them (Ardener, 1981; Diprose and Ferrell, 1991; Katz and Monk, 1993; Blunt and Rose, 1994). Through a refreshing critical (re)examination of spatial hypotheses, these works have denaturalized and de-essentialized commonplace perceptions concerning the (lack of) relation between spaces and genders (preconceptions that are not too different than those referring to the body). A related body of research is specifically concerned with the relations between types of masculine identities and types of spaces, which are urban/suburban or rural and natural. The latter are of specific relevance to us, because many activities and diversions backpackers undertake occur in, and in relation to, rural spaces and natural landscapes. These are constructed as locations that exist at a critical distance from industrialized metropolitan centres. Longhurst's (2000; also Morin *et al.*, 2001) works on masculine touristic spaces, and Woodward's (1998, 2000) works on militaristic masculine spaces, indicate that spaces are sites of engendering activities. More radically, they argue that interrelated interconstructions occur in these spaces, whereby spaces and bodies are *mutually engendered*. The romantic construction of 'Nature' as feminized allows contrastingly for the enactment and validation of masculinity in tourism. As historian White notes in a discussion of frontierism in western USA, 'men to match mountains – that is, men able to overcome and dominate a feminine nature' (White, cited in Quam-Wickham, 1999, p. 135).

It is worthwhile noting how various masculine images, which originally stemmed from different semiotic spheres of patriarchy relating to war, competitive sports and travel, are exchangeable in discourse. Such is evinced by the Israeli backpacker cliché 'we conquered Thailand', or with the designation of the backpackers as 'settlers' (*mitnahalim*) or 'conquerors' (*kovshim*), which is common among backpackers (Noy and Cohen, 2005a). The use of these and other tokens indicates that under the heavy influence of romanticist-colonial discourse, a diffusion of metaphors occurs – all of which relate to the masculine body and its movement in, and occupation of, designated spaces. Within the ludic context of tourism (Cohen, 1985), the fluidity of manly metaphors is heightened. Backpackers who describe how they 'traveled from one town to another, from one target to another' (using distinctly militaristic jargon), juxtapose different (neo)colonial registers. Enmeshing militaristic and touristic registers they create a 'militouristic' mode of travel. The militouristic fusion is possible because different spaces and discourses share the function of masculinizing men, evincing the abilities and skills of able and privileged male bodies to act competently: to cover distances and to overcome obstacles.

Trans/formed bodies: national ideologies and backpacking

Pursuing strenuous hiking activities builds on, and is a contemporaneous cultural successor to, an embodied and enspaced tradition of trips and hikes conducted in Israel. As early as the second decade of the 20th century, groups of 'wanderers' had undertaken extensive hiking tours and field trips across the Land of Israel for a ritual through which people experientially got to 'know' the Land. As Katriel (1995, pp. 6–7) observes, travelling at length by foot was an 'important element in the complex of ritualized cultural practices which have been appropriated and cultivated during the Israeli pre-state . . . [it carries] a special aura in Israel public culture . . . as a native-Israeli form of secular pilgrimage'.

Indeed, a significant aspect of the emerging Sabra (native-Israeli) tradition was the performance of adventurous, sometimes highly risky, trips throughout the country. This quality further intensified with the shift from the ethos of the 'farmer' to the ethos of the 'warrior' (Shapira, 1999), whereby hiking and travelling absorbed the meaning of a quasi-military reconnaissance activity (Ben-Ari and Levi-Schreiber, 2000). These manly adventures, which in extreme cases included transgressing the borders of neighbouring (hostile) countries at considerable risk, were pursued vehemently by various youth institutions, including youth movements of German and English origins.

The dominant masculine quality of these embodied and enspaced manly rites touches on three additional issues. First, these travels bring to mind an observation made by Mosse (1996), who argued that in public social spaces the male body is continually pursuing tasks in the name of hegemonic ideologies, and particularly national ideologies. In hiking trips in Israel the male body functions semiotically as grounding, or as an intermediate: the body is the means through which the relation between the people and the land is forged. This relationship is bi-directional: the land assumes a (new) identity through the people who inhabit it, and the (Jewish) people assume a localized 'national body'.

Second, the type of hegemonic body that is arrived through the exhausting, and yet invigorating, activities of hiking constructs and legitimizes a particular type of masculinity (from a variety of possible alternatives: see Connell, 1995). Gender-informed commentators of that period observe that immigrants from Muslim countries ('Oriental Jews', also colloquially called '*mizrahi* Jews'), did not share the European romanticist-colonial heritage. They did not hold with the view that patriotism is ideally pursued and performed through participation in strenuous travelling activities (Katriel, 1995). Hence, a hierarchy was established within various masculinities, one which is effective nowadays. According to this cultural hierarchy, Jews of European descent (*Ashkenazi* Jews) assume the top hegemonic ranks.

Finally, the demanding and masculinizing activities were part of a national project of transforming the diasporic Jewish body. The bodywork that was performed in and through adventurous travel was to achieve a transformative aim: transfiguring the feminine and weak image of the diasporic Jew into a well-built, competent, heterosexual Israeli body (Mosse, 1996, pp. 151–154; Boyarin and Boyarin, 1997; Boyarin *et al.*, 2003). This was in line with a few early Zionist ideologists who thought that the invention of a stronger, healthier heterosexual 'Muscle Jewry' would overcome the stereotype of the Jewish male as effeminate. Around the turn of the 19th century, Nordau famously called to establish the 'New Jew', who will be a 'strong-chested, tautly jointed, boldly gazing me' man (Nordau, 1900, cited in Presner, 2003, p. 283). Along this vision, we can conceptualize the spaces of the Land of Israel as an ideological (national) *gymnastic hall*, wherein the 'New Jew' will practice and train through exhausting outdoor activities.

Yet, while the field trips of the Israelis are conducted mostly *within* the confines of the homeland, the backpackers undertake adventures *outside* the spaces of Israel. This geographical transposition is meaningful because the Jewish male body thus far acquired its (national-ideological) meaning through hiking within national spaces and through the interrelation between national spaces and national bodies. Yet, the backpacking trip takes place in extranational touristic spaces. These are located at a great distance from the initial spaces in, and with regard to, which the new Israeli identity was formed. From a postcolonial perspective, Massad (2000) critically indicates that the exilic Jewish body could have earned its manhood only within the confines of the Land of Israel:

> The corporeal self perception of the Israeli Sabra is always already delimited within this space-time compression outside of which 'he' cannot exist. Israel as a colonial/postcolonial space-time, however, allows the existence of new postdiasporic Jewish bodies only as holograms. . . . If they exit (in the Zionist lexicon 'descent from') the Israeli space-time continuum, these bodies lose their new corporeality, and revert back to their pre-Israel diasporic condition . . . to being the 'feminine schleimel' that he [the Israeli Sabra] was before.
>
> (Massad, 2000, pp. 339–340)

An interesting question thus arises concerning the construction of hegemonic masculinity among Israeli youths who are travelling *outside* Israel. If the male body outside the borders of the homeland is as 'hologramic' as Massad (2000) suggests it is, and if, outside the national landscapes, it regresses to its exilic 'feminine schleimel', the stories of adventures in, and conquests of, the Third World will be ridden with this anxiety.

Backpackers' Narratives

This research is based on 41 interview conversations (Kvale, 1996) I held with Israeli backpackers who had recently (within 5 months) returned from 'the great journey'. The interviews took place in Israel, usually at the backpackers' homes (or, to be accurate, at their parents' homes), which were commonly located in large cities. The interview conversations were in-depth and open-ended, and typically lasted between 1 and 3 hours (Fontana and Frey, 2000). The backpackers with whom I met were middle-class, secular Jewish Israelis, aged 22–25, half of whom were women (21) and half men (20). All but two had been born in Israel. They all travelled for at least 3 months in the countries typically frequented by Israelis in Asia (mostly India, Nepal and Thailand) and in South America (mostly the Andeans, Argentina, Chile and Brazil), in a trip that took place shortly after completion of their obligatory and lengthy military service in Israel (3 years for men and approximately 2 for women).

I reached these veteran backpackers through employing a sampling method that is known as 'snowball' sampling, by which interviewees referred me to friends and acquaintances of theirs, and those friends and acquaintances gave me further names, and so on (Heckathorn, 1997; Noy, 2007). The first few backpackers I met through joint acquaintances and through several visits I made to a photography store located in the centre of Jerusalem which backpackers frequented in order to develop the many reels of film they had taken during the trip. The main advantage of the snowball sampling procedure is that the researcher is led along active social chains of friends, acquaintances and even siblings, who, in this case, regularly exchange backpacking travel information and experiences.

The interview conversations were semi-structured, giving priority to spontaneous expression and narratives of experience. This method is most appropriate to the aims of the research, namely to learn about backpackers' travel experiences and perceptions, and to explore the ways they narratively shape and communicate their experiences. In line with works on tourists' performances, I presently conceptualize the act of narration of one's travel experiences as a 'tourist performance' in and of itself (even if off-site performances: see Edensor, 2000; Noy, 2004a; Bruner, 2005). Indeed, as a backpacker exclaimed in the beginning of one of the very first interviews, 'whoever comes [to my] house, I immediately prepare him a cup of coffee and sit him down to hear my trekking and traveling stories!' By so indicating, the backpacker constructs the event of the interview as a routinized (and ritualized) opportunity to present himself or herself publicly, and to embody the cultural capital he or she has gained whilst backpacking.

Indeed, sharing stories of adventure and risk frequently is something that the backpackers enjoyed doing, a fact which was obvious from the pattern of participation in the interviews (they wilfully and with no exception consented to partake in the interview), as well as from the nature of the interview interaction itself (they enthusiastically shared detailed travel stories, apparently celebrating the opportunity that fell in their hands to tell their eventful recollections to an eager audience).[1]

Travelling and trekking: the male body mediating transformation

> To receive a [masculine] initiation truly means to expand sideways into the glory of oaks, mountains, glaciers. . . . We need wilderness and extravagance.
>
> (Bly, 1990)
>
> Masculinity required proof and proof required serious effort.
>
> (Kimmel, 1996)

In the backpackers' narratives hiking is commonly viewed as the emblem of outdoor activities, which are themselves the emblem of the entire backpacking trip (Noy, 2005). These outdoor activities embody a linear and progressive ascension, which aims at reaching a peak that is simultaneously topographical and experiential. They assume their emblematic (metonymized) status by showing the exchange between the physical and symbolic realms in (backpacking) tourism (Harrison, 2002; Bruner, 2005). Along the hiking trail the body continuously moves ('travels') forward and onward, engaging in strenuous, demanding and challenging activities, seamlessly collecting experiences and photographs. The physical difficulties backpackers confront and surmount are one part of the story. The other part consists of feelings of highest reward and satisfaction, which are endowed upon the successful completion of the tourist 'task'.

The following extract from Uri's story shows how meaningful indeed is the experience of hiking competently. The narrative concerns reaching and crossing a high-altitude mountain pass, in the region of the Everest Base Camp Reserve, in Nepal.

> URI: We decided that we're climbing that mountain. I mean the one that's harder to climb. And this is already truly a serious operation. We had to take with us – to plan everything. It's five thousand and eight hundred meters high. It's something that most [backpackers] don't climb. We left early in the morning. . . . And we said we'll make it to the mountain, then we'll stop for a rest and have breakfast. And this is what we really did. We had breakfast and we really left very very early because there's a weather problem there. Everyday, sorta in the middle of the day, clouds appear. [They] simply ascend up the wadi and block the entire vision. So it's also very dangerous, because in fact if you're stuck somewhere that steep and suddenly clouds appear, you can't see anything. And so you miss on the entire scenery. So this is why we had to leave very very early. At the break of the day. . . . [The mountain] had a very steep part which was made of huge rocks. So we reached the- We climbed up until that rocky part. There we decided that we're taking our backpacks off, and the rest of the heavy gear, and we're starting to climb without gear. 'Cause actually we had to get to the top, and to return, [and] we didn't want to take heavy things with us. On us. So we begun climbing and we were literally climbing with our hands and legs. . . . [Reaching the Pass] was fascinating, simply fascinating. It's a point where you see Everest and all these huge mountains, and the sun is setting behind you, and then everything simply gets covered with a kinda red line. It's a really fascinating thing in its appearance. Really pretty. . . . The view was impressive and I said [to myself]: 'this is like a once-in-a-lifetime experience'. . . . I descended to the town of Namche, where I was already looked at as one of *the* veterans. There were already stories being told there about me, and there I told everyone about my adventures. And so I was – I was kinda of an attraction. It was nice – [they] sought my advice and asked me [questions], and [called me] like – (in English) 'the crazy Israeli'.

This extended extract, wherein Uri describes parts of a trek he hiked alone for over 6 weeks, illustrates the physical difficulties backpackers endure during the lengthy hike, the drama embodied in ascending high-altitude mountain passes and the sense of fulfilment and satisfaction that a successful backpacker performance endows. We also learn about the narrative stylization of adventure stories, wherein suspense, drama and surprise work together in creating worthy and tellable stories, which transpire against the appealing background of soaring snowy peaks.

Stories of this type typically describe a lengthy and strenuous ascent, at the end of which a particularly spectacular view is visible or 'gaze-able'. The ascent is described as physically challenging, mentally demanding and, in so far as it requires meticulous preparations, it also demands the careful attention of the intellect. Together, these features endow the climb with a unique status, which Uri describes in the militarized term 'operation'.

The peak experience which is narrated concerns reaching a high-altitude pass. It typically lies at the heart of romanticist stories of adventure. The narrators describe how they successfully and resourcefully overcame immense predicaments and obstacles (Elsrud, 2001). From Uri's narrative we can see that these stories are clearly dramatic, and their heroes – the narrators themselves who are acting as characters within the heightened realm of adventure – are shaped according to heroic patterns of manly stories of travel, adventure and valour (Green, 1993; Campbell, 2004; Rank, 2004).

According to these masculine meta-narratives, the hero's movement across physical space has a social direction: from the familiar to the foreign, from the everyday to the sublime, exotic and authentic. After successfully grappling with, and overcoming, many obstacles, a deeply meaningful and (trans)formative experience awaits the male hero. It is a transcendent, 'once-in-a-lifetime' experience (as Uri puts it), which is intimately related to the natural and sublime spaces wherein it is consumed. In the backpackers stories Nature is the emblematic embodiment of the 'Other'. Nature supplies both the scenery and the setting in and against which – quite literally – the hero is constituted.

In Uri's narrative, representations of Nature recur: the huge boulders that are nearly insurmountable and the ominous clouds that threaten to rob the ascender of the prize of ascension (the spectacular views). These are concrete manifestation of Nature, which amount to tests and trials that the able male body is required to surmount. Indeed, there is a need for a variety of qualities to be possessed and actions to be taken on behalf of the hero in order to pursue the aim in a successful manner, including stamina, resourcefulness and self-discipline.

The topographic peak conflates with the phenomenological peak, and immediately after consuming these twofold peaks the narrative turns to describe the descent from the mountain. This is the return travel, whose direction is from the realm of the transcendent to the realms of the familiar and the social. In these stories the peak experience is located in, and defined by, a liminal moment, which lies between the movement away and the movement back, between ascending and descending, and between the experience and its recollection and recounting.

Moreover, Uri's extract clearly illustrates the prestige that is gained by the protagonist who returns from foreign and risky spaces. It has been noted repeatedly that a tight hierarchical social structure exists among backpackers (Riley, 1988; Elsrud, 2001; Sorensen, 2003). This hierarchy is based on the overall length of the trip and the many adventurous experiences backpackers undergo whilst travelling. Uri proudly indicates that his mesmerizing adventures had an instantaneous effect: he immediately acquired an outstanding status within the backpacker community. This status is stressed by Uri and is described in two different ways. The first is the phrase 'one of the veterans'.[2] The expression indicates that prestige is correlated with a state of being accomplished in the particular practice of backpacking. The point is that according to processes of 'hierarchization' (Sorensen, 2003), adventure-undertaking transforms into experience, and experience transforms into esteemed cultural capital.

The second expression that stresses Uri's accomplishments and their socio-cultural value or capital is 'crazy Israeli'. This expression is uniquely uttered in English, which amounts to a linguistic 'code switching' (Hymes, 1975, pp. 66–67). It performatively indicates that voices of others entered the narration in the capacity of validating the argument made by the narrator. In this case, Uri illustrates that his reputation exceeded the limited social circle of Israelis, and was admitted (even) by English-speaking backpackers (specifically by backpackers from New Zealand: see Morin *et al.*, 2001).

Upon returning from excursions to guest houses the backpackers have a ready audience to share with, and to recount to, their adventurous experiences. The deep and rewarding gratification they speak of stems from the successful performance of adventurous excursions, the narratives which they freely share and compare with fellow travellers. Satisfaction emerges from transgressing outstanding physical difficulties. This is apparent in the following two excerpts. The first of which is drawn from an interview with David, who backpacked for 7 months in South America. In the following excerpt he tells of the famous Machu-Picchu trail in Peru. The second excerpt is from an interview with Guy, who backpacked in Asia for 5½ months. Guy contrasts two different modes of backpacking: one, of which he is disapproving, is more leisurely, and the other, which he praises, is more adventurous.

> DAVID: You can hire local porters there. That is, you pay them about a buck a day, and they'll carry all your equipment on their back. So you can like walk freely . . . and hike the hills there quite leisurely. We decided not [to hire porters]. That is, we came in order to have an experience. So everyone took his own backpack on his back, and this added to the overall experience. That is, you know, after it's done, *all the pride* of returning like that to town, saying 'we did the four-day trek with the backpacks on our backs, an' all.' So it was – it was a wonderful trek.

> GUY: We saw that once you complete the trip – all that pride [that you feel] that you're not just lying about, but that you came here, you've traveled all that distance just to sit in some restaurant and tell your friends how much pot you smoked. I think that this was our greatest pride: that we pursued the trip *the way it should be done*. Not just wasting time moving from one site to another not doing anything in between, but really making the most of this period.

David commences by making a point about how backpackers can make travel life easier for themselves. He indicates that during the trek he and his companions *could* have made use of commonplace tourist services (porters, in this case). David explicitly notes that the price of these services, at least in monetary terms, was negligible, and by no means was the reason the group did not hire local porters. Rather, the masculinizing experience, which David seeks to establish, concerns precisely the right to *refuse* any such assistance. This refusal is particularly meaningful in the backpacking context. In the eyes of backpackers, services of this type are associated with bourgeois tourists, who are not manly enough to carry their valises by themselves (they are 'spoiled' as other backpackers indicate).[3] Hence, receiving help could have potentially robbed the experience of its manly qualities. The weight of the pride, which is experienced upon the completion of the task of hiking and travelling, is correlated with the weight of the heavy backpacks that the backpackers are carrying on their backs and with the amount of physical effort they exert.

Moreover, David has proved worthy of a deeply meaningful masculine experience also because he and his companions hiked the path quickly, covering the distance in only 4 days (less than the average time). Later in the interview, when he talks about his military service, David mentions that during the trip he faced an alternative that was not viable during the obligatory service: to relax and let go of the body discipline and have someone else carry his personal gear. It is against this background that the decision to *refuse* the porters' services, and to *voluntarily* carry the group's entire gear throughout the mountainous trail, achieves its highly gratifying and masculinizing effect. As another backpacker puts it: '[T]he habits we have are from the army, [but in the trip] you're doing it the way you like.' Male backpackers' bodies are inscribed with machismo patterns of movement and conduct, which the backpackers easily carry (over) to civic contexts, i.e. (backpacking) tourism. In other words, the 'way you like' (the civic and voluntary mode) and the militaristic (obligatory) mode are in effect identical.

From Guy's assertion a dichotomous distinction arises between the travellers, on the one hand, and those who 'smoke pot', on the other hand. Underlying this distinction are two resources – *body* and *time* – and the patterns of using them efficiently. The manly claim that is expressed in Guy's extract is also established by the fact that he is referring to a doctrine or to a hegemonic norm: there is a *correct or right* way of doing things, an accepted code by which those who wish to attain the symbolic capital engendered in backpacking need to abide. The expression 'the way it should be done' echoes an accepted masculine norm (which is not cited directly: see Noy, 2007). The reverse form, i.e. the manner which is *not accepted*, is presented in negative light, and includes the verbs 'to sit', 'to smoke pot', to 'tell about it', to waste time and not to do anything. These descriptions clearly answer to the category of *passivity*, which is constructed as having cultural association with femininity and weakness. Passivity does not supply for proof of masculinity (Kimmel, 1996).

Guy contrasts these passive verbs with active and assertive verbs such as 'making the most' of the time. The duration of the trip is presented as a period in which one should by no means rest or relax, but to the contrary. There is a pressing need to actively 'do' or 'perform' or accomplish backpacking, to *seize* the backpacking tenure. And the more this is pursued along the narrative of the ideal backpacker, the better. Production and gratification are inter-correlated in the manly stories, indicating that there are preferred ways of acquiring status and manhood. In these tight and hierarchical circumstances 'lying about' and 'wasting time' is a near sin.

In this way too, backpackers of the type of David and Guy differentiate themselves from the 'mass tourist'. They imply that some of the backpackers have 'gone bourgeois' and are acting like conventional tourists (Noy, 2005). Furthermore, since tourism is about the collecting of experiences (Bruner, 2005), and since backpacking is commonly viewed as a 'once-in-a-lifetime' experience, the youths' attempts to condense the trip and pack it with events are only sensible.

When Alon, who also praises the merits of hiking strenuously, describes the famous Machu-Picchu trail in Peru (as did David), he mentions that there are two ways to get to the Hidden Inka city: by foot and by train. His description indicates that worthy and rewarding experiences are only to be encountered when travellers 'truly exert efforts and do not take some *tour* (uttered in English), that transports them in the train'. Akin to David and Guy, Alon too contrasts the different gen-der/masculine alternatives tourists face when pursuing backpacking. Uttering the word '*tour*' in English and not in Hebrew, helps to sharpen the contrasts between tourists' commercialized patterns of travel and transportation (and their discursive correlates), and those of the backpackers, which are supposedly more 'authentic'. The latter create experiences that are more 'truly' masculine, because they are registered in the backpackers' bodies by way of notable physical effort. Because hegemonic masculinity requires proof, and proof requires considerable effort, in the backpackers' stories 'tourists' amount to a feminine ('softish' and passive) cat-egory of travellers, against which backpackers can appreciate and validate physical effort and the fruits it carries in terms of masculine identities.

Note that the words referring to 'taking it *easy*' (in Guy's extract) and to 'taking a *tour*' (in Alon's extract) are not uttered by the backpackers in English coincidentally. In the capacity in which they are performative 'code switchers', they indicate that the narrators are making use of the lingua franca of modern tourism (i.e. interna-tional English). In the context of tourists' language, international touristic English is a resource that tourists can productively draw upon. In the present case, David and Guy (and to some degree Uri too) are employing *vocabularies of leisure* which are incon-gruent with the backpackers' codes and ethos of manly endeavours and adventures.

In line with Richards and Wilson (2004) and Welk (2004), the excerpts above lend support to the observation that backpackers construct their identity in contrast to *other backpackers* as much as they do so vis-à-vis 'tourists' in general. These find-ings illustrate recent developments in backpacking tourism, concerning the prolif-eration of this form of tourism and its impressive raising heterogeneousness. The contemporary social scene of backpacking necessitates that the youths distinguish themselves not only from 'tourists' (which was traditionally the case: see Riley, 1988) but primarily from other types and groups of backpackers (Noy, 2006). The latter, I mentioned earlier, have 'turned bourgeois'.

From these and other narratives a normative male image emerges which encom-passes the successful, sometime virtuous, performance of romanticist-adventurous masculinity. This type of male body is characterized by self-restraint, self-discipline, outstanding physical abilities and cohesive social relationships (Klein, 1999; Ben-Ari, 2001). These qualities assist the backpacker hero in the task of competently over-coming the challenges and impediments that await him. The return from the nearly supernatural heights at which most of the backpackers hike are described in nearly mythic terms, which construct these sites and spaces as literally extraordinary.

Shortly after Uri's account, he indicates that when he returned from the trek, 'people looked at me there . . . they thought I returned from Mars'. Thus, the hero in the men's tall tales is constructed as if returning from a space or state of utter alterity. As Elsrud (2001) observes of male backpackers, 'through establishing a (mythologized) image of Otherness, a story about self-identity can be told' (p. 606). While the context of every day remains unchanged, the hero undergoes profound, transformative experiences (Bruner, 1991). As yet another backpacker indicates when he recalls descending from the Annapurna Circuit Trail in Nepal: '[Y]ou return to civilization, you return to yourself.' The first half of this parallel structure evokes the binary tension between the ordinary and the extraordinary, or between the familiar and the exotic. Interestingly, it does so by contrasting the *social realm* (inhabited by people) with an alterity that is constructed as non-human ('Mars' and 'the crazy Israeli', the latter metaphor evoking Otherness via an 'unnatural' or 'deviant' psychic state). The second half of the utterance, the expression 'you return to yourself', is commonly evoked in the narratives I researched in the form of bodily transformations, whereby the body of the traveller 'departs from itself' only to 'return to itself' transformed. As a whole, this expression tells the story of rites of masculinity in a nutshell, and implies why (backpacking) tourism should be its vehicle.

Hegemony and resistance: additional male voices

The voices of the backpackers we heard thus far unanimously express congruence with the normative and hegemonic masculine model. Yet, in most of the interviews I conducted, various degrees of oppositions to, and rejections of, the ideal male image were apparent. In fact, in only one-third of the interviews backpackers did not express resentments, oppositions and complaints with regard to the male ideal and to the strenuous efforts that they had to exert in order to stand up to it. In two-thirds of the interviews (and in all of the interviews with female backpackers) the narrators expressed overt or covert objections with regard to the normative challenges they had to face and stand up to.

In regard to the 'hegemonic group', i.e. backpackers' whose narrative and images were in complete agreement with the ideal ethos, it is interesting to note that during their obligatory service in the army they all have served in elite fighting squads. All of these backpackers indicated that certain skills, which came handy to them during the lengthy trip, were initially learned in military training (such as climbing). Ethnically, this group is expectedly composed of *Ashkenazi* (European) youths exclusively, a fact which brings to mind the hegemonic status of Ashkenazi Jews in Israeli society, past and present (Kimmerling, 2001).

In contrast to the stories narrated by the 'hegemonic group', the stories of most of the male (and female) backpackers I interviewed can be characterized by the ambivalent position they express. In most cases the male body does not stand up to the normative masculine expectations, which is one of the reasons a few of the backpackers reject the hegemonic ideal altogether. In such cases, where there is a considerable difference between the ideal image of the adventurous traveller and the actual performance of the male (and female) body, the narrators tell about minor bodily incidents which did not permit their bodies to pursue the backpacker goal to its idealic and hegemonic end (Noy, 2003, forthcoming). Their bodies, then, do not represent or embody the ideal backpacker. These backpackers mention that they suffered needlessly during the trip and particularly so during outdoor excursions, that they did not feel well (they were nauseous and/or vomited), that they slipped and tripped while hiking, that they lost their way and a whole variety of additional somatic symptoms suggesting incongruence with the competent image of the reconnoitring lone traveller.

This is the case with Tal, who tells an amusing incident which occurred to a friend and travel companion of his while they neared the peak of a trail in the Salar Salt Desert in Argentina:

TAL: Near the end there's a rock there that's about a meter and a half, which you simply need to grab with your hands and climb. You climb a sorta mountain step, which is about fifteen meters [high]. And this guy, Dan, like reached the last rock, sorta puts his hands on top (laughs) and he simply freezes. [He] starts shouting: 'I have a paralysis, I can't climb, I have a paralysis!' (laughs) And I remind him of this anecdote every time I see him. Every time! 'I have a paralysis.' That was really hilarious.

The humour that is expressed in this strip is related to Dan's (Tal's friend) bodily malfunction, due to which Dan was not able to conclude the climb and reach the sought-after peak. Tal is in fact describing a momentary paralysis of a hysteric type, which made his friend's hands immobile and ineffective. The laughter stems from an anxiety that the unexpected paralysis aroused. Discussing humour in tourist contexts, Dann (1996) notes that 'while humor can sometimes relieve anxiety, it does not exist without it' (p. 107). The surfacing of the paralysis in and of Dan's body prevents him (and the rest of the group) from progressing along the expected route in the normative direction of the summit. It calls to mind the fact that the trail is actually unidirectional: the travellers are expected to proceed onward and upwards. Turning backwards and returning in this one-way course are socially sanctioned movements. A female backpacker expressed this point poignantly when she narrated of her physical difficulties and said she wanted to quit the trek: 'I wanted to return but they (her friends) didn't let me.' The betrayal of Dan's body and his bodily refusal to withstand the many manly challenges backpacking embodies, suggests an incongruence between his *individual body* and the *normative ideal*. This incongruence is what sparks the lively laughter (which is embodied as well), which illustrates the expression of feelings and emotions rather than their denial.

The 'really hilarious' anecdote Tal narrates, which takes place shortly before the group is supposed to reach the climax of the trail, is not recounted as a peak experience in the normative sense, and it is not the climax of a romanticist travel narrative (Elsrud, 2001; Noy, 2004b). Rather, it is told as an implied *counter-peak experience*. According to the norm, the body is the source of extreme pleasure, which stems from the competent performance of the body's organs. The body should not be the source of anxieties and of moments of embarrassment and amusing bodily dysfunctions (some of which are not amusing at all, as we shall shortly see). Neither paralysis nor laughter is among the bodily experiences that are typical of hegemonic masculine narratives. Instead, romanticist sublime experiences are expected to be recounted, which include elation, satisfaction, fulfilment and deep pride (as Uri, David and Guy demonstrated). Incidentally, the fact that the anecdote is told repeatedly in post-trip contexts suggests that the group's shared recollections of the trip (and to some degree the group's identity) are constructed by way of implicit resistance to the romanticist ideal engendered in the backpacker norm.

This type of anxiety reaffirms the gender construction of the activity of hiking and of the spaces within which it is pursued. The trail is often referred to by the term *tsir* (literally meaning 'track' or 'way' yet connoting militaristic register), which is located in a space that is called 'the field' (*hashetah*, again, clearly connoting militaristic register). These words stress the quality of the spaces and routes that facilitate a particular type of engendered activity; they stress the predominantly active dimension of the endeavour of 'doing trekking'. This type of 'militouristic' discourse suggests that hiking is not about pleasure as much as it is about a particular type of 'bodywork', one which transpires in the 'field' and carries with it unique experiential value and cultural capital.

Later in Tal's story, he relates to female backpackers and expresses a typical negative evaluation: '[M]ost of the women – like just the mere thought of sleeping in a sleeping bag makes them feel uneasy.' Still further in the story Tal surely enough notes that he himself 'does not like sleeping in sleeping bags'. A picture thus emerges wherein behaviours that do not accord with the masculine norm are rendered as having stereotypically feminine attributes.

We can see that between stories conveying impressive masculine performances, on the one hand, and bodily incidents and minor accidents, on the other hand, a hierarchic continuum of masculinity is constructed. In a few cases, confronting the masculine norm is done explicitly and frontally, and indicates a basic rejection of the gender hierarchy. In the following excerpt, Ron locates himself socially vis-à-vis the backpackers' community. He states his beliefs about the trip apropos discussing the effect the service in the Israeli army had had on his trip.

> RON: People who I really didn't like are those who talked about trekking: 'we hiked thirty kilometers per day. We carried thirty kilos on our backs. aam [sic] We climbed this [mountain] in two hours. We climbed this [mountain] in three hours. Like, the most important point for them is how fast they hiked and how much they carried and how long they hiked. Like, it's the kind of long walks [that are] walked simply in order to [be] completed. And I think that if you feel that you're walking [only] in order to complete the path then you're missing out. Whoever walks in order to complete the trek and doesn't enjoy it – it's a shame. You can simply do it by bus. Save the effort. It's not that we didn't enjoy the effort. There were moments when we did. We felt really good each time we arrived at the summit of the Pass. Believe me – you feel [like] the king of the world. Like I've accomplished something awesomely great.

In order to substantiate the claim Ron is making, he is citing the collective backpacker norm. The normative voice illustrates a distinctly masculinist-militaristic mode of participation and conduct. According to the norm, hiking trails engenders a challenge that needs to be confronted and overcome in a manly manner. Inspired by the modern scientific ethos of quantification, the backpackers' performances too are quantified ('thirty kilometers . . . thirty kilograms . . . two hours'). The backpackers' performance equations, consisting of the variables duration, weight and length, affirm the accomplishment of the 'mission', and indicate how much effort and sweat were invested. Since the performances are quantified, they supply firm validation to their narrators' tales of masculine adventure and conquest (after all, it is hard to argue with numbers). All this effort results (at the end of the excerpt) in a unique and elevated sense of gratification, evoked in the expression 'king of the world'.

Ron commences the assertion by positioning his backpacker identity contrastingly in relation to the collective norm. As mentioned earlier, with the proliferation of backpacker populations in the last decade of the previous century, on the one hand, and the heterogenization of the range of experiential possibilities and travel preferences, on the other hand, more and more backpackers assert their identity vis-à-vis other types and groups of backpackers (Ateljevic and Doorne, 2004; Cohen, 2004; Richards and Wilson, 2004). This change is true to both global backpacker contexts and to local (Israeli) backpacker populations (Noy and Cohen, 2005a; Noy, 2006). Yet, interestingly enough, following the harsh critique Ron makes with regard to the instrumental mode of travel, he indicates that he and his companions were also seeking peak experiences. Hence, the differences that arise between the norm Ron evokes and criticizes and Ron's own perspective refer to the *way* in which peak experiences are to be obtained.

In this light we understand Ron's emphatic description of the truly uplifting experience he had upon reaching the summit. The last two sentences ('...you feel [like] the king of the world. Like I've accomplished something great.') are important because they show that giving up on the masculinist mode of travel does not necessarily entail giving up on the rewarding experience. Ron asserts that to the contrary, an immense sense of gratification and personal empowerment can be experienced without the exertion of strenuous physical effort. He, and backpackers like him, can also be (manly) 'kings of the world', and should not give up on the backpacker cultural capital because they did not adhere to the mode of 'travelling by foot'.

The injured hegemonic body or 'the body slowly, slowly shuts down': insights from Brian's body-story

I wish to use the remaining space of this chapter to explore in some length one narrative recounted by Brian about adventurous hiking in Bolivia. The narrative sheds further light on the backpacker masculine norm, from a particular perspective of a person – a body – which had *inadvertently* deviated from the norm. It is interesting to note that the insight or morale which Brian expresses could not have been attainable if some unexpected harmful event had not occurred. In other words, if the regular course of action had taken place, Brian's body and Brian's story would have both supplied an embodiment of the hegemonic masculine norm. Indeed, Brian notes that he served in the Israeli army in an elite infantry unit, and throughout his tale he repeatedly mentions intense training in long-distance navigating, survival and reconnoitring training, mountain climbing and many additional exceptionally difficult challenges he had to overcome during the military service.

Yet, the story he tells is illuminating precisely because a dramatic and negative turn occurs, in the shape of an inexplicable life-threatening pathology. Due to this accident the entire trip was abruptly stopped. While backpackers' stories regularly include episodes of risk, these eventually appear as surmountable challenges which test and validate the hero's abilities. Yet the plot line in Brian's story depicts a traumatic experience, which hues the narrative in post-traumatic shades. While hiking, Brian experienced a sudden and severe deterioration in his health, and the state of his body exceeded the common descriptions of painstaking physical challenges. It included, over and above headaches, dizziness and nausea, acute symptoms of numbness of hands and legs, breathing difficulty, loss of vision and even temporary loss of consciousness. The trek and the trip were abruptly terminated and Brian was evacuated to the USA and later to Israel. Because the medical examinations did not yield a clear diagnostic picture that could account for his malady, Brian was quite insecure and somewhat anxious about his health when we met and conversed, 5 months after he returned (was sent back) from the trip.

Brian describes himself before the trip and notes:

BRIAN: I really liked traveling. I traveled a lot here (in Israel). I always enjoyed a sense
of utter personal security while wandering around everywhere. . . . I served in the army
and I did very dangerous things, aa [*sic*] traveled around a lot. I worked my body a
lot. . . . I was in infantry and more than once I had experienced a real life threat there.
And I also saw people getting killed right near me, but I was – somehow I had the
knowledge that I myself am truly fine and healthy deep inside, and that my body can
perform anything I ask of it – [this was] a very powerful knowing. I think that it made
me deeply arrogant. Looking at things like, I mean – I can conquer the world.

Brian's tale begins with his passion for, and skills of, travelling and hiking in Israel,
an activity which reached its climax during his active service in the army. Brian's
body performs hegemonically as it encounters and surmounts life-threatening situations time and again in the service of the nation. Definitely the 'chosen body' (Weiss,
2002), Brian's body is the emblem of Jewish Israeli masculinity. His body repeatedly
proved itself and its outstanding abilities, and thus generated a unique sensation of
self-assuredness, captured in the expression 'a sense of utter personal security'. The
many near-death moments he experienced did not weaken his body (or soul), but to
the contrary proved how durable the body is 'deep inside'. In the introduction to his
story, Brian suggests that the adventurous trip initially amounted to yet another challenge, which, in light of the above, by no means seems difficult or unattainable.

It is worth noting that Brian's words have a touch of hindsight to them. They
suggest that the narrator and the protagonist are not in fact the same person.
The retrospective recapitulation communicates a message, which says that the
traumatic experience endured during the trip outdid earlier experiences, and over-
shadowed Brian's 'hegemonic-military body'. At this early point we already learn
that the experience truly humbled Brian and taught him a lesson in the shape of
overcoming his 'deeply arrogant' self-esteem.

The body that emerges from the extract is a 'buddy' or an 'ally', which is utterly
reliable and obedient. The body-buddy delivers whatever is demanded of it, and can
perform 'anything I ask of it'.[4] Brian's body-buddy endures ultra-masculine trials and
rites demanding exceptional stamina with a particularly rewarding outcome. It supplies Brian with a deep and rare sense of complete personal safety and security. More
than that, the body's abilities in fact endow a sense of invincibility. This powerful
'knowing', as Brian puts it, emerges not only because the body is extremely physically
able, but also because of the type of *relationship that emerges between the body and the self.*

Internalizing and embodying hegemonic masculine discourse brings about a
split between two entities: the body and the hero.[5] This is evinced quite plainly in
the words 'anything *I* ask of *it*': the subjectivized 'I' (self) is distinct from the objectified 'it' (body). The second is expected to conform to nearly superhuman (super-
man) tasks, a conformity or obedience that brings about a sense of gratification in
the first. Hence, we witness a *replication of macropower relationships*, which are perpetuated by the national-militaristic discourse of hierarchic obedience and submission.
Here the body is instrumentalized in the same way that the person or soldier
is instrumentalized and mobilized in national-militaristic contexts. As Longhurst
(1995) points out with regard to both tourists and their researchers, hegemonic
masculinity is characterized by 'the dominant/subordinate structure of the relation
between the mind and body' (p. 97); the body 'it' is the servant of the self 'I'.

Yet, this schism between Brian and his body changes during the story. While the physical injuries and painful psychological experiences he endured in combat have only strengthened his sense of personal security, the mysterious life-threatening trauma his body endured during the trip had a transformative effect. The male 'body-buddy' ceased obeying its master and a breach in the contract of subordination and obedience appeared. The body was hurt from within, from its interior (its 'deep inside'),[6] and has failed Brian for the first time.

Brian continues with the beginning of the actual narrative:

> BRIAN: We were in a pretty spot there. I remember dogs and cats and ducks all playing together. A really beautiful trek. And slowly, slowly I began feeling a serious shortage of breath. Even now I shudder when I think about it because every time the experience – it's like I can't take another breath. Just like that. And the hands gradually grow numb, and I felt it happening to me the way they described it would in the army. I remember that a man who loses – a man who's gonna die, slowly, slowly his body's peripheries grow numb. That's how it is in case of dehydration and loss of blood. The body slowly, slowly shuts down its systems, one by one. I felt it reaching [my] breathing, I couldn't see well, my hands were numb. . . . I could see death approaching. . . . It's something that I guess I'll carry with me for the rest of my life. . . . I simply lay there on the ground. I couldn't walk.

The description of the escalation of Brian's health begins in a pastoral and harmonious natural setting, which suggests a stark contrast to what follows: the collapse of a mechanic system. Indeed, Brian narrates the story of his body's shutdown in accordance with utterly disembodied militaristic discourse: the body is a machine, and its death is a technical process through which mechanic and electric units seize to function (cf. Martin's [2001] work on the female body as a reproductive machine). The process is spatial and its direction is from the 'peripheries' to the centre, or from the limbs (outside) to the lungs and heart (inside). We learn how badly the body is hurt when Brian ends the description with an observation: he could not walk. In the context of the masculine tradition of national travelling and hiking (see above), this handicap means more than a limited disability; in the capacity in which it indicates the lack of agentive movement, it amounts to a symbolic death.

In addition, between the lines we hear the possibility that a disease was lurking within Brian's body, i.e. inside the 'chosen body', a disease of which outbreak sheds retrospective light on the body's biography. Or is it the extranational space in which Brian and his companions travelled which rendered the body vulnerable and 'hologramic' 'from the inside', as Massad (2000) suggested?

In any case, an unexpected bodily transformation occurs. While other male and occasionally female backpackers indicate that their bodies 'adjusted' and 'acclimatized' to high-altitude destinations, thus indicating that an inner bodily change occurred, Brian's body failed to adapt to the new environment. His body refused to undergo inner transformation, a refusal which granted Brian a refreshing perspective. This perspective deviates from the normative and linear or progressive hegemonic track of Israeli youth, which Brian now views as 'deeply arrogant'.

Towards the end of the story, after he was evacuated to a nearby town (and then sent back to Israel), Brian reveals in a touching way the emotions that overwhelmed his body:

BRIAN: In the end I called home. I was obviously very emotional. And up until then, *never in my life did I* [cry]– some friends of mine in school died. One in a terrorist attack, two had cancer. All the kids in my class could cry but I could never cry. Also in the army I faced death and I never cried. . . . And then, when I called home and talked to my mother I burst into tears and I could hardly control myself. Somehow it opened something. Since then crying comes much more easily to me. It's something that – something that opened there.

Immediately after his successful evacuation, Brian establishes a reassuring connection with home (mother/homeland), whereby a burst of uncontrolled emotions is described as erupting from *within the body*. Although Brian's until-then hegemonic body did not undergo the sought-after transformation, his story, like other backpackers' stories, includes an impressive personal change and growth (Noy, 2004b). He gave up on check-marking yet another site of masculinity, but he gained a refreshing perspective and a new spectrum of bodily behaviours (such as crying). Brian is not 'deeply arrogant' anymore, and while he gave up on the sense of being the invincible 'king of the world', he can now express more emotions. Although the experience which he narrates is surely not typical, similar to many backpackers and tourists, Brian too 'accepts the invitation to become a better person' in and through tourism (Rojek and Urry, 1997, p. 4).

The two extreme states that Brian describes, that of being near death during the trek and that of bursting into tears while talking with his mother, share two important features: they are both *embodied states* of *loss of control*. During the trek Brian mentions that he lost his bodily mobility and spatial orientation, and during the conversation with his mother, too, he says that he could 'hardly control' himself (i.e. his body). Both states are bodily and hence essentially inexplicable. Indeed, Brian indicates that '[s]omehow it opened *something*'. In both cases the site of the transformation is interior, located amorphously deep within the male body ('something that opened *there*'). In both of these inter-correlated instances, the hegemonic masculine discourse, according to which the body is always under complete control, is rejected. This temporal lapse brings about a permanent bodily transformation. When Brian recounts his backpacking adventures and says 'I'll carry with me for the rest of my life', he indicates how the unusual backpacking experience he had undergone was absorbed both in his body and in his biography.

Conclusion

Backpackers' narratives of travel and adventure are embodied texts that shed light on the ways hegemonic masculinity is constructed and pursued in this tourist (sub)culture. Listening to their narratives illustrates the particular relations between bodies (tourist bodies) and spaces (touristic spaces). In this regard, this chapter deals with the semiotics of the interrelations of gender and embodiment in global backpacking tourism, and offers a contribution to the 'empirical possibilities of an embodied account of tourism' (Johnston, 2001, p. 181).

To begin with, the travel narratives powerfully illustrate the crucial role reserved for the body in the consumption and construction of gender identities in tourism in general and hegemonic masculinity in particular. The backpackers' post-trip narratives are embodied through and through. They supply a lively experience of how ventures and adventures are pursued in a manly rite of passage. The masculine body that progresses from one backpacker destination to another, check-marking on the way entire continents and subcontinents, is engaged in a 'mission', whereby it accomplishes a demanding physical challenge. The experiential reward of the intense 'bodywork' is twofold: experientially, backpackers indicate a deep sense of gratification and fulfilment upon completion of the lengthy trip. This experience is the accumulated result of various demanding activities that are pursued during the lengthy trip. The sense of gratification and self-fulfilment is oftentimes expressed it terms of a true personal transformation (Noy, 2004b).

Socially, the narratives backpackers recount endow the youths with *symbolic and gender capital of hegemonic masculinity*. The travellers are transformed from youths to (young) adults, and upon returning to the homeland they join a new collective of veteran backpackers. Hence, socially, their inner sense of fulfilment and transformation is expressed in terms of social systems and collective identities. This new affiliation is crucial within the heated politics of identity in present-day Israeli society. We should keep in mind that the backpacking trip, which is undertaken shortly after a duration of obligatory service in the army, is the first civic endeavour backpackers undertake as adults. Hence, the sites they visit and the trails they walk symbolically amount to the first footsteps they make in the world of 'grown-ups' and in its institutions.

As far as images of hegemonic masculinity are concerned, the masculine backpacker body heroically confronts and surmounts primordial 'authentic' wilderness (Nature), which is constructed as a 'militouristic' (romanticist and semi-militaristic) challenge. While overcoming Nature, the trip constructs and shapes the body, and its sense, abilities and limits. This act of overcoming nature is symbolic and has at least two additional aspects: first, the romantic hero receives or absorbs something of the profundity and exoticism of Nature (or Native) that it transgresses and overcomes. As Green (1993) notes in the epigraph of this chapter: 'the Western traveler became himself creative and divine' (p. 52). All of this occurs in tourist contexts where familiarity and alterity are institutionally juxtaposed. It is through this contrastive juxtaposition that one assumes a sought-after identity. '[B]odies involved in the tourism process do undergo change', and they do so 'through the reflexive play of the Other, as a category and as Body' (Veijola and Jokinen, 1994, cited in Johnston, 2001, p. 189).

The second symbolic aspect that is related to overcoming Nature (Other) concerns gender. The romantic construction of touristic destinations and spaces is feminized, and as such it endows the traveller with a sense of competent masculinity. In fact, the very act of travelling, i.e. of materializing one's mobility rights in public spaces, is itself a demonstration of cultural dominance and sovereignty (Pratt, 1992; Minh-Ha, 1994; Mazali, 2001). This is particularly so with backpackers who are emphatically romanticist tourists (at least the backpackers of the type interviewed for this study).

Yet, not all the narratives male backpackers recount describe spatial manly accomplishments. In fact, two-thirds of the male backpackers (and all of the female backpackers) evinced different degrees of discord in relation to the hegemonic norm by which they were required to adhere. In these instances too subversion was manifest in and through the site of the body. These backpackers did not celebrate the strenuous work they had to perform in the name of normativity; nor were they enthusiastic about the patriarchic discourse that splits the tourist into a conforming (instrumental) body and a disembodied traveller. From the richness of practices entailed in modern backpacking tourism, and from the varied gender character-istics they embody, these disillusioned backpackers tailor their own leisurely set of engendering practices and experiences (Uriely *et al.*, 2002; Cohen, 2004).

The singular complexity which characterizes the backpackers whose words were presented above stems from the transposition of embodied colonial practices from national territories (the territories of the youths' homeland wherein these practices were initially pursued) to extranational touristic spaces. While a few accounts support Massad's (2000) hypothesis concerning the 'hologramic' state of a body that exists in its constituting national spaces, other accounts indicate that a physical departure does not necessarily entail a symbolic departure. In other words, the 'hologramic' anxiety of the backpackers' bodies is reduced or eliminated as a result of the construction of tourist enclaves and spaces which resemble those of the homeland or motherland. Additionally, through these long-haul trips, which are pursued collectively, a 'new Israeli' arguably emerges (Haviv, 2005) who is not the Sabra Massad (2000) discusses.

Regarding the travellers' home society we can learn that it did not undergo changes that are typical of post–Second World War societies, whereby embodied endeavours of the national-colonial sphere gave way to the spheres of competitive sports. The transformation Kimmel (1996) notes, observing that 'the geographic frontier was replaced by the outfield fence' in the USA (p. 141), does not accurately describe the large-scale ideologies and institutions that are influential in Israel. Rather, as geopolitical frontiers in and around Israel have not been 'replaced' and clearly demarcated, hegemonic masculinity is (still) pursued through neocolonial-militaristic practices. Backpacking is thus viewed as a 'national sport', wherein exotic and faraway spaces are its arena. The travellers' bodies, and the body of the nation state, are both correlatively incomplete and unfinalized; they are both still being negotiated on macrospheres and microspheres.

Acknowledgement

This chapter is partly based on a lecture titled 'Trekking Stories and the Emplotment of Masculinity and Nationality', presented in the 17th Annual Conference of the Association for Israel Studies, 16 May 2001, Washington.

Endnotes

[1] See Elsrud (2001) and Sorensen (2003) concerning similar observations about backpack-ers. In relation to interviewing men, see Schwalbe and Wolkomir (2001), and Arendell (1997), which I teach in masculinity classes and which the students find very helpful.
[2] The Hebrew phrase Uri uses is *mivatikey ha-dor* (lit. of the elders of the generation), which is somewhat archaic and of high register. The phrase connotes precisely the tradition mentioned earlier, that of Sabra ritualistic hiking.

³ An additional reason for which David stresses that money was not an issue when refusing porters' services concerns the fact that bargaining and getting the 'best deal' are also activities that backpackers regularly boast about. By indicating that it was 'about a buck a day', David establishes the fact that his companions were good bargainers, and that money was really not the issue.

⁴ For similar references to the male body, i.e. as a reliable and faithful companion, see Hammond and Jablow (1987) and Sherrod (1987).

⁵ Feminist theoreticians of tourism and travel have noticed the price women pay for materializing their right to travel. A split within the traveller occurs, as is the case with Brian. Blake (1990) notes that 'split between traveler and lady . . . pervades women's travel narratives' (p. 354).

⁶ With respect to interior (unobserved) bodily changes, which are socially constructed as transformative, see Weiss (1997).

References

Aitchison, C. (2001) Theorizing other discourses of tourism, gender and culture: can the subaltern speak (in tourism)? *Tourist Studies* 1(2), 133–147.

Ardener, S. (ed.) (1981) *Women and Space: Ground Rules and Social Maps*. St Martin's Press, New York.

Arendell, T. (1997) Reflections on the researcher–researched relationship: a woman interviewing men. *Qualitative Sociology* 20(3), 341–368.

Ateljevic, I. and Doorne, S. (2004) Theoretical encounters: a review of backpacking literature. In: Richards, G. and Wilson, J. (eds) *The Global Nomad: Backpacker Travel in Theory and Practice*. Channel View Publications, Clevedon, UK, pp. 60–76.

Ben-Ari, E. (2001) Tests of soldierhood, trials of manhood: military service and male ideals in Israel. In: Maman, D., Ben-Ari, E. and Rosenhek, Z. (eds) *Military, State, and Society in Israel: Theoretical and Comparative Perspectives*. Transaction Publishers, New Brunswick, New Jersey.

Ben-Ari, E. and Levi-Schreiber, E. (2000) Body-building, character-building, and nation-building: gender and military service in Israel. *Studies in Contemporary Judaism* 16, 171–190.

Blake, S.L. (1990) A women's trek: what difference does gender make? *Women's Studies International Forum* 13(4), 347–355.

Blunt, A. and Rose, G. (1994) *Writing Women and Space: Colonial and Postcolonial Geographies*. Guilford Press, New York.

Bly, R. (1990) *Iron John: A Book about Men*. Addison-Wesley, Reading, Massachusetts.

Bourdieu, P. (1977) *Outline of a Theory of Practice*. Cambridge University Press, Cambridge.

Boyarin, D., Itzkovitz, D. and Pellegrini, A. (eds) (2003) *Queer Theory and the Jewish Question*. Columbia University Press, New York.

Boyarin, J. and Boyarin, D. (eds) (1997) *Jews and Other Differences: The New Jewish Cultural Studies*. University of Minnesota Press, Minneapolis, Minnesota.

Bruner, E.M. (1991) The transformation of self in tourism. *Annals of Tourism Research* 18(2), 238–250.

Bruner, E.M. (2005) *Culture on Tour: Ethnographies of Travel*. University of Chicago Press, Chicago, Illinois.

Butler, J. (1993) *Bodies That Matter: On the Discursive Limits of 'Sex'*. Routledge, New York.

Campbell, J. (2004) *The Hero with a Thousand Faces* (commemorative edition). Princeton University Press, Princeton, New Jersey.

Clifford, J. (1992) Traveling cultures. In: Grossberg, L. Nelson, C. and Treichler, P. (eds) *Cultural Studies*. Routledge, London, pp. 96–116.

Cohen, E. (1985) Tourism as play. *Religion* 15, 291–304.

Cohen, E. (2004) Backpacking: diversity and change. In: Richards, G. and Wilson, J.

(eds) *The Global Nomad: Backpacker Travel in Theory and Practice*. Channel View Publications, Clevedon, UK, pp. 43–59.

Connell, R.R. (1995) *Masculinities*. Polity Press, Cambridge.

Csordas, T.J. (1990) Embodiment as a paradigm for anthropology. *Ethos* 18(1), 5–47.

Dann, G. (1996) *The Language of Tourism: A Sociolinguistic Perspective*. CAB International, Wallingford, UK.

Diprose, R. and Ferrell, R. (eds) (1991) *Cartographies: Poststructuralism and the Mapping of Bodies and Spaces*. Allen & Unwin, North Sydney, Australia.

Douglas, M. (1966) *Purity and Danger: An Analysis of Concepts of Pollution and Taboo*. Praeger, New York.

Edensor, T. (2000) Staging tourism: tourists as performers. *Annals of Tourism Research* 27(2), 322–344.

Elsrud, T. (2001) Risk creation in traveling: backpacker adventure narration. *Annals of Tourism Research* 28(3), 597–617.

Featherstone, M., Hepworth, M. and Turner, B.S. (eds) (1991) *The Body: Social Process and Cultural Theory*. Sage, London.

Fontana, A. and Frey, J.H. (2000) From structured questions to negotiated text. In: Denzin, N.K. and Lincoln, Y.S. (eds) *Handbook of Qualitative Research*, 2nd edn. Sage, London, pp. 645–672.

Foucault, M. and Gordon, C. (1980) *Power/Knowledge: Selected Interviews and Other Writings, 1972–1977*. Harvester Press, Brighton, UK.

Frank, A.W. (1991) For a sociology of the body: an analytical review. In: Featherstone, M., Hepworth, M. and Turner, B.S. (eds) *The Body: Social Process and Cultural Theory*. Sage, London, pp. 36–102.

Green, M.B. (1993) *The Adventurous Male: Chapters in the History of the White Male Mind*. Pennsylvania State University Press, University Park, Pennsylvania.

Grosz, E.A. (1994) *Volatile Bodies: Toward a Corporeal Feminism*. Indiana University Press, Bloomington, Indiana.

Hammond, D. and Jablow, A. (1987) Gilgamesh and the Sundance Kid: the myth of male

friendship. In: Brod, H. (ed.) *The Making of Masculinities: The New Men's Studies*. Allen & Unwin, Boston, Massachusetts, pp. 241–258.

Harrison, J.D. (2002) *Being a Tourist: Finding Meaning in Pleasure Travel*. The University of British Columbia Press, Vancouver.

Haviv, A. (2005) Next year in Kathmandu: Israeli backpackers and the formation of a new Israeli identity. In: Noy, C. and Cohen, E. (eds) *Israeli Backpackers and Their Society: A View from Afar*. State University of New York Press, Albany, New York.

Heckathorn, D.D. (1997) Respondent-driven sampling: a new approach to the study of hidden populations. *Social Problems* 44(2), 174–199.

Hymes, D. (1975) Breakthrough into performance. In: Ben-Amos, D. and Goldstein, K.S. (eds) *Folklore: Performance and Communication*. Mouton, Hague, pp. 11–74.

Johnston, L. (2001) (Other) Bodies and tourism studies. *Annals of Tourism Research* 28(1), 180–201.

Katriel, T. (1995) Touring the land: trips and hiking as secular Pilgrimages in Israeli Culture. *Jewish Ethnology and Folklore Review* 17, 6–13.

Katz, C. and Monk, J.J. (eds) (1993) *Full Circles: Geographies of Women over the Life Course*. Routledge, London.

Kimmel, M.S. (1996) *Manhood in America: A Cultural History*. Free Press, New York.

Kimmel, M.S. (2002) Foreword. In: Gardiner, J.K. (ed.) *Masculinity Studies and Feminist Theory: New Directions*. Columbia University Press, New York, pp. ix–xi.

Kimmel, M.S. and Messner, M.A. (2004) *Men's Lives*, 6th edn. Allyn & Bacon, Boston, Massachusetts.

Kimmerling, B. (2001) *The Invention and Decline of Israeliness: State, Society, and the Military*. University of California Press, Berkeley, California.

Klein, Y. (1999) 'Our best boys': the gendered nature of civil-military relations in Israel. *Men and Masculinities* 2, 47–56.

Kvale, S. (1996) *Interviews: An Introduction to Qualitative Research Interviewing*. Sage, Thousand Oaks, California.

Longhurst, R. (1995) The body and geography: gender, place and culture. *Journal of Feminist Geography* 2, 97–105.

Longhurst, R. (2000) Geography and gender: masculinities, male identity and men. *Progress in Human Geography* 24(3), 439–444.

MacCannell, D. (2001) Tourist agency. *Tourist Studies* 1(1), 23–37.

Martin, E. (2001) *The Woman in the Body: A Cultural Analysis of Reproduction*. Beacon Press, Boston, Massachusetts.

Massad, J. (2000) The 'post-colonial' colony: time, space, and bodies in Palestine/Israel. In: Afzal-Khan, F. and Seshadri-Crooks, K. (eds) *The Pre-Occupation of Postcolonial Studies*. Duke University Press, Durham, North Carolina, pp. 311–346.

Mazali, R. (2001) *Maps of Women's Goings and Stayings*. Stanford University Press, Stanford, California.

Messner, M.A. (1995) Boyhood, organized sports, and the construction of masculinities. In: Kimmel, M.S. and Messner, M.A. (eds) *Men's Lives*. Allyn & Bacon, Boston, Massachusetts, pp. 102–114.

Minh-Ha, T.T. (1994) Other than myself/my other self. In: Robertson, G., Mash, M., Tickner, L., Bird, J., Curtis, B. and Putnam, T. (eds) *Travellers' Tales: Narratives of Home and Displacement*. Routledge, London, pp. 9–26.

Morin, K.M., Longhurst, R. and Johnston, L. (2001) (Troubling) Spaces of mountains and men: New Zealand's Mount Cook and Hermitage Lodge. *Social and Cultural Geography* 2(2), 117–139.

Mosse, G.L. (1996) *The Image of Man: The Creation of Modern Masculinity*. Oxford University Press, New York.

Noy, C. (2003) Narratives of hegemonic masculinity: representations of body and space in Israeli backpackers' narratives. *Israeli Sociology* 5(1), 75–102.

Noy, C. (2004a) Performing identity: touristic narratives of self-change. *Text and Performance Quarterly* 24(2), 115–138.

Noy, C. (2004b) 'The trip really changed me': backpackers' narratives of self-change. *Annals of Tourism Research* 31(1), 78–102.

Noy, C. (2005) Israeli backpackers: narrative, interpersonal communication, and social construction. In: Noy, C. and Cohen, E. (eds) *Israeli Backpackers and Their Society: A View from Afar*. State University of New York Press, Albany, New York.

Noy, C. (2006) Israeli backpacking since the 1960s: institutionalization and its effects. *Tourism Recreation Research* 31(3), 39–54.

Noy, C. (2007) *A Narrative Community: Voices of Israeli Backpackers*. Wayne State University Press, Detroit, Michigan.

Noy, C. (forthcoming) Traversing hegemony: gender, body, and identity in the narratives of Israeli female backpackers. *Tourism Review International*. Theme Issue: Female Traveler II 11(2).

Noy, C. and Cohen, E. (2005a) Introduction: backpacking as a rite of passage in Israel. In: Noy, C. and Cohen, E. (eds) *Israeli Backpackers and Their Society: A View from Afar*. State University of New York Press, Albany, New York, pp. 1–44.

Noy, C. and Cohen, E. (eds) (2005b) *Israeli Backpackers and Their Society: A View from Afar*. State University of New York Press, Albany, New York.

Pratt, M.L. (1992) *Imperial Eyes: Travel Writing and Transculturation*. Routledge, London.

Presner, T.S. (2003) 'Clear heads, solid stomachs, and hard muscles': Max Nordau and the aesthetics of Jewish regeneration. *Modernism-Modernity* 10(2), 269–296.

Quam-Wickham, N. (1999) Rereading man's conquest of nature: skill, myths, and the historical construction of masculinity in western extractive industries. *Men and Masculinities* 2, 135–151.

Rank, O. (2004) *The Myth of the Birth of the Hero: A Psychological Exploration of Myth*, (trans. G.C. Richter and J.E. Lieberman). Johns Hopkins University Press, Baltimore, Maryland.

Richards, G. and Wilson, J. (2004) The global nomad: motivations and behavior of independent travellers worldwide. In: Richards, G. and Wilson, J. (eds) *The Global Nomad: Backpacker Travel in Theory and Practice*. Channel View Publications, Clevedon, UK, pp. 14–39.

Riley, P.J. (1988) Road culture of international long-term budget travelers. *Annals of Tourism Research* 15(3), 313–328.

Rojek, C. and Urry, J. (eds) (1997) *Touring Cultures: Transformations of Travel and Theory*. Routledge, London.

Schwalbe, M. and Wolkomir, M. (2001) The masculine self as problem and resource in interview studies with men. *Men and Masculinities* 4(1), 90–103.

Shapira, A. (1999) *Land and Power: The Zionist Resort to Force, 1881–1948*. Stanford University Press, Stanford, California.

Sherrod, D. (1987) The bonds of men: problems and possibilities in close male relationships. In: Brod, H. (ed.) *The Making of Masculinities: The New Men's Studies*. Allen & Unwin, Boston, Massachusetts, pp. 213–240.

Sorensen, A. (2003) Backpacker ethnography. *Annals of Tourism Research* 30(4), 847–867.

Turner, B.S. (1996) *The Body and Society: Explorations in Social Theory*, 2nd edn. Sage, London.

Uriely, N., Yonay, Y. and Simchai, D. (2002) Backpacking experience: a type and form analysis. *Annals of Tourism Research* 29, 520–538.

Urry, J. (1990) *The Tourist Gaze: Leisure and Travel in Contemporary Societies*. Sage, London.

Veijola, S. and Jokinen, E. (1994) The body in tourism. *Theory, Culture and Society* 11, 125–151.

Weiss, M. (1997) Signifying the pandemics: metaphors of aids, cancer, and heart disease. *Medical Anthropology Quarterly* (New Series) 11(4), 456–476.

Weiss, M. (2002) *The Chosen Body: The Politics of the Body in Israeli Society*. Stanford University Press, Stanford, California.

Welk, P. (2004) The beaten track: anti-tourism as an element of backpacker identity construction. In: Richards, G. and Wilson, J. (eds) *The Global Nomad: Backpacker Travel in Theory and Practice*. Channel View Publications, Clevedon, UK, pp. 77–91.

Woodward, R. (1998) 'It's a man's life!' Soldiers, masculinity and the countryside. *Gender, Place and Culture* 5(3), 277–300.

Woodward, R. (2000) Warrior heroes and little green men: soldiers, military training, and the construction of rural masculinities. *Rural Sociology* 65(4), 640–657.

5 The Emergence of the Body in the Holiday Accounts of Women and Girls

JENNIE SMALL

Introduction

The body has, for the most part, been absent from the academic discussion of the tourist experience. However, when Australian women and girls were asked to discuss their holiday experiences at different stages of the life course, an emergent theme was the physical experience of a holiday. This chapter discusses a study employing the research method, memory-work, in which different-aged women and girls wrote about, and collectively discussed, their good and bad holiday experiences, and it reveals the many ways in which the body was evident in their memories. Johnston (2000, p. 181) argued that 'the study of tourism within the social sciences has been built on Western hierarchical dualisms and tends to produce hegemonic, disembodied and masculinist knowledge'. This chapter thus describes a study which produced a different kind of knowledge of tourism and holidays, the knowledge and understanding of *women*. In recognition that there is no single women's voice, an attempt was made in the study to 'factor in the multiplicity of women' (Burman, 2002, p. 1205) by examining the experiences of women of different ages and their experiences of holidays over the life course. It was assumed that the tourist experience is socially and historically constructed, contingent on time and social context. Different age groups at different historical times are likely to have different experiences of tourism and holidays. It was also assumed that when gender intersects other subjectivities, not all women are equal. In other words, if women are Other, then there are 'Other' Others.

As a form of leisure with the implied notion of choice, tourism can be a site of contestation and resistance to existing stereotypes of gender. Through leisure women can become more confident and affirmed in their identity to enable them to 'resist oppression in all aspects of their lives' (Henderson *et al.*, 1996, p. 8). On the other hand, the holiday might be a site for the reinforcement of gendered subjectivities. The study looked for patterns of good and bad holiday experiences, commonalities and differences with the aim of developing a *theory* of women's experiences. The research was exploratory, rather than hypothesis-testing; grounded in the sense that theory was

Table 5.1. Memory-work research participants.

Memories	12 years	20 years	40 years	65+ years
At age 12	✓	✓	✓	✓
At age 20		✓	✓	✓
At age 40			✓	✓
At age 65+				✓

constructed inductively. In the patterns which emerged, the *embodiment* of the holiday experience was a strong theme across all age groups and at different historical times.

The women and girls who participated in the research differed in terms of age/family life stage[1] and historical time. The participants were aged 12 (26 participants), 20 (25 participants), 40 (18 participants) and 65+ (17 participants). The women aged 40 and 65+ were mothers. Those aged 40 had at least one child under the age of 15. The participants shared certain identities: race and ethnicity (white, Anglo-Australian), socio-economic class (middle-class), sexuality (heterosexual) and able-bodiedness. The study examined the relationship between holiday experiences and age (individual time)/family life stage (family time) and historical time. Current holiday experiences were studied as were memories of holidays at younger ages (see Table 5.1). Through studying memories of good and bad holiday experiences at four different ages, the research examined how Australian women and girls socially construct their holiday experiences over the life course.

The research method employed was the feminist social constructionist method, 'memory-work', developed by Haug *et al.* (1987). The premise of memory-work is that women's memories of their life experiences are the basis of their knowledge and, through examining memories, we can understand how women construct themselves into, and through, existing social relations. Respecting different types of knowledge, the method aims for consciousness raising and empowerment for women. There are three phases to memory-work:

Phase 1: The individual participant writes a memory.

A group of 4–5 same-aged participants was formed and each member wrote a memory about a *good holiday experience* and a *bad* (or 'not so good') *holiday experience* at a specified age.

Phase 2: The group meets and analyses the memories.

The collective looked for commonalities and dissimilarities in the memories, clichés, contradictions and silences. The method at this stage allows for the social nature of the production of the memories to be realized.

Phase 3: The researcher[2] analyses the collective analysis.

While phase 2 was concerned with how the collective made sense of the memories, phase 3 was where I, the researcher, made sense of them.
I transcribed the tape and related the discussion to those of other collectives (same-aged and different-aged) looking for general themes and patterns.
A further analysis was made of the collective's analysis by relating it to the academic literature and tourism industry practice.

Embodiment of the Tourist Experience

A major theme which emerged from the cross-sectional (across age groups) and 'longitudinal' (over the life course) analyses of the collective discussions was the *embodiment of the tourist experience*. Although expressed differently at different ages/family life stages and historical times, embodiment was a theme common to all age cohorts. The term 'embodiment' is used by Turner (1996, p. xiii) to capture 'the notions of making and doing the work of bodies – of becoming a body in social space'. The holiday was remembered as bodily movement, a sensual experience, an emotional experience and bodily appearance. It is significant that the body is not part of the traditional academic tourism discourse.

Bodily movement

Physical activity was a part of holidays at all ages but the meaning of physical activity varied at different ages. Holidays at age 12 were remembered for the *pleasure* and *fun* of bodily movement.

> KRISTINA [age 12]: [Holiday at age 12] From the moment I arrived on Plantation Island, Fiji, and spotted the pontoon with the sun sparkling down on it, I knew it was going to be one of the highlights of my holiday. After a delicious breakfast, I would swim out through the sparkling warm water and you would be able to see the bottom of the water as it was so clear. When I reached the pontoon, I climbed up the ladder and stood up on the surface of it. I would feel very proud and look out over the water and feel like I'm on top of the world! You could also dive off the pontoon into the water and that was heaps of fun too.

> JESSIE: *Oh yeah, I agree because when I went to Fiji I dived off a pontoon too, and I thought it was fun.*[3]

> BARBIE [age 20]: [Holiday at age 12] She settled, feet first onto the slide and waited a moment or two before she headed off down the slide. It was great. She could feel the water and her body as if they were moving as one down the cool slide. She took a deep breath in and hit the water at the bottom and made it safely to the other side. Barbie felt happy again. She was at last having some fun.

Holidays can offer opportunities for physical activity for girls and women of all ages. Squire (1995) in her analysis of earlier women tourists in the Canadian Rockies found that tourism offered the women the opportunity for physical exercise that would have been unacceptable at home. Grace Seton-Thompson (cited in Squire, 1995) explained in 1900:

> It is [a] pleasure to use your muscles, to buffet with the elements, to endure long hours of riding, to run where walking would do, to jump an obstacle instead of going around it, to return, physically at least, to your pinafore days when you played with your brother.
>
> (Squire, 1995, p. 8)

The benefits of physical activity surpass the health benefits. Through physical activity, the body can be liberated. As Wearing (1998) says:

When women do make the effort to refuse what they have been told they are and to reach towards their potential in the area of bodily movement and the use of space, there is some evidence from the leisure literature of a corresponding increase in self-confidence and a new and exciting awareness of bodily power. For example, women who participate in outdoor adventures such as rock climbing, canoeing, camping, bush walking, scuba diving, body-building and weight-lifting report emotional, physical and psychological benefits.

(Wearing, 1998, p. 110)

A renegotiation of the boundaries for women's use of their bodies in space leads to 'a femininity that is expansive rather than constrictive' (Wearing, 1998, p. 112) and 'indicates a possible change in subjectivities for women away from that predicated on the fragility of the female body' (p. 113). The benefit of using the body gives women control over their bodies rather than being the object of men's gaze and control. Despite others' findings (Henderson and Bialeschki, 1993; Little and McIntyre, 1995) of possible negotiation and resistance to the feminine discourse of women and physical activity, in this study, by the time the women had reached age 20, subordination to the feminine discourse was more evident. After age 12, bodily movement was only rarely highlighted as a positive holiday experience. The centrality of physical activity in childhood holidays compared with its peripheral position in adult holidays reinforces findings from leisure studies that female participation in physical activity declines after childhood (James, 1995; Roberts, 1996). By age 20, bodily movement was replaced by social interaction as the key ingredient of a good holiday experience.

> OTHER (Kristen's group) [age 20]: [Holiday at age 20] You go away and you're with your friends so . . . you don't feel like you have to go skiing.
>
> KIMBERLEY: Yeah, like you don't have to do anything.
>
> OTHER: Mmm.
>
> OTHER: You're on holidays, you decide you're different. You don't need to do anything.
>
> OTHER: No problem.
>
> KIMBERLEY: Yeah.

There was only one woman in the study whose holiday involved organized sport (an interstate trip to represent her university). However, her memory of the trip related to bad relations with her teammates. The fact that she did not get to play her sport *at all* was only mentioned as an afterthought.

The discourse of femininity can be said to discourage bodily movement and encourage the control of bodies in space. Wearing (1998) cites the findings of Young to explain women's constraints in using their bodies in space:

> Constraints begin to appear as soon as they are told not to get hurt, not to get dirty, not to tear clothes and not to attempt dangerous challenges. In order to transcend such prescriptions a conscious effort is needed. Boys have been encouraged to use space quite differently from an early age – they see it as their natural right to throw their bodies into the available space, to get dirty and to attempt challenging bodily tasks.

(Wearing, 1998, p. 110)

Parents' concern for the physical safety of girls in public spaces has been seen as responsible for limiting girls' use of space and thus leisure activities (Kelly, 1987;

Henderson and Bialeschki, 1993; McRobbie and Garber, 2000). Boys' derogatory comments, girls' attitudes to their bodies and girls' underrating of their competence are other explanations for girls decreasing physical activity as they age. A connection between personal use of space and self-esteem has been noted by Garret (cited in James, 1995), with low self-esteem being related to limited use of space. Holidays at age 12 provided a space in which physical activity was legitimate. Holiday locations away from urban areas and holiday environments which were enclosed, such as a resort or a ship, provided a space where the girls could explore more widely and safely than they could at home. They could experience a freedom from parents in a safe environment that might not be so easy in the home environment. Holidays were thus a time to develop independence and self-esteem, to be in control.

At age 40, a *relaxed* body was the key to a good holiday experience. It was not so much that the women were constrained by the feminine discourse of a controlled body in space, but rather that they were resisting the feminine discourse to be forever active in looking after others, a discourse to which they subscribed in their everyday home lives. The holiday could provide a space where the body was not challenged.

> JEAN [age 40]: [Holiday at age 40] They [female friend and self] relaxed in the suck and surge of the pool, roughly the size and shape of a jacuzzi. The pool bottom was full of loose stones, and they laughed a lot and fell about. The seas, the rocks, the salt mist and the natural beauty was food for the soul, and Jean's weary body could feel itself renewing.

> SUSIE [age 40]: [Holiday at age 40] The spa offers us gym, lap pool and any type of facial, massage or beauty treatment possible, all of which so far have been used and enjoyed. Kids are not allowed in there so it's very peaceful and the atmosphere is encouraged.

> Later
> ANNIE: *We all enjoy a relaxing holiday.*
> CARLY: *So lying on a beach with a book (*ANGELA: *preferably without kids) rather than climbing Mount. . .*

A study of women's holiday experiences at age 40 not only identifies what was being sought (a 'relaxed' body) but also illuminates that from which they were escaping (an 'exhausted' body). The 'leisure gap' referred to by Henderson *et al.* (1996) is most apparent at this stage of the life course. The women's negative memories portrayed the work (of their bodies) in preparing for a holiday, maintaining the holiday and, on return, unpacking the holiday which increased their already-high, everyday, domestic workload. At age 65+, bodily movement was associated with difficulties related to ageing. The tourism industry, through its services and facilities, could either facilitate or hinder physical movement.

> JANE [age 65+]: [Holiday at age 65+] The bedroom had a double bed in it, but the bed was so low I knew I'd never get out of it, with my arthritic knee . . .

> SUSAN *[age 65+]: [Holiday at age 65+] Well, I could hardly get up the ladder [of the plane] with the weight of my knapsack (*JANE: *Yes, yes) pulling me back. I say, this was only a couple of years ago. I had this crook leg coming on then (*JANE: *Yes) so I wasn't exactly spry.*

> JANE: *Oh I know, isn't it awful.*

> SUSAN *[age 65+]: [Holiday at age 65+] They [tourism industry] all knew when they wrote the brochures [for Italy] that we were going to have to have long walks (*LOU: *Mmm;* OTHER: *Mmm).*

And one couple that was on that tour . . . he had just had a hip replacement and she had just had
a triple bypass (LOU: Mmm; AMELIA: Oh, that's not fair, is it!) and had no idea that the buses
wouldn't drive them up to the Baptistry in Florence (AMELIA: Mmm) or up to St Peters in Rome, no
idea at all.

LOU: That's right.

JANE: That's dreadful, isn't it!

AMELIA: Mmm.

SUSAN: Because it really was horrendous. I mean, it was horrendous (JANE: Mmm). I mean, I was,
I almost couldn't cope with that.

There are physiological losses which occur in the process of ageing but physical and
sensory disabilities may prevent travel and holidays as much through structural inad-
equacies (such as unsuitable transport and accommodation, and inappropriate tour
planning) as from any inherent lack of ability on the part of the women to enjoy a
holiday. It is useful to refer to the disability studies literature which understands disability as a social construction (Begum, 1992; Bickenbach *et al.*, 1999). As Ferri and
Gregg (1998) state, in reference to the writing of Asch and Fine: 'Gender and disability are both social constructions, understandable only within the contexts and relationships that give meaning to the terms' (p. 429). It is important that the embodied
nature of growing older is not ignored in a tourism discourse of 'successful' ageing.

Sensual experience

It was evident from this study that a holiday was not only a kinaesthetic experience
but was also a complex sensual encounter. The instructions for writing the holiday
memory suggested that participants 'might find it helpful to think, not only of the
visual sights, but also, sounds, smells, tastes, and touch'. In the women's and girls'
memories it was apparent that the visual sense dominated but that many holiday memories were associated with other senses: sounds (the crisp sound of snow,
animals), smells (salt water, animals, toilets, flowers), taste (food and drink) and touch
(weather, pebbly beaches). The report of strong bodily sensations by women backpackers in different travel contexts led Elsrud (1998) to suggest that 'intensified bodily
sensations appear when clock-time is moved out of focus and living becomes a "being
in the present"' (p. 321). The traveller has the time to listen to the body, 'to let the
body do the talking, creating and signalling its own rhythmical time' (p. 323).

Traditionally our understanding of the tourist experience has privileged the
visual (which interestingly has more to do with the mind and masculinity) over
the body and other senses (which are related more closely to femininity). Until
recently the holiday has been portrayed as a 'sensory void' (Dann and Jacobsen,
2002, p. 211). The findings in this study support those of Selänniemi (cited in Dann
and Jacobsen, 2002): 'Everything in mass tourism is not about looking at places, or
to put it more exactly, to see places. The sense of sight is not exclusive in experiences
of the vacation' (p. 210). A gendered understanding of the holiday must go beyond
Urry's (1990) visual gaze. Urry's (2002) revised edition of *The Tourist Gaze* is more relevant in an understanding of women's and girls' experiences. While acknowledging
that the typical Western tourist experience is visual, Urry in the later edition of his
text also recognizes that 'there is nothing inevitable or natural about this organising

power of vision' (p. 146). As he claims: 'There are . . . complex connections between bodily sensations and socio-cultural "sensescapes" mediated by discourse and language' (p. 152). In the study reported here, the sense of touch was present in both positive and negative memories. Physical comfort and discomfort resulted from the air temperature, the feeling of clothes, bluebottle stings, the texture of the ground, etc. Physical discomfort was a particularly strong theme for holidays at age 12.

> JACKIE *[age 12]: [Holiday at age 12] I know when I got the bluebottle, I got it just on my thigh and I couldn't sit down because it really hurt and like we went to the theme park the next day and most of the rides you had to sit down on them and it really hurt. So I didn't quite enjoy that day.*

When the tourism industry was insensitive to the physical needs of many of the older women aged 65+, physical discomfort was the consequence. Illness also emerged as a theme in many of the memories but was most dominant for the current 12-year-olds and the 65+ women recalling holidays at age 40.

The sense of taste was represented in the pleasures and, to a lesser extent, the displeasures of certain food and drink for all age groups, particularly in the memories of holidays at ages 12 and 20. While much of the feminist literature on the body (e.g. Bordo, 1989, 1992) focuses on women's contradictory and problematic relationship with food leading to eating disorders, there was no evidence of this in the holiday memories. While the women (and girls?) may have been committed to a discourse equating slimness with sexual attractiveness and consequent dieting in the home environment, there was no evidence of restraint during holidays. If anything, holidays were a time for indulgence. At age 12, holidays were seen as a time for treats. Holidays were a time to resist the discourse of a healthy body.

> RUTH [age 40]: [Holiday at age 12] There was always a packed picnic lunch made by her mother to eat en route and the purchase of a special kind of boiled lolly selection at Central Station, never duplicated anywhere else. . . . These holidays meant lots of picnics and bush-walking. She and her family would be out all day, her dad with a backpack of chops or sausages to grill somewhere in the bush for lunch. The smell of sizzling meat never failed to whet the appetite, the meat accompanied by thick slices of bread and butter, washed down with our treat purchased in the village of our choice of soft drink. Hers was always Cottee's Passiona and the taste of it today still evokes those mountain memories. For her parents, a boiled billy of black tea, always with a gum leaf added for extra flavour and accompanied by a slab of home-made cake. . . . On those days when her father and brothers were attempting a longer than usual hike, she and her mother would walk to the village to choose a cream bun for morning tea or call at the milk bar to choose a bag of lollies from an enormous selection.

Holidays also offered opportunities to experience different tastes. It was evident that food and beverage preferences were cultural, with different meanings at different ages and historical times. In discussing alcoholic beverages, the current 20-year-olds cited cocktails, in particular 'Illusions'; the 40-year-olds remembered 'Harvey Wallbangers'; and those 65+, 'Pimms' (or, in the USA, 'Boxcars'). Offal, which was a delicacy for one older woman at age 12, is unlikely to be considered a treat by current 12-year-olds. On the other hand, ice cream remained a constant favourite! It is uncertain whether women's special relationship to food accounts for the emergence of food as a theme in their holiday memories. Women, traditionally, are responsible for the preparation of meals and the family's diet. They also may be highly conscious of food in their battle for desired body shape. The findings from the 12-, 20-, and 40-year-old groups support Richards's (2002) contention that 'food is central to the tourist experience' (p. 3). However, it is difficult to know where to place the women and girls in the food tourism model of Hall and Sharples (2003). They were not special interest tourists, not the consumers of what is termed these days the 'gastronomy tourism product' (Fields, 2002, p. 36), but neither were they disinterested in the food at the destination.

The senses least likely to be present in the women's and girls' memories were hearing and smell and they were less likely to appear in the memories of the younger groups than the older groups. These senses appeared more often in the written memories than in the discussion. It is uncertain whether age differences were a result of differences in accessibility to sensations or ability to articulate sensations. It is only recently that tourism scholars have considered the olfactory as a component of the tourist experience. If the sense of smell is superior in women than men (Synott cited in Dann and Jacobsen, 2002), the traditional denigration of this sense in the tourist experience is also a denigration of women's experience. Dann and Jacobsen (2002), while highlighting the role of the olfactory in the tourist experience, also report the difficulty in articulating smells and our need to rely on 'the help of those with a special gift for words . . . who are particularly adept at evaluating and conveying their lived impressions of places and peoples' (p. 215). Having stated that smells are learned and women have a superior sense of smell, one might then question why Dann and Jacobsen (2002) omit from their discussion (with the exception of Jan Morris) any female writers 'with a special gift for words' to express their olfactory 'lived impression of places and peoples'! Ironically, even when male tourism scholars venture across the binary to the woman's position – the body – it is male knowledge of the body which is presented as the norm.

A theory of tourist experiences also needs to account for sensual changes (and their associated meanings) which occur with age. Discourse may not create the senses but it helps us 'make sense' of the senses. Veijola and Jokinen (1994) explain: 'When you hear, see, smell, sense and taste, you are in a context, connected. Thoughts may wander around and emotions vary, but a person has become a part of the unity, become a participant' (p. 140). Being part of the unity is apparent in the following holiday experience recalled from 1925:

SUSAN [age 65+]: [Holiday at age 12] Summer at the Lake was sheer heaven. . . . A pump outside the door delivered the sweetest water one could ever drink, and visitors from town declared it a beautiful nectar. . . . Every day they donned their pure wool bathing suits, neck to knee (OTHER: neck to knee), with a waist to knee all round skirt as well. Susan's mother's bathing suit had sleeves to the elbow, but Susan's was more modern, with only a bit of a sleeve covering her shoulders (OTHER: Oh). How hot and scratchy they were, and how heavy when one walked out of the water, with all that sodden mass of material. And how itchy as they dried. But oh to be swimming in that refreshing cold lake. . . . The beauty of the night noises to a city child are still fresh in Susan's mind. Whip-poor-wills, owls and the lonely call of a loon from the lake. The lake, they knew her every mood. Early morning while it was still dark, rowing off quietly into the middle of the lake to be there before the sun rose. Rowing noiselessly so as not to disturb the fish, the fowl and the birds, the glory of watching the sun rise behind the trees, the ducks swimming and from their night time nesting spot, the geese flying overhead.

Emotional experience

According to Freund (Wearing, 1998), emotions are always in some way embodied as they are expressed through the mind and body acting as one. Memories of emotions experienced during holidays clearly situate the body in the holiday experience. Wearing's (1998) assertion that leisure spaces have the potential 'to contribute to the expression of emotions in a positive way under the emotionally constrained circumstances of contemporary society' (p. 123) also applies to tourist spaces. Although there were age and cohort differences in terms of *which* emotions were remembered from holidays at different ages, holidays were emotional experiences for all age groups. Tourism sites allowed for the expression of positive emotions, such as happiness and joy.

> RACHEL [age 40]: [Holiday at age 12] Rachel's parents decided that they should climb St Mary's Peak. . . . A real sense of achievement was experienced and an overwhelming sense of happiness at doing this sort of thing with her mum and dad. . . . At night Rachel and her mum and dad sat in the caravan and played games and cards. They all had a great time. And Rachel wished they could do this at home too. Rachel felt happy. There was a sense of newness in all they did. Also relaxation and contentment.

> LORNA [age 65+]: [Holiday at age 65+] Lorna took her elder grandchild on a trip to San Francisco and Yosemite National Park. This was the most special time of her trip. To be together with this precious child she has loved for so much of her life, for the next four days, is something she knew would live in her heart forever. . . . When they arrived back home in Seattle, the feeling in Lorna's heart was almost overpowering. She had been on this same trip with her late husband just a few years earlier and she was so thrilled to be able to show this same beautiful part of the world to her granddaughter.

There was also the excitement of adventure, particularly remembered in holidays at age 12 by the older groups of women.

> *TOPSEY [age 65+]: [Holiday at age 12] We were encouraged to make the most of everything.*
>
> *GILLIAN: Absolutely.*
>
> *ELEANOR: We had adventures all the time, didn't we?*
>
> *GILLIAN: Mmm, oh yes, and secret things.*

If adventure is to be found beyond everyday, common routines, as Goffman (cited in Mitchell, 1988) claims, holidays can offer opportunities for women and girls to experience emotions which cannot be experienced at home. Adventure is part of the traditional masculine discourse rather than an element of femininity. Mills (1991) highlights the historical silence on women and adventure. According to Mills (1991), even in women's travel writing of the colonial period, adventure could not be highlighted as it would be read as odd or false. However, as Simmell (cited in Wearing and Wearing, 1992) says, adventure offers the possibility for personal expression and identity development:

> Adventure is a dropping out of the turmoil of everyday existence to experience a new 'something alien, untouchable, out of the ordinary', 'an island of life which

determines its beginning and end according to its own formative powers' (Simmel, 1965, p. 248). The adventurer sets challenges, the achievement of which brings satisfaction and a sense of personal control. The experience extends beyond the island of the adventure to everyday life through reflection.

(Wearing and Wearing, 1992, p. 13)

The tourist site was not always positive. It could also be the location for negative emotional experiences:

> JOAN [age 40]: [Holiday at age 40] They arrived at the camping ground. . . . Now to unload the car. The children started to pull out all the gear. And Joan's husband said, 'Stop! Let's do this in an organised manner'. And Joan could already start to feel the tension. . . . And then we started to put up the tent, and Harry [husband] said, 'I can do this without instructions' – new tent, hadn't done it before. So, lo and behold, we ended up in a huge argument, very frustrated . . . and in the end everyone was yelling at each other. It was just horrible.

Many of the recalled negative emotions are part of the discourse of femininity: shame, guilt, embarrassment, fear and hurt.

> MONICA [age 20]: [Holiday at age 20] The most negative memory of Monica's about this trip was when she was sitting on the lounge in the house, having just argued with her mother for the umpteenth time. Monica felt hot and bothered in the humid rainy weather. She felt annoyed that she may be missing out on the fun . . . she saw that all her friends would be having while she was stuck in a crumbling house in the rain. Every noise seemed to irritate her, from the chirping of the birds, to the grating sound of her mother's voice. And there could not possibly be a holiday experience more dreadful. Monica felt that tiredness one feels when there are just so many things seem to get in . . . seem to get on one's nerves. She saw herself as the only one in the family who seemed to be dissatisfied with the situation and hence . . . selfish and guilty. In essence, that particular afternoon Monica was left feeling rather sorry for herself.

> CARLY [age 40]: [Holiday at age 20] *I didn't tell my parents everything, that's for sure (ANNIE: Oh, no; SARAH: Oh, no, certainly didn't, no . . .). I was sprung when I had a boyfriend in Switzerland. (ANNIE: Oh wow) . . . I think I told a little white lie and I said I was going somewhere else. And my father found out. And he tracked me down in Switzerland. Oh, it was just horrific coming back. It was horrific. He met me at the railway station. Oh, I felt so ashamed. So bad!*

> OTHERS: *Mmm, Mmm.*

> JEAN [age 40]: [Holiday at age 40] *When I went away with Mum to New Zealand, I remember I went out one night, just in a motel where we were . . . had a few drinks with some other people on the tour. And I felt really guilty about getting in, back to the room, after midnight. You know, even at this age, like two years ago (OTHER: Mmm). Still felt like I'd done the wrong thing by Mum. . . . Oh it was just like being 17! I felt dreadful.*

In the mind/body dichotomy, it is the mind associated with rationality, thinking, perception and learning which has been foregrounded in the academic study of the tourist experience. In this study, the cognitive experience of learning about a destination was rarely mentioned, and when it did feature, it was only in holidays at 65+ years that such experiences were positive memories. The emotional experience of holidays was not limited to the duration of the holiday; it was often long-lasting. A number of women in recalling holidays at younger ages reported reliving the *emotion* of the experience and also the sensations. Many women 'could still' taste/smell/feel/hear and see the elements of the holiday. The memory-work session was in effect an embodied experience of the past!

Bodily appearance

As Hopwood (1995) says, for women, physical appearance signifies femininity, sexual attractiveness, success and power. In this study the body 'as project' appeared in the memories of holidays at different ages, but particularly in holidays at age 20. Shilling (2003) describes the body project:

> In the affluent West, there is a tendency for the body to be seen as an entity which is in the process of becoming; a project which should be worked at and accomplished as part of an individual's self identity.
>
> (Shilling, 2003, p. 4)

Clothes are part of the body project and were a particular focus of the memories of the 40- and 65+-year old women reminiscing about the holidays of their youth, at age 20. The high level of detail suggests the relevance of clothes to the holiday experience. The positive experiences related to clothes which made the women feel good.

> FRANCES [age 65+]: [Holiday at age 20] The shoes and high-heeled sandals purchased in Surfers [holiday destination] were absolutely gorgeous, beautiful soft leather, pale pink, blue, all the colours of the rainbow, with beads or pretty decorations and when worn to dances at home were the envy of every girl who saw them. . . . Frances purchased a pair of . . . gorgeous, silver dance sandals for herself which were very stilt and just a small ¼ inch strap around the heel and across the ankle and a ¼ inch strap across the toes with rhinestones across the strap. They were beautiful shoes, and danced in for many years. From when she first purchased those silver shoes, Frances felt like Cinderella every time she wore them.
>
> BARBIE [age 20]: [Holiday at age 20] Once settled, sunscreened and sexy in her new bikini, Barbie made her way proudly to the surf. However, she was taken aback at the size of the waves. Ken had no hesitation and dove straight into the water, and Barbie riskily followed. She was soon overawed at the sight of her bikini still on her body having survived a major disaster of a massive wave. This added security of non-moving swimwear made Barbie positively delighted. Her confidence was radiating and even Ken described her as 'captivating'. It was the only time in her life Barbie felt the absolute centre of attention and confident in a swimsuit!

The fondness with which the women remembered their clothes, such as the bikini, can be understood within the women's contemporary experience of their body.

> CARLY [age 40]: [Holiday at age 20] We'd have . . . the inciest, winciest, tiniest, weeny bikini (OTHERS: Yes, Mmm) . . . remember the ones . . . they're just strings (OTHER: Mmm, mmm). It was an Indian cotton one (OTHER: Yeah) and it was just strings and had those little dingleling bells on the back (OTHERS: Mmm, Yes).
>
> SUSIE: I'm sure we had those.
>
> CARLY: And the bra the size of an egg cup.
>
> ANNIE: Yes, nothing.
>
> SARAH: That's right, very, very brief.

CARLY: *Wouldn't fit on my big toe now!*

While the women reminisced fondly about the clothes of their twenties, clothes were also remembered as problematic. They could be physically uncomfortable (especially if one were sunburned) or could be considered inappropriate for the occasion.

> TOPSEY [age 65+]: [Holiday at age 20] [On arrival at a tropical island, walking from the jetty to the guesthouse] It would have been a lot more comfortable if Topsey and Marina [friend] had worn more suitable shoes as they tripped along in their flimsy, black, patent leather, strappy sandals and both in nylon stockings. Can you imagine, in 1955!

> LOU [age 65+]: [Holiday at age 20] On one night she was invited to a dance in the local hall. She went in a long dress and looked totally out of place. Others were not dressed up as they said. So that was a big mistake.

> OTHER: Mmm.

> . . .

> SUSAN: *But, you know, how dreadful in those days if you were dressed incorrect (*AMELIA: *Yes;* OTHER: *I know). You see nowadays it doesn't matter.*

Such embarrassment was not apparent in the memories of the current 20-year-olds:

> KIMBERLEY *[age 20]: [Holiday at age 20] Like I rock up and like, yeah, I'm in my jeans OK, it's OK, and everyone's in their North Sydney gear, like (*OTHER: *Yeah), the tight black pants, big heels, little boppie tops, like leather jackets (*OTHER: *No way!) and stuff. I was just sitting there going . . . 'I'm a sloth' . . . and it was all the people from like North Shore (*OTHER: *Yeah). It was just unbelievable. It was just like going to North Sydney (*OTHER: *Mmm). It was just ridiculous you know. All the girls there, you know, trying to pick up and stuff. All the guys were leering at them and stuff.*

Clothes in the 1950s required maintenance:

> CARMEN *[age 65+]: [Holiday at age 20] On holiday, I don't remember, but we must have had to locate the hotel ironing rooms.*

> FRANCES: *The petticoats were the worst of all (*OTHERS: *Yeah, Mmm). Oh yes, it was the first thing we did when we got on holidays (*OTHER: *Yeah). You took your clothes out and ironed everything you owned (*OTHERS: *Yes, Mmm) and hung it up so you didn't have to iron the rest of the holidays. You can get changed quicker then!*

At age 20, the women saw themselves as the objects of the gaze of others and themselves. Citing Bartky, Wolff (1990) refers to the ' "panoptical male connoisseur" in women's consciousness' (p. 126). The power of the gaze is explained by Foucault (1980):

> [T]here is no need for arms, physical violence, material constraints. Just a gaze.
> An inspecting gaze, a gaze which each individual under its weight will end by interiorising to the point that he is his own overseer, each individual thus exercising this surveillance over, and against himself.

> (Foucault, 1980, p. 155)

The women in this study could be seen to be the 'bearers' of power (Foucault, 1979) in taking on themselves an agreed-upon bodily appearance which would be observed. As Richards (2002) said: 'The surveillant gaze may become even more crucial on holiday, as bare flesh is exposed to the view of strangers on the beach' (p. 4). Outside the privacy of the home space which occurred on holiday women could find themselves in the unpleasant situation of having their femininity threatened by others' gaze. They experienced embarrassment when that which was normally hidden was exposed.

FRANCES *[age 65+]: [Discussing Japanese toilets] Squatting over a hole and no doors – nothing.*

LORNA: *Yes, they walk past you.*

FRANCES: *I would never have gone.*

LORNA: *Oh, it's horrible.*

As Bordo (1989) says:

Through the exacting and normalizing disciplines of diet, make-up, and dress – central organizing principles of time and space in the days of many women – we are rendered less socially oriented and more centripetally focused on self-modification. Through these disciplines, we continue to memorize on our bodies the feel and conviction of lack, insufficiency, of never being good enough.

(Bordo, 1989, p. 14)

Ganetz (1995) refers to 'womanliness as a masquerade':

This very obvious element of the masquerade, of 'dressing up', has prompted some researchers to suggest that femininity and, by extension, women's clothes, are actually a mask – something that conceals something else. What this 'something else' is, is much disputed: according to some of the post-modernists who most enthusiastically promulgate the theory, it is 'emptiness'. Femininity is nothing in itself, it is not a biological core or essence.

(Ganetz, 1995, p. 78)

As Ganetz states, the problem with this theory is that 'pleasure and satisfaction in the aestheticizing of one's own body is made invisible, as is subjectivity, or the possibility of expressing and finding oneself' (p. 79). In this study, memories of 'aestheticizing' the body were, for the most part, enjoyable. There can also be a pleasure in resisting dominant images of the body, but there was little evidence of such confrontation in the memories. There is debate as to the extent of the opportunities for subversion (Bordo, 1993). The argument that all women, including the most subordinate, can resist the dominant discourse of the female body is countered by the claim that such an approach 'fails to account for the success and durability of this precarious male dominance' (Holland *et al.*, 1994, p. 35).

It was apparent in discussing holidays at age 20 that some of the older women were quite critical of what they saw as the androgynous appearance and behaviour of 20-year-olds today: 'Girls don't look like girls.' Boëthius (1995) discusses the ambivalence that adults have about youth:

By criticizing the young . . . adults defend their own more disciplined way of living while trying to convince themselves that by becoming adults they have not lost or renounced anything important.

(Boëthius, 1995, p. 50)

The discourse which identifies women with the body rather than the mind and which favours the young woman's body over the older woman's perhaps explains the joy in recollection of clothes at age 20.[4] From the vantage point of the intervening years, the older women could appreciate what they had then and what is denied to them now. If the older women can dislike the fashions of young women today, their loss of youth is not as painful.

For the current 20-year-olds the body project also included 'the suntan'. Gibson and Yiannakis (1999) similarly found the 'sun lover' role prevalent in young adulthood. They and other researchers (Towner, 1995; NSW Cancer Council cited in Wood, 2003) have confirmed that the incidence of sunbaking is higher for women than for men. Rojek (1993) says:

> Successful tanning requires the consumption of sun-tan lotion and the abandonment of work. It is, quintessentially, a transformative activity. Often the process literally involves the shedding of skin to acquire a new look. Display and appearance determine tanning activity . . . the tan is one of the most accessible and universal signs. It instantly conveys health, leisure, vigour and sophistication.
>
> (Rojek, 1993, p. 190)

Although Rojek (1993) sees tanning as non-work, the body project does require effort. Competence can be associated with tanning. A common expression, and one used by one of the women, was 'working' on a tan.

> NICOLE [age 20]: [Holiday at age 20] Nicole enjoyed sunbaking and had decided that she would work on her tan this holiday. For the first week, Nicole went to the beach every day in the morning. She would alternate between swimming and sunbaking, before heading home for lunch. Then she would stay home all afternoon reading before heading out for some exercise in the early evening.

Today in many Western countries, the holiday is closely associated with the suntan. Urry (1990) says: '*The* ideal body has come to be viewed as one that is tanned' (p. 38). The meaning of a suntan is socially and historically constructed. Although there is a shared meaning of the suntan in Western countries, it does not so clearly mean 'holiday' in Australia as it does in northern European countries. Educational programmes about skin cancer have also changed the meaning of a tan, especially in countries with a high incidence of skin cancer such as Australia. However, many of the current 20-year-olds were resisting the medical discourse of the dangers of suntanning, in preference to accepting the fashion discourse of a tanned body. It was also apparent that the suntan was not a feature of the memories of the other age groups of women.

Absence of the body

As stated above, in different ways the body was present in the holiday experience. However, in other unexpected ways, the body was absent. From the 86 women who took part in the study and their hundreds of holiday memories, it might have been expected that female bodily processes such as menstruation, pregnancy, breastfeeding and sexual behaviour would have featured. Pregnancy and breastfeeding were never mentioned and in only three instances did menstruation figure. When the topic was raised it was 'dealt with' quickly and quietly 'disposed of' with little fuss. Despite the identification of holidays with the 'four Ss' (sun, sand, sea and sex), sexual behaviour figured only in memories of holidays at age 20, and even then it was more allusion than direct comment. Such observation confirms Davidson's (1996) finding that sexual relationships did not feature in women's discussion of holidays. Holland *et al.* (1994) refer to 'the careful social construction of disembodied sexuality' (p. 24). Sexuality must be concealed in order to be considered respectable and decent. It is possible that female bodily processes and sexual behaviour were irrelevant to women's holiday experiences. However, the collective's response to the raising of such matters (quiet dismissal) suggests that the women were relegating female bodily processes and sexual behaviour to the private sphere and, in doing so, were reinforcing patriarchal control of women's bodies. Tinkler (1995) confirms that for those growing up between 1920 and 1950 'the external and also internal dimensions of the female body were cross-cut by a public/private division such that the breasts and genitalia, the changes of adolescence, menstruation and pregnancy were not publicly discussed' (p. 185). Despite changes in the construction of girlhood and womanhood, the private/public division still appears to exist.

Conclusion

In examining the socially constructed body, the question remains whether the body is no more than discourse. In this study, the women's and girls' experiences reflected a materiality, a physicality, a *lived* bodily experience: bodily movement, the pain of sunburn, the sensation of happiness and fear. It is difficult to consider the body as simply a blank slate to be inscribed. It is alive: a breathing, digesting, defaecating, sleeping, menstruating, lactating organism. Physical processes and sensations are not independent of discourse, but neither are they the consequence of discourse. Harper (1997) refers to 'the ongoing tension between the body as constructed and the body as experienced, the body as an inscribed exterior and the body as a lived interior' (p. 161). Grosz (1993) deals with this tension by connecting the 'two' bodies. Grosz (1993) explains the body 'as a kind of *hinge* or threshold: it is placed between a psychic or lived interiority and a more sociopolitical exteriority that produces interiority through the *inscription* of the body's outer surface' (p. 196). To avoid the dichotomous, mutually exclusive categories of mind and body, new terminology is required. Grosz (1994) suggests that 'some kind of understanding of *embodied subjectivity*, of *psychical corporeality*, needs to be developed' (p. 22). The body is matter but it is not a fixed essence on which the social is inscribed. As Holland *et al.* (1994) say: 'The material body and its social construction are entwined in complex and contradictory ways which are extremely difficult to disentangle in practice' (p. 22). In terms of the women's and girls' tourist experiences, the body is the matter to be adorned, the seat of physical activity, illness, discomfort, smells, sounds, taste, 'as well as of the social images and meanings of these' (Holland *et al.*, 1994, p. 34). However, as Bordo (1989) says, the body is more than 'a *text* of culture'. It is also 'a *practical*, direct locus of social control' (p. 13). The body is gendered and aged.

Contemporary consumerism's emphasis on 'pleasure, desire, difference, and playfulness' (Turner, 1996, p. 2) is enacted in the tourist experience. The tourism industry recognizes the body in tourism through the various senses: sight (attractions); smell (flowers, food, etc.); sound (music, birds, animals, etc.); taste (food and drink); touch (climate, massage, comfort of accommodation, etc.); and kinaesthetics (movement of the body in snorkelling, skiing, etc.). The tourism promotional literature is emotionally charged to attract the tourist. The tourism discourse constructs the tourist body as slim, tanned, young, Caucasian, female and bikinied. Underlying the discourse are power relations. The body is at the core of different types of tourism: sex tourism, sports tourism, health tourism, snowbird tourism. Hargreaves (1986) comments: 'The body is clearly an object of crucial importance in consumer culture and its supply industries' (p. 14). Tourism is an industry in which the body is central to its purpose. Given that the selling of tourism by the tourism industry involves the commodification of the body, Shilling's (2003) reference to the body as an 'absent presence' is even more significant in tourism studies than in many other fields of study. Veijola and Jokinen (1994) claim:

> [O]ne starts to feel that tourism researchers (including us) have, in analysing the authentic, the undestroyed and the nostalgic in tourism, squeezed their subject too tight – without ever really embracing it. Or embracing only rhetorically, ignoring the body.
> (Veijola and Jokinen, 1994, p. 126)

In recent years a feminist interest has been developing in the commodification (and exploitation) of women's bodies in the promotion of tourism. None the less, the gendered body is an under-researched area of tourism (McCabe, 2002) as is the aged body. To emphasize the biased perspective of the literature, Jokinen and Veijola (1997) have 're-metaphorised' the postmodern tourist in ways which are 'not based on *implicitly* sexed bodily and imaginary morphologies' (p. 23). They have provided an alternative perspective to those of the 'great names' in tourism studies by putting the body back into tourism.

The privileging of the mind over body is perhaps more evident in tourism studies than in other fields, as scholars have struggled to be taken seriously, to be seen as engaging in a legitimate topic of scholarly endeavour. In making the field academically 'respectable', writers, including those taking a social constructionist approach, have maintained a separation of body and mind ignoring the body in favour of the mind. Culture has dominated the body; the male has dominated the female. Scholars can be accused of elitism in shunning the hedonistic 'beach' tourist in favour of the 'cultural' tourist. They have ignored the fact that many tourists travel for corporeal reasons rather than for improvement of the mind or to experience authenticity of others' lives. They have also failed to acknowledge that even the 'cultural' tourist has a body!

No holiday experience can be understood without reference to the body, since it is through the body that the holiday is experienced. Indeed, a definition of tourism implies a body which travels from the home region to another geographical space and stays overnight at the destination. And it is the body in proximity to a particular place, person or event at the destination which allows for a tourist to be 'corporeally alive' (Urry, 2002, p. 155) and for 'intense moments of co-presence' (Urry, 2002, p. 150) to occur. The physical experiences on holiday (an extraordinary event) can, in turn, illuminate the everyday experiences of the body at home. The women's and girls' memories of movement, senses, emotions and appearance clearly situate the body in the holiday and demonstrate that the holiday is both a site of bodily compliance and resistance to gendered discourse.

Endnotes

[1] Chronological age can be related to income, family life stage, ability/disability, etc. In examining one form of identity, one must be aware of other linkages. In this study, chronological age (individual time) coincided with family life stage (family time)

(Hareven, 1982). References to age imply a family life stage. At ages 20 and 40 the family life stage was specified for participant eligibility.

2 In the original application of the method (Haug et al., 1987), all participants engaged in phase 3. However, such democracy is not always possible, especially when the method is used in student research.

3 Non-italicized quotations are from individual written memories (phase 1). Italicized quotations are from the collective discussion (phase 2)

4 The meaning of clothes in holidays at ages 40 and 65+ contrasts with the 'sexy' meaning at age 20!

> JEAN [age 40]: [Holiday at age 40] At the bottom [of the hill] the pandanus palms were interspersed with large rocks. Here they undressed. Barbara was wearing black knickers and looked very fit and tanned. Jean was wearing most unflattering pink knickers which seemed to exaggerate her white flab but really she could not blame the knickers. . . . They took photographs of each other. Jean felt a bit self-conscious of her out-of-condition shape, but Barb said 'It was art and not to worry'!

> LOU [age 65+]: [Holiday at age 65+] [Describing the dress she took when she travelled interstate for a wedding] And it's in jersey, silk jersey.

> SUSAN: Oh lovely, so it travels well.

> JANE: Very attractive, yeah.

> LOU: And you can roll it up into a little ball (SUSAN: Aah!) and it just doesn't crush or anything.

> . . .

> AMELIA: So that it would travel perfectly.

References

Begum, N. (1992) Disabled women and the feminist agenda. *Feminist Review* 40, 70–84.

Bickenbach, J., Chatterji, S., Badley, E. and Ustin, T. (1999) Models of disablement, universalism and the international classification of impairments, disabilities and handicaps. *Social Science and Medicine* 48, 1173–1187.

Boëthius, U. (1995) Youth, the media and moral panics. In: Fornäs, J. and Bolin, G. (eds) *Youth Culture in Late Modernity*. Sage, London, pp. 39–57.

Bordo, S. (1989) The body and the reproduction of femininity: a feminist appropriation of Foucault. In: Jaggar, A. and Bordo, S. (eds) *Gender/Body/Knowledge: Feminist Reconstructions of Being and Knowing*. Rutgers University Press, New Brunswick, New Jersey, pp. 13–33.

Bordo, S. (1992) Anorexia nervosa: psychopathology as the crystallization of culture. In: Curtin, D. and Heldke, L. (eds) *Cooking, Eating, Thinking: Transformative Philosophies of Food*. Indiana University Press, Bloomington, Indiana, pp. 28–55.

Bordo, S. (1993) Feminism, Foucault and the politics of the body. In: Ramazanoğlu, C. (ed.) *Up against Foucault: Explorations of Some Tensions between Foucault and Feminism*. Routledge, London, pp. 179–202.

Burman, J. (2002) Gender/tourism/fun? *Annals of Tourism Research* 29(4), 1205–1207.

Dann, G. and Jacobsen, J. (2002) Leading the tourist by the nose. In: Dann, G. (ed.) *The Tourist as a Metaphor of the Social World*. CAB International, Wallingford, UK, pp. 209–235.

Davidson, P. (1996) Women's leisure: the woman's perspective of holidays. MA thesis, Royal Melbourne Institute of Technology, Melbourne, Victoria, Australia.

Elsrud, T. (1998) Time creation in travelling: the taking and making of time among women backpackers. *Time and Society* 7(2), 309–334.

Ferri, B. and Gregg, N. (1998) Women with disabilities: missing voices. *Women's Studies International Forum* 21(4), 429–439.

Fields, K. (2002) Demand for the gastronomy tourism product: motivational factors. In: Hjalager, A. and Richards, G. (eds) *Tourism and Gastronomy*. Routledge, London, pp. 36–50.

Foucault, M. (1979) *Discipline and Punish: The Birth of the Prison* (trans. A. Sheridan). Peregrine Books, Harmondsworth, Middlesex, UK.

Foucault, M. (1980) The eye of power. In: Gordon, C. (ed.) *Power/Knowledge: Selected Interviews and Other Writings 1972–1977 Michel Foucault* (trans. C. Gordon, L. Marshall, J. Mepham and K. Soper). Pantheon Books, New York, pp. 146–165.

Ganetz, H. (1995) The shop, the home and femininity as a masquerade. In: Fornäs, J. and Bolin, G. (eds) *Youth Culture in Late Modernity*. Sage, London, pp. 72–99.

Gibson, H. and Yiannakis, A. (1999) Patterns of tourist role preference across the life course. In: Foley, M., Frew, M. and McPherson, G. (eds) *Leisure, Tourism and Environment: Participation, Perceptions and Preferences*. Leisure Studies Association, Eastbourne, UK, pp. 85–95.

Grosz, E. (1993) Bodies and knowledges: feminism and the crisis of reason. In: Alcoff, L. and Potter, E. (eds) *Feminist Epistemologies*. Routledge, New York, pp. 187–215.

Grosz, E. (1994) *Volatile Bodies: Toward a Corporeal Feminism*. Allen & Unwin, St Leonards, Australia.

Hall, C.M. and Sharples, L. (2003) The consumption of experiences or the experience of consumption? An introduction to the tourism of taste. In: Hall, C.M., Sharples, L., Mitchell, R., Macionis, N. and Cambourne, B. (eds) *Food Tourism Around the World: Development, Management and Markets*. Butterworth-Heinemann, Burlington, Massachusetts, pp. 1–24.

Hareven, T. (1982) The life course and aging in historical perspective. In: Hareven, T. and Adams, K. (eds) *Ageing and Life Course Transitions: An Interdisciplinary Perspective*. Tavistock, London, pp. 1–26.

Hargreaves, J. (1986) *Sport, Power and Culture: A Social and Historical Analysis of Popular Sports in Britain*. Polity Press, Cambridge.

Harper, S. (1997) Constructing later life/constructing the body: some thoughts from feminist theory. In: Jamieson, A., Harper, S. and Victor, C. (eds) *Critical Approaches to Ageing and Later Life*. Open University Press, Buckingham, UK, pp. 160–172.

Haug, F. *et al.* (1987) *Female Sexualization: A Collective Work of Memory* (trans. E. Carter). Verso, London.

Henderson, K. and Bialeschki, M. (1993) Negotiating constraints to women's physical recreation. *Society and Leisure* 16(2), 389–409.

Henderson, K., Bialeschki, M., Shaw, S. and Freysinger, V. (1996) *Both Gains and Gaps: Feminist Perspectives on Women's Leisure*. Venture Publishing, State College, Pennsylvania.

Holland, J., Ramazanoğlu, C., Sharpe, S. and Thomson, R. (1994) Power and desire: the embodiment of female sexuality. *Feminist Review* 46, 21–38.

Hopwood, C. (1995) My discourse/my-self: therapy as possibility (for women who eat compulsively). *Feminist Review* 49, 66–82.

James, K. (1995) The perceived ownership of recreational space: implications for participation of adolescent women. In: Simpson, C. and Gidlow, B. (eds) *Proceedings ANZALS Conference 1995*. ANZALS and Department of Parks, Recreation & Tourism, Lincoln University, Canterbury, New Zealand, pp. 110–115.

Johnston, L. (2000) (Other) bodies and tourism studies. *Annals of Tourism Research* 28(1), 180–201.

Jokinen, E. and Veijola, S. (1997) The disoriented tourist: the figuration of the tourist in contemporary cultural critique. In: Rojek, C. and Urry, J. (eds) *Touring Cultures: Transformations of Travel and Theory*. Routledge, London, pp. 23–51.

Kelly, J. (1987) *Freedom to Be: A New Sociology of Leisure*. Macmillan, New York.

Little, D. and McIntyre, N. (1995) Constraints and opportunities: women's involvement in adventure recreation. In: Simpson, C. and Gidlow, B. (eds) *Proceedings ANZALS Conference 1995*. ANZALS and Department of Parks, Recreation & Tourism, Lincoln University, Canterbury, New Zealand, pp. 123–127.

McCabe, S. (2002) The tourist experience and everyday life. In: Dann, G. (ed.) *The Tourist as a Metaphor of The Social World*. CAB International, Wallingford, UK, pp. 61–75.

McRobbie, A. and Garber, J. (2000) Girls and subcultures. In: McRobbie, A. (ed.) *Feminism and Youth Culture*, 2nd edn. Macmillan, Basingstoke, UK, pp. 12–25.

Mills, S. (1991) *Discourses of Difference: An Analysis of Women's Travel Writing and Colonialism*. Routledge, London.

Mitchell, R. (1988) Sociological implications of the flow experience. In: Csikszentmihalyi, M. and Csikszentmihalyi, I. (eds) *Optimal Experience: Psychological Studies of Flow in Consciousness*. Cambridge University Press, Cambridge, pp. 36–59.

Richards, G. (2002) Gastronomy: an essential ingredient in tourism production and consumption? In: Hjalager, A. and Richards, G. (eds) *Tourism and Gastronomy*. Routledge, London, pp. 3–20.

Roberts, K. (1996) Young people, schools, sport and government policies. *Sport, Education and Society* 1(1), 47–57.

Rojek, C. (1993) *Ways of Escape: Modern Transformations in Leisure and Travel*. Rowman & Littlefield, Lanham, Maryland.

Shilling, C. (2003) *The Body and Social Theory*. Sage, London.

Squire, S. (1995) In the steps of 'genteel ladies': women tourists in the Canadian Rockies, 1885–1939. *The Canadian Geographer* 39(1), 2–15.

Tinkler, P. (1995) *Constructing Girlhood: Popular Magazines for Girls Growing Up in England, 1920–1950*. Taylor & Francis, London.

Towner, J. (1995) Understanding gender differences in the usage of Victoria's surf beaches. In: Simpson, C. and Gidlow, B. (eds) *Proceedings ANZALS Conference 1995*. ANZALS and Department of Parks, Recreation & Tourism, Lincoln University, Canterbury, New Zealand, pp. 76–82.

Turner, B. (1996) *The Body and Society: Explorations in Social Theory*, 2nd edn. Sage, London.

Urry, J. (1990) *The Tourist Gaze: Leisure and Travel in Contemporary Societies*. Sage, London.

Urry, J. (2002) *The Tourist Gaze*, 2nd edn. Sage, London.

Veijola, S. and Jokinen, E. (1994) The body in tourism. *Theory, Culture and Society* 11, 125–151.

Wearing, B. (1998) *Leisure and Feminist Theory*. Sage, London.

Wearing, B. and Wearing, S. (1992) Identity and the commodification of leisure. *Leisure Studies* 11(1), 3–18.

Wolff, J. (1990) *Feminine Sentences: Essays on Women and Culture*. University of California Press, Berkeley, California.

Wood, M. (2003) Teens the target in anti-tan campaign. *Sun-Herald*, 16 November, 55.

6 Life's a Beach and then We Diet: Discourses of Tourism and the 'Beach Body' in UK Women's Lifestyle Magazines

FIONA JORDAN

Introduction

As a pursuit in which many of us engage and as one of the largest global industries, the power of tourism to influence numerous facets of our daily lives is indisputable. We are likely to spend at least some of our leisure time planning for our next holiday, possibly saving up for a special trip, browsing through brochures and Internet sites, watching travel-related television programmes or reading travel magazines. These activities are often regarded as a pleasant adjunct to the holiday itself and as Ateljevic (2000) points out, the omnipresence of such tourism imagery in popular cultural forms has resulted in 'the multiplication of tourist consumption spaces and places' (p. 378). There is, however, another form of holiday preparation which is often less visible and potentially less enjoyable, that of physically preparing our bodies for the ritual of public display. It is that aspect of embodied tourism that is the central concern of this chapter.

Previous research has indicated that the predominant imagery of tourism, as represented in the cultural forms referred to above, portrays the holiday as a site of freedom and fantasy where 'norms' are suspended, and where we are free to 'let our hair down' and behave in ways that we might not dare to at home (Uzzell, 1984; Crick, 1989; Urry, 1990; Clift, 1994). Such 'pleasure propaganda' (Rughani, 1993, p. 12) offers the opportunity to escape to a world that contrasts with the humdrum existence of our everyday lives. However, in enticing us with promises of excitement, and sometimes the possibility of romance, it should be noted that such imagery is also creating its own norms and social rules. As Dann (1996, p. 79) comments: '[T]he images define what is beautiful, what should be experienced and with whom one should interact.' For all those beautiful people seen frolicking on beaches, there are many others whose physical forms are excluded from the dominant representations of tourism.

In this chapter the potential connections are explored between representations of tourism in the popular cultural form of UK women's 'lifestyle' magazines and body imagery. First, I will contextualize the study with reference to previous research into tourism marketing literature and, in particular, its reliance on a narrow range of stereotypical images. In theorizing the discussion of the links between tourism and body image I draw on the work of Foucault on the power–knowledge–sexuality triplex and the power of the collective social gaze. I then move on to discuss the findings of a study, carried out jointly with Cara Aitchison, of the discourses of tourism as articulated in UK women's magazines. This research, carried out primarily during 2001 but updated on a smaller scale annually, focused on the ways in which women's bodies were portrayed in the context of the holiday. I centre the discussion on topics relating to the creation of what is often referred to in the magazines as a 'beach body' or a 'bikini body'. I identify three key themes of female bodily representation: the homogenized beach body; the sexualized 'beach babe/beach beauty' body; and the disciplined (bikini boot camp) body. I conclude with more questions than answers, but highlight some issues for further exploration.

Getting Away from It All? (Re)presenting the Peoples and Places of Tourism

It is, of course, unsurprising that in advertising holidays, tourism marketeers rely on images of happy, healthy smiling people having fun and escaping the pressures of everyday life. Pictures of miserable people sheltering from the elements in windswept landscapes are unlikely to sell holidays – or indeed any other services. However, it is also important to recognize that in the promotion and consumption of such images, power relations are continually being played out. As Aitchison (2001, p. 4) points out, there is a need to go beyond accepting that images are simply the product of economic imperative and to acknowledge their major role in 'the cultural construction of places and people as gendered sites and sights'. The nature of tourism and the micro-social interactions that take place in the holiday context are thus shaped by our readings of tourism iconography whether we are aware of this or not. Through this process, our attitudes to the people and places of tourism are influenced by what Hughes (1992, p. 31) describes as a 'geography of the imagination' in which 'the fusion of tourist representations and marketing philosophy blurs the boundaries between reality and fiction through the commodification of place imagery'.

In constructing this geography of the imagination, tourism marketeers often rely on stereotyped images of people and places with which the reader can readily identify (Ryan, 1991). The use of such stereotypes to mediate the relationships between people in 'host' nations and tourists has been discussed by a number of writers (Mathieson and Wall, 1982; Albers and James, 1988; Smith, 1989; Pearce, 1994). I contend, however, that it is not simply the physical landscape of tourism or its 'host' communities that are commodified, but that each person's engagement with tourism imagery shapes their own embodied identity as a tourist. The (re)presentation of tourists in marketing (and other) literature thus informs our performances and practices as tourists. This is not to suggest that human beings are passive recipients of cultural messages, but simply that these do play a key role in shaping our identities.

Previous studies of tourism brochures have revealed them to be reliant on a narrow range of images, often symbolizing hegemonic masculinity, femininity and heterosexuality (Enloe, 1989; Clarke, 1993). Urry (1990, p. 142) identifies three predominant images in material produced by tour operators: 'the family holiday' (nuclear family), the 'romantic holiday' (heterosexual couple) and the 'fun holiday' (same-sex group looking for [sexual] partners). Research has shown that there is (certainly in many UK brochures) an absence of tourists from ethnic minority groups, of tourists with disabilities or disfigurements, of obese people or of older people (Uzzell, 1984; Jordan, 1998, 2004). In particular, the portrayal of women in tourism marketing literature is characterized by passivity and their use as a sexually alluring decoration (see, e.g. Kinnaird and Hall, 1994; Swain, 1995; Marshment, 1997; Pritchard, 2001). The predominant imagery is of the sexualized female body and feminized landscapes (Pritchard and Morgan, 2000a). As Pritchard and Morgan (2000b) point out, tourism imagery therefore tends to privilege the male, heterosexual gaze.

Tourism providers frequently construct women socially and culturally as the embodied objects of the sexualized gaze. What has been subjected to less attention is the portrayal of tourism in the wider media and popular cultural forms (Carter and Clift, 2000; Shaw *et al.*, 2000), which may also be highly influential in determining our sense of self as tourist. This chapter draws on imagery from the popular cultural form of women's lifestyle magazines, slimming and health magazines, and teenage and story magazines to explore the (re)presentation of tourism as a form of embodied practice. The key focus here is on the portrayal of what is commonly referred to in these magazines as the 'beach body' or 'bikini body', and the centrality of this body form in (re)creating and (re)inforcing (hetero)sexualized norms of bodily display in the holiday context.

Representing the Beach as a Site of Seduction

In tourism marketing literature and in tourism-related artefacts such as postcards, there is a tendency to portray the beach as a particular place of bodily display and of sexual possibility (Rojek, 1993). Such characterization is often linked to its role in facilitating romantic encounters and as a site of 'holiday romance'. Stereotypes of the 'Latin lover', the exotic siren and the saucy, voluptuous 'kiss me quick' hat-wearer by the sea abound; the combination of holidays as times of freedom and relaxation, and the daring act of being semi-clothed or unclothed in a public place, create the beach as 'a place of adventure and sexual possibility' (Rojek, 1993, p. 189). In this space there is the potential, and indeed possibly the expectation, that with the shedding of clothes comes public licence to display the sexual body for the sexualized gaze of others: be they local people or other tourists. Such acts of liberation serve to perpetuate the notion of what Shields (1991) has termed the 'carnivalesque' nature of the beach as unregulated space. Through these processes, the beach becomes one of the touristic 'sites of seduction' referred to by Ryan and Hall (2001) and thus a uniquely sexualized space.

However, when exploring the beach as a place of sexualized embodiment and display, it is important to acknowledge whose bodies are the primary objects of such display and representation. As Rojek and Urry (1997) contend, the tanned female body is not only the central focus of much of this imagery, but has also assumed an almost trophy-like, ornamental status. There is clearly a gendered dynamic at work in the (re)production of sexualized tourism imagery and the consequent (re)creation of the seductive and embodied practices of beach display. As Enloe (1989), Richter (1994) and Marshment (1997) highlight, the reliance of tourism literature on linking sex and tourism, with the tanned female body as the primary focus, reflects the gendered power relations at play within the organizations producing the materials. As Pritchard and Morgan point out:

> Thus, vacations are marketed as hedonistic experiences, where sex is often a part of the trip, whether within the framework of a romantic (heterosexual) getaway for two or the chance of a romantic encounter with a fellow tourist or local.
> (Pritchard and Morgan, 2000a, p. 125)

The wider media in the UK are also increasingly reinforcing the sexualized themes promoted in tourism marketing literature. What is of primary interest here is that where touristic spaces are constructed as sexualized all of those who consume such spaces are doing so in a sexualized environment. Each tourist, therefore, who dares to bare their body on the beach is potentially offering their physical being for scrutiny (or even critique) by all those who share the space. The power of this type of social gaze and its link with physicality and body image is explored in the next section.

Who Are You Looking at? Surveillance and the Gaze

Central to my specific analysis of the 'beach body' and its place in popular culture is the work of Foucault (1976, 1977, 1984a,b), examining the ways that power, discourses, sexuality and surveillance serve to direct how we (re)produce and (re)present our bodies. Foucault (in his later writings) conceptualizes power as being a fluid entity (re)produced through discourses and exercised through social surveillance in different situations. For Foucault, discourses that influence bodily (re)production are articulated through complex interplays between images, text and language. The ways that we as human beings (re)interpret these discourses influence our relationships with our bodies and how we manage and mould them.

Foucault links the power of discourses with the creation and promotion of certain sexualities. He argues that at the end of the 18th century the body began to be considered as a social object of power and as a project for the individual to manage. According to Foucault, the intervention of politics, economics and ideologies in the sex and sexuality of social and individual bodies resulted in a 'technology of sex' comprising 'different tactics' applied in various ways with 'the objectives of disciplining the body and that of regulating populations' (1976, p. 146). This was generally carried out in the name of promoting the health and continuance of the population. What it also resulted in, however, was an 'objectification of the body' (Sawicki, 1991) in which individuals were encouraged to take responsibility for manipulating their bodies to ensure that they conformed to social expectations of what was acceptable. The social pressure to measure up to socially sanctioned bodily ideals was (and is) exerted not by physical threat, but by the less explicit coercion of the surveillant gaze of one's peers. This, Foucault argued, resulted in the production of 'subjected and practised bodies, "docile" bodies' (1977, p. 138). Thus, one's body becomes a project in which self-surveillance in accordance with established social norms leads one to strive for a certain body image through engaging in practices such as diet and exercise.

When viewed in these terms, the body becomes the subject of a powerful disciplinary collective gaze, which encourages individuals to be socially responsible in curbing their excesses of appetite (both sexual and corporeal) in order to gain control of their bodies. Foucault (1984a, p. 101) points to the development of dietetics and the use of diets and regimens as encouraging modes of socially approved bodily self-management. In classical Greek societies it became accepted that those who 'had the proper, necessary, and sufficient concern' (1984a, p. 108) for their bodies would display this through practising regimens of diet and exercise. These ideas have obvious resonance with contemporary work in sociology and social and cultural geographies of the body image. These studies (examples include Featherstone *et al.*, 1991; Tuana and Tong, 1995; Duncan, 1996; Lupton, 1996; Corrigan, 1997; Fox, 1997; Valentine, 1999) have highlighted the links between the physical and social constructions of the body and the role of popular culture and the media in creating bodily social norms. Additionally, there are potentially useful parallels between Foucault's ideas on excessive behaviour as being condoned in certain spaces and times, and notions of hedonistic spaces in tourism where the suspended norms of everyday life condone touristic excesses.

Foucault's work on the power–knowledge–sexuality triplex therefore provides a potentially useful conceptualization of power as (re)produced through the discourses of sexuality objectifying the sexual body. Applying these ideas in the context of tourism it can therefore be argued that tourism literature creates sexualized discourses that serve to portray the female body as the accepted object of the unquestioned, sexualized gaze. This promotes bodily 'norms' for the display of the physical form within the spaces and places of the holiday and particularly on the beach, arguably the most overtly sexualized of these.

Study Methodology

The interest that Cara and I developed in exploring the representations of tourism (or more specifically the female embodiment of the tourist) in women's lifestyle magazines was piqued by a general impression of seasonal body panic that appeared to be engendered in many popular cultural forms in the UK each spring. Whilst neither of us is a regular consumer of women's lifestyle or diet magazines, a cursory glance at magazine fixtures in newsagents or supermarkets is sufficient to raise one's awareness of this issue as summer approaches. Having become aware of headlines highlighting the need to diet into a bikini, television advertising for diet products and services that featured beach scenes, as well as daytime television programmes that encouraged women to diet to fit into swimsuits, we became interested in analysing the interrelationship between the portrayal of the beach in such cultural forms and the focus on body image and bodily preparation for summer.

With the help of a small grant secured from the institution where we worked, we purchased a sample of 50 magazines in the spring of 2001. Our approach to the research was informed by previous studies examining the influence of magazines on various aspects of women's lives, such as their leisure (see, e.g. Bolla, 1990), their body image (see, e.g. Tiggemann and Pickering, 1996), health information and advice (Bonner and McKay, 2000) and their occupations (see, e.g. Massoni, 2004), as well as by studies exploring the portrayal of women in tourism literature (see, e.g. Marshment, 1997; Pritchard, 2001). We chose to examine the portrayal of tourism in women's lifestyle magazines because of their central cultural role as 'ubiquitous "everyday" agents in the process of gender socialization and construction' (Massoni, 2004, p. 49).

When selecting the sample we drew on classifications used by the Advertising Standards Agency to categorize the women's lifestyle magazine market: 'women's interest (general)'; 'teenage and story'; and 'slimming and health'. Of the 50 magazines purchased, the majority fell into the first of these categories. The magazines were purchased as a purposive sample in that the majority had a reference to summer and/or the beach on the front cover, but our observations suggest that this was reflective of the messages articulated in the majority of the magazines. Within the purposive sample we endeavoured to ensure that there was a good cross section of titles representing both the high-spend, high-fashion market and the more general weekly gossip or chat magazines.

In analysing the magazines we initially undertook content analysis, defined by Bryman (1988) as 'the quantitative analysis of the communication content of media' (p. 12), to determine categories of image for the purposes of directing our discourse analysis. Such categories included advertisements, slimming features, competitions, travel features, hair and beauty features and fashion features. Our primary method was not, however, content analysis, but critical discourse analysis in which we sought to identify 'the intricacies of communicative practice' and what they 'reveal about power relations' (Macdonald, 2003, p. 3). Discourse analysis functions by identifying themes and patterns in data but in a much less scientific and rigid manner than pure content analysis. Our aim was to deconstruct the tourism-related images and text in the magazines in relation to their portrayal of tourism generally and the (female) tourist in particular.

The findings presented here are based on our reading of these images and are thus inevitably coloured by our subjectivities. We quickly identified that the overwhelming focus of tourism-related imagery in the magazines, and across the spectrum of articles and advertisements, was the embodied female tourist. In particular, emphasis was almost exclusively placed on acquisition, maintenance and presentation of what was ubiquitously referred to as the 'beach body' or 'bikini body'. In order to discuss significant aspects of this beach or bikini body, we identified three key areas of bodily representation: 'the homogenized beach body'; the sexualized 'beach babe/ beach beauty' body; and 'the disciplined (bikini boot camp) body'.

The homogenized 'beach body'

The most striking facet of the discourses of the tourism-related imagery permeating the magazines was the sameness of the imagery portraying what was frequently described as the 'beach body'. Culturally created and ascribed with homogenized characteristics in order to invent and promote an idealized femininity, the 'beach body' was the primary focus of attention across all features and advertisements. It was held up by the magazines as something to which all women should aspire. There were defining characteristics that were common to the vast majority of images. The 'beach body' was female, almost exclusively white, UK clothing size 8–10, slim or thin, toned and sometimes muscular, often tanned and frequently used as a canvas for the display of beach fashion and summer cosmetics.

Previous research has shown that women's magazines have been generally more concerned with the domestic (or private) sphere of women's lives than with their appearance in public spaces (Bonner and McKay, 2000), but by contrast the 'beach body' was most often posed outdoors against a backdrop of white sand and blue sea. This was not, however, a casual outdoors or active embodiment of femininity. Rather, this body was planned for and rigorously prepared for display. Generally the poses in which women modelling the beach body were reflective of the alluring, passive supine, sexualized and available 'woman in swimsuit' image identified by Marshment (1997) and Pritchard (2001) as being prevalent in tourism brochures. In this respect, there appeared to be complicity (possibly unconsciously) between holiday promotional literature and the magazines that claimed to 'assist' women in attaining this ideal.

The aspirational aspect of the 'beach body' pervaded the text of the magazines across all categories. The requirement to possess this physical form prior to legitimate bodily display on holiday was reinforced by the text that accompanied the pictures. Women were overtly encouraged to engage in a regime of bodily preparation well in advance of the summer. In many articles there was a count-down to the summer with a staged process of body self-management set out to achieve the ultimate goal. The need for such advance planning was generally sig-nalled by the shedding of clothes, catalysed by the onset of warmer weather and the advent of holidays. An article in *Shape Health and Fitness*, June 2001, contained this illustrative advice:

> Have you noticed how there seems to be a national body panic at this time of year? The onset of warm weather sparks a sudden enthusiasm to get in shape for our holidays and prepare to bare flesh. After piling on jerseys and comfort-eating our way through the colder months, it's no surprise bikinis are such a scary prospect for many of us. But you don't have to go to the gym, lift enormous weights, or live on celery to sculpt your body into a tantalising vision of bikini-clad loveliness.
>
> (Waterman, 2001, p. 63)

Similarly, the introduction to a *Top Sante* free slimming magazine, May 2001, states:

> Like most people, as the temperature rises I get really hot and bothered about stripping off the layers and revealing flesh that hasn't seen the light of day for months. Then when skimpy summer clothes start filling the shops, the panic really sets in – a flabby waistline and untoned legs are not something I wish to share with everyone else! . . . So go for it! Start straight after Easter and you could have a brand new beach body by 1 June.
>
> (Kellow, 2001, p. 1)

The links between the public licence of semi-nudity in the beach context and the creation of the female body as an object of social surveillance (Rojek and Urry, 1997) were overtly articulated in these magazine discourses. The message was clear. In order to be comfortable as the object of the gaze when on holiday, women need to ensure that their bodies conform to appropriate norms of physicality. To assist with this, the magazines contained a wide variety of articles on physical preparation ranging from diet through to the application of fake tan. The pre-holiday grooming requirements stipulated were stringent and involved waxing, plucking, smoothing, dieting, exercising, conditioning, exfoliating, oiling and fake-tanning to name but a few. Bolla (1990), in her study of the media portrayal of women's leisure, highlighted the significance of such imagery in shaping women's views of what is or is not acceptable:

> Women who read magazines receive both explicit and implicit messages through advertisements depicting leisure about what their own leisure should be like. For example, advertisements illustrating women participating in various leisure activities explicitly tell women about the acceptability and desirability of those activities.
>
> (Bolla, 1990, pp. 242–243)

In the context of the beach, the discourses of the women's magazines enunciate explicit messages about acceptable embodied identities, which may contribute to what is described by Bordo (1993) as the 'tyranny of slimming' (p. 481).

In the sample of magazines studied here, the 'beach body' was marked out as a slim, female form attainable by those women prepared to undergo the required self-surveillance to attain the socially acceptable ideal. The body in this context was also designed as a vehicle for the display of what were often referred to in the magazines as 'beach fashions'. An article in *Vogue*, March 2001, centring on the 'fantasy island' of Mustique illustrated the concept of the body as canvas for display:

> Relaxed chique prevailed as bare-foot beach babes donned a colourful array of designer bikinis and sarongs. Chanel sunglasses, Burberry headscarves and La Perla swimsuits were the key items to have.
>
> (Falcon, 2001)

In this text the body is regarded as a vehicle for the promotion of feminized fashion ideals, the key objective being to draw the gaze of others in holiday spaces. As Featherstone *et al.* (1991), Craik (1994) and Sparkes (1997) point out, the beach body, when decorated and painted in this context, becomes a passive and objectified vehicle for display.

The sexualized 'beach babe/beach beauty' body

Valentine (1999) draws attention to the body as an object of desire and the links between cultural and historical portrayal of sexually desirable body shapes and women's body image. She contends that forms of popular culture play a central role in determining 'the idealised standard of female beauty' (p. 331). Drawing on what Lupton (1996) describes as the 'sex, health, beauty triplex', Valentine highlights the role of popular culture in promoting the slim and sexualized (female) body as the means to attaining a successful sexual relationship. This too was clearly articulated in the discourses of the magazines in this study. The association of holidays with sexual licence was a strong theme permeating the features both implicitly and explicitly. In *Red*, March 2001, for instance, a story on long-term relationships highlighted the perceived exotic and erotic nature of the holiday with the claim that 'sex is an appealing prospect in a hotel in Antibes; less so back home after an argument over the phone bill' (Gibson, 2001, p. 69).

A number of magazines contained special holiday features focusing on the sexual possibilities of travel. The magazine *19*, April 2001, for example, included a series of features highlighting the different possibilities offered by various types of holiday: 'Let's get piste: Three reasons to go skiing'; 'Ski yourself slim'; 'The best girlie holidays – bond with your mates, but hide the snaps from your boyfriend'; 'The most romantic holidays – share some magic moments with your bloke'; 'The best party holidays – shake your booty with your buddies baby'. Throughout, implicit messages reinforced the notion of the holiday as a site of sexual liberation. Such portrayals have clear parallels with the linking of sex and tourism in holiday promotion literature as discussed earlier.

Photographs of the beach often signified the sexualized nature of the 'beach body' through the semi-pornographic poses of the models, a number of which echoed those in UK men's magazines (Jordan and Fleming, 2005). In some images, bikini-clad women were photographed in sexually alluring poses on the beach at sunset or dusk, evoking the possibility of night-time sexual adventure on the 'pleasure periphery' of the beach. The accompanying text made repeated references to the ideal of becoming a 'beach babe' or 'bikini babe', the inference being that the ideal beach body was a sexually desirable one. In some features the various elements of the sexually desirable female form were articulated. An advertisement in *Marie Claire Health & Beauty*, February 2001, for instance, featured a photograph of a woman in beachwear with the strapline: 'Red hot lips, bare shimmering flesh. Feel the heat of Rio this season!'

There were also repeated references to the links between feeling strong (in control of one's body) and sexy. One illustrative article in *Shape Health and Fitness*, May 2001, stated: 'Give us just five weeks and we'll make you stronger, sexier and slimmer well before summer.' Similarly a feature in *Top Sante Health and Beauty* magazine, May 2001, read: 'You'll feel sexier – as your shape changes and your confidence increases so will your libido. Say no more!' The implication of such features was often that a disciplined approach to self-surveillance and the (re)production of one's body would result in the creation of a sexually desirable body and that in feeling sexy a woman would feel stronger. There are obvious parallels here with Foucault's conceptualizations of a power–knowledge–sexuality triplex through which social surveillance serves to (re)create and (re)enforce bodily ideals through self-surveillance (Foucault, 1984a,b).

The disciplined (bikini boot camp) body

In many of the magazines in this study the attainment of the beach or bikini body was planned out with almost militaristic precision. The measurability and arithmetic nature of self-surveillant body management was clearly visible. The ultimate goal of the beach body was outlined as a series of calculable improvements in calorie reduction, amount of weight lost, reduced size of various body parts and the time taken to achieve this. The beach body was thus presented as an objective project to be managed in a coordinated and regimented manner. The most direct link between the body project and military discipline was articulated in the form of bikini boot camps in two of the magazines. In *Shape Health and Fitness*, May 2001, for instance, women were motivated to follow celebrities in engaging in an active body management campaign:

> You hear it all the time: if an exercise plan isn't fun, you just won't do it. So, why would anyone willingly enlist in a boot-camp programme, when it brings to mind a gruelling workout, and a wild-eyed drill sergeant barking to drop and give him 20? Believe it or not, you can do a military-style programme that's as fun as it is effective. . . . The stars agree. All Saints are said to have done boot-camp training with trainer Nicki Waterman . . . and Mel C and even Robbie Williams have taken to the tough face of training in order to get fit.
>
> (2001, p. 72)

Such discourses are reflective of Bordo's ideas that the reading of the slender body highlights the measurable and mechanistic tendencies of the diet culture:

> Fat, not appetite or desire, is the declared enemy, and people begin to measure their dietary achievements by the numbers on the scale rather than the level of their mastery over impulse and excess.
>
> (Bordo, 1993, p. 467)

However, in the magazines, control over one's own excessive appetites was also celebrated in many forms. In the general interest magazines the (female) celebrity body was the focus of much attention. That particular summer, Geri Halliwell, a former Spice Girl (an all-female pop group), appeared on a wide variety of magazine front covers being fêted for her significant weight loss. Geri's devotion to yoga was said to be central to her control over her body and the text of articles praised her for her exemplary devotion to the body project. In the magazines, celebrity bodies such as Geri's were held up as both desirable and attainable role models for women who aspired to a beach or bikini body. The message here appeared to be that with hard work and control any woman could earn the right to have her body displayed for the gaze on holiday.

Spring 2001 also saw the launch of the magazine *Celebrity Bodies*, described as fusing 'the popularity of dieting mags with the voyeurism of Hello!' (available at: www.guardian.co.uk). This magazine presented the diets and body maintenance secrets of 'the stars'. Naturally its first front cover featured the newly shaped and sculpted Geri Halliwell under the strapline 'Geri: the TRUTH behind this body'. Wood (2001) highlighted the concern about this new type of magazine stating: '*Vogue* is clearly about dreaming of glamour, whereas *Celebrity Bodies* claims you can have it if only you follow the meal plans.' The concern voiced in this debate is not that women are passive and malleable dupes, but that body iconography as signified in such popular cultural forms can, in some instances, insidiously contribute to an undermining in body confidence on the part of women who find it problematic to attain the celebrity body ideal. There are obvious links here to Foucault's notions of the 'docile body' as a self-surveillant social project in response to societal norms.

This theme of bodily control being equated with strength, success and happiness was also articulated in many of the health and slimming magazines, which often published the emotive stories of those who had triumphed over their own excessive desires. It was interesting that in a number of instances the motivation for weight loss directly related to bodily display in the holiday context. One illustrative narrative came from the *Woman's Own Diet Special*, 2001, and tells the story of a woman who has lost 8 stones (note here also the measurability of success):

> Previously I used to dread the hot summer days because they'd make me feel so uncomfortable, and I just couldn't cope. And of course, I didn't like wearing shorts because I was so big. Instead I'd be melting inside my leggings and baggy T-shirt. And I've never been on a plane because I was always too scared of getting stuck in the seat – I even used to worry that it would happen when I went to the cinema. But next year F and I are hoping to take the children on holiday to Disney World in Florida. Who knows, I might even wear a swimsuit for the first time in 15 years.
>
> (2001, pp. 58–59)

The explicit link to the difficulties of being unclothed in public space and the trials of presenting one's allegedly imperfect body for social scrutiny are clearly visible here. Reference is made to the problematic issue of wearing a swimsuit when not in possession of the requisite 'beach body'. What is also of interest is the valorization of taking control and thus earning the right to display one's body. The implication in such articles is that a 'beach body', and therefore by definition a disciplined one, exemplifies appropriate social control and responsibility that can then be rewarded by public approval. This discourse was reinforced in many of the magazines, through the association of slimness with strength, health and well-being. When describing the potential benefits of a pre-summer diet and exercise plan *Top Sante Health and Beauty* magazine, May 2001, states:

> The benefits after six weeks. You'll be physically and mentally stronger as a result of the exercise you have been doing. Your body has become accustomed to its higher energy output and as a result will be working more efficiently. You'll be fitter, more toned and slimmer – particularly if you've stuck to the healthy eating regime. So wear your swimsuit with pride and enjoy your holiday!
>
> (2001, p. 23)

As Bordo (1993) contends, the 'beach body' therefore represents more than a simple feminized ideal of beauty. This body symbolizes 'correct attitude' according to socially and culturally ascribed norms. The photographic images of slim and toned women that accompany the article demonstrate a body that was clearly under control and from which excesses had been banished. The discourses that promoted it also reflect Foucault's (1984a) conceptualizations of modes of socially approved bodily self-management. To diet and exercise one's way to a beach body is to achieve the ultimate social approval: the sexualized (male) gaze exercised on the semi-clothed female form in public space.

Concluding Comments

The key cultural messages conveyed throughout the women's magazines are of uniformity, aspiration, discipline and sexual attractiveness. In this way moral social surveillance is practised and the female body becomes public property, openly subject to social and sexual scrutiny. The dominant discourses of these women's magazines define the appropriate physical female form for display in the holiday context. The implicit message is that without such a body women should not be happy to be unclothed in the public spaces of tourism. In order to prepare for the social gaze of those (men) who inhabit the strictly circumscribed embodied worlds of tourism, women are encouraged to engage in strict self-management regimes in the private spaces of the home. The homogeneity of such imagery reflects the findings of studies into magazines in the USA which concluded that

> . . . the ideology of women's magazines has remained remarkably stable during the past five decades. Through words and images, mainstream women's magazines have consistently supported traditional gender roles: the importance of youth, beauty, and (heterosexual) romance.
>
> (Massoni, 2004, p. 51)

The body is treated as a manageable and malleable entity over which it is suggested that all women really should have control. The celebrity beach body is repeatedly held up to be the ideal. Often this celebrity body is a slim, toned, tanned and well-groomed one. Here too, however, there are very strictly defined parameters of physical acceptability. These are delineated both by the inclusion of images of those female celebrities whose bodies fit the idealized femininity determined by the magazines, and by the public castigation of those whose body management is perceived to be out of control – by having gained weight or being too thin.

The celebrity beach or bikini body is held up as a benchmark for the embodied female tourist to guide the consumers of the magazines and show explicitly what the acceptable feminine form should be. A cultural agenda is thus established, promoting an idealized tourism physicality. King *et al.* (2000, p. 341) point out that in previous studies 'the media's portrayal of a slim "ideal" body for women has been linked to the increasing prevalence of dieting disorders and body image disturbance in general'. Their research suggests that women who have high body dissatisfaction are more strongly affected by media imagery. They support the idea that the media is unlikely to be the sole determinant of dieting disorders but suggest that the links between media presentations of the body and dieting disorders need to be more fully explored.

Women are offered the possibility of attaining the ultimate beach body through a process of self-surveillance and discipline. The production of the beach or bikini body is often treated as a project. There is the suggestion that everyone can have an appropriate beach body if they are prepared to devote the time, energy and financial resources required. To make this more attainable to those without personal trainers or the time to devote 3 hours per day to yoga the body is broken down into separate tasks.

Often women will be encouraged to adopt a military-style approach to the production of the beach body. The 'bikini boot camps' promoted by some of the magazines are symbolic of this. The message is that conformity to a body management regime is required and that achieving one's physical ambition may necessitate temporary deprivation in the pursuit of the greater goal. The physical parameters of the beach body are defined in measurable terms by weight, dress size, measurements of waist, bust, legs, etc. Thus, targets can be set and progress towards them charted in terms of loss of weight or inches or clothing size. Frequently, too, the time allowed for the body transformation to be completed is established, with 6 weeks often being designated as the ideal time span in which to prepare for beach display. Separate features are devoted to hairstyles for the beach, how to attain a flat stomach, how to treat cellulite, the best methods for removing body hair and so on.

The right to display one's female form in the public space of the holiday is something that is shown to be earned by hard work and determination. Women are encouraged to have pride in their achievements by buying smaller clothes or earning the right to display. Naturally, given the commercial as well as the cultural orientation of these magazines, the majority of these suggestions are linked to the purchase of relevant cosmetic products, evaluated in the features according to their ability to assist women in these self-management and self-presentation activities.

But what of those who do not conform to the beach body ideal? A report by the British Medical Association (2000) highlighted the significant role played by the media in portraying acceptable body shapes and thereby influencing young women's attitudes towards food and eating. The findings of this study suggest that in the popular cultural forms of the UK women's lifestyle magazines there is a clear association between the holiday and the appropriate embodied identity of the female tourist. Absent from the discourses of the magazines were all bodies that did not conform to this feminized beauty ideal. I suggest that in an adaptation of Foucault's power–knowledge–sexuality triplex, there may be a 'power–tourism–sexuality' triplex in operation here. The concern is to what extent this may be impacting on women's holiday choices and experiences. Whilst this issue was not within the parameters of this particular project, I conclude that more research into the relationship between tourism, body image and women as tourists would be a valuable next step.

Acknowledgement

This chapter is based on a research project jointly undertaken with Professor Cara Aitchison, Professor of Human Geography, University of the West of England, Bristol.

References

Aitchison, C. (2001) Theorizing other discourses of tourism, gender and culture: can the subaltern speak (in tourism)? *Tourist Studies* 1(2), 133–147.

Albers, P.C. and James, W.R. (1988) Travel photography: a methodological approach. *Annals of Tourism Research* 15, 134–158.

Ateljevic, I. (2000). Circuits of tourism: stepping beyond the 'production/consumption' dichotomy. *Tourism Geographies* 2(4), 369–388.

Bolla, P.A. (1990) Media images of women and leisure: an analysis of magazine advertisements 1964–87. *Leisure Studies* 9, 241–252.

Bonner, F. and McKay, S. (2000) Challenges, determination and triumphs: inspirational discourse in women's magazine health stories. *Continuum: Journal of Media and Cultural Studies* 14, 133–144.

Bordo, S. (1993) *Unbearable Weight: Feminism, Western Culture and the Body.* University of California Press, Berkley, California.

British Medical Association Board of Science and Education (2000) Eating disorders, body image and the media. Available at: www.bma.org.uk

Bryman, A. (1988) *Quantity and Quality in Contemporary Social Research*, Vol. 18. Routledge, London.

Carter, S. and Clift, S. (2000) Tourism, international travel and sex: themes and research. In: Clift, S. and Carter, S. (eds) *Tourism and Sex: Culture, Commerce and Coercion.* Pinter, London, pp. 3–19.

Clarke, A. (1993) Everybody loves somebody: significant signs in leisure and tourism. In: Brackenbridge, C. (ed.) *Body Matters.* LSA Publication No. 47, Leisure Studies Association, Eastbourne, UK, pp. 55–64.

Clift, S. (1994) Romance and sex on holidays abroad: a study of magazine representations. Working Paper No. 4, Christ Church College, Canterbury.

Corrigan, P. (1997) *The Sociology of Consumption.* Sage, London.

Craik, J. (1994) *The Face of Fashion.* Routledge, London.

Crick, M. (1989) Representations of international tourism in the social sciences: sun, sex, sights, savings and servility. *Annual Review of Anthropology* 18, 307–344.

Dann, G. (1996) The people of tourist brochures. In: Selwyn, T. (ed.) *The Tourist Image: Myths and Myth Making in Tourism.* Wiley, Chichester, UK, pp. 61–82.

Duncan, N. (1996) Renegotiating gender and sexuality in public and private spaces. In: Duncan, N. (ed.) *Bodyspace: Destabilizing Geographies of Gender and Sexuality.* Routledge, London, pp. 127–145.

Enloe, C. (1989) *Bananas, Beaches and Bases: Making Feminist Sense of International Politics.* Pandora, London.

Featherstone, M., Hepworth, M. and Turner, B. (eds) (1991) *The Body, Social Process and Cultural Theory.* Sage, London.

Foucault, M. (1976) *The History of Sexuality: An Introduction*, Vol. 1. Pantheon, New York.

Foucault, M. (1977) *Discipline and Punish: The Birth of the Prison.* A. Lang, London.

Foucault, M. (1984a) *The Use of Pleasure: The History of Sexuality*, Vol. 2. Penguin, London.

Foucault, M. (1984b) *The Care of the Self: The History of Sexuality*, Vol. 3. Penguin, London.

Fox, K. (ed.) (1997) *The Physical Self: From Motivation to Well-being.* Human Kinetics, Champaign, Illinois.

Hughes, G. (1992) Tourism and the geographical imagination. *Leisure Studies* 11, 31–42.

Jordan, F. (1998) Shirley Valentine: where are you? Tourism provision for mid-life women wishing to travel alone. In: Aitchison, C. and Jordan, F. (eds) *Gender, Space and Identity: Leisure, Culture and Commerce.* Leisure Studies Association, Eastbourne, UK, pp. 69–88.

Jordan, F. (2004) Gendered discourses of tourism: the experiences of mid-life women travelling solo. Unpublished PhD thesis, University of Gloucestershire, UK.

Jordan, F. and Fleming, S. (2005) Making sense of *Nuts* and *Zoo*: the construction and projection of homogenised masculinity. In: Caudwell, J. and Bramham, P. (eds) *Sport and Active Leisure: Youth Cultures.* Leisure Studies Association Publications, Eastbourne, UK, pp. 133–152.

King, N., Touyz, S.W. and Charles, M. (2000) The effect of body dissatisfaction on women's perceptions of female celebrities. *International Journal of Eating Disorders* 27(3), 341–347.

Kinnaird, V. and Hall, D. (1994) (eds) *Tourism: A Gender Analysis.* Wiley, Chichester, UK.

Lupton, D. (1996) *Food, the Body and the Self.* Sage, London.

Macdonald, M. (2003) *Exploring Media Discourse.* Arnold, Abingdon, UK.

Marshment, M. (1997) Gender takes a holiday: representations in holiday brochures. In: Sinclair, M.T. (ed.) *Gender, Work and Tourism.* Routledge, London, pp. 16–34.

Massoni, K. (2004) Modelling work: occupational messages in *Seventeen* magazine. *Gender and Society* 18, 47–65.

Mathieson, A. and Wall, G. (1982) *Tourism: Economic, Physical and Social Impacts.* Longman, London.

Pearce, P. (1994) Tourist resident impacts: examples, explanations and emerging solutions. In: Theobold, W. (ed.) *Global Tourism: The Next Decade*. Butterworth-Heinemann, Oxford, pp. 103–123.

Pritchard, A. (2001) Tourism and representation: a scale for measuring gendered portrayals. *Leisure Studies* 20, 79–94.

Pritchard, A. and Morgan, N.J. (2000a) Constructing tourism landscapes: gender, sexuality and space. *Tourism Geographies* 2(2), 115–139.

Pritchard, A. and Morgan, N.J. (2000b) Privileging the male gaze: gendered tourism landscapes. *Annals of Tourism Research* 27(4), 884–905.

Richter, L.K. (1994) Exploring the political role of gender in tourism research. In: Theobold, W. (ed.) *Global Tourism: The Next Decade*. Butterworth-Heinemann, Oxford, pp. 146–158.

Rojek, C. (1993) *Ways of Escape: Modern Transformations in Leisure and Tourism*. Macmillan, Basingstoke, UK.

Rojek, C. and Urry, J. (eds) (1997) *Touring Cultures: Transformations of Travel and Theory*. Routledge, London.

Rughani, P. (1993) Tourism: the final brochure. *New Internationalist*, July, pp. 7–12.

Ryan, C. (1991) *Recreational Tourism: A Social Science Perspective*. Routledge, London.

Ryan, C. and Hall, M. (2001) *Sex Tourism: Marginal People and Liminalities*. Routledge, London.

Sawicki, J. (1991) *Disciplining Foucault: Feminism, Power and the Body*. Routledge, London.

Shaw, G., Agarwal, S. and Bull, P. (2000) Tourism consumption and tourist behaviour: a British perspective. *Tourism Geographies* 2(3), 264–289.

Shields, R. (1991) *Places on the Margin: Alternative Geographies of Modernity*. Routledge, London.

Smith, V.L. (1989) *Hosts and Guests: The Anthropology of Tourism*, 2nd edn. University of Pennsylvania Press, Philadelphia, Pennsylvania.

Sparkes, A.C. (1997) Reflections on the socially constructed physical self. In: Fox, K.R. (ed.) *The Physical Self: From Motivation to Well-being*, Human Kinetics, Leeds, pp. 3–110.

Swain, M.B. (1995) Gender in tourism. *Annals of Tourism Research* 22, 247–266.

Tiggemann, M. and Pickering, A.S. (1996) Role of television in adolescent women's body dissatisfaction and drive for thinness. *International Journal of Eating Disorders* 20, 199–203.

Tuana, N. and Tong, R. (eds) (1995) *Feminism and Philosophy: Essential Readings in Theory, Reinterpretation, and Application*. Westview Press, Boulder, Colorado.

Urry, J. (1990) *The Tourist Gaze: Leisure and Travel in Contemporary Societies*. Sage, London.

Uzzell, D. (1984) An alternative structuralist approach to the psychology of tourism marketing. *Annals of Tourism Research* 11, 79–99.

Valentine, G. (1999) A corporeal geography of consumption. *Environment and Planning D: Society and Space* 17, 329–351.

Wood, G. (2001) We're just dieting for it. *The Observer*, Sunday, 1 April. Available at: www.guardian.co.uk/Archive

7 The Sensual Embodiment of Italian Women

Martine Abramovici

Introduction

This chapter is positioned within the critical turn in tourism studies (Ateljevic *et al.*, 2005), producing what is now claimed to be the 'new' tourism research (Tribe, 2005). This critical turn is reflective of the field researchers' overdue shift in thought to a more reflexive and embodied approach (Phillimore and Goodson, 2004). Issues that were either marginalized or simply not researched have now moved to the mainstream within this multidisciplinary field, which has come to be perceived as a significant realm for understanding broader issues of culture and society (Urry, 2002; Hall *et al.*, 2003). In contrast to more positivist approaches, and through paradigms of post-structuralism and post-feminism, the critical turn embraces many research topics, such as gender, race, politics, culture, sex and the body.

Within these broader debates, two closely connected and key issues in this chapter are the recognition of the sensuality and embodiment of the tourist experience (Franklin and Crang, 2001) and my embodiment as a woman, thus challenging the perceived neutrality of disembodied constructions of tourism knowledge (Veijola and Jokinen, 1994; Aitchison, 2001; Johnston, 2001). Along with new research topics, new frameworks and metaphors have emerged in tourism enquiry and I am engaging here with two frameworks known as embodiment and performance. The embodiment framework addresses issues concerning me and the embodiment of gender as a social construction, whilst the performance framework, originating from Goffman and recently used in tourism (Edensor, 2001), addresses issues of sensuality and embodiment.

The focus of this chapter is the gendered perception of women in Italy. While issues of body and performance have been addressed in tourism in recent years, this has been limited to the Anglo-Saxon context. Thus, this study fills the gap through its empirical context, providing an insight into the strikingly different 'Southern mentality' of Mediterranean societies. In order to research the symbolism of Italian women and tanning, the structural context of Italy is studied, and in particular the way society shapes the material sensuality of the female body. I therefore explore the beach as a stage for the 'tanning' performance, to study cultural issues of body and identity in Italy. My positionality and embodiment as a woman in Italy (physically being there to carry out my research) is also discussed as the key aspect of my methodology (which consists of ethnographic analysis, document analysis and in-depth interviews). Throughout the chapter I strive to portray the extent to which women's bodies reflect the pressures of their society, the power of the media, the prevalent male gaze and what is expected of them in this context. Italy is a visual country where the postmodern reality of consumerism and the importance of aesthetics and appearances is ever present and, as such, represents an 'ideal' empirical context in which the material body is a focal point of society.

I open the chapter with a theoretical presentation of the way social identity is linked to the body in contemporary Western consumer society, revealing the body as individualized, reflexive and metamorphosed. I then move to a discussion of the corporeal turn in tourism studies, introducing the concept of performance, and explaining my research framework through my own embodiment before presenting an overview of Italian structural forces. Studying tanning in the context of Italian society, it is necessary to understand the way this society shapes the sensual embodiment of Italian women and their desire to appear beautiful, youthful and tanned. Following this, I discuss sensuality as perceived at the beach 'stage', where the body is 'paraded' or shown, the actors performing within the socially constructed reality of gender in Italy.

The Body and Social Identity

Although interest in the body is not new, the position of the body within contemporary culture reflects an unprecedented individualization of the body, as growing numbers of people are increasingly becoming concerned with the health, shape and appearance of their own bodies as expressions of individual and social identity (Shilling, 2003). Consumption has become one of the basic ways in which Western society is structured and organized today so that choices over purchase of goods and services become interpreted as statements of identity (Lash and Urry, 1987; Featherstone, 1991). Detrez (2002) affirms this to be especially true of women. She explains that if all social relation is the place of 'exchange' where each 'delivers' the self for evaluation by others, the physical part, as opposed to the language part, is more important for women than men.

Since bodily conduct is recognized as an important means for socially classifying and categorizing individuals in Western societies, individuals increasingly invest into bettering and maintaining their bodies (Howson, 2004). The body is emerging as a powerful consumption 'object', modelled and transformed in society through muscle-building, tanning, aesthetic treatments, plastic surgery and general body grooming (Borel, 1992). In this light, the body can be described as a perfect raw material which can be worked on to comply with the image of the ideal body as defined by society.

The French sociologist Bourdieu (1984) underlined the relationship between body and identity among the 'new' middle class in his study 'Distinction' 20 years ago. He argued that the right clothing, the right style and the right taste were used as signals to others, to the outside world, representing one's social status and cultural capital. Duret and Roussel (2003) argue, however, that in recent years the number of people concerned with their bodies has spread well beyond the narrow confines of the middle class to become a generalized reality of Western society. The link between visual appearance – in particular notions of youth and beauty – and a sense of self-worth has been emphasized as a general characteristic of Western consumer society (Duret and Roussel, 2003).

Furthermore, in the case of women, sociologists contend that today it is not only their individual identity which is linked to their physical appearance, but also the identity of their couple or family. In his book entitled *La domination masculine*, Bourdieu compares the male-dominated Kabil society in Algeria with Western European society, where he argues that 'in much the same way that in the less emancipated societies women were treated as exchange goods for men to accumulate social capital through marriages, today they also bring an important contribution to the production and reproduction of the family's symbolic capital' (1998, p. 135). Thus women are positioned within the realm of the public eye, their role being to be attractive to look at. In this light, the social world functions as a market of symbolic goods dominated by the masculine vision, where 'to be', for women, is 'to be seen' and this by the masculine eye or the eye which has been trained by the masculine vision (Bourdieu, 1998). This determines not only the relations of men to women, but the relations of women to themselves (Wolf, 1991; Kaufmann, 2001).

As well as being young, beautiful and sexy, the ideal woman is also shown to possess either a creative or a senior managerial job, and a passionate fulfilled life (Shilling, 2003). Physical beauty, as portrayed in the media then appears to be tightly linked to social success. The body is actually more than linked to success: one could say that it has become the external sign of success in Western consumer society. As sociologist Detrez (2002) argues, being in control of one's own body signifies, or is perceived to signify, being in control of one's life.

The availability of numerous means for controlling, or having someone control, one's body, as described and publicized in the media, stimulates among individuals a heightened degree of reflexivity about what the body is (Crossley, 2001). The increasingly reflexive ways in which people are relating to their bodies can be seen as one of the defining features of our culture (Shilling, 2003). With the decline of formal religious frameworks in the West which constructed and sustained existential and ontological certainties residing outside the individual, and the massive rise of the body in consumer culture as a bearer of symbolic value, there is a tendency for people to place evermore importance on the body as constitutive of the self (Featherstone, 1995). Lipovetsky (1983) and Kernan and Domzal (2000) explain this as an advanced narcissistic state resulting from the 'emptiness' characteristic of postmodernism, an empty space, they argue, left by the loss of religion, ethnicity, occupation, address and politics as reference points in our society. This space is today taken up by the worship of the body. However, gazing in the mirror at a fitness centre or at home reflects looking at the image perceived by others. It is therefore not a pure narcissistic view, according to sociologists Duret and Roussel

(2003), but rather represents 'looking for the self' through the images of others. In finding the self, one forges an identity, the aim being to throw off an image of success, as described earlier. Individuals appear to have developed a new relation to their private sphere whereby hedonism and research of pleasure have become legitimate.

In order to promote the possibility of developing one's identity in a unique fashion amid a mass practice where all individuals are on the same quest, a body of literature explains that society offers an innumerable combination of options from an ever-growing field of possibilities, from lifting weights to wrapping bodies in seaweed, jogging on athletic tracks, attending weekly weigh-ins, receiving beauty treatment or appealing to cosmetic surgery (Borel, 1992; Detrez, 2002; Gimlin, 2002; Black, 2004). Borel (1992) argues that it is through the multiplication of these options that the mass practice conserves its illusionary aspect of being a means for subjective auto-construction of one's self and identity. The growing global movement in metamorphosing the body reflects the extent to which people feel the need to comply to the latest beauty criteria in order to feel happy and at ease in society. The desire of belonging to a particular social group, or more precisely to the 'right' social group, the 'successful' one, appears to guide today's individuals, and more particularly women, in their quest towards body metamorphosis.

Embodiment and the Corporeal Turn in Tourism Studies

In the tourism field, the corporeal turn has been expressed with the recognition of 'the body' as enabling a sensory tourist experience at a much deeper level than the passivity of the 'tourist gaze' (Urry, 2002). Since the body is now considered as active and perceived as a significant component of the tourist experience, three theoretical dimensions have emerged concerning the tourist body: a sensuous awareness in the context of experiencing places and 'the doing' of tourism; a cultural awareness of embodiment whereby social meanings of power and ideology are inscribed; and an awareness of the limits of subjectivities, identity and practices of encountering the world of discursive experience (Ateljevic *et al.*, 2005). The spaces in which people move and the encounters that take place reflect an 'embodied' dimension where people have real emotions, perceptions and feelings linked to their physically 'being there' (Crang, 1997; Edensor, 1998, 2001; Crouch, 2001; Crouch *et al.*, 2001; Perkins and Thorns, 2001; Doorne and Ateljevic, 2005).

The corporeal turn became a reality in tourism research through the use of many different frameworks and here I will introduce the two frameworks of performance and embodiment which I used in my research. Embodiment of the researched has been discussed in tourism through the metaphorical mobilizations of performance (Crang, 1997; Edensor, 1998; Crouch, 2001; Crouch *et al.*, 2001; Perkins and Thorns, 2001; Doorne and Ateljevic, 2005). Thus, Ateljevic and Doorne (2004, p. 1) affirm that 'the emergence of theoretical perspectives that conceptualize tourism as performance moves beyond the passive gaze of the visual towards the embodiment of acts of production and consumption', whilst Edensor (2001, p. 59) argues that by harnessing the metaphor of performance, tourist studies can escape the 'theoretical straightjacket which has bounded them for so long', and continues that tourism should, as such, be understood by its immersion in the everyday life as opposed to a separate field of activity. Edensor broadens this argument to the 'extreme' and shows how the whole of social life can be considered as performative. In much the same way, Franklin and Crang (2001, pp. 17–18) claim that 'the cultural competencies and required skills that make up tourist cultures themselves suggest a "Goffmanesque" where all of the world is indeed a stage'.

Goffman's (1959) work – the origin of performance theory – sheds light on the fact that both individuals and groups are the actors in both individual and group performances when they meet. He explains that these performances take place on specific stages, that the performer and performing groups are each other's audiences and that they play different roles frontstage and backstage. In the tourism field, Edensor (1998) has expanded this tourist performance metaphor, particularly in his examination of the different performances taking place upon the Taj Mahal stage. Along the same lines, Doorne and Ateljevic (2005) study backpackers in Fiji, where this time the resort is the stage and the actors perform 'backpacking'. In the research presented in this chapter, the performance stage I study is the beach and the actors perform 'tanning'. My interest in studying this stage is to highlight the extent to which sensuality is as an essential part of the performance. Although there are studies of tourism and sensuality (Harvey, 2005), there is no extant research which links the performance metaphor with sensuality.

Embodiment, however, does not concern only the researched, but also the researcher herself, as expressed for example by Veijola and Jokinen (1994), Johnston (2001) and Aitchison (2001) in the tourism and leisure fields. These researchers challenge the perceived neutrality of disembodied constructions of tourism knowledge, described by Aitchison (2001, p. 139) as 'othering machines' and by Johnston (2001, p. 181) as reflecting 'Western hierarchical dualisms', producing hegemonic, colonial and masculinist knowledge. Veijola and Jokinen (1994, p. 149) explain that it is the Cartesian separation of mind and body whereby 'only the pure mind, free from bodily and social subjectivity' is at work in analysing and interpreting data, which lies at the heart of the disembodied, discursive, rationalized existing literacy in academia. They challenge traditional 'scientific objectivity' and 'the absence of the body from the corpus of the sociological studies on tourism', explaining the richness and deeper value which comes from writing tourism into the duration of time and sexed body, actually 'being there', and writing from a complete, holistic approach including one's body, one's sex, one's gender, one's values and one's knowledge.

Following the feminist lead of scholars such as Rose, Hooks and Hallaway, tourism researchers Ateljevic *et al.* (2005) acknowledge the impossibility of divorcing themselves from the context that informs their (value-laden) analysis and privileges them with their social position of authoring and the associated power to be able to speak. Grosz (1994) refers to the body as the inscriptive surface reflecting the researcher's positionality in terms of race, gender, age, class and sexuality, as well as choreography of knowledge. Swain (2004, p. 102) also makes specific reference to the feminist influence in using the framework of embodiment, engaging with feminist and postcolonial perspectives of the body, although she assures her readers by affirming that 'don't worry, this chapter is not all about me'. Her argument engages intersectionality and the body, and describes the embodied approach as one that will inform all qualitative tourism in useful ways, not just feminist research. While Swain extends the issue of reflexivity beyond feminist analysis, her use of embodiment theory can potentially categorize reflexivity as the domain of primarily feminist researchers according to Ateljevic *et al.* (2005).

My own embodiment

As the embodied author of this chapter on women in Italy, I will introduce the choreography of my personality and cultural background. I am a woman, and given the gendered perception of women in Italy, this gives me an insider's perspective. Brought up with both English and French languages and cultures at home – being born to an English father and a French mother – I spent my childhood in spaces as physically and culturally diverse as Kiribati, Afghanistan, Tunisia and Morocco. Since my parents loved adventure and discovery, we travelled the countries in which we lived at length and I developed an ease at adapting to diverse cultural and social settings. Anchored in Rome, Italy, by the age of 13, I moved into teenage years and young-adulthood engaging with Italian cultural ways. This part of my life is particularly significant for my research as during these years I became fluent in the Italian language. Understanding the ins and outs of Italian society (as well as the language) was a critical feature of my research which took place solely in Italian; not only was in-depth interviewing made feasible but Italian academic material, popular writings, newspapers and all other forms of media were also within reach.

At the age of 19, I moved to France, where I resided for 12 years, followed by New Zealand for a period of 8 years. In both countries, it is through university and research that my intellect was stimulated, and that my postmodern, feminist and critical outlook on research developed. So it is within the French and New Zealand cultural and social expectations, and through personal, academic and research experiences, that I evolved as a grown woman, weaving the values and choices of the choreography of my life towards a cosmopolitan identity.

In terms of my positionality in carrying out my research in Italy, I feel enriched by my teenage and young-adult years in Italy which resulted in cultural intimacy and enabled me to better understand the Italian ways and better communicate with Italians (Denzin, 1997). My 'foreign' experiences on the other hand (foreign to Italy that is) resulted in cosmopolitan lenses (see Swain, 2005) and enabled a better understanding of the Italian context, for I can 'see' the context. As an outsider, I am very aware of the way men look at women in Italy, of the language of the body, of the way men and women relate to each other and, more particularly of interest to this study, of the pressure of society on women. Being a citizen of the world and possessing 'different' values gives me a deeper observation of the context and of the gendered construction of women, through my own embodiment and perceptions as a 'local cosmopolitan'.

During the last 2 years I have been based in Rome and have travelled considerably within Italy, 'soaking in' the local culture, through innumerable informal chats, interviewing women in depth and observing the society in which I live. My embodiment, ethnographic observations and general communication have enabled me to merge into Italian society and position myself within the Italian cultural scene as an Italian woman with multicultural post-feminist theoretical lenses.

Sociocultural Conditions in Italian Society: Politics, Work, Media and Social Expectations

Women and politics

In order to contextualize the social and cultural conditions of lives of Italian women, I will begin with some statistics on women and politics. With a few exceptions, the Italian parliament is a famously male domain, as the Italian anthropologist Di Cristofaro (1993) explains – only 10% of parliamentarians are women and for a 52% electorate this is the lowest percentage in the European Union (ISTAT, 2004). A recent survey by the Italian national statistics organization ISTAT analysed how much television time was dedicated to male and female governmental ministers: for every 4 hours of masculine chat, 7 minutes were spent interviewing women ministers (Hopkinson, 2002). According to Jones (2003, p. 118), a British journalist writing on Italy, 'it is not that there aren't many successful women in Italy, it's that they're never in the hungry public eye unless they come with heaving cleavages'. He explains that it is hard to think of any female role models in Italy other than those confined to the role of television confectionary.

Mernissi (2005), a writer from Morocco, visited Italy in 2005 and commented on Italian television and women in power quite neatly:

> Whilst you continue to represent the Arab woman as submissive and veiled, at home (Morocco) as I entered a café near the Rabat university for an appointment with a colleague, I discovered that the whole clientele, mainly male, was watching Al Arabioa, the new rival of Al Jazeera, because Mai Al Khalifa had appeared on the screen. She is not a singer, nor a belly-dancer, but an intellectual who writes books and is one of the first women to have obtained an official position at the Ministry of Culture in Bahrein. And like her, in other nations of the Gulf region, other women have taken on important political roles. . . . In your country, in Italy, have you ever had a Minister of Economy who is a woman?

The gendered aspect of Italian politics is underlined in the Shadow Report, an alternative report to the Italian government's official report describing the Italian situation 10 years on from the United Nations conference on women held in Peking in 1995, and presented in New York by Italian feminist organizations in October 2004 (Marsili, 2005). This report places Italy 73rd out of the 183 states surveyed around the world, in terms of female representation in political institutions, a position which clearly disadvantages Italian women vis-à-vis their European neighbours. The objectives defined in Peking have not been reached and although the official (ISTAT, 2004) view is that more and more women are asserting themselves in social and cultural fields, according to the Shadow Report, this is taking place in the context of poor material conditions for women as a result of government policies. In other words, the official Italian documents (as presented by the Italian government) focus solely on the structural elements of legislation in Italy today and make no reference to the sociocultural contexts which constrain women's lives.

Women, work and maternity

Together with the statistics on female political representation in Italy, employment figures also reveal the extent of gender inequity in the country and again the statistics place Italy below the European average. Only 48% of women are employed in Italy (ISTAT, 2003), a low figure which compares with the European average of just over 60% (and a UK figure of 64%). According to ISTAT, 20% of working women in Italy give up their jobs when the first child is born. According to Italian sociologist Piazza (2003), women who do not want to give up their jobs and become dependent wives confess to feeling a strong pressure in this direction from their families and husbands. Social historians Bravo *et al.* (2001) and anthropologist Di Cristofaro (1993) provide a very thorough overview of the Italian feminist movements and outline how Italian legislation has evolved in favour of women. They explain, however, that the law is not enforced and that women do not have equal rights in everyday life. Women are thus held aside from important and senior managerial positions, be it in private companies or public and political jobs.

Within marriages or partnerships, the onus remains on the women to sacrifice their careers, explains Piazza (2003), whose research reveals how society expects women to look after the home, husband and children. In their article on the quality of life of Italian women in the province of Rome, the Italian research group Ricerche Economiche e Sociali (EURES) (2005) argues that no differences have been noted between non-working women and working women in terms of the time they spend in domestic work. Their figures indicate an average of 15.5 weekly hours dedicated to children for non-working mothers as opposed to 14 for working mothers, and an average of 13.9 weekly hours to domestic chores for non-working women, as opposed to 12.9 for working women. When women find time short for accomplishing all household chores, EURES affirms that more often than not extra help is found in paid staff rather than in other family members, in particular their husbands.

Although Italian law incorporates some of the most generous terms anywhere for maternity leave – 5 months' fully paid leave, followed by an optional 7 months' paid leave at 30% of full salary (P.R. INPS Istituto Nazionale Previdenza Sociale, Rome, 2006, personal communication), as in so many areas of Italian life, the obstacle to the securing of citizens' rights has been the application and enforcement of the law. I would suggest that there is a widespread practice in small firms and workshops to hire women only on condition that they do not get pregnant.

Traditionally, it has been the grandmother, or any other female family member, who has stepped in to look after young children should the need arise if the mother has returned to work. In today's Italy, however, families have shrunk and working mothers now have fewer family members with whom to leave their children. Yet, the caretaking system (as offered by Italian government) is not keeping up with these changes in family structure, and therefore working is not a viable and easy option for women since there are too few nurseries and childcare facilities in

Italy today (De Gregorio, 2005). On 8 March 2004, women's day, the *Il Messagero* newspaper printed a front-page promise from Ciampi, the head of state, to give more support to women in terms of maternity leave and child support policies, thus underlining the seriousness of the issue of working mothers (Lombardi, 2004). The article explained the way state help and financing have so far been directed mainly at pensioners and is in need of a redirection towards childcare services. Ciampi argues that there are too few mothers, and too few children in Italy, and that this represents a dying society. The childcare services are openly criticized in this article and are used to justify the difficulty for mothers to combine work and children, and their choice not to have children. In 2004 the Arcidonna Association (a feminist organization) published official figures which indicated a shortfall of 6000 nurseries in Rome, 8000 in Bologna and similar numbers for most Italian cities (De Gregorio, 2005); they argued that the social services are not progressing and, as a result of this, Italian society is witnessing the return of women to their homes (De Gregorio, 2004). The difficulty for women to combine work and mother-hood may explain why Italian birth rates are the lowest in Europe. According to Hopkinson (2002), Italian women produce on average 1.3 children, a figure lower than industrialized countries such as Austria, Denmark, Germany, Hong Kong, Greece, Luxembourg and Spain (all with 1.5), whilst France and Britain averaged 1.8, the USA 1.9 and African women between 6 and 8.

Women and social expectations

The barriers to the greater engagement of women in politics and work are not related solely to the structural conditions of childcare and legislation but, more profoundly, to the social expectations of women. Becoming a mother is a major decision in Italy where everything is done for children (Piazza, 1999, 2003). As the protagonists of Italian life, their smallest wishes are satisfied and although there is no academic literature (either international or Italian) on this subject, both my ethnographic and document analyses confirm the depth of this statement. It is quite natural for parents to offer their grown-up son or daughter a floor in their house or to buy an apartment, or house, for their children. In the same way, it is not uncommon for a mother to cook dinner for her son and his wife when they so wish, or to make home-made dishes to be frozen and used throughout the week for their grandchildren's meals. Similarly, finding a job in society for the grown-up children is often a family affair, the children benefiting from links and ties made by their parents or extended family. It appears clearly then that although children may get jobs, marry and move out into homes of their own, they do not ever become a separate unit.

Today, although the size of the family may have changed, the traditional family ties have not. Journalist Richards (1994) argues that the most stable rela-tionship of all in Italy remains between mother and son. *Mammismo* has none of the connotations of 'mother's boy' in English-speaking countries: it merely means that sons are spoiled by their mothers, which they almost always are according to my ethnographic research. The model of the Madonna and Child persists as the stereotypic Italian relationship as 'time and again, when sons sin, in their mothers'

eyes they can do no wrong' (Richards, 1994, p. 141). Even nowadays few men
leave home until they marry and one often meets single men in their thirties still
living with their mothers. Hopkinson (2002) confirms this and indicates that 70%
of the 8 million Italian 18- to 34-year-olds live with their parents and that among
those over the age of 30 two-thirds are male. The strength of the mother–son relationship greatly prejudices the successful fulfilment of subsequent relationships, as
men exchange one 'mother' for another when they marry.

It is true that as an unspoken part of the social contract and marriage arrangement, Italian women today are increasingly getting their own way (Piazza, 2003).
In postmodern Italy, it is the woman who takes the decision to delay having children and, having done so, to limit the family. Not that the 'new Italian woman' has
exchanged femininity for feminism, but she has exchanged the desire to be *mamma*
for a more holistic desire of being a woman, according to my many interviews
and informal conversations. However, the 'new man' has scarcely arrived in Italy;
Italian men still largely regard it beneath their dignity to wash up, change nappies,
do the shopping or help with the housework or cooking. The invisibility of the
'new man' is illustrated by the call of the head of state, Ciampi, in the *Il Messagero*,
inviting men to start 'giving a helping hand' at home (Cocace, 2004). This fact is
also clearly illustrated in everyday life by the way 'technical' operations are carried
out. If a woman is accompanied by any man at all, relative, friend or colleague,
and a technician has been called upon for help, the custom is for the technician
to address the man, not the woman. I have personally experienced this custom on
numerous occasions of which I will recount a few.

I received an electrician in my home for three consecutive visits, during my
husband's absence, and a final visit was necessary to finish the work in progress.
This time, my husband happened to be present, and the electrician automatically
addressed him. Having followed the operation to date, I was better informed to
answer and naturally intervened, but appeared to be unheard by the electrician.
A pattern took form from then on whereby the electrician questioned my husband,
I answered – to my husband, not the electrician – and my husband then proceeded
to repeat the information for the benefit of the electrician.

On another occasion, when I had a bad case of tendonitis and driving proved
too painful, my husband drove me to the recommended specialist. We were in the
waiting room, chatting away, when the doctor beckoned for me to come. Seeing
my husband, he asked him whether he would like to come in too, and we agreed to
this. There followed a scenario whereby the doctor spoke to my husband, explaining what the problem was as he prodded me. He told my husband this problem
was typical of women in their forties and continued to talk about women's health to
my husband. My husband and I were rather amused. Both our repeated attempts
to redirect the conversation between the doctor and myself led nowhere. In much
the same way as with the electrician, we ended up having a triangular conversation. At one point he even said to my husband 'When I put pressure on this point,
it will hurt' and when I showed signs that it did hurt, he looked at my husband in
a satisfied way, 'See?'

Such scenarios have been related to me by many a surprised foreign woman
living in Italy. When Italian women are asked about this attitude and whether it
is also part of their own lives, they explain that it is. Some do not mind, or rather

do not question this attitude, because it 'has always been this way'; other women feel angry and frustrated as they try to convince the technician that although they are women they do understand the topic being discussed and that they are in fact the ones dealing with the particular issue at hand. One woman told her plumber that he could explain the problem to her rather than phone her husband, who was not in, because she had a degree in physics. For an answer she received a puzzled look.

My informal interviews, in-depth interviews and personal experiences all echo the concept of Mediterranean masculinity as described by Irena Ateljevic and Derek Hall (Chapter 9, this volume). Masculinity is seen to be about men 'performing' for other men, showing them that they are competent and that they know how to deal with the problem at hand. The pressure of society is for men to accomplish acts that prove their virility and this is done in part by proving their value as a man to other men. My research underlines the fact that if a man were to speak to a woman in preference to the man accompanying her, he would not only come across as not performing strong masculinity, but would also be implying that the other man is incompetent or, at any rate, a man undeserving of the respect of other men.

Beauty and objectification

The centrality of the male figure as the decision maker, the main protagonist and the possessor of 'the gaze' is further reproduced by the media. Anna Bravo, an Italian researcher from Torino, in a presentation to the Italian feminist organization Paese delle Donne, described the feminine body as a public space, more objectified than ever before (Giuffrida, 2005). She speaks of the male gaze as the neutral gaze in Italian society – so that women themselves look at their own gender through the male gaze. One of the most powerful cultural media to perpetuate the male gaze in Italy is television, through which the woman's role appears clearly submissive and objectified for men's eyes. The concept of *velina*, an active part of most Italian television programmes, speaks for itself. A *velina* is a young woman who appears on television as a mixture of a soubrette and chorus girl. Aspiring candidates must be aged between 18 and 26, be attractive and happy to dress in very revealing clothes. In his ethnographic account of Italy, journalist Jones (2003) describes how in 2002, 10,000 girls applied for the *Striscia la notizia*, the most popular Italian programme of political satire, where two beautiful girls cavort around whilst the others, mainly men, talk politics. As many as 80% of the candidates were university students.

This issue of Italian women and television coverage was discussed in the Shadow Report I mentioned above. The feminist organizations that participated in the writing of this document wrote of the demeaning effect of these highly sexualized and objectified women's images as portrayed on television. Zardo (2004), who specializes in Italian culture at French universities, describes women on television as semi-nude young 'mermaids' with interchangeable faces but identical bodies, all moving in the same sensual and sexualized way, with nothing to say. He admires Berlusconi for having understood that this 'mermaid' represented national desire and for introducing her into every programme, whatever the content. Italian journalist Severgnini, writing about the scantily dressed young women who accompany virtually any talk show on Italian television, suggests that stamps and coins should carry pictures of this new icon, 'Miss Semi-nude' (2005, p. 96).

The consequences of visual rather than literary culture are evident everywhere in Italy where it is often hard to find anything that is remotely ugly, be it the architecture, the art or the peoples' clothing and grooming (Jones, 2003). This appears to be very reflexive of the postmodern era, where the consumer trend of Western society is shown to be elevating the threshold in terms of the body and appearances. It is perhaps significant that Italy produces the world's most esteemed fashion retailers, be they for the high street or the catwalk (e.g. Versace, Armani, Valentino, Max Mara, Benetton, Diesel, Dolce & Gabbana). According to the French Fashion Institute (IFM), Italy produces 37% of the EU's fashion wear, represents 62% of European fashion exports to the USA and is positioned as the world's third largest fashion exporter, after China and Hong Kong (IFM, 2003).

However, there is virtually no Italian academic literature on fashion and its sociocultural impacts, or on the way bodies are objectified in lifestyle and feminine magazines. Pritchard and Morgan (2005, p. 55) argue that representations of women's bodies in fashion magazines are 'grounded in wider gendered power relationships, so that women are burdened with men's meaning and interpreted through masculinist discourse in these magazines'. They also argue that women are represented as passive and sexually available in the context of tourism marketing literature and confirm the absence of studies of the fashion industries. Thus, whilst a number of marketing studies on Italian aesthetics have been undertaken, these focus on the actual clothing rather than on how women are represented. Morace (2004), writing on Italian marketing, describes the Italian way as elegant and fashionable, exerting a strong influence on all other nations. Fashion in Italy, he explains, is a way of life, it is seen to represent the creativity and ingenuity of Italians: it is embedded in their roots and their philosophy of life, and is the result of Italian history, art and culture.

Italian passion for beauty goes well beyond art, architecture and fashion, into the depths of morality – so argues Severgnini (2005) in his book describing 'what goes on inside Italian minds'. He discusses the confusion between what is good or 'goodness' and that which reflects beauty: only in Italian is there such an expression as *bella figura*, literally translated as 'beautiful face/figure'. The meaning of the expression, however, is 'good impression', so that here creating a good impression with others is equated to looking beautiful to them. In these terms, the English expression 'never judge a book by its cover' does not translate in Italian because there you *do* judge a book by its cover, and politicians by their smiles, professionals by their offices, secretaries by their styles, lampshades by their designers, cars by their lines and people by their titles.

The overwhelming importance of beauty may be felt from the moment one lands on Italian territory, at the airport. On entering the cellphone boutique at the Malpensa airport of Milan, for example, it becomes very quickly apparent that the women selling the phones know very little about the difference between one cellphone and the next; however they all have another quality in common. They are beautiful, and this is why they are there. According to Severgnini (2005), when telephone companies select their sales employees, the criterion is beauty, rather than technical knowledge, because that is what the public wants. A beautiful body is worth more than a bright mind in the marketplace, argues Bravo (Giuffrida, 2005), in her feminist talk on women and work in Italy. In other words, customers are willing to sacrifice the information they could be getting to help them with their purchase, for the joy of seeing beauty and being served with a smile. This is the country where aesthetics has more power than ethics (P.R. Casa Internazionale delle Donne, Rome, 2005, personal communication).

Sensuality and Performance: Tanning

Sensuality is an important part of each and every moment of the day in Italy. I will try to portray the extent to which this characteristic is an integral part of being Italian, before focusing on the sensual performance of tanning at the beach. Being based in Rome, much of my fieldwork has been carried out in and around this city; however, since I have links in Bologna, Venice and Naples, I have done a good part of my fieldwork in those cities too, as well as in many of the smaller towns and villages in the regions of Tuscany, Umbria, the Abbruzzi and Emilia Romagna. I will describe a few key spaces and experiences which illustrate the importance of sensuality and the way it influences all experience of life in order to better contextualize the 'tanning game'.

First, I will start with the very characteristic consumer society activity of shopping, then discuss the dynamics of fitness centre changing rooms, before moving onto the Italian activity of parading in the streets. The buying experience in Italy is a physical experience where time is taken to look, touch, feel, smell, listen and discuss before buying a product. People like to look inside a lamp, around it, underneath it, and caress the base before they decide whether they like it or not. When purchasing a table, measurements are taken, but most of the time and energy goes into touching, getting a physical feel for the table, running one's hand along the entire length and back. A carpet will be felt in much the same way – although even this is not sufficient, for the wool needs to be smelt too. A suitcase will be touched whilst listening to the vendor's long explanation about its innumerable qualities. Food must be poked, smelled, talked about and thought about, before making its way into the trolley. When purchasing a clothing article, feeling and touching with one's hands is a prelude to bringing the material up to one's cheek to see how soft it really is. Using one's senses is the most important part of checking whether a garment is right and fits well. Clothes shopping is carried out under the gaze of the other women in the shop who proceed to give their advice and may comment on which garment looks better. This is a nation representing a real challenge for e-commerce, a nation where shopping and purchasing is carried out through one's senses, without which the fun, enjoyment and life are gone.

I leave the shopping scene now and move to fitness centres and more particularly to the women's changing room: one big room, shared by all, with open showers and close quarters. Women come into the changing room after swimming or following a class at the gym to better their bodies, and here, after showering, they get ready to re-enter the outside world. The shower is prepared with many products, different towels and special shower shoes. It is a slow process whereby the hair is massaged and treated at length and a lot of talking and exchanging information on product qualities goes on. On coming out, the body is dried and anti-cellulite cream is applied with much sensuality on each and every naked body to be seen, mainly on thighs, buttocks, breasts and tummies. This anti-cellulite massaging of the body lasts about a quarter of an hour and is carried out whatever the age or the size of the woman. The same pattern is then followed by all, which is to put on underwear and shoes and move to the hairdryers and mirrors. The scene here is then mainly high heels, with beautiful matching underwear and bras, highlighted by the solarium-tanned bodies, drying of hair, shaking of hair from side to side, some adding special creams, and all this done with much sensuality, be it in the actual drying or in checking out one's reflection in the mirror. This is followed by a make-up session and here too time is taken to check out the general effect of the make-up at different intervals during the application. Finally the dressing of the body takes place, and before each woman leaves, there is a stop at the mirror to check out the final look. Important to this whole experience is the looking on of the women who check out the other bodies, creams and so on. There is both a sharing of womanly ways and a competitive look, as other women are 'eyed up' through the male gaze. The performance in the changing room is carried out for the benefit of the other women; however, these women look at each other through the lens of the male gaze.

The last scene I would like to describe, as representative of Italian lifestyle and sensuality, is one that takes place in the streets, in fact on the main street of a village, town, city quarter or beachfront. It is the stroll where one shows oneself to the world and one observes others, called the *struscio*. The best translation would be 'parading' although this word does not carry with it the sensual connotation of the Italian *struscio*. Talking and gossip are an essential part of these strolls where one learns everything about everybody whilst the eye searches and scrutinizes every detail. The competition is high among the women who are walking to be seen, and the men look on whilst showing off their own woman, who is at their arm. Fashion is at its highest here, as is the tanning competition and the sensual walk. The walk is a slow one where every movement can be given charm, character and, above all, sensuality.

These three types of experience express the 'Southern' passion and outlook on life – reflecting the Italian sensuality and joy for life and their desire to live experiences to their fullest. These descriptions are important to better contextualize and understand the beach, for they form the backdrop and set the scene for the beach, the stage on which the tanning performance takes place. The whole game of tanning can now be seen in the context of Italian society, as described in the first part of this chapter.

The beach: tanning the body

Most religions associate the celestial with light and brightness, and grant the sun a place of honour as such. In our civilization where pagan belief is based on the everyday life, worshipping the sun is articulated round the corporeal movement, based on bodily pleasure and pleasurable sensations (Kaufmann, 2001). On arriving at the beach, the sand, as described by my interviewees, feels hot and soft under their feet and is beautiful because it reflects the heat of the sun. The first contact with the sun is made, the sun worshipper has emerged and the desire to lie down and take it in the heat is awakened. It is necessary to be lying immobile in order to feel the sensations produced by the sun. The pleasure is immediate as the body starts to absorb the heat. Several participants spoke of the feeling of being touched, the sun stroking their body. All described the wonderful feeling of the whole body relaxing and the brain functioning on slow mode. This feel-good effect is perceived by the women as a reward for all the stress and tensions of everyday life.

The mention of how 'good' they felt after a session in the sun was also developed by the participants, all of whom discussed how having a darker tan affected their image, boosted their morale and consequently their inner happiness. Once the height of the tan is reached, the tanning session is still considered important for the image because it keeps up the 'tanned' status they have worked hard to obtain. The sun gives pleasure, but it also generates hard work to regain the tan every year, and to keep it going throughout the summer. The element of competition is very real, both at the beach and afterwards in strapless dresses or other light clothing accompanying this season. For this reason, many women choose to prepare for the summer by going to the solarium before the start of the 'bikini and strapless dress' challenge. It is much easier to make 'an entrance' at the beach with a tanned body, explain my participants, the tan representing a form of clothing, without which one feels 'naked' and vulnerable to the gaze of the other beach-goers.

Tanning is a major feature of the beautiful body as seen in the Italian media. Publicity for tanning products can be seen across all newspapers, magazines, television advertisement spots and other public spaces. One particular advertisement speaks of the body as 'a temple': 'Your body is your temple, the body is a sign, an ideal of beauty, you must feel attractive to yourself before being able to feel attractive to others, the cult of tanning has one idol only: yourself, for this unique rite celebration, you need a grand talisman' and here follows the name of the product (La Repubblica Salute, 2005). This advertisement is particularly representative of tanning publicity in Italy. Another typical advertisement reads: 'The heat invades the body, the brain relaxes, the cream smells good, I drift into a second state and want to be disturbed no more.'

Having introduced the importance of tanning, I will now analyse the actual act of tanning, through the framework of performance. The stage then is the beach, and the actors prepare to walk onto the scene, they prepare for looks. They park their car backstage, where the pressure to perform is not felt, and prepare for the frontstage. At the top of the beach, preparing to become frontstage performers, they will observe the beach to take in who is there, how the bodies are arranged on the beach and where the best spot is. They will also take in the women's appearances on the beach, their bikinis, tans and body shapes, with a competitive eye for the incoming women, and an appreciative eye for the incoming men. They are looking at their audience. The looking is directed towards the newcomers from those already on the beach scene. The new characters walking onto the beach stage are sending visual signals to the audience through their costumes and props: the way they are dressed, the way they look, and the way they walk towards their chosen spot.

Bodies are mainly lying down, looking relaxed, and onlooking eyes are half closed, appearing to dreamily float over the beach scenery in an aimless and nearly sleepy fashion. However, these eyes are working hard, they are gathering important information. The beach has been described, in fact, as an advanced laboratory for experimenting both 'being looked at' and 'looking at' (Corbin, 1988). There is, to this effect, no public area more structured by appearances and looks than the beach (Kaufmann, 1998). Goffman (1959), in his analyses of looks and their importance, could not have been more accurate today, in describing the beach scene at the start of his book. The hero (taken from a novel) imagines the different ways in which 'the beach' is watching him, and tries to create carriage and attitudes within himself to be seen in the way he dreams of being seen, by those already at the beach.

Back to Italian beaches, it appears clearly that as soon as the spot is chosen, the creaming up begins. This is done in a very open, uninhibited and sensual way. The whole body is creamed up with slow, massaging gestures. Arms go up, bodies twist and bend, and legs open up as necessary. The tanning may now begin, tanning being considered an activity in its own right. As one mum said to her enquiring child: 'Leave me alone, can't you see I'm tanning?!' The lying down position engages all women to pull up the bottom part of the bikini in order to tan the buttocks when lying on their tummies. This ensures that when parading along the beach at a later time, if the bikini shifts a little with the walking movement, there will be no visible white, or untanned, skin. In much the same way, when lying on their backs, women will detach the straps of the top of the bikini so as not to have white marks when wearing a dress or light top at a later time in the day. It is also essential to lie at some point in a fetal position so as to ensure no white lines at the back of the legs where these meet the buttocks. Hair is tied back because a white neck is not a sought-after feature either as it can ruin a beautiful evening outfit worn with done up hair.

The standing up position triggers a different scenario for the actors. Since tanned buttocks are considered more attractive than white buttocks, the women who have a good tan can remain with the bikini bottom in the 'pulled-up-over-the-buttocks' position. The tanned buttocks also signify a regular beach-goer, a connoisseur, and hence mean more respect from the onlookers, or the audience. On the other hand, those with white buttocks pull their bikini back down into the 'normal' position at this point. Movement brings on yet more modifications of the script. When walking down to the waterline or along the beach, only the young, slim, toned and tanned buttocks may remain unveiled. They are then paraded for all to see. This is a sign of beauty and beach success for the parading character. When, on the other hand, the movement is directed towards the refreshment area, or beach bar, which is usually situated at the top of the beach, props are used. In this situation, the bikini is in 'normal' position for all characters, and a pareo or costume cover-up is worn, very short, transparent and tied just below the bikini line on the hips; whether one is tanned or not, the pareo should be matching the bikini. The characters check each others' bikinis and pareos out on this part of the stage. The importance of the choice of the bikini is revealed here. The women I interviewed owned anything between five and 15 bikinis for the summer and explained that they often changed bikinis several times during a day at the beach. Wearing a wet bikini is not perceived as comfortable, and to this effect, parents are often seen to make their children change swimsuits when coming out of the water.

To complete this overview of Italian beaches and women's tanning performance, I will add that, on the whole, water is not a big attraction at the beach, where it appears very clearly that 'working on the tan' is the main reason for being there, along with parading and observing. Tanning is clearly not considered a secondary effect or natural consequence of being at the beach but rather it is an activity in its own right and is respected as such. Finally, it is important to point out that, although the script is not always easy and represents hard work for the actors, my perception is that the actors are enjoying themselves, 'having fun' through their performance at the beach. I lived this through my own embodied experience and also got confirmation from my interviewees.

Conclusive Reflections

In this chapter, I have shown the value of embodiment in research, positioning myself as a woman in Italy, living and 'being there'. I have acknowledged my critical view (being both multicultural or 'different' from Italians) and my portrayal of the performance of Italian women through my critical feminist lens. As a researcher, I feel it is important to underline the fact that the Italy illustrated in this chapter represents a deep reflection of my own interests, issues and interpretations in life. The analysis is not simply based on an ethnographic study enriched by interviews, but comes from the depths of my own embodied position, which takes the research a step further into understanding the sensual embodiment of Italian women.

The chapter has also reviewed the importance of the body in Western society, the importance of beauty in Italian society, the patriarchal and masculinist ways of Italian society, and the sensuality and passion with which life is lived in this country; all of this created the necessary context for my analysis of the tanning performance of Italian women at the beach. The underlying structure of Italian society and values can be felt through women's performances on Italian beaches, their bodies reflecting the pressures of society, the power of the media, the prevalent male gaze and what is expected of them in this context. Using the metaphor of performance, I have tried to depict the sensuality of creaming up at the beach, of arranging one's bikini and of parading. Above all, I have tried to underline the importance of Italian society's embedded male gaze, a gaze which is even appropriated by other women when looking at female bodies.

References

Aitchison, C.C. (2001) Theorising other discourses of tourism, gender and culture: can the subaltern speak (in tourism)? *Tourist Studies* 1(2), 133–147.

Ateljevic, I. and Doorne, S. (2004) Theoretical encounters: a review of backpacker literature. In: Richards, G. and Wilson, J. (eds) *The Global Nomad: Backpacker Travel in Theory and Practice*. Channel View Publications, Clevedon, UK, pp. 50–76.

Ateljevic, I., Harris, C., Wilson, E. and Collins, F. (2005) Getting 'entangled': reflexivity and the 'critical turn' in tourism studies. *Tourism Recreation Research* 30(2), 9–21.

Black, P. (2004) *The Beauty Industry: Gender, Culture, Pleasure*. Routledge, London.

Borel, F. (1992) *Le vêtement incarné: les métamorphoses du corps*. Calmann-Levy, Paris.

Bourdieu, P. (1984) *Distinction: A Social Critique of the Judgement of Taste*. Routledge & Kegan Paul, London.

Bourdieu, P. (1998) *La Domination Masculine*. Editions du Seuil, Paris.

Bravo, A., Pelaja, M., Pescarolo, A. and Scaraffia, L. (2001) *Storia sociale delle donne nell' Italia contemporanea*. Editori Laterza, Bari, Rome.

Cocace, P. (2004) Ciampi: piu figli e sostegni alle donne. *Il Messagero* 126(67), 8 March.

Corbin, A. (1998) *Le Territoire du vide. L'Occident et le désir du rivage, 1950–1840*. Flammarion, Paris.

Crang, P. (1997) Performing the tourist product. In: Rojek, C. and Urry, J. (eds) *Touring Cultures: Transformations of Travel and Theory*. Routledge, London, pp. 37–54.

Crossley, N. (2001) *The Social Body: Habit, Identity and Desire*. Sage, London.

Crouch, D. (2001) Spatialities and the feeling of doing. *Social and Cultural Geography* 2(1), 61–75.

Crouch, D., Aronsson, L. and Wahlstrom, L. (2001) Tourist encounters. *Tourist Studies* 1(3), 253–270.

De Gregorio, C. (2005) I servizi sociali diminuiscono e le donne tornano a casa. *La Repubblica*, 4 January.

Denzin, N.K. (1997) *Interpretive Ethnography: Ethnographic Practices for the 21st Century*. Sage, Thousand Oaks, California.

Detrez, C. (2002) *La construction sociale du corps*. Editions du Seuil, Paris.

Di Cristofaro, G.L. (1993) *Identita e cultura: per un' antropologia della reciprocita*. Edizioni Studium, Rome.

Doorne, S. and Ateljevic, I. (2005) Tourism as a performance: enacting backpacker tourism in Fiji. In: Jaworski, A. and Pritchard, A. (eds) *Tourism, Discourse and Communication*. Routledge, London, pp. 173–198.

Duret, P. and Roussel, P. (2003) *Le corps et ses sociologies*. Nathan, Paris.

Edensor, T. (1998) *Tourists at the Taj: Performance and Meaning at a Symbolic Site*. Routledge, London.

Edensor, T. (2001) Performing tourism, staging tourism: (re)producing tourist space and practice. *Tourist Studies* 1(1), 59–81.

EURES (Ricerche Economiche e Sociali) (2005) *La provincia si racconta: la qualita della vita delle donne nella provincia di Roma*. Conference Rome, Palazzo Valentini, 10 March. Ufficio Stampa EURES, Rome.

Featherstone, M. (1991) *Consumer Culture and Postmodernism*. Sage, London.

Featherstone, M. (1995) *Undoing Culture: Globalization, Postmodernism and Identity*. Sage, London.

Franklin, A. and Crang, M. (2001) The trouble with tourism and travel theory? *Tourist Studies* 1(1), 5–22.

Gimlin, D.L. (2002) *Body Work: Beauty and Self-image in American Culture*. University of California Press, Los Angeles, California.

Giuffrida, A. (2005) Non negare il valore cognitivo delle esperienze del corpo. *Il Paese delle Donne on line*, 23 June.

Goffman, E. (1959) *The Presentation of Self in Everyday Life*. Doubleday Anchor, New York.

Grosz, E. (1994) *Volatile Bodies: Towards a Corporeal Feminism*. Indiana University Press, Bloomington, Indiana.

Hall, D., Swain, M.B. and Kinniard, V. (2003) Tourism and gender: an evolving agenda. *Tourism Recreation Research* 28(2), 7–11.

Harvey, N. (2005) Backpacking in Fiji: an investigation into the heterogeneity and performances of the postmodern nomad. MSc thesis, Auckland University of Technology, New Zealand.

Hopkinson, L.P. (2002) *Italy: Some Facts and Figures*. Arti Tipografiche Toscane, Cortona, Italy.

Howson, A. (2004) *The Body in Society: An Introduction*. Polity Press, Cambridge.

IFM (Institut Français de la Mode) (2003) Etude annuelle 2003. IFM, Paris.

ISTAT (Istituto Centrale di Statistica) (2003) Rapporto sull' Italia. Il Mulino, Rome.

ISTAT (Istituto Centrale di Statistica) (2004) Rapporto sull' Italia. Il Mulino, Rome.

Johnston, L. (2001) (Other) Bodies and tourism studies. *Annals of Tourism Research* 28, 180–201.

Jones, T. (2003) *The Dark Heart of Italy*. Faber & Faber, London.

Kaufmann, J.-C. (2001) *Corps de femmes, regards d'hommes: sociologie des seins nus*. Bussière, Paris.

Kernan, J.K. and Domzal, T.J. (2000) Playing on the post-modern edge: action leisure as self-identity. In: Woodside, A., Mazanec, J. and Opermann, M. (eds) *Consumer Psychology of Tourism, Hospitality and Leisure*. CAB International, Wallingford, UK.

La Repubblica Salute (2005) Il Culto dell'abbronzatura. *Il settimanale di chi vuole vivere bene* 11(458), 22 July.

Lash, S. and Urry, J. (1987) *The End of Organised Capitalism*. Polity Press, Cambridge.

Lipovetsky, G. (1983) *L'ere du vide*. Gallimard, Paris.

Lombardi, M. (2004) Piu servizi, il bonus per i figli non basta. *Il Messagero* 126(67), 8 March.

Marsili, M. (2005) Le Politiche di genere in Italia dopo Pechino. *Il Paese delle Donne on line*, 29 April.

Mernissi, F. (2005) In una delle mie ultime visite in Italia, non sono riuscita a vedere un solo canale TV non occidentale. *Republica delle donne*, 15 October, 25.

Morace, F. (2004) *Estetiche Italiane, Italian Ways*. Future Concept Lab, Milan, Italy.

Perkins, H.C. and Thorns D.C. (2001) Gazing or performing? Reflections on Urry's tourist gaze in the context of contemporary experience in the Antipodes. *International Sociology* 16, 185–204.

Phillimore, J. and Goodson, L. (2004) *Qualitative Research in Tourism*. Routledge, London.

Piazza, M. (1999) *Le ragazze di cinquant'anni: amore, lavori, famiglie e nuove liberta*. Oscar Mondadori, Milan.

Piazza, M. (2003) *Le Trentenni: fra maternita e lavoro all ricerca di una nuova identita*. Saggi Mondadori, Milan.

Pritchard, A. and Morgan, N. (2005) 'On location': re(viewing) bodies of fashion and places of desire. Conference Proceedings of the International Conference on Critical Tourism Studies, Dubrovnik, Croatia, 30 June–3 July.

Richards, C. (1994) *The New Italians*. Penguin, London.

Severgnini, B. (2005) *La Testa degli Italiani: Una Visita Guidata*. Rizzoli, Milan.

Shilling, C. (2003) *The Body and Social Theory*. Sage, London. [First published in 1993]

Swain, M. (2004) (Dis)embodied experience and power dynamics in tourism research. In: Phillimore, J. and Goodson, L. (eds) *Qualitative Research in Tourism*. Routledge, London, pp. 102–118.

Swain, M. (2005) Gender analysis in tourism: personal and global dialectics. Conference Proceedings of the International Conference on Critical Tourism Studies, Dubrovnik, Croatia, 30 June–3 July.

Tribe, J. (2005) New tourism research. *Tourism Recreation Research* 30(2), 5–8.

Urry, J. (2002) *The Tourist Gaze*. Sage, London. [First published in 1990]

Veijola, S. and Jokinen, E. (1994) The body in tourism. *Theory, Culture and Society* 11, 125–151.

Wolf, N. (1991) *The Beauty Myth: How Images of Beauty Are Used Against Women*. Vintage, London.

Zardo, F. (2004) Come sopravvivere agli italiani: anche voi potete farcela. Castelvecchi, Rome.

8 Bodies, Carnival and Honey Days: The Example of Coney Island

CHRIS RYAN AND HUIMAN GU

Introduction

In the introduction to his photographic essay on Coney Island, Stein (1998, p. 5) writes:

> Coney Island is a cultural icon of contradictions and complexities, a fantasyland of the past with a seedy present and an irrepressible optimism about its future. It's the poor man's Riviera, the real Disneyland. It's where the human polar bears still cavort, mermaids parade, the snake charmer offers up her albino python, and burly men stuff themselves to the max at Nathan's hot-dog eating contest every Fourth of July.

It might be said to be the Blackpool of America, a forgotten yet living incarnation of an age of simple, hedonistic pleasures from a rougher period characterized by immigration, an expanding and unchecked industrial growth built on sweatshops and ghettoes – it encapsulates a sense of carnival with unashamed expression of the body in all its forms: beautiful, grotesque, flamboyant, shy. In his review of Stein's work Lindsay (1998, p. 13) asks:

> Who are these people staring out so intently from the pages of this book? The sun shines flat on their imperfections . . . they seem to be operating in a hermetic world, beyond the purview of late-twentieth century exhortations. The Coney Island shown here is the last outpost of a forgotten culture, where exhibitionism retains its human scale and its original spontaneous flaws.

Yet, while Coney Island is thus represented as an image of the past, it flaunts itself still in the present. It thrives outside the mainstream, perhaps because it represents a form of yearning located apart from the postmodernistic angst of style where form becomes substance only in the knowing way of Urry's (2002) ludic playing tourist. As captured by Stein, those cavorting on the sea, exposing ripe over-suntanned bodies on the beach or boardwalks, engaging in a Mardi Gras-type parade exposing bust and bottom – these are not role-playing people who artificially create an entity between role and self through acting a part – they are the part, they are the whole, for these might be said to be their 'honey days' in the sun.

This chapter takes Stein's photographic essay as its starting point, but does not want to present a dry analysis of photographic content but rather capture its spirit and the body of Coney Island. It seeks to do this through presenting a short history of Coney Island to reveal the tumultuous past that pervades its present spirit, to then contextualize this within Bakhtin's concept of the carnivalesque to further highlight the importance of the body and, through a fleeting reference to the work of Trauer and Ryan (2005), to suggest a formulation of intimate holidays as 'honey days', as periods of healing through recognition of sex, the body and a tantric essence which underlies the experience of a place like Coney Island. This chapter is thus a reaction to the photographic essay of Harvey Stein; and like many reactions it is not linear, but meanders, partly purposelessly, but in its very musings it is hoped that the disparate thoughts form a commentary upon the holiday body exposed not only as a subject of gaze, but also as a sociological phenomenon.

A Brief History of Coney Island

The first European to land on Coney Island was Henry Hudson, in 1609, but the area was subsequently occupied by the Dutch, who in turn permitted a group of English dissenters led by Lady Moody to settle there. They established relations with the local Indians, the Bear Band, and after various skirmishes, ambushes and the like, in 1654 an Indian named Guttaquoh was declared by the settlers to be the owner of the land, and who thereby had the power to sell it to the English for two guns, 3 pounds of powder and 15 'fathoms of wampum' (a form of bead work). Not that the guns were of much use to the Bear Band, for in 1655 they were wiped out by rival Mohawk Indians (Stanton, 1997). For much of the intervening years until the 19th century the population remained small, outnumbered by the local rabbits (or coneys) until in 1824 the first hotel was built by the Coney Island Road and Bridge Company (Stanton, 1997). By the fourth decade of that century tourism began to make its mark, driven by a new fad of the middle and higher social classes to take the sea air and bathe in the sea for the sake of their health, and by the immigrant working classes of New York who sought an escape from the sweatshops, heat and violence of that city. A small steamer brought growing crowds from Manhattan down the river, and local entrepreneurs quickly spotted the potential to make money. At a fare of only 50 cents for the 2-hour ride, the combination of a scenic destination, absent law enforcement and low cost enabled gamblers, roughnecks and opportunists to set up at the west end of the bay at Norton Point. Their antics, noisiness and drunkenness shocked the more refined classes by then holidaying in the new and more expensive hotels at the centre of the bay.

These latter classes, as noted above, drawn by the novelty of sea bathing were duly advised by the guardians of public morals that 'the bathing dress should be made of woollen fabric . . . as it retains the heat of the body and therefore prevents a too rapid evaporation. Maroon and blue are the proper colors as they resist the corrosive and bleaching effects of salt water' (the advice of Dr Durant recorded by

Stanton, 1997). Fully clothed, and thus 'respectable', they discovered the joys of a bodily freedom not wholly accorded to them in other social contexts, in spite of the extra weight caused as body-covering woollen bathing suits absorbed the water. By the 1860s Coney Island had none the less acquired a less than desired reputation as Mike Norton, a New York politician of influential power, acquired land. Unfortunately his was a reputation based on shady practice, of selling poor-quality foods to the Civil War Federal Army, and being on the take through dubious property deals, and giving protection to those providing gaming and prostitutes. Initially helpless due to the lack of a large enough police presence on the island, things only subsequently improved for residents when John McKane was elected constable in 1868. Although a speculator, he appreciated that deals could only prosper in the longer term when honestly undertaken. Through a manipulation of property deals he was able to attract more wealthy and honest businessmen to the island, of which one of the more famous was Charles Feltman, who had built his wealth upon the invention of the hot dog. Feltman began further property development, built gardens and restaurants, and in 1878 built the 100 ft iron pier. Other businessmen followed, and in 1898 the Manhattan Beach Hotel was built, an imposing hotel of 258 superior rooms, financed by monies made during the railway boom and created to take advantage of new road and rail links to New York. At the same time, a second resort based on Brighton Beach, to the west of the Manhattan Hotel, came into being to extend the claims of fashion and make the resort yet more available to the growing middle managerial classes. By the late 1890s Coney Island was poised for its second leap into history.

In 1895 the adventurer and inventor of a rubber suit for life saving, Captain Paul Boyton, arrived in Coney Island. He soon opened Sea Lion Park complete with one of the world's first thrill rides, a boat launched down a slide whereupon it skipped across a lagoon with diminishing height and speed. It was an instant hit! The Park also featured the Flip Flap Railroad, a scary ride where, through centrifugal force, those daring enough to risk life and limb were shot around a 25 ft-diameter loop. Most people preferred to watch! The Funfair and Theme Park had arrived. Boyton's success inspired another Coney Island entrepreneur to also develop a theme park, and within months George C. Tilyou had established his steeplechase-horses ride, combining the thrill of a ride along an undulating course across streams and hurdles with an opportunity for betting which horse might win 'the race'. Unfortunately the steeplechase was destroyed in a major fire in 1907, along with much else of Tilyou's Park; but a second park arose from the ashes, bigger, better and using the new technologies of its day. Another success was the Pavilion of Fun, where the knowing would watch as an unwary female had gusts of wind blow her skirts up to, and perhaps over, her knees, exposing underwear and legs, while the dilatory male would suffer the indignity of a clown using an electric stinger on his buttocks. In an age where middle- and upper-class young women were chaperoned, and men would hunger for a sight of a lady's ankles, Tilyou provided opportunities for closer contact. Young women would cling to young men on the steeplechase metal horses as they cavorted over the course, The Mixer would throw people higgedly-piggedly together in a mass of humanity; ages and genders mixed. The Human Pool Table had the same effect, except that the cunning could perhaps select with whom they might be thrown together. This combination of human contact, moving floors and exciting rides was to characterize the park until the 1920s.

But the body was celebrated in other ways – as a source of curiosity and in ways calculated to incur a frisson of horror. Coney Island was also famed for its freak shows. Samuel W. Gumpertz built Lilliputia with midgets, and in successive years encouraged hairy women, armless women, dog-faced boys, the albino man – a selection of individuals who, while exposed to public gaze as oddities, according to Stanton (1997), yet none the less appreciated the sense of community Gumpertz provided, the source of income obtained and the sense of personal worth through no longer living in conditions of brutal fear or victimization. This tradition lasted into the mid-1950s when the Wonderland Circus and Palace of Wonders finally closed its doors.

Coney Island, however, not only presented a world where social conventions were contravened, where social classes mixed in new democratic ways and where taboos on intergender mixing were broken, but it also offered another fantasy world made possible by new advances in engineering as well as physics. In a period when many towns still lay dark at night, Coney Island was a fantastic city of light where electric light bulbs blotted out the sight of the stars. In 1903 Boyton sold Sea Lion Park to Frederick Thompson and Elmer 'Skip' Dundy, who renamed and 'ref(r)amed' the Park as Luna City. Its attraction lay in a new fairyland of 250,000 light bulbs, and crowds thronged at the wonder of this 'electric Eden'. A year later Dreamland Park was built and boasted a million light bulbs in an arabesque fantasy of towers and minarets. Spectacular free shows were mounted and the Burning Building and Hell Gate took full advantage of new ways of taming fire to produce shows that could be repeated in safety.

As an easily accessible and cheap attraction, Coney Island continued to do business, albeit adversely affected by the recession of the 1930s and further fires that, for example, in 1932, created significant damage to the boardwalks. In this decade the area struggled, and in 1933 Luna Park went bankrupt, initially traded under bankruptcy, was restructured and then sold to new owners. The depression was not, however, the sole explanation for Coney Island becoming a more faded pleasure. Its very success had generated imitators. Even in faraway Sydney, a Luna Park opened in 1935, but this was not the first in that continent. The first was built in 1912 in St Kilda, and another opened in Adelaide in 1930. Other fairs and parks had opened in the USA, all made accessible by a new road system constructed in response not only to a public works programme for the unemployed, but also to a slowly growing mass ownership of automobiles. The cinema had, by the 1930s, escaped its silence and was embracing colour as a new mass medium of entertainment. Coney Island was beginning its move from being at the cutting edge of social, technological and democratic change to take a more modest place in a contemporary world. Finally, in 1946 Luna Park was to close, but a brief revival of post–world war relief brought a reprise for the Island, and in 1947 Coney Island beach attendance was over 5 million (Stein, 1998). By the 1960s, however, Coney Island had returned to a former, more disreputable reputation of being the haunt of gangs as besieged Afro-Americans discovered in turn the delights of the resort away from the ghettoes of Harlem. However, their presence scared many white Americans away and it was estimated that by the mid-1960s about half the visitors to the Park were from the ghettoes of New York and other north-eastern US cities (Coney Island USA, 2005). By the 1980s, though, Coney Island began to emerge as if from a slumber. Coney Island USA was founded by Dick Zigun, and slowly the heritage it represented was recognized. In the 1980s and 1990s various buildings were officially designated as heritage landmarks (Stein, 1998). But just as physical assets are so named, so too did behaviours and atmosphere continue, as if the Island was marooned in some time capsule. Nathan's famous hot dog eating competition commenced in 1916 with the opening of Nathan's Hot Dog stand, and still continues. The Island continues its role not only as the playground of New Yorkers, but also as a home for new waves of immigrants, and in 2005 became a major place of residence for Russian immigrants from the Soviet Union – so much so that an area of Brighton Beach is locally known as 'Little Odessa'.

Possibly the best known continuation of Coney Island tradition of body exposure, apart from the sunbathing on the beach, is the annual Mermaid Parade (see Fig. 8.1). The parade takes place the first Saturday after the summer solstice – a date that in itself resonates with myths derived from more pagan times. Anyone can participate so long as prior registration is made and the entrant complies with the second requirement: that one must dress as a mermaid. In addition there are floats, cars and music, but all based on the theme of the mermaid. The first Mermaid Parade was held in 1983, and in more recent years, as is often the case, the parade has become more professional and commercial. This is evidenced by the establishment of a web site, but it retains its community associations as it is sponsored, at least in part, by Coney Island USA, the community's arts association. As that association states with reference to a display in the Coney Island Museum:

> Mr Beeber (a mini train) is able to convey a sense of solitude that is redolent of nostalgia but in a way still remarkably bereft of mawkish sentimentality, even as he pays homage to Coney Island's ultimate artificiality and plasticity.
>
> (Coney Island USA, 2005)

Comments that might be extended to much of the resort.

Fig. 8.1. Scenes from Mermaid Parades. (Available at: http://nosebleed.com/brooklyn bizzarro/coney/mermaid.html)

The Carnivalesque

Consistent through this reading of Coney Island and its history runs a motif of the importance of the body on holiday. Coney Island represents an epitome of the carnivalesque with its references of lewdness, lasciviousness, sensuality, farting, grotesqueness of breaking down social convention to offer a release from the restricting rules that normally bind and dictate behaviours. Such themes are not new within the literature of leisure and tourism. Rojek (1993) makes reference to the importance of the carnivalesque in his analysis of contemporary leisure, as does Ryan (2005) in his work on tourism experiences. In sociological writing, the term 'carnivalesque' is best associated with the work of Bakhtin, yet, as Hitchcock (1998, p. 78) argues, to understand Bakhtin, one must start 'with the unconsummated nature of his own tissue, a body that for most of his life painfully reminded him of its fleshly imperfections'. From an early age Bakhtin suffered from osteomyelitis, a bone disease that causes inflammation of nerve endings, and which in 1938 led him to have his right leg amputated. Not that the osteomyelitis was restricted to that part of his body; by 1920 the disease had spread to his left shin, a hip joint and his right hand, all of which was exacerbated by typhoid and banishment to Kazakhstan by the Stalinist regime. For Hitchcock this continual, daily reminder of bodily malformation is an important determinant of Bakhtin's writings of the grotesque, the beautiful soul in a body, the body as source of 'I' in communication and dialogue.

Bakhtin's work on *Rabelais and his World* presents his thoughts on the importance of the carnivalesque. It is a complex analysis. At one level it represents the social importance of the condoned role reversal based on Fool's Days of the Medieval Period, of the jester who can taunt the king and remind him of his earthly nature. The carnival represents a social release where dominant social and political powers permit modes of expression of self and body as escapes from repression of the system imposed upon people and the ways in which they are socially controlled. Channelled safely into the expression of the vulgar, into festive occasions of drinking, fornication, dressing up, expressions of sensuality and sexuality, they permit the oppressed to criticize, to be free of the form of oppression if not the substance. Carnival is the playful body in rebellion. As Eco (1984, p. 6) notes, Bakhtinian carnival is 'an authorized transgression'.

It might be said that many holiday locations have represented this valuing of the bodily fun, sensuality and sexuality, of escapes of not only responsibility but also social systems that constrain. Travis (1993, p. 149) reports the *North Devon Journal* in June 1849 as admonishing the 'over 400 of the human swarm of Swansea' who invaded Ilfracombe by pleasure steamer:

> Many of them went on board drunk; and what shocked our townspeople more . . . there were women – that ever we should have to write – women who were tumbled aboard in a state of – we cannot write that name of shame – a state not to be mentioned.

Similarly, Sprawson (1992, p. 29), in his history of bathing notes:

> In the Victorian coastal resorts, when the sea was normally 'black with bathers', the females did not venture beyond the surf but lay on their backs, waiting for

the approaching waves, with their bathing dresses in 'a most degage style. When the waves came', commented one onlooker, 'they not only covered the bathers, but literally carried their dresses up to their necks, so that, as far as decency was concerned, they might as well have been without any dresses at all'.

Little surprise that the promenades could be thronged with interested male onlookers! Thus, even today, Blackpool remains famous for its kiss-me-quick hats, the occasional revelation of how prostitutes work the streets during the summer by the British tabloid press and additionally how 18–30 holidays have been referred to by the Birmingham comedian, Jasper Carrot, as 'knocking' or 'bonking' holidays. Benny Dorm (1998) exposes the reality of the beach as the last resort, cable television shows *Ibiza Uncovered* – the tradition of the carnivalesque remains strong. Coney Island, not only in its funfairs but also on its beaches, represented a sense of freedom and hedonistic delight in basic pleasures of feeling sun, sea and sand on the body. It also exposed the body to the gaze of others, and in its funfairs opened up the opportunity of the body being felt by, and feeling, others. It was unalloyed fun, especially for the young; periods of escape from the constrictions of work, whether of factory or office, of the stifling conventions of middle-class respectability that sought to enforce its social norms of proper behaviour. Little wonder, in a USA that so embraced an anti-alcohol movement, that in the 1920s it was to adopt prohibition as federally enforced social policy, that a location like Coney Island was a place of escape, of fun, of bodily and social release. Shields (1991, p. 95) summarized the carnival of the beach as being vulgar:

> It is this foolish, impudent, undisciplined body which is the most poignant symbol of the carnivalesque – the unclosed body of convexities and orifices, intruding onto and into others' body-space (which) threatens to escape, transgress, and transcend the circumscriptions of the body.

Thus, various themes are implicit in the conceptualization of the carnivalesque. As Russo (1994, p. 8) explains, the grotesque body of the carnival is 'open, protruding, irregular, secreting, multiple and changing; it is identified with non-official "low" culture or the carnivalesque, and with social transformation'. The carnival represents the ever-present threat of the alternative, of the dominion of the unruly, the unwashed, the working class, if not the underclass. It is an alternative society based not on the planning of the future, but on the enjoyment of the moment. Carnival is the promotion of the body and its carnal needs to the fore, an expression of uncontained display. Thus, the complexities of Bakhtin's analysis come to the fore, because for Bakhtin carnival is an alternative to revolution. For Bakhtin, revolution is a violent form of subversion wherein violence is the price paid for the abolition of difference (Ozouf, 1988). Bakhtin (1986, pp. 134–135) writes that the distinguishing mark of violence is its absence of laughter, there is 'no Gogolian laugh' that is joyful, festive, but which is not frivolous, satirical, cynical and negative (Jung, 1998). Carnival thus need not be solely carnal; nor is it wholly all playful or ludic for it states an opposition to a dominant normative, social and political mainstream (see Caillois, 1979). Carnival is, on the contrary, life-affirming, and arguably that attribute represents an important component of holidaying, whether at locations such as Coney Island, or the more salubrious surroundings of luxurious hotels. The importance of carnival is the empowerment of the non-violent through a rejection of violence and the adoption of dialogue. The role of dialogue, and types of dialogue, are of vital importance in Bakhtin's sociology. His concepts infuse the idea of carnival. Bakhtin (1984, p. 3) makes reference to Rabelais' images as having 'a certain undestroyable nonofficial nature. . . . These images are opposed to all that is finished and polished'. The carnival is rough in outline and character, it is unfinished – the discourse is subjective with 'depth, complexity, and inexhaustible resources' (Bakhtin, 1984, p. 44).

The implications of these perspectives are many, paradoxical and complex. Coney Island encapsulates many of these perspectives, as do many other holiday locations. The body is a performance space, it is displayed and enjoyed, it is carnal, but engages in dialogue that goes beyond the carnal. In a world of business it challenges the formal by emphasizing fun. Its presence forces the formal structures of the world to engage with the fact that alternative modes and manners of life exist. Ferguson (1990, p. 67) argues that the bourgeoisie world was 'built first upon the renunciation of fun' for it is unreasonable to have fun. Fun thus insinuates itself into the life of reason. But what the modern world does is that it locates fun into specific social and physical spaces, and so the Coney Islands of this world become as separate worlds within the world. It needs to be reinforced that historically the engagement and dialogue of Coney Island was very important to the development of industrial New York State in the 19th century. As Martin Scorsese was to demonstrate in his 2002 film *Gangs of New York* (based on Herbert Asbury's book) the violence directed at the then recent immigrants was real, socially unsettling and engaged characters involved in the history of Coney Island such as Boss Tweed. The film concentrates a number of different events from different periods across the 19th century, and the character of Happy Jack in the film is based upon Happy Jack Mulraney, a thug who belonged to the Gophers, a gang occupying the area of 7th to 11th avenues and from 14th to 42nd streets, Manhattan Island, known as Hell's Kitchen, in the 1890s. Yet, Coney Island was a location where all classes mixed; it presented a democratizing force bound by a belief in new technologies, mediated by fun, that existed in juxtaposition to both the violent reality of migrant life and established older white Anglo-Saxon protestant classes. It was a place of discourse that in Bakhtin's terminology was multi-temporalized, hypertemporal and polyglot. It was a heteroglossia, another speech in another tongue – and Coney Island in its artificiality and plasticity still continues in that tradition as evidenced by events like the Mermaid Parade. However, as Baudrillard (1998, p. 152) pointed out, to enter into discourse is a process whereby agendas tend to be set by the dominant groups:

> For this is the exigency which lies at the bottom of 'free' time: *that we restore to time its use-value*, that we liberate it as an empty dimension to fill with its individual freedom. Now, in our system, time can only be 'liberated' as object, as chronometric *capital* of years, hours, days to be 'invested' by each person 'as he pleases'. It is already, therefore, no longer in fact 'free', since it is governed by its chronometry by the total abstraction which is that of the system of production.

Ryan (2005) argues that there is an inherent paradox in holidays – in that it is the reward for work, it is the condoned period of non-employment where the non-employed has dominance over the employed, but in this scenario the language is that of the workplace – not the alternative of the carnival. By its process of dialogue, the carnival becomes commodified, it has its values based upon the economic, not on an alternative system of healing 'honey days' as described below. Baudrillard (1998) also reinforces the notion of the commodification of the body, for as he writes: 'In the consumer package, there is one object finer, more precious and more dazzling than any other – and even more laden with connotations than the automobile. . . . That object is the BODY' (Baudrillard, 1998, p. 129). The body is represented as capital and as fetish (or consumer object) in which there is 'deliberate investment' (Baudrillard, 1998, p. 129). For Baudrillard the body is the erotic, a generalized set of signs, as well as being the abode of desire. The body is also commodified, most notably the feminine body in the way in which it is used and manipulated by the world of advertising. The predominance of the commercial world is now also seen to invade the grotesque, as a world of fashion that has created ciphers of the female body as a subject of neutral gaze, as a coat hanger upon which to display clothes, in short the paradox of the denial of femininity to display the female body now seeks new means to draw attention upon itself. In 2005 the fashion designer John Galliano was 'the talk of Paris' (McDowell, 2005, p. 23). Under the headline 'Le Freak C'Est Chic' McDowell describes how Galliano sent 'a crew of giants, identical twins, fat women, body builders, old men and even dwarves down the catwalk'. McDowell goes on to state that on a play upon notions of romance, Galliano created bizarre couplings such as that of a corpulent waiter and modern geisha. The commodification inherent in the modern world thus intrudes upon the carnival and changes the nature of the discourse as the alternative modes are harnessed to serve the needs of the commercial. But the dialogue continues to be subversive as the commercial is also seen to incorporate the grotesque. Thus too with the Mermaid Parade. Featured on web sites, organized with increasing professionalism, aimed at generating interest and visitor numbers, it continues to challenge both participant and observer by reference to older traditions, thereby creating new hybrids of being.

Honey Days

Trauer and Ryan (2005) argue that in the experience of any destination a key component overlooked in the marketing literature is that the visitor experience is often determined by the presence of significant others. By making reference to intimacy theory and the work of Piorkowski and Cardone (2000) it is argued that four types of intimacy exist: physical intimacy (actual contact), verbal intimacy (exchange of words and communication), spiritual intimacy (sharing beliefs) and intellectual intimacy (sharing reflection and disclosures of knowledge). Underlying such experiences must be a sense of trust, and their work explores various modes of intimacy, including the access by the visitor to MacCannell's (1976) backstage through involvement with those native to a location who themselves have intimate histories of family and other ties with a given place. Developing themes derived from this work, but wishing to emphasize the Bakhtinian concept of fun, body as performance and site of rebellion, the concept of the body engaged in the honey days of holiday is proposed. The concept of the spatially and demarcated space wherein knowledge of another's body is potentially important is socially condoned in the space of the honeymoon. The wedding has its component of the carnival when the newly married couple is farewelled for their honeymoon complete with decorated vehicle be-ribboned, and in Western society trailing a chain of old tin cans to rattle behind their car. Jokes are made that are sexual in implication; the honeymoon is expected to be a consumption of lust within an environment of love, trust, passion and body revelation. But this socially accepted carnival is also repeated by lovers who may not be married (at least to each other) or by those of the same sex; and the basic tenets of sexual play, bodily exposure, passion, shared reflection, shared hot and tender moments may be experienced by many. By their nature these too are moments of isolation from a wider world, yet have new potentials and realities.

Grace (1996, p. 5) argues that for Bakhtin the carnival represented freedom, creativity and invention, and no matter how fleeting the moment 'its participants experience an altered sense of reality that held potential for renewal and change'. In such circumstances, the body becomes the text of the meeting, but engages in a dialogue that comes to involve the meeting of minds, of mutual respect, tenderness and love in its confirmation of a sense of being. It is the triumph of being over the confines of social restriction and of simple rationality. Truly these romantic interludes might be called 'honey days' for they can be literally and metaphorically sticky, but they also possess a healing power for those involved. However, this romantic idyll shares only the concentration upon the body with the above interpretations of carnival, for carnival is rough-hewn, lustful and not seeking the tender moment, although it might encapsulate the tenderness of the shared passivity of a semi-drunken state. Thus, the romance of a Coney Island is a romance bequeathed upon it by the gaze of a present upon a heritage of the past, a heritage emasculated in the Mermaid Parade in part by the nature of its organizers, who none the less remain in thrall to rougher times. 'Honey days' represent a gentler form of holidaying of the intimate; but they equally share with the carnival a sense of being beyond the norm, of being in its romance and tenderness of bodily encounter, a contrary way of seeing the rational, money-driven world. Holidays possess potentialities to criticize the contemporary world by restoring the body and emotions to the fore of the human condition, and thus the dialogue identified by Baudrillard becomes the means by which that latter world dominates the alternative and commodifies the holiday to make it safe. All holidays are approved transgressions of work, yet retain the ability to subvert.

Conclusion

The work of Baudrillard and of other commentators such as Edensor (2000) has demonstrated that the verities of one generation are changed as society changes. There is a danger that sites such as Coney Island increasingly seem anachronistic in the early 21st century. The holiday camps of Butlins and others in the UK have sought to reposition and reshape themselves as the *Hi de Hi Campers* no longer wish to gaze at knobbly knees or have 'a knees up' at the bar. Each succeeding generation of social commentators builds upon the previous generation, shaped to a large degree by the experience of their own younger days, and while postmodernistic analysis owes much to the observations made in the period 1960–1980 by commentators such as

Foucault, increasingly the mélange of de-differentiation is absorbing new shapes and forms under the pressure of new world orders, technologies and changing views of the world. Coney Island lives today as Lindsay (1998, p. 13) notes, a 'last outpost of a forgotten culture, where exhibitionism remains its human scale and its original spontaneous flaws'. The honey days are pushed increasingly into the privacy of bedrooms, yet these too can be commercialized in a world of 'dogging', readers' wives DVDs and the other paraphernalia of the lower social classes as caught by the *Sunday Sport* in the UK – that also encapsulate a new, raw, rough sense of bodily escape.

Carnival continues, but perhaps increasingly less centred upon the holiday than in the leisure time of weekends and evenings of a more mobile class, communicating by cellphone and text messaging. Throughout the motifs of the romantic holiday or the commodified rawness of the carnival as, for example, demonstrated by the buskers on Sydney's Darling Harbour, the continued essence of the body remains not far below the surface. Harvey Stein's photographic essay is not only a homage in praise of days past and present at Coney Island, but in its study of hairy-chested, bearded men, of men with beer-gut bellies over skimpy speedoes, of lovers entwined in each other's arms, of preachers holding crosses and promising eternal salvation on renunciation of the devil, of sun worshippers and painted 'mermaids', his work remains an evocation and a questioning of what it means to relax, to be comfortable with the body, to display, to gaze and be gazed upon. It captures the very meaninglessness of being free, its purposelessness in terms of rationality, and hence its very humanity in its viewing of holidaymakers in Coney Island.

References

Bakhtin, M.M. (1984) *Rabelais and His World*. Translated by Hélène Iswolsky. Foreword by Krystyna Pomorska. Indiana University Press, Bloomington, Indiana.

Bakhtin, M.M. (1986) *Speech Genres and Other Late Essays*. In: Emerson, C. and Holquist M. (eds) (trans. V.W. McGee). University of Texas Press, Austin, Texas.

Baudrillard, J. (1998) *The Consumer Society: Myths and Structures* (trans. C. Turner). Sage, London.

Benny Dorm (pseudonym) (1998) *Beach Party: The Last Rseort*. Hodder & Stoughton, London.

Caillois, R. (1979) *Man, Play and Games* (trans. M. Barash). Schoken Books, New York.

Coney Island USA (2005) Available at: http://www.coneyisland.com/

Eco, U. (1984) The frames of comic 'freedom'. In: Seboek, T.A. (ed.) *Carnival!* Mouton, Berlin, pp. 1–9.

Edensor, T. (2000) Staging tourism: tourists as performers. *Annals of Tourism Research* 27(2), 322–344.

Ferguson, H. (1990) *The Science of Pleasure*. Routledge, London.

Grace, D. (1996) Gummy worms and butt jokes: student video production as a site of pleasure and resistance in the elementary classroom. Unpublished doctoral dissertation. University of Hawaii, Hawaii.

Hitchcock, P. (1998) The Grotesque of the body electric. In: Bell, M.M. and Gardiner, M. (eds) *Bakhtin and the Human Sciences*. Sage, London, pp. 78–94.

Jung, H.Y. (1998) Bakhtin's dialogical body politics. In: Bell, M.M. and Gardiner, M. (eds) *Bakhtin and the Human Sciences*. Sage, London, pp. 95–111.

Lindsay, D. (1998) After the end: Coney Island lives on. Introduction by H. Stein, *Coney Island*. W.W. Norton, London, pp. 7–8.

MacCannell, D. (1976) *The Tourist: A New Theory of the Leisure Class*. Macmillan, London.

McDowell, C. (2005) Le Freak C'Est Chic. *Sunday Times Supplement*, 23 October, p. 23.

Ozouf, M. (1988) *Festivals and the French Revolution*. Yale University Press, New Haven, Connecticut.

Piorkowski, G.K. and Cardone, S.S. (2000) *Too Close for Comfort: Exploring the Risks of Intimacy*. Perseus Publishing, Boulder, Colorado.

Rojek, C. (1993) *Ways of Escape: Modern Transformations in Leisure and Travel*. Macmillan, Basingstoke, UK.

Russo, M. (1994) *The Female Grotesque*. Routledge, London.

Ryan, C. (2005) *The Tourism Experience*, 2nd edn. Continuum Books, London.

Shields, R. (1991) *Places on the Margin*. Routledge, London.

Sprawson, C. (1992) Everything going swimmingly. *The Independent Weekend*, 23 May.

Stanton, J. (1997) Coney Island History Site. Available at: http://naid.sppsr.ucla.edu/coneyisland/

Stein, H. (1998) *Coney Island*. W.W. Norton, London.

Trauer, B. and Ryan, C. (2005) Destination image, romance and place experience: an application of intimacy theory in tourism. *Tourism Management* 26(4), 481–492.

Travis, J.F. (1993) *The Rise of the Devon Seaside Resorts 1750–1900*. University of Exeter Press, Exeter, UK.

Urry, J. (2002) *The Tourist Gaze*, 2nd edn. Sage, London.

9 The Embodiment of the Macho Gaze in South-eastern Europe: Performing Femininity and Masculinity in Albania and Croatia

IRENA ATELJEVIC AND DEREK HALL

Introduction

In response to social science debates, it has been claimed that a wave of new tourism research (Tribe, 2005) is creating a 'critical turn' in tourism studies (Ateljevic *et al.*, 2005, 2007) that marks an ontological, epistemological and methodological shift (Phillimore and Goodson, 2004). This shift has created several conceptual implications, offering new theoretical lenses and frameworks. It is within this emerging critical school of thought that this chapter is positioned. One of the key concepts we engage with is that of 'embodiment'. Recognition of 'the body' beyond the passivity of the tourist gaze has created three main theoretical concerns:

1. It has introduced sensitivities and a sensuous awareness in the experience of place and 'the performance' of tourism.
2. It draws to the tourism debate a context of representation in which culture is inscribed and with it power and ideology are given spatial reference: the body defines the limits of subjectivities, identities and practices of encountering the world as discursive experience.
3. We can emphasize the reflexive situating of critical perspectives, which seek to encounter the very essence of subjectivity itself.

As part of this post-structural deconstruction of tourism, the cultural complexities of gender, race, class and ethnicity in the production and consumption of tourist spaces and experiences have become critical in our understanding of tourism phenomena. A focus on the body does not simply translate into sensuality (feeling and doing) and biology (sex, race), but more importantly into the cultural performances and power relations of human interaction. Embodiment becomes a framework that refers

> . . . to the values, perceptions and gestures that are inscribed in and through the body and how we live these experiences through our bodies as men and women. Thus the

> body is engendered – inscribed with gender specific meanings that reflect the social, cultural, economic and political milieu of its experience.
>
> (Wearing, 1996, p. 80)

The body becomes significant in relation to 'the social systems which construct it in terms of values, morality and social laws' (Hall *et al.*, 2003, p. 8), allowing for a more reflexive, fluid and contingent definition of gender and other social categories. These dimensions of embodiment have been discussed through metaphorical mobilizations of performance and encounter. Franklin and Crang (2001, pp. 17–18) claim:

> [T]he cultural competencies and required skills that make up tourist cultures themselves suggest a 'Goffmanesque' where all of the world is indeed a stage.

Crouch (1999, 2001; Crouch *et al.*, 2001) uses the idea of embodied practice through the metaphor of the encounter, a process in which 'the subject actively plays an imaginative, reflexive role, not detached but semi-attached, socialised, crowded with contexts' (Crouch, 1999, p. 12). The process mixes elements of spatiality, subjectivities, gender, race, class with emotional dimensions of humans as poetic beings. Further, embodiment and creation of the knowledge of the world cannot be separated from notions of power/ideology and micro-politics of cultural negotiation.

Within this new configuration has come the pressing need to challenge the perceived neutrality of disembodied constructions of tourism knowledge (Veijola and Jokinen, 1994; Coleman and Crang, 2002; Aitchison, 2003). We acknowledge the impossibility of divorcing ourselves from the context that informs our (value-laden) analysis and privileges us with our social position of authoring and the associated power to be able to speak (Aitchison, 2001). Grosz (1994), for example, positions the body as an inscriptive surface, whereby a researcher's positionality in terms of race, gender, age, class and sexuality creates a choreography of knowledge. Swain (2004) links the project of embodiment to its feminist influences. In doing so, she raises questions about the 'perceived neutrality' of what has been predominantly Western, masculinized knowledge about the tourist experience. She notes the limited use of reflexivity in tourism research, citing Veijola and Jokinen (1994) as providing the seminal account in opening up a reflexive line of inquiry. Swain specifically uses embodiment theory not only to address issues of 'the disembodied authoritative perspective of objective science' (p. 110), but also to expose power dynamics and difficulties in the intersectional relationship between the researcher and the researched. This argument also contends that researchers cannot position themselves in categories of insider and outsider (Nast, 1994), but rather should acknowledge that they are always an interlocutor charged with the final act of interpretation and representation of knowledge (McLafferty, 1995).

Telling a 'Story'

Engaging with the post-structural framework of embodiment, this chapter employs an auto-ethnographic narrative approach of two authors with considerable tourism (research) experience in south-eastern Europe (SEE), specifically Croatia and Albania. An embodiment framework helps us to understand the role of tourism in transforming the identities and roles of women and men in the Balkans, focusing particularly on the cultural construction and communication of femininity and masculinity in tourism practices and experiences, driving gendered performances and multiple subjectivities. The juxtaposition of two narratives by one female (Croatian) researcher and one male (Western) researcher helps us to critique how our own embodied subjectivities as insiders/outsiders/interlocutors intersect with the people we interact with. Gray (2003) argues that the use of 'stories' is a crucial part of our research practice to gain an understanding of culture and the social.

Irena Ateljevic was born in a small Adriatic fishing/tourist village and spent her first 27 years 'breathing and living' tourism in Croatia in the context of Yugoslavian communism, and since then has lived and worked abroad as a tourism academic in the 'West'. Her interlocutor position in the 'third space' of insider–outsider dialectics brings the complexity of reflexivity into her feminist theoretical gaze of tourism development and the macho Croatian society. On the other hand, Derek Hall's narrative of negotiating and experiencing the dominant constructions of masculinity and femininity in the Balkans is exemplified through his roles as a Western researcher, tourist and tour leader. He interacted with both female and male (Albanian) tourist guides in Albania, especially during the constrained circumstances of Stalinist authoritarianism. The two contrasting experiences of Albania as the epitome of a totalitarian socialist regime and Croatia as a 'Westernized version of the European East' reveal significant ethnic, ideological and gender variations of power relations deeply embedded in their specific cultural heritages.

Existing literature: the absence of embodiment

Almost a decade ago Weiner (1997) could argue that in general there had been relatively little discussion of women's and men's productive and reproductive roles in postcommunist Central and Eastern Europe (CEE). For SEE in particular, and specifically in relation tourism, little appears to have changed that position. Although the level of debate in, and concerning, social and cultural consequences of economic restructuring has generally improved, notably in relation to processes of mobility, labour migration and ethnicity (e.g. Kasimis *et al.*, 2003), and although a number of gendered studies have focused on violence and conflict in the territories of former Yugoslavia (e.g. Albanese, 2001; Carpenter, 2005), gender critiques of production and consumption relations in tourism from the region remain scant. Individual studies and collections of gender-aware evaluations of tourism (e.g. Kinnaird and Hall, 1994, 1996; Swain, 1995; Swain and Momsen, 2002) have rarely embraced empirical observations from, or theoretical perspectives explicitly relating to, gendered dimensions of tourism in CEE and specifically in SEE.

Exceptions have included the work of Ghodsee in Bulgaria, Devedzic working in pre-Yugoslav war Montenegro and Scott examining the role of migrant Romanian (and other CEE) women in northern Cyprus. Despite the gender stereotyping so prevalent in the hotel and catering industry, Ghodsee (2003) has argued that in the case of Bulgaria, state support and encouragement for viable economic sectors such as tourism, with perceived relatively high wages and employing a 'critical mass' of women, can help to ease women's burden within transition processes. This is perhaps more a reflection of the lack of considered viable alternatives to tourism than of notional positive attributes for female employment of tourism per se.

The intersection of gender and ethnic differentiation is a critical Balkan theme, raising issues of identity. In pre-Yugoslav war Montenegro, Devedzic (2002) saw coastal tourism development transforming gender relations and roles to varying degrees amongst Slavic Montenegrins and Muslim ethnic Albanians, two distinct and contrasting patriarchal SEE host societies. In the Ulcinj region, just north of the Albanian border:

> The tribal structure of both ethnic groups that has existed in the interior
> patriarchal villages indicates some unique social relations built on a warrior past
> and tradition....Glorification of the man-warrior has encompassed a gender-related
> hierarchy of power and authority of men...men have been subordinated only to
> older men, while a woman is subordinate to both men and older women and has no
> rights to make decisions....Simultaneously with the patriarchal order, an 'Oriental'
> one has been present among the majority of Albanians as well, which has only
> further strengthened the existing family and social structure.
>
> (Devedzic, 2002, p. 145)

Although the erosion of such patriarchy had begun long before tourism was brought to the region, the latter was seen to collide with remnants of 'tradition', offering a vehicle for the personal and structural transformation of women within transition processes. But while both ethnic groups were drawn into tourism work, the Montenegrin women found a greater sense of independence and identity through such an employment route than did their ethnic Albanian counterparts. The latter, almost paradoxically, appeared to distance themselves from the notion of tourism employment being an extension of feminized domestic work, preferring to participate within the tourism economy as 'mediators', notably in the travel agency business.

The gender-expressed ethnic and religious faultline has also been documented within the context of tourism employment in northern (Turkish) Cyprus. Here, migrant Romanian (and Russian) women have found employment in those occupations considered 'unsuitable' by local women, notably as casino croupiers (Scott, 1995, 1997, 2003). Although (Muslim) northern Cypriot women's participation in the tourism labour force has increased in recent years, the persistence of clear areas of cultural proscription has resulted in a division of female labour highlighting women's dual role and identity in SEE and the eastern Mediterranean.

Yet, in gendered appraisals of development processes within SEE, little attention has been paid to embodied approaches of analysis. There are opportunities both for embodied approaches to the reality of gendered tourism experience, and for the establishment of an appropriate culturally sensitive theoretical framework within which to situate and interrogate wider issues of tourism, gender and power relations in the region. In practical terms, there is a basic need for women's unfettered access to land and property (e.g. Hartl, 2003; Overbeek, 2003), and appropriate evaluations to support this. The pivotal role of women in tourism, and of tourism in 'transition' development processes (e.g. Hall, 2004; Hall and Roberts, 2004), places considerable responsibility on the industry's development and management, and its collaboration and partnership with other social and economic development sectors. It also emphasizes the need for the reflexivity of embodied evaluations and their critical importance in informing policy and praxis.

The role and position of SEE women as tourism consumers is minimal and, unsurprisingly, is not represented in the literature. Yet, it is likely to articulate strongly domestic (family) relationships and remnant patriarchal power structures. Although domestic tourism and recreation has been marketized and opportunities of access to formerly subsidized services have decreased for many, theoretical improvements in opportunities for travel have increased access to international tourism. Yet, in terms of their domestic family relations and responsibilities, when or if on holiday, women's positions are unlikely to have improved. Indeed, with the greater likelihood of opting for self-catering, unserviced types of accommodation because of cost considerations, many SEE women's positions of access to 'leisure' while on holiday are likely to have deteriorated since 1989 (Hall, 2001).

Personal narrative of negotiation and experience: the case of Albania

Derek's narrative of negotiating and experiencing the dominant constructions of masculinity and femininity in the Balkans is exemplified briefly through his roles as researcher, tourist and tour leader, focusing on the 1974–1991 period, for four basic reasons:

1. It is the major period of my experience as a tourist and tour leader in Albania.
2. It represents a period of control, both in the authoritarian and scientific sense: tourism was heavily prescribed and few external influences penetrated the otherwise near-hermetically sealed borders of the country.
3. It represents a period during which informal, if not formal, attitudes gradually changed within the country, prior to the final collapse of communism in 1991.
4. Narratives of tourism during this period are poorly documented.

Two sets of arguments are put forward through empirical exemplification. First, that the authoritarian nature of the Albanian Stalinist state, while relatively male-dominated in terms of positions of power, did manage to suppress, within egalitarian ideals, the gender-specific excesses that were to be unleashed after the fall of communism in 1991 (resurgence of the blood feud, the trafficking of women, religious and domestic subjugation) (see, e.g. Weyr, 1992; Lazaridis, 2000) although land privatization and the mass emigration of Albanian men have had an empowering effect for women (see, e.g. Nicholson, 2004). In other words, the macho was mediated and subjugated by ideological (super-)imposition. Second, that the ethnic, ideological and gender tensions of relations with foreign visitors under such circumstances were revealed through the embodied expressions of outward appearance and use of shared language.

The cultural performance of the encounter here acts as a metaphor for negotiating explicit gender, cultural, racial and ideological differences, while also embracing complicit, sometimes paradoxical and occasionally illicit, commonalities of intellectual and professional mores, within the acting out of tourism-based relations. My first experience of SEE took place in the revolutionary year of 1968 as a student of geography and social anthropology. I was a volunteer of a 2-month overland expedition to Turkey. Driving through virtually the whole length of the then Yugoslavia, from Krapina to Niš, across Bulgaria, Thrace and the Bosphorus to Anatolia (Bedford, 1969), I discovered places and cultures of which I knew virtually nothing. The personally formative experiences and encounters and the reading I undertook (such as almost learning by heart Hoffman's (1963) *The Balkans in Transition* while sitting on an upturned bucket in the back of an overloaded Morris J2 minibus) generated a thirst to learn more about ideology and propaganda, their philosophical and ethical underpinnings.

The paradox of state socialist societies being ruled in the name of the working people, but in practice for the benefit of a different type of elite to that experienced in my own society, made me want to know more about what this actually meant to those people in whose name it was being undertaken.

My long-standing obsession with Albania (e.g. Hall, 1975, 1984, 1994) stems from this time. Without diplomatic relations and with individual foreigners' travel to and within this small Balkan country proscribed, conventional attempts to undertake research in Albania were virtually impossible for a UK citizen. One way to gain access to decision makers and to be able to interact with Albanians on a daily basis was to become a tour group leader, a role that I took up on an occasional basis in the 1980s and early 1990s, after more than a decade and a half of travelling to the country as a tourist. A major ethical issue for Westerners researching into a number of state socialist societies was the means by which original empirical (and other) source material could be secured. Official channels were often obstructive and misleading. On the other hand, particularly in the more authoritarian societies, we researchers found ourselves assuming an often self-censoring position since in some circumstances making (unofficial) contact with individuals could place the latter at risk.

Under these circumstances, reflexivity and sensitivity were highly important, if not always productive, qualities to imbue and apply. There certainly persisted stories – not all apocryphal – of naive or selfish academics causing very major problems for citizens of particular regimes through their blind pursuit of empirical research materials.

The Albanian Balkan Stage

There is a dearth of published research on the negotiating roles, intermediary positions and relative power of such tourism actors as tour guides, tour company representatives and tour group leaders. The specific roles of overland expedition leaders receive some consideration in a standard introduction to tourism employment opportunities (Collins, 2004, pp. 35–37), but this is purely descriptive. Pizam and colleagues' potentially interesting work on tour guides' perceptions of tourists (Pizam and Sussmann, 1995; Pizam and Jeong, 1996) does not, unfortunately, bring any focus or reflexivity to the negotiating positions of the guides themselves. Guerrier and Adib's (2004) work on the gendered identities of overseas tour reps finds that, unremarkably, in roles where the boundaries between work and play are ambiguous, reps reveal masculinities and femininities that comply with 'traditional expectations'. Young male reps are portrayed as 'laddish' – in relation to their engagement with alcohol and sexual relationships with guests – while the emphasis of female reps' roles is placed on being providers of emotional labour and taking control of guests' perceptions. The authors conclude that in these roles of negotiation within tourism, men and women appear to construct different work identities. In my experience, such differences were – indeed needed to be – expressed far more subtly in the Stalinist context of tourism performance in Albania.

The Albanian authorities' 'prescriptive' approach to tourism development incorporated a number of distinctive characteristics that attempted to ameliorate three tensions which appeared to be inherent in the performance of international tourism within a Stalinist political economy. First, tourism's need for flexibility and the ability to respond to changing consumer demands could not be easily accommodated within the Stalinist organizational model. Albturist's adoption of pre-planned, limited-scale, group-based circumscribed tourism (based on the Soviet Intourist model but taken further) obviated the need for such flexibility and placed responsibility on Western tour companies and Albanian embassies to educate and filter potential visitors.

Second, as a service industry, requiring both initial capital and human resources, tourism might have appeared to be an irrelevant diversion from the major socio-economic priorities of state socialism for such an economy of shortage. However, by promoting the role of Albanian culture and heritage for tourist consumption through closely managed prescription, foreign tourists could be presented with a 'good face' of the country, and perhaps even be imbued with a sense of the (self-perceived) superiority of Albania's development path, thereby conferring on tourism and its interlocutors an important ideological role.

Third, the encouragement, however low key, of foreign, especially Western visitors to the country, might have appeared to ordinary Albanians to be privileging just those people – 'capitalists, revisionists and fascists' – against whom, for decades, the indigenous society had been galvanized. Through the delicate selection and supervision of foreign visitors and the preclusion of any meaningful interaction with the host population, the validity of the state's xenophobic rhetoric for domestic consumption could be preserved, and the protection of foreign guests secured. In the 1970s, for example, and in some cases also through the 1980s, no US, Greek, Yugoslav or South African citizens were allowed entry, and certain employment groups – notably journalists and clerics (Albania declared itself 'atheist' in 1967) – were also prohibited (Hall, 1994, pp. 132–134).

The Encounter as Research: But for Whom?

The roles of a tour leader (also referred to as a tour escort or tour manager) are characterized by a delicate balance of interests, acting as an intermediary and liaison within and between at least four sets of actors in a web of cross-cutting (if largely transient) relationships: the tour company and destination tourism organizations, the tour company and its clients on the tour, destination tourism organizations or local guides and the tour group, and members of the tour group themselves. Within this mosaic, the tour leader is placed at the fulcrum of cross-cultural performance.

The tour leader travels with the group he or she is leading, and may be closely interacting with them for up to several weeks at a time, normally accompanying the group for the whole tour, acting as an escort, guide, source of information, assistance and reassurance for the tour group both collectively and individually. It is a role that combines the spontaneity of the mass package tour 'rep' with some degree of the place-specific knowledge and experience held by local guides, but often spread across a much wider geographical context. These interlocuting roles require, above all, an ever-ready physical presence. Bridging the (cultural, perceptual, ideological) spaces between tour members and local tourism employees and officials is thus an explicitly embodied function of the tour leader.

The deliberate separation of tourists from the host population was institutionalized in an attempt to forestall any ideological, cultural or financial contagion passing from foreigners to locals. Tourism infrastructure – hotels, transport, guides – represented an instrument of policy and symbol of political philosophy expressed in a two-way process of exclusion. In Albania tourists were debarred from using public transport unescorted, being almost hermetically sealed within state-owned tourist transport which was rendered explicitly exclusive and inaccessible to the 'host' population (Hall, 1984, 1990, 1994), thereby privileging the Albanian guides and drivers.

As contact with 'ordinary Albanians' was proscribed (any contact with foreigners had to be reported by Albanians to the authorities), the next best thing was adopting a role that required interaction on a regular basis with Albanian tourism workers, and preferably those for whom tourism employment was not their prime job. Language teachers recruited as foreign tourist group guides thus provide the focus of this all too brief appraisal. They could be attached to a foreign tourist group for up to 2 weeks, travelling in the same (Albturist) bus, escorting, protecting and eating with the group, but staying in the same hotel in inferior accommodation or in a nearby lower-quality establishment.

If, in the view of Franklin and Crang (2001, pp. 17–18), the cultural competencies of required skills making up tourist cultures are 'Goffmanesque', on this world stage of negotiation the (often mutually reinforcing) roles of tour leaders and tour guides bear an affinity not so much to stage managers but to the compilers (or at least interpreters) of the programme notes for the performance. The performance in the case of Stalinist Albania saw prescriptive tourism being stage-managed by the destination state (abetted by the Western source tour company), with both local guides and tour leaders perhaps being merely the puppeted ushers and usherettes of the cultural auditorium. None the less, the relationship between the two role players acts to lubricate the locomotion of collective sequential experience. It smoothes around the edges of the forbidden interstices of personal relationships in a choreography of embodied cultural juxtaposing. In less prescribed circumstances the tour leader–local guide relationship may have the flexibility and expansiveness to be one of performance producer and director.

Indeed, the tour leader acts as a pivotal interface of race, gender, economic and social power relations, not only on behalf of the tourists in his or her care and of the tour company, but also endeavouring to protect the local guides from the naive behaviour of members of the tour group. For, in such prescribed circumstances – and this can apply in a number of cultural contexts – the local guides may be the sole (prescribed) means for members of the tour group to interact meaningfully with members of the 'host' population.

The tour leader–local guide relationship is a performance encounter rarely expressed in the literature. From my viewpoint as a male tour leader, 'friendship' was usually easier, more relaxed with the female than male Albanian guides, if only because of the very explicit gender demarcation lines established both by the then contemporary communist mores and by traditional codes of honour (*besa*). The tensions of cultural, ideological and gender differences could be expressed through relatively mild joking relationships in public, while a shared language helped to develop mutual knowledge at a more individual level. For example, having located for me Tirana's irregularly opened philatelic shop, one guide subsequently presented me with a gift of several sets of early post-war Albanian postage stamps whose Western monetary value was far greater than she perhaps could have imagined and certainly could have afforded. Had this gift been part of a family heirloom or ascertained at great personal cost? I never found out, but the act of kindness did follow an incident when she (unusually) publicly harangued me for the persistent lateness of two members of my group.

However suppressed and disguised, male guides usually appeared subliminally imbued with a macho, competitive instinct, needing to express, in public, their controlling, dominant role (vis-à-vis the tour leader) in relation to the group and its activities. One or two were, however, able to reveal a frailer aspect of their personalities in private, such as when one was suffering from a persistent headache and consumed most of my supplies of aspirin in the apparent absence of any Albanian analgesic at his disposal. The men's attitude to female tourists was often ambivalent: both schoolmasterly and fraternal. In later years, younger male guides – of whom there were few until the later 1980s – expressed a greater interest in hitherto taboo subjects such as contemporary Western music which, publicly, they appeared particularly inclined to discuss with the younger female members of the group. Indeed, in 1990 one female tour member was able to claim to have had an intimate relationship with a guide (whom I knew) on a previous recent visit. If true, this certainly was a predictor of the imminent demise of the country's political (and moral) fabric.

Compliant Bodies (Outwardly)

The requirement of foreign tourist bodies to be compliant with Albanian norms became an important element and significant focal point of the performance. In an ideologically 'pure' economy of shortage that became particularly acute following the final withdrawal of Chinese support in 1978, there was room neither for wasteful fashion nor a capacity to accommodate contagion effects from outside the country's borders. For a period covering almost a decade, intending visitors were forewarned that certain types of outward appearance were not acceptable to the Albanian authorities. This meant that flared or 'tight' trousers, Cuban heels, 'short' as well as 'extra-long' skirts, 'decolleté' necklines, full beards and long hair would not be permitted.

At the country's points of entry, notably the land border crossing with Montenegro at Hani i Hotit and the country's Rinas (now 'Mother Thereza') International Airport just outside Tirana, a tailor and hairdresser would be on hand to advise newly arrived visitors of their sartorial obligations. Thus, the 'foreign body' came to represent compliance with official Albanian norms while the prescriptions were explicitly gendered: hair, beard, trousers for men, skirt length, neckline, heel shape and size for women. One outcome of this imposition had the effect of outwardly de-sexualizing group members.

This requirement clearly placed some of the intelligent Albanian guides, as the mediators and conveyors of such information and requirements, in a position they clearly did not enjoy. Under the gaze of portraits of Marx and Engels, whose flowing beards were mockingly full (the full beard proscription – there had to be bare flesh between sideburns and beard – was aimed at precluding the appearance of an Orthodox priest), guides would need to be close at hand to interpret for customs officers' detailed examination both of visitors' luggage and their bodily appearance.

For example, on one occasion I was considered by Albanian customs officials to be wearing unacceptably flared trousers. In fact, they were unfashionably baggy for the time, albeit less so than the pair worn by Enver Hoxha in the portrait beaming down on the newly arrived group in the customs hall. Under such circumstances, an acceptable equivalent item of Chinese-made clothing would be required to be purchased from customs and worn henceforth while in Albania. My height precluded this – all the Chinese trousers were far too short for me – and the customs officer eventually agreed, grudgingly, to allow me to wear an alternative pair of trousers taken from my luggage. Had this 'solution' not been forthcoming, I would have been required to undertake an immediate return across the border out of Albania. Thus, for several years, male travellers who had unwisely not heeded pre-trip recommendations had to submit themselves to haircuts, beard modifications and the purchase of Chinese clothing before they could proceed any further into Albania. By contrast, in my experience, few women were ever required to modify their appearance to meet official prescriptions, perhaps because they were sensibly better prepared, rather than as the result of any gender bias on the part of the Albanians.

Language and Body Spaces

When the role of language in articulating or constraining behaviour represents the prescribed formal dimension of communication, but where words are often best left unsaid, body language becomes a complicit medium of expression. There was always the implicit understanding that all interactions between the guides and foreigners would be overheard, and I was equally aware that I or any group member might say something (however inadvertently) that might compromise the guides. Thus, fascinating combinations of the use of the English language and employment of body language characterized the varying relationships different Albanian guides had with their tour groups and tour leaders.

For example, some of the English teacher guides would employ the tour leader and tour members not merely to help improve their own knowledge and usage of the language amongst native speakers, but also to explore facets of language as a medium for informal exchange and semi-illicit discussion. At its most mundane, this was represented by a female student teacher who claimed to be collecting English language phrases used to describe going to the toilet. She encouraged – usually male – members of the group to provide her with new examples that were not familiar to her (most

English language materials in Albania at the time were Chinese in origin). Whether true or otherwise, this opened up an inclusive avenue for the sharing of joking relationships with her. She would deliberately sit next to Australasian or Canadian members of the group in the Albturist tour bus some way back both from the senior teacher-guide and from the overseeing driver. After 2 days with the group, we were told by the senior guide that she was ill. She never rejoined, and was eventually replaced by a much more serious young man who rarely failed to leave the senior guide's side.

One mature English teacher-guide in particular enjoyed limericks as a medium of expressing the language of his pedagogy, and would encourage me (initially I was a little hesitant fearing an *agent provocateur*) to construct limericks about Albania, which, if he felt were appropriate, he claimed he would then employ in his classroom as a teaching medium, the geography of which his students could relate to.

As indicated by the (unknown) fate of the female student teacher, such linguistically choreographed exchanges risked transcending the boundaries of prescribed discourse by entering the realms of innuendo and double entendre, and had to be executed with care. Despite an official diet of British humour restricted almost wholly to the films of Norman Wisdom, my limericks appeared to be appreciated, I suspected, as very much an elitist, almost esoteric, intellectual entertainment that would surely have been officially taboo.

Personal Narrative of Negotiation and Experience: The Case of Croatia

In contrast to Derek who had his first experience of SEE as a Western student of geography and social anthropology, hence an 'outsider thirsty to learn about ideology of state socialist societies', Irena was born and raised within it. Born in 1965 on a small island called Murter, in Dalmatia (the central Croatian province on the Adriatic coast), at the beginning of golden times of tourism development in former Socialist Federal Republic of Yugoslavia (SFRJ). Our narratives cover approximately the same period of the communist past in this region, although my story also extends into the first years of the Yugoslav war. The focus on the 1960–1993 period is bounded by two crucial events that significantly determined my life and inherently symbolize the gendered core of the narrative:

- My mother going for her first summer holiday in 1960 to Murter, falling in love with my father and staying in the village forever.
- My marrying a Serb at the dawn of the Yugoslav conflict and consequently leaving to go into exile to New Zealand in 1993 to begin 'a new life' in 'another world'.

These events also neatly capture the era of the tourism boom and collapse in Yugoslavia in which tourism as the main economic and social agent became an embodiment of traditional performances of femininity and masculinity being continuously reproduced. Furthermore, my whole life appears to embody the tourism phenomenon: growing up in a house that was turned into an informal homestay 'tourism business' every summer; working in local tourism businesses from the age of 13 (waitress, travel agent and tour guide); taking tourism and economics studies at the university; running our own small family business with my husband.

While my personal account underpins the main thread of the narrative, the insight is derived from the lifelong cultural intimacy and observations of my community and the society in producing and consuming tourism experiences. The post-structural framework of embodiment allows me to integrate the complexity of national political history, traditional patriarchy and ideological structures of socialism with my subjectivity as the site of resistance. Speaking of structures, it is important to stress that the decentralized 'socialist market economy' of Yugoslavia had a unique position within CEE and SEE. Being part of the non-aligned movement and serving as a buffer zone between the Eastern and Western blocs, the SFRJ had a strange mix of socialist and capitalist structural elements. With borders open to both blocs, by the end of the 1980s it was generating international tourism receipts equivalent to the total for the rest of CEE and the Soviet Union (Hall, 2004).

Performing masculinity and femininity in Croatia

The Croatian coastline together with its islands ranks among the most intricately indented coastlines in the world. Of 1185 islands, islets, cliffs and reefs, only 67 are inhabited (Brusic, 2004). It is important to briefly reflect on the historical background of this region as an important sociocultural context for further discussions on performance of masculinity and femininity in the Croatian patriarchal and macho society.

Croatian modern nationalism, which also characterized the most recent war in the area, originates from a sideshow of the Napoleonic wars. In 1809, Napoleon created the 'Illyrian Provinces' from territory ceded by Austria, comprising a part of Slovenia, a part of Croatia (roughly the regions around the capital Zagreb) and Dalmatia (the Adriatic coast). This gave the Croats and Slovenes first-hand experience of the new economic and political liberties that had inspired Western Europe. 'Illycrum', the name of the western Balkans in classical antiquity, underlined the pan-(southern) Slav sentiments and also aimed to overcome problems posed by regional differences among Croats themselves. Cultural and political differences were not always successfully bridged, notably in Dalmatia where people considered themselves Dalmatians rather than Croats. The historical associations of Dalmatia with Romans and Venice had created a collective consciousness based around 'preferred' images of Mediterranean identity, in contrast to more Central European and pro-Austrian mentalities derived from the domination of the Habsburg Empire (Austria–Hungary) over continental Croatia.

The Croat national movement was used by Austrian absolutism in its struggles against the Hungarians as well as a counterweight to the Italian *risorgimento*, since the Venetians nurtured a claim to Dalmatia. This gap between Mediterranean and Central European associations continues to shape the cultural landscape of Croatia, and only becomes bridged in anti-Serb nationalism. Strong and united Croatian national identity becomes important when necessary to distance itself from pejorative Balkan connotations as illustrated in Hall's (2002) study of Croatian tourism branding efforts following the Yugoslav wars. Yet, in social performances to enhance the macho male figure, Dalmatian men often ridicule the 'continental guys' as too soft, being associated with a more serious, reserved and 'liberal'

Central European mentality. In contrast, the pride of a more macho, 'Southern' outlook resembles the Italian character of expressive behaviour, passion for food, good life and a predatory machismo for the voracious seduction of women (see Abramovici, Chapter 7, this volume).

With their stony bare landscape and scarcity of fertile soil, the Dalmatian islands historically provided a limited economic base for peasant society, mostly organized around fishing, small-scale boat-building, olive cultivation and limited sheep farming. The upheavals of the 20th century stimulated many Dalmatians to migrate to Western Europe and to the 'promised lands' of the New World (particularly the USA and New Zealand). However, the phenomenon of mass tourism reversed the trend of depopulation, and the rapid tourism growth began in the early 1960s. Initially, the coast became popular as a summer holiday destination for the domestic (mostly urban) Yugoslav population (Vukonic, 2005). A lack of accommodation facilities saw the local population becoming widely involved in tourism, renting their own rooms, apartments and houses to tourists.

Initial domestic demand was followed by the rapid growth of international tourism in the late 1960s and early 1970s. Croatia received over 80% of tourists in Yugoslavia, registering 68 million nights and 10 million tourists in 1988, the peak year of 30 years' continuous tourism growth (Hall, 2003). The significance of small-scale, local involvement in tourism is illustrated in the fact that by 1987, the *registered* private accommodation providers together with camps comprised two-thirds of the overall accommodation capacity in Croatia (Institut za Turizam, 2005; Ateljevic and Weber, 2006).

It is this era that provides the context of my story presented here. My village is a typical representative of small communities scattered around the Dalmatian islands that experienced the tourism boom. By the mid-1980s the village population of around 1700 was experiencing tourist flows of up to 10,000 in the peak season months of July and August (Ateljevic and Doorne, 2003). I was born to a Dalmatian father and a *purger* mother (*purger* is a local, often derogatory, expression for people born in the capital city of Zagreb). My mother came to this village in 1960 to spend a family holiday and they stayed in the house that was to become my grandparents'. Interestingly, my parents embodied the tourist development of that time as my mother's family was representative of urban-dwelling domestic tourist, and my father's was one of those local entrepreneurial households that turned their house into an informal homestay tourist business. My father was a local teacher, his father was a captain on local ships and his mother had a typical gendered role of subsistence agricultural work and running the household, which, with tourism development, turned into extended domestic work. My father, single and attractive (tall, fit and olive-skinned) embodied the typical Dalmatian macho man, *galeb* (seagull), a local term symbolically used for men getting their 'catch of fish' (women!).

Dramatized by the war experience in the capital city of Zagreb, my mother fell in love with the 'local boy' and the 'whole romantic vision of the island life' (as expressed in her own words). She married my father in the autumn of that year and her 'tourist' role of play changed into the responsible position of work as a daughter-in-law and the 'main woman' of the house. When the tourists who flooded local streets, cafés and beaches in the summer deserted the island at the

end of the season, her husband continued his life as usual, working during the day
and playing cards in the evening with his male friends in a local *trattoria*. She found
herself in the isolation of lonely evenings with responsibility for the household.
My father simply replaced the role and position of his mother with his new wife,
ensuring his image of 'a real man' who never 'gives in' to his wife. The first years
were particularly difficult as her 'outsider' position of being a *purgerica* of Hungarian
origin (her mother was Hungarian) who wore too liberal clothes (e.g. short skirts)
did not give her easy access to patriarchal and enclosed women's networks. The
gaze of rural (particularly older) women – who experienced a harsh life of poverty
and water shortages (e.g. the laundry was washed in the sea), worked on the land,
went to church and wore traditional black clothes (mourning dead members of the
extended family) – expressed suspicion and disapproval of this 'city girl'.

In an intensely patriarchal society, where 'the birth of a son' is always to be
celebrated (to the extent that a woman is commonly expected to bear children
until she produces a son), men play the central role. The intergenerational family
businesses and properties are always inherited patrilineally. So, when women get
married it is generally expected that they will move into their husbands' houses:
into the living space where the extended family makes rules and creates expectations of what is perceived to be the proper behaviour of 'a good wife, mother and
daughter-in-law'. Small and isolated communities create a very critical gaze that is
regularly focused on young girls and women.

While houses increasingly have separate flats for two generations, everyday life
is shared through regular family meals and grandparents' care of young children.
Close family relationships reflect a deep-seated suspicion and mistrust of socialist state institutions and banks, to the extent that today the extended family has
become the main reference for financial, social and emotional support (Ateljevic
and Doorne, 2003; Ateljevic and Weber, 2006). In the conditions of continuous
political upheavals and the corrupted socialist state, social and personal stability could only be ensured by women's commitment and duty to keep the family together. One of the most famous Yugoslavian/Croatian feminists, Slavenka
Drakulic (1993, 1996), argues that this collective consciousness is so strong and
characteristic of the Balkans that people use a different pronoun – 'we' instead of 'I'.
Despite the socialist quotas and the communist claims of equity between gender
and class, in Yugoslavia it remained deeply embedded in patriarchal discourses
of domination and could not easily shift axes of power and traditional gendered
performances, particularly in smaller towns and peripheral areas.

During the Second World War, the communist partisans invested heavily
in organizing women, whom they needed to secure the logistics for guerilla warfare, including food and nursing care for the wounded. In 1944, they formed an
organization called the Anti-fascist Front of Women (AFZ), which included a few
educated communists but mostly consisted of uneducated rural women. These
were mobilized for many different tasks after the war: clearing ruins, educating
other women, popularizing basic ideological concepts, witnessing for 'the people' at
trials of quislings; they were the symbolic representation of a new order in which
women's bodies gained respect and dignity. The AFZ had several million members
when the Communist Party had only a few hundred thousand. After the break
with Stalin, this huge political body was suddenly dissolved by the party, who felt

it was a potential danger; and the curious mixture of patriarchal and consumerist attitudes towards women slowly took over. Svetlana Slapsak (2001), one of the early feminist activists in Yugoslavia, arguing that the history of Balkan women shows that the combination of patriarchy and ideological pressure has produced a specific, subversive women's culture, describes her experience when, at one of the first feminist meetings in the 1970s, some older women who had been AFZ activists appeared, tears in their eyes.

Within the 'loose' ideology of the Yugoslav state, strong patriarchy continued to reproduce traditional gendered roles clearly manifested in the tolerance of religious practices – Catholic (for Croats) and Orthodox (for Serbs). While there were no public holidays at Christmas and Easter, the religious rituals of baptism, christening and church weddings were regular events in my village. In a country with strong historical ties with the Roman church where today 90% of the population claims to be Catholic (Statisticki Ured Hrvatske, 2003), marriage represents one of the key social goals. I can vividly remember the growing panic in my family as my older sister was approaching the age of 25 and was still not married. As a teenager I remember internalizing this fear, which, despite my university studies, focused me strongly on getting married as my primary life goal.

Strong family values put the pressure on women to fulfil their biological role and to produce children, whilst the trophy of the macho Dalmatian man is earned by two key performances: producing a son and continuous seductive behaviour towards women. Facilitated by the Mediterranean climate of mild weather, the macho skills are learned in public spaces of communal conviviality. The sexual and romantic affections are overtly expressed through local folk singing, dancing, jokes, flattering, sexual comments and open approach of sexual proposals. Folk dancing, however, which used to be one of the regular social practices in public community life for expressing affections of love and romance between men and women, had almost completely disappeared by the mid-1970s. The performance is always public as the macho identity is primarily to be earned in the eyes of other men.

Young women happily submit to the whole game, feeling empowered by the bodily performance of the overobsession with grooming, slim bodies and fashion, flaunted in cafés and promenades. The performance of femininity is not only controlled by the male overt display of heterosexuality but also by women's critical gaze competing and inspecting each other in constant re-evaluations of 'looking good', often judged (and envied) on the basis of clothing brands and overall style. This performance for female eyes becomes particularly important as married women grow into middle age, when in the increasing absence of the male attention, most of their bodily self-esteem is gained from the approval and essential envy of the female community (friends, colleagues, neighbours). Success in their lives is assessed by excessive material values embodied in expensive clothes and how well you 'maintain' yourself (in addition to cars and houses). In such a context, intangible values such as travel do not represent a strong priority. Living in the coastal areas of Dalmatia is regularly used as an excuse for the low interest in international travel, apart from shopping purposes. I remember that most of my teenage and family travel was focused around shopping tours to Trieste (Italy) for cheaper goods of coffee and more fashionable Italian clothes.

Whilst the roles and performance of married women change to the more 'serious' status of the primarily dedicated mother and wife who performs 'the appropriate' behaviour for the closer community of extended family and female friends, the masculinity of married men needs to be continuously restated. In the camaraderie of male companionship displayed in endless hours spent in cafés (beginning in early morning) and excessive drinking (which often finishes in long nights of singing local Dalmatian songs) the machismo is incessantly exercised. Teasing jokes about sex, women and politics in which the 'penis and balls' always have the central reference are the main themes of their conversations, whereby the real performance is particularly tested in the summer months. The availability of single female tourists creates the pool in which the 'local *galeb* can fish', while the tourist crowds ideally distort the otherwise close scrutiny of a small community in which adultery is not easily forgiven. Whilst married men need to play it more subtly, young single guys proudly exhibit their macho potential in public by creating often-excessive sexual stories. Such exerted masculinity of Dalmatian *galebs* is so well recognized that it is often commented on in national newspapers as an important tourist attraction. In my village it even resulted in annual competitions whereby the local guys would organize a gathering at the end of summer to provide detailed accounts of their sexual experiences and subsequently elect the 'winner' of the most 'trophies' who then would be publicly announced. These obsessions with 'women hunting' and erections as a primary symbol of masculinity deeply penetrate men's psyche in which the feminine side and soft, romantic emotions are never to be explored, understood and displayed. Not surprising then that the first gay parade to be held in the Croatian capital Zagreb, in 2002, required tight police security as some 200 people were subjected to jeering and heckling from bystanders and at least 15 persons supporting the event were beaten up after it (BBC News, 29 June 2002).

The patriarchal values quickly, visibly and abhorrently surfaced at the time of growing nationalism in the late 1980s as right-wing, sexist and racist ideas were established as a legitimate part of 'democracy' – a form of democracy characterized by the presumption of male supremacy and the absence of women's voices in public political spaces (Slapsak, 2001). The patriarchal censorship of women, and nervous reactions to women's voices, grew with nationalism. This attitude became uncontrolled, random and rabid, and only became worse with the state of war and the very real endangering of men at war. The clearest example of this mentality is certainly the case of the five Croatian women writers and journalists (Slavenka Drakulic, Rada Ivekovic, Jelena Louric, Vesna Kesic and Dubravka Ugresic) who were publicly accused of being 'witches' and of 'raping' Croatia. Three of the five had to leave Croatia, and now live abroad. Their main 'crime' was that they were less patriotic than expected, and resisted the nationalistic manipulation of the rape issue, insisting that women who were raped be seen first as women, not primarily as Muslim, Croatian or Serb (Slapsak, 2001). The new political elite built on patriarchal values of aggressive nationalism and machismo put a priority on the nation first, which reduced women to producers of 'the nation'. The discourse of 'dying nation fear' of a small nation with low birth rates was reinforced by legislative changes. For example, the first government of independent Croatia under the presidency of Franjo Tudjman introduced the policy of paying rewards to Croatian mothers who gave birth to more than two *Croatian* children (emphasis added as the policy was only aimed at ethnic Croatian mothers) (Novi List, 29 June 1997). The patriarchic women cheerfully supported the patriotic movement to the extent that some public, political figures stated their pride of 'not giving birth to children but to little Croats' (Stipic, 1997).

Patriotism was the key reference used by the new political elite, producing historical myth of origin which served to provide the sense of continuity of a nation, whereas in social terms, the new bourgeois lifestyle, a complete opposition of communist ideas of social equality, referred back to Austro-Hungarian heritage (Pisac, 2004). My own 'destiny' of being married to a Bosnian Serb attests to those difficult times when my family and friends treated me as a betrayer of the nation, albeit pitifully seen to be an 'innocent and brainwashed' victim of a Serbian husband. Although it was commonly expected of women to take their husbands' surname, I was seen to have unfortunately 'lost' mine (Croatian) to a Serbian surname. Interestingly, this nationalistic attitude only appeared when the war started. We were married in Sarajevo at the time when Yugoslavia still existed and all our Croat, Serb and Muslim friends happily danced at the wedding. However, in the nightmare of warfare between Croats and Serbs, as a 'mixed' married couple losing the 'neutral' Yugoslav grounds, we suddenly faced the crisis of national and ethnic identity. Although we ran successful businesses together (restaurant, café and model agency), it was primarily seen as a Serbian business on Croatian soil, and as such it was under the constant threat of abuse by Croatian nationalists. The Croatian female co-owner and wife did not count as long as she stayed married to a Serb. I had to submerge my own national origins that could not be passed on to our child. The social norm had it that the child takes the ethnicity of the father, even though it would make my daughter's life extremely difficult if we stayed in Croatia. The patriarchal values married with nationalism deeply penetrated my personal life and I became caught between my nation and my husband. It was 1992 when we lost our business to my husband's friend whom he invited to come from Bosnia in order to give a 'Croatian face' to the business. But he rather took it over, without compensation, which was easy at the time when the law was not really on the side of the Serbs living in Croatia. That was also not a time when you could always count on old friends from the socialist past of Yugoslavia. It was time to leave the country and we did.

Final Reflections

This chapter has aimed to articulate a number of key arguments. First, we described the general value of embodied approaches to the reality of gendered tourism experiences that reveal the complexity of gender, cultural, ethnic, racial and ideological differences of every society. Second, we pointed to the lack of embodiment studies in the area of the Balkans and generally within the CEE and SEE regions, whereby the historical narratives of the past communist era are poorly documented. Third, in aiming to fill this gap our personal accounts revealed the cultural complexities and extreme variations of experiencing tourism in the context of socialism within the SEE region. Two key differences emerged.

First, Derek's narrative has shown that the authoritarian nature of the Albanian Stalinist state managed to suppress, within egalitarian ideals, much of the inherent machismo of this part of the Balkans, while Irena's narrative of the Croatian experience proved the contrary. The 'loose' ideological structure of decentralized socialism in former Yugoslavia combined with the complex colonial history of Croatian nationalism reproduced an inherent machismo and deeply embedded patriarchy. In the context of tourism as the main economic and social agent, one of the most persistent characteristics of the cultural environment in Croatia remains gender performance of macho identity based on excessive expressions of heterosexuality and aggressive nationalist anti-Serb feelings.

Second, Derek's account illustrated some of the constraints and subtleties of embodied relations within the context of regulating Albanians in their contact with the foreign world. The complexity of ethnic, ideological and gender tensions of relations with foreign visitors were revealed through specific embodied expressions of the relationship between tourism 'officials' and visitors. On the other hand, Croatia with the open political regime of former Yugoslavia enabled locals to fully 'embrace' their foreign visitors in terms of business, consumption and sexual gratification. The ideological structure of communism did not principally disturb the traditional values and performances, but rather it has deepened the historical tensions of complex intersection of gender and ethnic differences.

References

Aitchison, C.C. (2001) Theorising other discourses of tourism, gender and culture: can the subaltern speak (in tourism)? *Tourist Studies* 1(2), 133–147.

Aitchison, C.C. (2003) *Gender and Leisure: Social and Cultural Perspectives*. Routledge, London.

Albanese, P. (2001) Nationalism, war, and archaization of gender relations in the Balkans. *Violence against Woman* 7(9), 999–1023.

Ateljevic, I. and Doorne, S. (2003) Culture, economy and tourism commodities: social relations of production and consumption. *Tourist Studies* 3(2), 123–141.

Ateljevic, I. and Čorak, S. (2006) Croatia in the new Europe: culture versus conformity. In: Hall, D., Marciszewska, B. and Smith, M. (eds) *Tourism in the New Europe: The Challenges and Opportunities of EU Enlargement*. CAB International, Wallingford, UK, pp. 288–301.

Ateljevic, I., Harris, C., Wilson, E. and Collins, F. (2005) Getting 'entangled': reflexivity and the 'critical turn' in tourism studies. *Tourism Recreation Research* 30(2), 9–21.

Ateljevic, I., Pritchard, A. and Morgan, N. (2007) *The Critical Turn in Tourism: Innovative Methodologies*. Elsevier, Oxford.

BBC News (2002) Croatian gays join first 'pride' march. BBC News, 29 June 2002.

Bedford, E. (1969) Turkish field studies. *South Hampshire Geographer* 2, 44–48.

Brusic, Z. (2004) Milenijski zivot u Tarcu i na Toreti. In: Majnaris, M. (ed.) *Kornati: Biseri Jadrana*. Copygraf, Zagreb, Croatia.

Carpenter, R.C. (2005) 'Women, children and other vulnerable groups': gender, strategic frames and the protection of civilians as a transnational issue. *International Studies Quarterly* 49(2), 295–334.

Coleman, M. and Crang, M. (eds) (2002) *Tourism: Between Place and Performance*. Berghahn, Oxford.

Collins, V.R. (2004) *Working in Tourism: The UK, Europe & Beyond. For Seasonal and Permanent Staff*, 3rd edn. Vacation Work, Oxford.

Crouch, D. (1999) Introduction: encounters in leisure/tourism. In: Crouch, D. (ed.) *Leisure/Tourism Geographies: Practices and Geographical Knowledge*. Routledge, London.

Crouch, D. (2001) Spatialities and the feeling of doing. *Social and Cultural Geography* 2(1), 61–75.

Crouch, D., Aronsson, L. and Wahlstrom, L. (2001) Tourist encounters. *Tourist Studies* 1(3), 253–270.

Devedzic, M. (2002) Ethnic heterogeneity and gender in the Yugoslav seaside tourist region. In: Swain, M.B. and Momsen, J.H. (eds) *Gender/Tourism/Fun(?)*. Cognizant Communication Corporation, New York, pp. 143–153.

Drakulic, S. (1993) *How We Survived Communism and Even Laughed*. Harper Perennial, London.

Drakulic, S. (1996) *Café Europa: Life after Communism*. Penguin Books, New York.

Franklin, A. and Crang, M. (2001) The trouble with tourism and travel theory? *Tourist Studies* 1(1), 5–22.

Ghodsee, K. (2003) State support in the market: women and tourism employment in post-socialist Bulgaria. *International Journal of Politics, Culture and Society* 16(3), 465–482.

Gray, A. (2003) Research practice for cultural studies: ethnographic methods and lived cultures. Sage, London.

Grosz, E. (1994) *Volatile Bodies: Toward a Corporeal Feminism*. Allen & Unwin, Australia.

Guerrier, Y. and Adib, A. (2004) Gendered identities in the work of overseas tour reps. *Gender, Work and Organization* 11(3), 334–350.

Hall, D. (1975) Some developmental aspects of Albania's fifth five-year plan, 1971–5. *Geography* 60(2), 129–132.

Hall, D. (1984) Foreign tourism under socialism: the Albanian 'Stalinist' model. *Annals of Tourism Research* 11(4), 539–555.

Hall, D. (1990) Stalinism and tourism: a study of Albania and North Korea. *Annals of Tourism Research* 17(1), 36–54.

Hall, D. (1994) *Albania and the Albanians*. Frances Pinter, London.

Hall, D. (2001) From the 'iron curtain' to the 'dollar curtain': women and tourism in Eastern Europe. In: Apostolopoulos, Y., Sönmez, S. and Timothy, D.J. (eds) *Women as Producers and Consumers of Tourism*

in Developing Regions. Praeger, Westport, Connecticut, pp. 191–207.

Hall, D. (2002) Branding and national identity: the case of Central and Eastern Europe. In: Morgan, N., Pritchard, A. and Pride, R. (eds) *Destination Branding: Creating the Unique Destination Proposition*. Butterworth-Heinemann, Oxford, pp. 87–105.

Hall, D. (2003) Rejuvenation, diversification and imagery: sustainability conflicts for tourism policy in the Eastern Adriatic. *Journal of Sustainable Tourism* 11(2/3), 280–294.

Hall, D. (2004) Key themes and frameworks. In: Hall, D.R. (ed.) *Tourism and Transition: Governance, Transformation and Development*. CAB International, Wallingford, UK, pp. 25–51.

Hall, D. and Roberts, L. (2004) Concluions and future agenda. In: Hall, D.R. (ed.) *Tourism and Transition: Governance, Transformation and Development*. CAB International, Wallingford, UK, pp. 217–226.

Hall, D., Swain, M.B. and Kinnaird, V. (2003) Tourism and gender: an evolving agenda. *Tourism Recreation Research* 28(2), 7–11.

Hartl, M. (2003) *Rural Women's Access to Land and Property in Selected Countries*. Food and Agriculture Organization of the United Nations, Rome.

Hoffman, G.W. (1963) *The Balkans in Transition*. Van Nostrand, Princeton, New Jersey.

Institut za Turizam (2005) *TOMAS: Stavovi i Potrošnja Turista u Hrvatskoj*. Institut za Turizam, Zagreb, Croatia.

Kasimis, C., Papadopoulos, A.G. and Zacopoulou, E. (2003) Migrants in rural Greece. *Sociologia Ruralis* 43(2), 167–184.

Kinnaird, V.H. and Hall, D.R. (eds) (1994) *Tourism: A Gender Analysis*. Wiley, Chichester, UK.

Kinnaird, V.H. and Hall, D.R. (1996) Understanding tourism processes: a gender-aware framework. *Tourism Management* 19(2), 95–102.

Lazaridis, G. (2000) Filipino and Albanian women migrant workers in Greece: multiple layers of oppression. In: Anthias, F. and Lazaridis, G. (eds) *Gender and Migration in Southern Europe*. Berg, Oxford, pp. 49–79.

McLafferty, S. (1995) Counting for women. *Professional Geographer* 47, 436–442.

Nast, H.J. (1994) Opening remarks on 'Women in the Field'. *Professional Geographer* 46, 54–66.

Nicholson, B. (2004) The tractor, the shop and the filling station: work migration as self-help development in Albania. *Europe–Asia Studies* 56(6), 877–890.

Novi List (1997) *Vladine Mjere za Odumirucu Hrvatsku Populaciju*. Novi List, 29 June 1997.

Overbeek, G. (2003) The income and property of women in the agriculture and tourism sectors. *International Journal of Agricultural Resources, Governance and Ecology* 2(2), 125–139.

Phillimore, J. and Goodson, L. (2004) *Qualitative Research in Tourism*. Routledge, London.

Pisac, A. (2004) Reading criminal tribunals: ICTY and the role of intellectual as interpreter of the national culture – The Drakulic Paradigm. Conference paper presented at the international conference: *Historijski mitovi u zemljama nasljednicama Jugoslavije*, Dubrovnik, 16–18 September 2004. Inter University Center, Dubrovnik, Croatia.

Pizam, A. and Jeong, G.-H. (1996) Cross-cultural tourist behavior: perceptions of Korean tour-guides. *Tourism Management* 17(4), 277–286.

Pizam, A. and Sussmann, S. (1995) Does nationality affect tourist behavior? *Annals of Tourism Research* 22(4), 901–917.

Scott, J. (1995) Sexual and national boundaries in tourism. *Annals of Tourism Research* 22(2), 385–403.

Scott, J. (1997) Chances and choices: women and tourism in northern Cyprus. In: Sinclair, M.T. (ed.) *Gender, Work and Tourism*. Routledge, London, pp. 60–90.

Scott, J.E. (2003) Coffee shop meets casino: cultural responses to casino tourism in northern Cyprus. *Journal of Sustainable Tourism* 11(2–3), 266–279.

Slapsak, S. (2001) Censorship in Yugoslavia, a personal story. In: Azhgikhina, N. and Tax, M. (eds) *The Power of The World II: Women's Voices and the New European Order*. A Women's WORLD pamphlet. Available at: http://www.wworld.org/publications/powerword2.htm

Statisticki Ured Hrvatske (2003) *Populacija Hrvatske*. Statisticki Ured Hrvatske, Zagreb, Croatia.

Stipic, M. (1997) Ponosna sam majka Hrvatica. *Globus*, 29 September 1997.

Swain, M. (2004) (Dis)embodied experience and power dynamics in tourism research. In: Phillimore, J. and Goodson, L. (eds) *Qualitative Research in Tourism*. Routledge, London, pp. 102–118.

Swain, M.B. (ed.) (1995) Gender in tourism. *Annals of Tourism Research* 22(2).

Swain, M.B. and Momsen, J.H. (eds) (2002) *Gender/Tourism/Fun(?)*. Cognizant Communication Corporation, New York.

Tribe, J. (2005) New tourism research. *Tourism Recreation Research* 30(2), 5–8.

Veijola, S. and Jokinen, E. (1994) The body in tourism. *Theory, Culture and Society* 11, 125–151.

Vukonic (2005) *Povijest Hrvatskog Turizma*. Prometej, Zagreb, Croatia.

Wearing, B. (1996) *Gender: The Pain and Pleasures of Difference*. Longman, Melbourne.

Weiner, E. (1997) Assessing the implications of political and economic reform in the post-socialist era: the case of Czech and Slovak women. *East European Quarterly* 31(3), 473–502.

Weyr, T. (1992) Women's economic hardship in Albania. *Albanian Life* 2, 24.

10 Encountering Scopophilia, Sensuality and Desire: Engendering Tahiti

ANNETTE PRITCHARD AND NIGEL MORGAN

Introduction

For many of us in the West our image of the South Pacific is of islands set in shimmering blue seas with endless white sandy beaches fringed by palm trees. If we probe a little deeper, we may think of thatch-roof bungalows, teeming natural abundance and even seductive, barefoot women in clinging *pareus* gazing out to sea. As Hall (1998) points out in his essay *Making the Pacific*, it does not take long to elicit such highly gendered images of these distant 'paradise' islands. Such clichéd associations are firmly rooted in the Western cultural imaginary and have long been nurtured by a host of explorers, travellers, writers, artists and more latterly by photographers and film makers. Indeed, nowhere is travel's intimate connection with scopophilia, sensuality and desire more apparent than in the West's making of Tahiti as a latter-day Eden. And this remains a remarkably durable imagery, preserved and promulgated by the 21st-century successors to the early European storytellers (the explorers, sailors and colonists) – today's travel writers and photographers. Thus, whilst in this chapter we once again traverse the relationships between landscape, representation, tourism and gender, this time we turn our attention to the South Pacific.

Whilst the main focus of the chapter is the engendering of Tahiti, we also aim to explore travel magazines as products of cultural discourses and inscriptions. Basing our discussion around an in-depth textual analysis of Tahiti features in *Condé Nast Traveller*, we argue that such travel and fashion features are discursive domains which set parameters around the presentation of particular social and cultural bodies. Thus, the chapter's contribution is twofold. First, it seeks to build on our earlier work on gendered landscapes (Morgan and Pritchard, 1998; Pritchard and Morgan, 2000a,b) by premising that the travel and fashion features of such lifestyle travel magazines (themselves powerful agents of cultural pedagogy) form another element in the circle of representation (Hall, 1997) and confirm the patriarchal, imperialist discourses embedded in masculine conceptions of adventure, conquest, pleasure and the exotic which have long framed representation of the South Pacific. We suggest that, just like other cultural forms (cinema, literature, tourism promotion, etc.) these lifestyle magazine features depict both women and landscape in racialized and sexualized terms, confirming 'that women and land are somehow analogous to each other' (Lewes, 2000, p. 3). Second, through our discussion of the magazine's fashion features we foreground and illustrate the intimate connections between tourism, the body and dress, connections which remain stubbornly marginal to tourism enquiry. However, we begin the chapter by briefly reviewing the relationship between the circle of representation and tourism, before rehearsing discourses in tourism which have emphasized the interplay between tourism, space, representation and social structures, experiences and identities.

Places of Desire, Bodies of Enchantment

In this chapter we will see how Tahiti has been constructed as an 'anthropological place' (Augé, 1995), rich in layers of human meaning built up through situated processes of historical memory and identity. For over two centuries a fertile European and Euro-American cultural imagery has fed upon and produced a variety of manifestations of Tahiti by non-Tahitians: explorers' accounts and sailors' stories, missionaries' tales, artists' paintings, anthropologists' descriptions, novels, plays, films, television series and even fashion designers have all played their part in crafting the discourses of primitivism and eroticism which frame contemporary representations of the islands. We will demonstrate, as we have elsewhere, how such representations of bodies and landscapes are grounded in wider gendered power relationships, so that both women and nature are burdened with men's meaning and interpreted through masculinist discourse and colonial narratives. At the same time, we will also show how racism draws on gender as a means of oppression, forming part of the 'wider discursive network' (Anderson, 1996) which has (re)made Tahiti an island of 'soft primitivism'. As a result, we intend to demonstrate that the ways in which landscapes and destinations are imaged reveals the power geometries of the international cultural industries and has significant implications for how those places and their peoples are perceived globally.

We believe that contemporary gendered and sexualized tourism landscapes can be seen as an extension of the deep-rooted Western view of space in which gender, sexuality and race are entwined – a view found throughout the history of colonialism and travel. Gender and race are both critical to this spatial construction, and representations of landscapes are grounded in the power relationships which characterize societies. Thus, despite the 'siren-like power' (Wernick, 1991, pp. 55–57) of the exoticized and eroticized feminine landscape, it is ultimately mastered by the masculine gaze of colonialists, geographers and traveller-explorers. Such construction of landscapes (particularly faraway landscapes) as feminine reveals a discourse in which 'masculinity, militarism, imperialism and science all come explicitly together in a fantasy of fieldwork in foreign lands' (Sparke, 1996, p. 215). This conceptualization of places and spaces as political and contested sociocultural constructions came late to tourism studies although it has now gained considerable ground. Key scholars who placed concepts of space and place at the centre of social, economic and political thought in the 20th century argued some time ago that there are no neutral or innocent spaces (see Hubbard *et al.*, 2004). In the early 1970s David Harvey was among the first geographers to suggest that social practices and processes create spaces, and that these spaces in turn constrain, enable and restructure those practices and processes (Castree, 2004) in what Soja (1989, p. 78) termed a 'socio-spatial dialectic'. As a result of such scholarship, the more widespread understanding of space today is that it is both a product and a medium, 'something that is brought into being according to how it is used, surveyed and invested with symbolic significance' (Cohen, 2002, p. 262), a mutable and culturally constructed mixture of representation and physical form. Spaces mean different things to different people at different times and represent, reinforce, idealize and naturalize sociocultural power relations. Such readings of spaces as cultural productions have been applied to a range of tourism landscapes (Ringer, 1998; Crouch, 1999; Morgan, 2004; Terkenli, 2004), many of which have been conceptualized as liminal places where dominant discourses and wider hegemonic sociocultural relations are resisted, contested or affirmed.

Of course, cultural and spatial production cannot exist in isolation and is inexorably intertwined in a continuous circle whereby language utilizes representations to construct meanings and discourses. This is known as the circuit of culture or the circle of representation (see Hall, 1997), a concept which is established across a range of research fields, and although it is presented in slightly different terms in each, the fundamental premise is that certain visual images circulate within a culture and become imbued with particular meanings, associations and values. This conceptualization recognizes that language, representation and meaning are ceaselessly connected in a continuous circle so that a set of discourses or frameworks embracing particular combinations of narratives, concepts and ideologies become so powerful that – reinforced over time by a variety of cultural forms – the images generated of different gazes come to constitute a closed self-perpetuating system of illusion or 'way of seeing' particular peoples and places. This can be seen in operation across a range of cultural forms and discourses, so that, for example, today's iconic images of Venice reproduced in postcards, tourism brochures and tourist photographs can be traced to the influence of Venetian artwork of the 17th century (Staiff, 1999), whilst – as we will see below – the 19th-century artwork of Gauguin continues to frame today's touristic representations of French Polynesia.

According to Hall (1997, p. 3), who wrote that culture 'is about "shared meanings", which may be produced at several sites and circulated through several different processes or practices', we can see tourism representation as a 'key moment' in the circuit of tourism discourse (see Morgan and Pritchard, 1998). In this circuit, different forms of media operate as agents of cultural pedagogy and scholars (e.g. Butler, 1990; Riley *et al.*, 1998; Busby and Klug, 2001) have discussed how news broadcasts, popular films and television shows act as shapers of international travel patterns, but the notion that lifestyle magazines and their travel writings and fashion features also form an element in the touristic circle of representation has not received such detailed attention. Yet, the framing of travel and fashion photography is often based on previous representations of the places where the shoots take place: in other words, travel and fashion shoots are texts about previous texts of place, just as are travellers' texts (Barnes and Duncan, 1992). If tourists select for their personal photographs images already seen in art, travel brochures, postcards, films and television shows, creating a 'hermeneutic circle' where they recapture images of landscapes and iconic buildings they are already familiar with (see Staiff, 1999; Urry, 2002; Jenkins, 2003), so too do fashion and travel photographers. Indeed the fashion industry as a whole has been described as 'a visual and remarkably compressed expression of various streams of modern culture . . . [including] politics, wars . . . major cultural events . . . arts, movies, theatre and literature' (Gronow, 1997, pp. 105–106).

As we said in our introduction, our second goal in this chapter is to further our explorations of the relationship between the fashion body and representations of tourism places (see Pritchard and Morgan, 2005, 2007). Fundamental to this discussion, of course, is the recognition that 'the body' as a sociological concept is a much more complex entity than the biological form that defines the human person and that social and cultural theorists (see Turner, 1984; Shilling, 1993) no longer regard the body as a simple material reality, but as an intricately constructed set of social discourses. Yet, although travel has intimate connections with desire, dress and sensuality, the overwhelming emphasis on 'the gaze' has underserved the embodied politics of travel and sexuality (Veijola and Jokinen, 1994). Discourses of sexuality and sensuality frequently frame the marketing of contemporary destinations, hotels and tourist resorts, sometimes in exoticized and occasionally eroticized language (Pritchard and Morgan, 2006). Moreover, arguably sex has always been part of tourism and the ritual conventions of the beach (that pre-eminent tourism site) and the bodies on display there also interpellate a sexualized subjectivity (Desmond, 1999; Abramovici, Chapter 7, this volume), whilst the media and cultural forces of globalization generate a wealth of material suggesting that sensual pleasures and the fulfilment of bodily desires are part of the tourism experience (Wang, 2000). Yet, despite this and the continued focus of Western culture on the body which has given corporeality a privileged symbolic position in discourse (Curry, 1993; Fisher, 2002), it is fair to say that too few tourism studies have focused on the body per se and that bodies have been taken for granted in tourism enquiry (some notable exceptions include Veijola and Jokinen, 1994; Jokinen and Veijola, 1997; Johnston, 2001).

However, if tourism studies have at least *begun* to address issues of embodiment (and the present volume is evidence of this), tourism researchers have largely failed to acknowledge body matters such as dress and fashion. Indeed, this echoes wider social science enquiry where it seems as though theories of the body overlook dress and theories of fashion and dress leave out the body (Turner, 1984). The study of fashion and dress has been doubly disadvantaged since not only has the long academic silence over the body marginalized the study of dress and clothing, but both these areas have in turn also been dismissed by 'serious' research fields as a frivolous feminine indulgence (Neissen and Brydon, 1998). Jukka Gronow (1997, p. 74) agrees with this assessment, noting that there is very little mention of fashion in the theories of post-industrial society and that it 'seems to have been too ephemeral and frivolous a social phenomenon to have been taken seriously'. As a result, fashion and dress remain underexplored within sociological and cultural studies, so that 'the *dressed body* as a discursive and phenomenological field vanishes and dress is disembodied' (Entwistle, 2002, p. 136). Despite this intellectual marginalization, fashion can be described as 'nothing more and nothing less than the systematic encryption, transmission, and interpretation of social meaning' (Solomon, 1985, p. xi). Certainly, dress (with its close proximity to the body) carries enormous social, cultural and political meaning and (un)dress has intimate connections with travel, sensuality and desire, closely bound up with broader social and historical concerns about the regulation of bodies in social spaces. Dress offers opportunities for social distinction and identification (Simmel, 1981) and for self-expression (Wilson, 1985); it is both a private and a social experience and 'any understanding of the dressed body must acknowledge the social nature of it – how it is shaped by techniques, attitudes, aesthetics . . . which are socially and historically located' (Entwistle, 2002, p. 134). To this significance must be added the notion that bodily fashion gives a symbolic rendering of the cultural categories it distinguishes; thus, fashion also has racial readings. Indeed, the very term fashion 'is rarely used in reference to non-Western cultures. The two are defined in opposition . . . Western dress is fashion . . . non-Western dress is costume because it is unchanging, encodes deep meanings and projects group identity and membership' (Craik, 1994, p. 18) – an issue we will return to below.

As we will see in our readings of the fashion and travel features on Tahiti in the following pages, the fashion industry (whilst often seen to challenge convention) also confirms cultural and social norms, and fashion photography is a practice which takes place within a closed universe where everything is a sign of something else or a text of a text – just like travel photography. Whilst in the fashion industry, somehow, 'in an almost mysterious way, a collective taste . . . is distilled out of a myriad of individual tastes' (Gronow, 1997, p. 110), there are clearly identifiable influences on design and we can explore the discursive formations which give meaning to (what first seem superficial and transient) fashion–travel iconographies. At the same time, the fashion industry as a whole is subject to an intensely select-ive process in terms of the influences of designers, fashion houses and buyers, and crucially, the designers themselves are influenced by the past and the 'exotic', with travel and tourism being important sources of designer inspiration (Gronow, 1997). The fashion image is therefore created, filtered and mediated through cultural and ideological structures and this 'Western-led' creative process clearly has significant implications for 'the kinds of gender, "racial" and ethnic identities or scripts that are sanctioned within these creative industries' (Nixon, 1997, p. 211).

Thus, the fashion and travel photographers (who are often the same individ-uals), stylists, travel writers and editors who contribute to travel magazines each play a role in constructing the individual features through a number of creative and technical choices – and, of course, creative choices are selective choices. First, the photographers and stylists could have chosen a range of landscapes and backdrops – but they selected the ones they did. In the case of fashion shoots, the stylist could have chosen any model (e.g. black or white), decided to combine any number of accessories with the clothes to be shown, chosen differing styles of make-up and hair for the models, or selected different or indeed no jewellery for them to wear. Whether it is a fashion or a travel feature, the photographer had to decide how to photograph each particular scene in terms of its composition and each creative, compositional choice affected the form of the final photograph. Then there were technical choices – how sharp did they want the focus to be – with 'scientific' precision or with a 'softer' effect, how much shade, shadow and highlights did they require, and then, at the printing stage, how did they decide to frame, crop, enlarge, lighten or darken the prints? Finally, the whole process was subject to the editorial decisions of the travel and fashion editors – some photographs were selected and some omitted whilst the layouts and page constructions are also the products of a number of choices: the page designers could have selected and combined any number of other photographs, but they selected the ones they did. 'The eventual photograph, then, is the result of creative choices that began at the very setting up of the tripod' (Howells, 2003, p. 161), but as we will argue below, in such features, these choices tend to confirm rather than to challenge the dominant metropolitan ways of seeing places and their peoples.

Yet, to unpick just how the travel and fashion features of such lifestyle magazines confirm or challenge the patriarchal and imperialist discourses which have long framed representation of the South Pacific, 'it is necessary to do something that style implicitly abhors: we must penetrate the surface of the image and place it within the social and historical setting of its development' (Ewen, 1991, p. 44). As any cultural artefact, texts are representations of ethnographic knowledge, sites of cultural production and the output of both social interaction and individual experience (see Jaworski and Pritchard, 2005). Travel writings and travel and fashion photography are dynamic, context-sensitive narratives, which are a discursive expression of the popular culture of the time. Just like any cultural artefact, however, these magazines are not merely a medium for the 'neutral' retention of images, and are more than ephemera, temporarily viewed and just as quickly disposed of. Travel and fashion photographs are narratives and ways of looking, a filter between the photographer's subject and the world: neither factual records nor innocent of value but legitimizers and arbiters of certain interpretations at the expense of others. Likewise, anyone who uses a camera (or writes travel journalism) is engaging with some theory of representation, and travel photographers 'respond to and refer to known visual forms, styles, discourses and meanings through the content and form of their visual images' (Pink, 2001, p. 27). Thus, as Pink (2001, p. 27) continues, in creating images which reproduce or reference 'conventional compositions and iconographies individuals draw from personal and cultural resources of visual experience and knowledge'. In this, there is no value-free position from which to see or to view – from the moment that they are framed, travel and fashion photographs define space and location and map position and situation, immediately suggesting social and spatial hierarchies and homologies.

Locating Tahiti in the Western Imagination

Tahiti is physically located in the centre of the Pacific Ocean in subtropical French Polynesia – it is the largest and most populated of the five archipelagos (consisting of 118 islands and atolls) which remain French territory in today's largely postcolonial world (see Henningham, 1992; Hall and Page, 1996; Hall, 1997; d'Hauteserre, 2005). Yet, such is the power which Tahiti exerts in the Western imaginary that it has come to stand for the whole of this Pacific territory and its very name overshadows its reality; indeed Tahiti Tourism's web site proclaims that

'Tahiti is the world's definition of paradise' (available at: www.tahiti-tourisme.com.
au). Thomas (1994) has argued that all instances of colonialism are unique although
they may share common characteristics and, in the case of French Polynesia, it
shares a key trope – which construes it as a Garden of Eden – which has been very
influential in historical and contemporary representations of the South Pacific. This
European-derived cultural imaginary of Tahiti as an Edenic paradise populated
by a childlike, libidinous, free and natural people dates to the very first encounters
between European voyagers and the islanders in the 18th century (Smith, 1984; see
also Kahn, 2003; d'Hauteserre, 2005). But, whilst the South Seas' emplacement in
the Western mind with Eden was established in the European voyages of the 18th
and 19th centuries, it was its reinforcement by writers such as Stevenson and artists
such as Gauguin that cemented its place in the Western imaginary. These associations can be traced to earlier painters such as William Hodges, who sailed with
Cook and whose painting *Tahiti Revisited* (1776) visualizes the island as a sensuous
paradise of noble and erotic savagery (Osborne, 2000). Such constructions of the
South Pacific islands are clearly imaginings of Eden which can themselves be found
in a range of biblical, Islamic and ancient mythologies, Renaissance explorations
and 18th-century fantasies of neoclassical Arcadia. In this romanticized ethnology
the dominant images quickly became those of palm-fringed islands set in dazzling
blue seas, bursting with flower-decked trees filled with bright birds and populated
by indigenous women and children who conveyed innocence and closeness to
nature through their associations with flowers, grass and palms. In fact, the perfect
metaphor for such tropical paradises became the palm tree itself; it soon came to
stand for 'the South' and, as such, is typically depicted not upright 'but lounging
across the frame, often heavy with fruit – as though swooning, yielding, "falling
back" across the path of the viewer; a feminised entity proposing a languorous
eroticism' (Osborne, 2000, p. 107).

The first European to encounter Tahiti was the explorer Louis-Antoine
Bougainville who anchored off its northern shore in 1768 and named the island
Nouvelle Cythère (New Cytheria) after the legendary birthplace of Aphrodite,
the Goddess of Love. Thus began the long history of aestheticizing Tahiti which
has proved such a remarkably durable imaginary. Indeed, the Edenic myth
remains intact today, despite the establishment of a French nuclear test site on
two of its uninhabited atolls and the building of an international airport there
in the early 1960s. Even the arrival of mass tourism and a shift to urbanization
which have resulted in landscape degradation and unemployment have hardly
dented our view of this paradise island. Whilst these changes mean that the
island looks less and less like the Gauguin-inspired myth that created its tourism
industry in the first place (now the island's major source of income), the fabled
island that is Tahiti, nurtured by writers, artists and Hollywood film crews,
remains as alluring as ever. In fact, Osborne (2000, p. 109) has adroitly commented that Gauguin's visual descendents – the tourism promoters and postcard
photographers – portray it either as an island forever preserved in a moment
prior to 'first contact' or as one already conquered 'yet somehow approached
eternally for the first time. . . . Tahiti . . . is never quite arrived at. It has become
a sign of something elsewhere and of something other than itself. Here paradise
is always the *prospect* of paradise.'

Following in the wakes of the 18th-century explorers were the missionaries and the colonists and in 1838 the islands became a French Protectorate, becoming in 1880 the French colony it remains today, albeit with greater autonomy since 1996. During the 18th century French Polynesia became part of the imperial colonial project (of which Gauguin himself was a key agent) and the islands and its people were constructed in the European imagination in ways which legitimized and valorized French colonial activity and nationalist self-promotion. The first appearance of these 'colonial subjects' as objects of spectacle occurred at the 1889 Exposition Universalle in Paris when people from the French colonies, including the Pacific, were brought to Paris and asked to re-enact their local customs in specially fabricated villages so that European visitors could 'experience' their world (Beckenbridge, 1989). In order to maintain the colonial project, however, it was necessary for the French to engender a sense of desire for the colony, and postcard and postage stamp images of luscious peaks and valleys and exotic Polynesian women served this purpose. At the same time, amongst 19th-century social scientists, Polynesia came to symbolize an older, idyllic stage of civilization through which Europeans had already passed: a trope which characterized its people as 'Noble Savages', simple and purer – a people before 'The Fall'. In this sociocultural (re)construction of place the feminization of the islands cannot go unnoticed; its women were seen as openly sexual, unnamed presences of difference, bodies within a space of exotic flora and fauna who came to embody availability and echoed the old stories of Polynesian women who supposedly offered themselves freely to the first European mariners. The islands themselves came to be symbolized by an innocent or sexualized femininity, becoming erotopias which were defined in relation to the West – a contrast of feminine, leisure, nature and adornment to masculine, labour, culture and fashion.

Such South Sea island clichés can be seen across a range of Western literary, musical and cinematic discourses, from H. de Vere Stacpoole's novel *The Blue Lagoon* (1908) to those of James M. Michener (which inspired the musical *South Pacific*). On screen they are most obviously typified in the various versions of *Mutiny on the Bounty*, notably those of 1935 (starring Charles Laughton), 1962 (starring Marlon Brando) and 1984 (starring Mel Gibson), whilst the 1980 film *Blue Lagoon* (starring Brooke Shields) and the UK television commercials for Bounty Bars (a coconut chocolate confectionary) are more overt examples of the elemental, untutored and hence eminently 'natural' eroticization of 'paradise'. In all of these discourses, the island women are constantly associated with a timeless realm of nature. Yet contradictorily, at the same time that woman is represented as natural, her very proximity to instinct and animality makes her the ultimate embodiment of untrammelled, unartified sexuality, a sexual force famously veiled in idealization in the work of Gauguin, whose aestheticization of her erotic charms has forever framed perceptions of the Tahitian woman. Thus, in visual representations of Tahiti we can see how discourses of primitivism and femininity combine so that the innocence associated with the Edenic trope prohibits a knowing, aggressive sexual allure. As Desmond (1999, p. 12) argues, women in the South Pacific are associated more with sensuous heterosexual romance than with sex per se and their image 'evokes the feminised lushness of the tropics: accessible, hospitable, beautiful, exotic and natural'.

In fact, Desmond's work on Hawaiian body materiality – which she suggests provides a 'non-threatening, alluring encounter with paradisical exoticism, a "soft primitivism"' (1999, p. 4) – is particularly relevant here. She draws on the Hawaiian scholar and activist Haunani-Kay Trask who has linked these imperialist visions of soft primitivism with gender, arguing that Hawai'i – the word, the vision, the sound in the mind – has become the fragrance and feel of soft kindness. 'Above all Hawai'i is "she", the Western image of the Native "female" in her magical allure. And if luck prevails, some of "her" will rub off on you' (Haunani-Kay Trask, quoted in Desmond, 1999, p. 11). Smith (1984) first used the term 'soft primitivism' to refer to the imagining of the Pacific as a lost Eden, connoting such attributes as childlike, libidinous, free and natural. Such images have their roots in a gendered, racialized and aestheticized 19th-century Caucasian imagery directly linking body, race and culture. When combined with ideologies of colonialism these produce imageries that merge the feminine and the exotic in colonial pleasure zones – as Torgovnick (1990, p. 17) says: 'Sooner or later those familiar tropes for primitives become tropes conventionally used for women.' Moreover, as the chapter will now explore, these discourses continue to exert significant power in contemporary cultural and travel spheres, as the memory of colonial consummations continues to resonate within tourism's wish fulfilments (Osborne, 2000).

Reading Tahiti in *Condé Nast Traveller*

In the preceding discussion, we saw how mythologies of Tahiti have long constructed it as an Edenic paradise – the home of 'natural' societies and of guiltless sexuality. In this section we provide an in-depth textual analysis of some of the Tahiti features in *Condé Nast Traveller*, exploring how the myths and fantasies circulating within the narratives of *both* the tourism and the fashion industries confirm and recycle the same heteropatriarchial, racial and colonial discourses, so that gendered and heavily sexualized representations of women are seen to exoticize and eroticize tourism destinations of the South Pacific. We focus on several travel features which have appeared in the magazine for this analysis (particularly Hughes, 1998; Browne, 2001; Chipperfield, 2004), together with a fashion feature *Living Colour* photographed on location at Tahiti's Le Mériden Hotel from the magazine's June 2003 issue.

Language of exploration and seduction

The language of 'truth', adventure, discovery – and above all seduction – dominates when travel writers describe Tahiti in *Condé Nast Traveller: Truth in Travel*. As is common with this writing genre of the globalized travel industry (see Jaworski and Pritchard, 2005), these writers often begin their articles by expressing a desire to eschew the usual travel clichés in a search for 'the real Tahiti' (Chipperfield, 2004, p. 189). Yet, ironically, by deploying this specific discursive device – positioning the writer as explorer/anthropologist – the travel journalists are using prototypical content and form which are conventionally recognized within this particular community of practice. Browne (2001), in searching for the 'South Specific', visits the 'remote Marquesas Islands', described by Chipperfield (2004, p. 191) as offering 'Polynesian authenticity'. The reader is told that whilst one of these islands – Nuku Hiva – 'is still wild and primitive', he or she is quickly reassured that there is no need to sacrifice Western comforts as the island has 'a smart new hotel' (Browne, 2001, p. 130). Yet, at the same time, it is clear that tourists to Nuku Hiva can derive cultural capital from visiting this – one of the more remote islands of French Polynesia. Unlike those (presumably less discerning Westerners) 'who flock' to Bora Bora:

> Travellers who . . . come to hike in the rugged interior and visit archaeological sites [on Nuku Hiva], learn something about traditional Marquesan culture and get a glimpse of how real Polynesians get along without having to fluff their grass skirts for the next fire-dance performance at a five-star resort.
>
> (Browne, 2001, p. 130)

These archaeological sites are described in some detail as places of primitive 'otherness', confirming the island as a place

> rich in pre-colonial archaeological sites such as ceremonial arenas (*meae*) where warriors were sacrificed and cannibalistic rites took place, sacred banyan trees, [and] ancient sculptures of gods in human form (*tiki*).
>
> (Browne, 2001, p. 132)

We can immediately see the extent to which the language of exploration dominates this article, constantly emphasized by the travel writer's affirmation of the physical remoteness of the destination; indeed, the sentence 'there was a satisfying sense of arrival in a strange land severed from the rest of the world' appears twice on the same page as it is also used in large red type to underline a photograph of 'Nuku Hiva's craggy landscape' (Browne, 2001, p. 130). The remoteness of the islands is reinforced by the subsequent reference to Gauguin who chose to 'end his life about as far away from "civilised" Europe as it was possible to get' (Browne, 2001, p. 130). Just how far we are from 'civilised' Europe is then further underscored by the anthropological tone of the following discussion of Marquesan culture. Browne is greeted by a 'beautiful bongo-playing transvestite' and he tells us that in 'French Polynesian culture it is accepted that some boys will be raised as girls'. Known as *mahus*, they are

> considered as *"thirdsex"*. It is thought this custom spans centuries, certainly predating any contact with Europeans. . . . *Mahus* are now a familiar sight in hotels and restaurants and are not to be confused with the more flamboyant and Westernised *raerae*, the transvestite prostitutes who hang around the bars of Papeete.
>
> (Browne, 2001, p. 132)

It seems, however, as though the anthropological tone which the writer deploys here cannot dampen his obvious enchantment with the 'exoticism' of Tahiti and its people. For him, to experience Tahiti is to experience an extravagant, otherworldly place; here he celebrates the colours of its landscapes and his own sense of adventure as a traveller in a hyper-real land:

> OH MY GOD, OH MY GOD, OH . . . MY . . . GOD! Every swoop and twist of the helicopter ride across Nuku Hiva, in the remote Marquesas Islands . . . brought

unexpected vistas: a red desert Grand Canyon, an emerald Swiss pasture; mysterious black jagged peaks bearded with twisted trees; shafts of cathedral light . . . impenetrable forests and waterfalls; . . . [to visit] Nuku Hiva is to enter the realm of unreality.

(Browne, 2001, p. 130)

Whilst Nuku Hiva is seen here as 'almost virginal' yet 'extreme . . . and challenging' (Browne, 2001, pp. 133–134) possibly overawing the Western traveller, the neighbouring Bora Bora is framed as an island of languid seduction. In a play on the song 'I'm gonna wash that man right out of my hair", from the musical *South Pacific*, Browne (2001, p. 135) writes that 'BORA BORA WILL WASH NUKU HIVA right out of your hair. . . . Mythologised and eulogised, sung about and danced about, Bora Bora is famous for being beautiful'. Given such an introduction (also later repeated in larger type as a heading for a photograph of 'Bora Bora's celebrated lagoon'), it is hard to resist this allusion to the ultimate 'it girl', because whilst Bora Bora may be perfectly formed we are warned not to 'look for depth in those baby blues or culture in her sculptured form' (Browne, 2001, p. 135). This clearly reinforces androcentric associations of (vapid) femininity with nature and echoes other travel journalists who write of 'the seductiveness of the islands', commenting that 'they are seminally beautiful, their arrangement of mountains, seas, sky, clouds, colour, climate and vegetation has defined beauty' (Hughes, 1998, p. 92). Land has become woman and woman has become land. As Browne (2001, p. 135) concludes: 'It is easy to fall for Bora Bora. A practised seductress – sailors through the ages have lost their heads at the sight of her – she is almost wholly dedicated to pleasuring tourists.' Even Tahiti's official tourist brochure equates 'the Island of Love' (Tahite Tourisme, 1996, p. 37) with a woman, telling prospective tourists that 'the Islands of Tahiti . . . have allured, inspired and enamoured a wide range of visitors . . . [since] [t]hese are islands of beauty, of love and of passion' (Tahite Tourisme, 1996, p. 3), whilst the official Tahiti web site welcomes visitors to 'Tahiti and Her Islands' (available at: www.tahiti-tourisme.com.au).

Feminist geographers and feminist scholars of the Pacific have elsewhere already argued that 'Tahitian women represent the enticing and inviting land to be explored, mapped, penetrated, and known' (Rose, 1993, p. 94). Our analysis here, however, demonstrates just how deeply these colonialist discourses have permeated the language of tourism and particularly travel magazine features – all of which consistently map the sensual topography of land and skin so that the women and the landscapes of the South Pacific become analogous. These are the paradise islands, which have 'long beguiled outsiders with [the] . . . promise of languid sensuality' (Chipperfield, 2004, p. 191). They have 'seduced the crew of the Bounty, captivated Gaughuin . . . inspired Herman Melville . . . W Somerset Maugham . . . Rupert Brooke, Jack London and James A Michener whose tales of the South Pacific spawned the Broadway musical' (Browne, 2001, p. 130). These cultural framings, together with referents such as Brando's *Mutiny on the Bounty* 'have all added to the allure of Polynesia as an Eden whose beautiful natives frolic beneath breadfruit trees, far from the constraints of the Western World' (Browne, 2001, p. 130). Here, this piece of travel writing collapses myth and reality, describing how

the myth of 'Tahiti and the Islands' as French Polynesia is now marketed is buoyed by the legendary beauty of the Polynesians themselves, in particular the *Vahine*, or island women. When the earliest European explorers reached the islands. . . . They wrote fragrant accounts of their encounters with raven-haired Tahitian women, whose favours were readily exchanged for fishing hooks. The most famous mutiny of all time, led by Fletcher Christian in 1789 from the *Bounty*, was fuelled by the men's reluctance to give up Eden and the Eves therein.

This, one of the island's most famous cultural referents, is constantly evoked in contemporary travel writing. Descriptions of the 'languidly obliging Vahine' – evidenced by the fathering of children by American GIs during the Second World War (Browne, 2001, p. 139) – are never too far away in these overwhelmingly eroticized and feminized descriptions of French Polynesia. We are repeatedly reminded of the open sexuality of the island women and how 18th-century European seafarers were

> [i]ncredulous at the bare-breasted abandon with which they were greeted, the sailors found the natives . . . welcoming beyond their hammock fantasies . . . the islanders were bemused by their visitors' . . . idea that sex should be neither communal nor public.
>
> (Hughes, 1998, p. 88)

Peter Hughes' *Atoll Story* (1998) and Bob Payne's *Beauty Beyond Measure* (1997) are both about the French Polynesian island of Moorea, and it is perhaps in these two articles that all the cultural referents discussed above can be most obviously seen to collide in highly gendered and sexualized descriptions of the South Pacific and its indigenous women. In Payne's article, readers are first introduced to the island by a full-page photograph of Moorean girls in short sarongs – their traditional dress – wearing flowers in their hair and around their necks. One of the girls has her face turned towards the camera, smiling. The accompanying text suggests that she is representative of all the women of the island who use 'antique traditions to tempt tourists'. This suggestion is confirmed in a conversation about the island's attractions between the travel journalist and an artist who moved there as a young man: 'When you are twenty-two and single and male . . . it is not the majestic beauty of the mountains . . . it is the women. It is this long hair, this velvet type of skin, this fragrance, like salted bananas' (Payne, 1997, p. 91). The intensity of this sexualized description is also underscored by the journalist's comment that this makes him wipe 'the tiniest bead of sweat from my forehead' (Payne, 1997, p. 91).

The choice of several photographs of women and young girls wearing flowers and carrying fruit to illustrate these two features also confirms the imperialist and androcentric discourses which have long eroticized the island women since they echo Gauguin's *Two Tahitian Women with Mango Blossoms* (1899) and *Tahitian Women with Flowers* (1891). Wayne Andersen (quoted in Nochlin, 1989a, p. 139) has argued:

> Gauguin used this image in Tahiti because the charm of it fitted in with his surroundings, and with his favourite myths about the Promised Land. In *Tahitian Women with Flowers*, a noble-featured Tahitian girl holds a tray of flowers beneath her bosom; the lushness of the presentation causes the breasts to appear as cornucopias from which all good things flow.

Such comparison of the desirable woman's body (specifically her breasts) with ripe fruit is one of the prime topoi of erotic imagery, as is the use of flowers as a metaphor for women's sexuality, or rather their genitals (Pollock, 1988). Thus, we can trace the fruit- or flower–breast metaphor in Tahiti's ethnology from Gauguin's paintings to today's travel photography, which continues to liken women's bodies to abundant nature. Yet, significantly for our discussion, not only are the women represented as highly desirable – epitomized once again by Paul Gauguin's paintings of 'dusky, voluptuous village girls [which] still travel the world as postcards' (Hughes, 1998, p. 88) – but Moorea itself is imaged as a beautiful young woman. 'Like the pretty girl next door, Moorea is Tahiti's enticing neighbor' (Payne, 1997, p. 91). Indeed, Tahiti, Bora Bora and Moorea are all described as 'the "It" girls amongst atolls. Like film stars, they can also be prima donnas, occasionally petulant' (Hughes, 1998, p. 88). The message is clear: Moorea and its women are there to be encountered and explored by the male travel journalist and his audience (who have to adopt a masculinist viewing position). At the close of Payne's article, the reader is left with the lasting image of this feminized destination and its exotic inhabitants, as he sees an unnamed young woman described simply as 'her' – presumably the epitome of Tahitian women – 'She was dressed in a red and white wrap-around *pareu*, sitting all by herself . . . the perfect image of paradise was locked in my head forever' (Payne, 1997, p. 91).

Visualizing desire and enchantment

As our analysis has so far made clear, there is much more to place representation in *Condé Nast Traveller* than the written word. Photography is central to this process and we will now shift our focus firmly onto the visual in order to scrutinize how issues of bodily materiality profoundly influence the structuring of gender and identity categories in today's globalized travel industry. The focus of this analysis is a fashion feature entitled 'Living Colour' which was shot entirely on location at Tahiti's Le Mériden Hotel. From its beginnings, tourism's visual culture has been a fellow-traveller of fashion and such fashion features also convey messages about particular parts of the world. Crucially, of course, these messages do not appear only in fashion, but rather as O'Barr (1994, p. 93) says: '[T]hey are part of a repeated discourse that informs our understandings of other places and people as it purports to be conveying information about products that are actually Western in manufacture. The[y] . . . borrow from our culture's ideas about others to promote these brands, but they simultaneously regenerate the very ideas about foreigners that they draw on.' At the same time, Gupta and Ferguson (1992) suggest that popular ideas of culturally and ethnically distinct places have become even more salient as their dimensions of difference have blurred in our globalized world. Since tourism works to cement and promote the notion that places have their own cultural identities and the fashion industry works to encourage cultural capital through the acquisition of fashion inspired by 'ethnic art', we could say that both industries promote the notion that the world is divided into numerous destinations, all containing their own peculiar life-worlds.

Significantly the subtitle to 'Living Colour' alerts us to the key cultural constructs of the Tahitian life-world: 'A century after the death of Gauguin the exquisite beauty of Tahiti and its people continues to exert their magic. Vibrant silk prints echo the island's exotic palette' (2003, p. 129). As this heading suggests, it is difficult to underestimate the continued influence of Gauguin on contemporary Western imaginaries of French Polynesia. Indeed, 'Living Colour' is direct testament to this – just like the frequent allusions to Gauguin in the travel writing we discussed above. The fashion feature consists of shots of five lone women, except for one photograph which shows six young boys playing together in a lagoon – itself an echo of the continuing discourse of soft primitivism which associates the French Polynesian islands with the childhood of humanity. The photographs are taken in natural settings and all the models wear dresses by major European fashion houses (available we are told from high-end stores such as Fortnum & Masons), although in two photographs they also wear sarongs of local cloth painted by local artists. The barefoot models each have hand-painted tattoos and none obviously wears make-up or nail varnish, although all are styled by two New York salons. Clearly the fashion team responsible for this shoot draws on the same cultural discourses which sees travel writers describe Tahitian women as 'dusky, voluptuous *village* girls' (Hughes, 1998, p. 88, emphasis added).

In the first photograph a model is partially reclining against a wall of woven reeds – she looks away from the camera, her face in profile and her long dark hair hanging naturally down her back. She wears a colourful silk kimono and a necklace of shells on a coconut thread – natural, locally abundant materials, yet like the dress, it is made by the European fashion house Missoni and used here as a 'prop' to signify Polynesian culture. In the second photograph (which is a double-page spread) another model is carefully posed reclining on a woven reed bed with a roll of twigs under the arm that supports her. She does not look at the camera either but gazes to one side, much as one might pose for a portrait painter. This time her voluminous, black hair is swept forward over her shoulder, softly framing her sultry, full-lipped face. She wears a locally made necklace, which (we are told) is usually worn by men – presumably it has also been appropriated here by the stylist as a signifier of Polynesian culture – and an anklet of Tahitian pearls. One strap of her dress hangs down, whilst the skirt is pulled up above the knee (exposing a hand-painted stylized Polynesian body tattoo). The whole composition exudes a languid yet unpractised sensuality: it merely hints at undress and communicates a casual, unknowing sexuality deliberately echoing Gauguin's painting *Queen of Beauty*, in which the Tahitian woman's 'confidence in her sexual powers is expressed in her languorous pose, her calm smile and sly side-long glance' (Bade, 1979, p. 19). In the third photograph the model kneels on a bed in a traditional *fare* bungalow. She gazes at the camera and once again, her long black hair loosely frames her full-lipped face, although this time she wears a more revealing silk backless spaghetti-strap minidress and a locally made necklace. In the last two photographs, two models are seen outside, one sitting on a rough wooden board with her back resting against a wall of coarsely hewn planks, the other sitting on a tree bough. As in the previous photograph, both these models gaze longingly at the camera with their sultry, full-lipped faces framed by long black hair fanned over their bare shoulders: a sense of stillness and yet expectancy seems to permeate all the compositions.

This is very clearly both a fashion shoot and a 'lesson' that instructs the reader about Tahitian women and the South Pacific; the exotically designed advertised commodity and the 'foreignness' of the models are intimately and explicitly related, echoing O'Barr's (1994) reading of a black lingerie model's connections with nature, service and African mystery. Each woman's hairstyle, jewellery and dress have been carefully orchestrated and they add up to a picture of a beautiful woman, an overlapping notion of beauty and femininity that is entwined in dress, hair, skin texture, fabric and the carefully choreographed interplay between artifice and nature. Bodies can be dressed in a variety of ways with fabric, body paint, tattoos, jewellery and make-up – and here we have all of these forms of adornment – with the hand-painted tattoos echoing those of the island women in Hodges' painting *Tahiti Revisited* (1776) and serving as metaphors for aboriginal culture. It is important to remember that artefacts (such as these tattoos, jewellery and dresses) are used by fashion stylists – just as they are by curators in ethnographic museums (Dicks, 2003) – to stand for an entire human culture, which can then be known and accessed by readers of these lifestyle magazines, through the purchase of clothing and fashion items. In this sense, dress is a socio-political, cultural and historical construction and fashion photography often confirms rather than challenges such associations.

Here, the dresses are constructive of the national communities of the Pacific and revealing as they do the lines of the women's bodies, the 'feel' of the photographs is very natural and unartified. Any fabric gives form to the human body, producing it as formal or informal, tailored or casual, and here in Tahiti we have a very casual style, emphasized by the 'natural' settings, where the dominant textures are palm fronds, reeds, stone and wood and the pre-eminent colours are natural hues. Whilst this tone works to consolidate the islands' appeal as places out of time, it is also a rural setting of innocence and the theme of contrasting rural innocence with urban sinfulness has a long history in popular imagery, especially in 19th-century art (Nochlin, 1989b). It seems, then, that the overwhelming message in any reading of this fashion shoot is that Tahiti is an island of natural abundance and its women are equally 'natural' and unpractised. Theirs is an innocent, barefoot sexuality – one which requires no obviously styled hair or make-up – and yet one which emphasizes the most frequently eroticized parts of the female anatomy: the feet, hair, hands and eyes (Brydon, 1998). Yet, of course, the irony is that here the essence of the island woman (inseparable from the island itself) is proclaimed at once as nature, as eternally pre-modern and yet also as a product of modernity, for she has been 'made-over' by the global fashion system.

Although there is no wider context or story for these photographs, the objects, details, arrangements and settings thus construct a story and an identity. But what emerges from the imagined narrative is specifically femininity and this is a femininity linked with eroticism, although not always through explicitly 'sexual' poses as the models' passivity and vulnerability are central to their construction as 'fathomless icons of femininity, passive repositories of desire' (Williamson, 1991, p. 102). Passivity and languor are the dominant tropes in imagining Tahiti, and beauty renders those so designated an object of another's desiring gaze. Most of these models recline on a bed, impassive and inert and, as Cixous notes (in Pollock, 1992, p. 20), in patriarchal cultures, 'woman if you look for her . . . [s]he is always to [be] found in or on a bed'. Thus, in the ceaseless exchange between the colonial discourses of Tahiti and the visual texts analysed here, the fragility and lassitude of island women are read off from graphic signs: the lowered head, averted eyes with heavy lids and free-falling hair softly framing the face. And, of course, such photographic poses bear a marked resemblance to those of Gauguin's paintings, notably *The Queen of Beauty* in which the island woman 'reigns in a mysterious and exotic paradise, far removed from the reality of Tahiti in Gauguin's day' (Bade, 1979, p. 122). Even then, his vision was a fantasy, 'the composition derived from a long European tradition of reclining female nudes' (Bade, 1979, p. 122) which evoked a mysterious and languid sexuality.

Just like any artist, in choosing a backdrop, styling a model and framing a photograph, a fashion team is simultaneously making technical and also representational choices; they are crafting meanings which result from the way the model is positioned and creating symbolic procedures which constitute part of the social practice of composing a photograph. They also contribute to how femininity is socially, sexually and psychologically constructed. As the feminist art historian Griselda Pollock has said of paintings: these are 'economically and culturally determined, be they technical – the legacy of conventions, traditions and procedures – or those social and ideological connotations of subject' (Pollock, 1988, p. 83). We believe that art history and the study of tourism's visual culture has much in common and, especially in view of the influence of artists such as Gauguin on Tahiti's ethnology, it is instructive to explore the relationship between art, colonialism and tourism discourses. Interestingly, several scholars (notably Bade, 1979 and Pollock, 1992) have discussed how art and art history have remained resistant to discourse analysis – just as have the fashion and tourism industries. Indeed, Nead (1988, p. 4) has commented how art 'has been allowed to remain in a social and political vacuum [even though] to identify art as an historical discourse is to insist on its part in the production and reproduction of power and domination'.

Bearing this in mind, Pollock's (1992) fascinating exploration of how masculinist and imperial narratives dominate the work of Paul Gauguin (and his role in the colonial project) throws light on the importance of the colonial–tourism dialectic in mythologizing Tahiti. The expatriate French artist lived in Polynesia from 1891 until 1893 and then again from 1895 until his death in 1903, and his depictions of Polynesian women as dark virginal beauties – he liked to see himself as a 'corruptor of purity [and his] . . . taste was for innocent young girls' (Bade, 1979, p. 19) – have to be seen as part of an imperial imaginary directly linking body, race and culture. Central to this colonialist trope which has for so long haunted the Western masculine imagination is the contrast between the chaste white woman of home and the erotic, highly sexed dark woman of far away. Gauguin's Tahiti 'exhibits all the symptoms of this ambivalent but escapist fantasy of a sexually permissive, naturally fertile world of sights, sensations and free pleasures' (Pollock, 1992, p. 46) which so permeated the 19th-century imperial project. It is also relevant that at this time, art was dominated by the iconic figure of the femme fatale – a figure which looms large in the mythology of Tahitian women. In the period when Gauguin was at his most prolific, women were seen almost exclusively through the eyes of men and were construed as malignant, threatening, destructive and yet fascinating, often as voluptuous temptresses characterized by thick sensuous lips, sultry features and lush tresses. Indeed, the femme fatale's hair was her most effective and lethal weapon (Bade, 1979) and art historians note that loose hair is a powerful and effective symbol of illicit desire (Nochlin, 1989b), a suggestive sign of allowed disorder, conventionally a sign of woman's sexuality (Pollock, 1988). It is no coincidence that all of the models in the Tahiti fashion shoot have their long, flowing hair swept prominently forward and, as such, their resemblance to Rosetti's femmes fatales with their 'sultry features and ballooning black hair' (Bade, 1979, p. 14) is remarkable.

We can thus argue that in the spaces – such as these magazines – marked out for visual and notional sexual consumption these women's bodies are laid out, opened up and offered to view while their clothes function to reveal a sexualized anatomy. The models rarely return the viewer's gaze – a convention which confirms the viewer's right to look and appraise – whilst their downcast eyes also serve to offer the female face for the viewer's uninterrupted surveillance. When they do look into the camera, this merely seems to confirm the gaze of the masculine spectator in 'the sexual politics of looking . . . [which] function around a regime which divides into binary positions, activity/passivity, looking/being seen, voyeur/exhibitionist, subject/object' (Pollock, 1988, p. 86). In such ways are women both denied a representation of their desire and pleasure and are constantly occluded so that to look at and enjoy the sites of patriarchal culture women must assume a masculinist position. Indeed, feminist scholars have long argued that 'woman' has become so central to visual representation and so powerful has this regime proved to be (e.g. in art, photography and the cinema) that we no longer recognize it as representation at all; thus, 'the ideological construction of an absolute category woman has been effaced and this regime of representation has naturalised woman as image, beautiful to look at, defined by her "looks"' (Pollock, 1988, p. 121). As we have argued elsewhere, men are rarely featured as the object of tourism's sexual and voyeuristic gaze (Pritchard and Morgan, 2005), echoing other systems of visual representation in which 'women's main symbolic value is to men – we *are* the language that is spoken on posters and screens, inasmuch as "Woman" is an image' (Williamson, 1991, pp. 25–26).

Of course, in the imperialist project, gender combined with race in the wider discursive network of oppression, and Fanon (1984) has argued that the white male (post)colonialist gaze imposes a white mask on the construction of black people as animalistic, immoral, lascivious and promiscuous. In exploring the relationship between blackness and colonialism, he conceptualizes the 'body as mask', and for women such body masks are patriarchal, reflecting male notions of womanhood and femininity. In representation, women are 'trapped' in a visual space which defines them in terms of their body and appearance, yet which opposes this essence to the superior white male spirit of the intellect. This is a superior spirit which is manipulated by the beauty of womanhood, the mask which acts as a 'vehicle to dazzle men to their destruction' (Tseelon, 1995, p. 12 in Shilling, 1993). For hundreds of years there has been what Michèle Le Doeff describes as an 'imaginary portrait of "woman", a power of disorder, nocturnal, a dark beauty, a black continent, sphinx of dissolution . . . an internal enemy who corrupts and perverts' (Williamson, 1991, p. 142). As a result, we should see both the paintings of Gauguin and the travel and fashion features as less an individual man's personal fantasies or romantic obsessions and rather as symptoms of, and sites for, the renegotiation and redefinition of femininity and sexuality within a complex web of social and gender relations. This concept of the body as mask can be seen in the framing of the fashion shoots we discuss here, in tourism marketing brochures and in the ubiquitous postcards featuring Tahitian women. Interestingly, one of the individuals who currently monopolizes postcard production in French Polynesia elaborates on how he stages his shots to achieve the most marketable mix of the exotic and the familiar, employing very few fully Tahitian women 'because the men who visit Tahiti want a woman that they already possess in their head or their libido. They want one who looks like women they are used to. They don't want her skin to be too dark, her nose too broad, or her thighs too strong.' For these reasons, he often uses a French model but, he says: 'I put a crown of leaves on her head and a coconut-leaf basket in her hands to give her a Tahitian look. That's all it takes' (Kahn, forthcoming). Such admissions give an additional dimension to the reading of representations of island women in postcards and of fashion shoots: it is the aestheticized, imagined island woman who is desired, not the reality of contemporary Tahitian women.

Conclusion

At the outset, we said that in this chapter we would return to our earlier explorations of the relationships between landscape, representation, tourism and gender and, at the same time, further explore the intimacy between tourism and dress. Looking at Tahiti through the lens of the photography and journalism in *Condé Nast Traveller*, we have analysed travel magazines as products of cultural discourses and inscriptions and suggested that their travel and fashion features should be seen as fellow-travelling discursive domains which set parameters around the presentation of particular social and cultural bodies. Both have been seen here to confirm the patriarchal, imperialist discourses embedded in masculine conceptions of adventure, conquest, pleasure and the exotic which have long framed representation of the South Pacific. Moreover, both the travel and the fashion industries draw on the same discourses to depict both woman and landscape in racialized and sexualized terms.

Lifestyle magazines such as *Condé Nast Traveller* are thus agents of cultural pedagogy creating economies 'of desires and dreams' (Gronow, 1997, p. 174). Through its pages we have seen how style and fashion code our understanding of the past and our expectations of the future, reinforcing 'the notion of people as saleable objects' (Ewen, 1991, p. 50). Of course, the reader of the magazine is not a passive receiver of these images. Rather he or she is an active audience who 'searches out the meaning, drawing on the "bricolage" of meaning systems (Levi-Strauss 1966) which comprise the cultural baggage one takes to any situation' (Uzzell, 1984, p. 82). Yet, the fashion photographs and the travel features are links between the readers' desires to escape their busy, everyday metropolitan lives and depictions of typical idyllic settings and luxurious tourism resorts to which they could escape. Jenkins (2003, p. 324) suggests that one way of seeing the circle of representation might be as an outward spiral, 'where each successive whirl of the spiral increases the audience of a tourist destination image and adds another layer of symbolic meaning'. Certainly, we believe that such fashion features set in 'faraway' places add another layer of symbolism and draw in another readership and audience to the circle of tourism representations as active participants. Just like travel features, they too draw on established metropolitan discourses of place and peoples and, as we have previously noted (Morgan and Pritchard, 1998), being a circular process, this is in no way a linear relationship, but a continuous process of cultural production and reproduction, where the media-makers, the audience and the indigenous peoples all play a part in creating meanings through the dialogues between individuals and the images and symbols they perceive (Ryan, 1999). It is important, however, to recognize that, despite the importance of these dialogues, hegemonic 'dominant ideological practices and discourses shape our vision of "reality"' (Kincheloe and McLaren, 2000, p. 310).

This leads us to conclude that there remains a pressing need for a complex, interdisciplinary and fine-grained exploration of tourism's role in the colonial project (see Crick, 1989; Nash, 1989) which embraces more non-Western-trained and positioned researchers. In this, Pollock's challenge to art historians to confront art's interconnectivity with imperialism could equally well be thrown down to tourism researchers. She has said that art history's continued desire to uncritically celebrate the great masters 'only confirms its collaboration with that European project, exposing not only the gender, but also the colour of art history' (Pollock, 1992, p. 72). We could justifiably contend that there have been surprisingly few such analyses in a tourism research field which remains dominated by business prerogatives and resistant to decolonization. It has often been argued that the tourism academy too rarely articulates questions of gender and sexuality, but for how much longer can it also afford to be complacent about the interrelationship between colonialism, sexuality and aesthetics – both in terms of tourism theory and practice? In terms of the former, there is an urgent need for those of us who undertake tourism research to engage in a debate over the neocolonial domination of research practice: so far there has been scant recognition of the consequences of the tourism academy's Western epistemological empire. As a result, too many key research issues, including 'power relations, initiation, legitimization and accountability continue to be addressed in terms of the researchers' own cultural agendas, concerns and interests' (Bishop, 2005, p. 111) and too few alternative experiences, meanings, voices, epistemologies, authenticities and world views are recognized. In much the same way, as work has finally begun in art history to understand the discursive narratives which underpin art, so too must we advance this agenda in our field of tourism to champion what Mackie (2000) describes as analyses of the political economy of representation.

In our analysis here, we have explored the travel writers' and fashion photographers' intertextual framing of Tahiti which continually draws on history, art, literature, stage, music, cinematic and tourism advertising storylines to portray Tahiti as an Edenic paradise, populated by alluring, siren-like Eves. Central to this travel–fashion iconography is 'the European-derived cultural imaginary of Polynesia . . . [which] reaches back . . . to the first encounters of European voyagers and islanders' (Desmond, 1999, p. 11). Tahiti shares much in common with the paradise stories of Hawaii, Jamaica, Bali, Indonesia, Goa and a host of other places around the world where 'hundreds of different counter-territorializing movements work to point to the hidden or obscured faces of the paradise stories (Soguk, 2003, p. 49). Interestingly, of course, whilst travel magazines such as *Condé Nast Traveller* express a desire to move beyond the travel clichés as they search for 'truth in travel', travel writing and photography on Tahiti is permeated by colonial discourses and one of the most recurring cultural referents is the mutiny on *The Bounty*. Indeed, we see such features as an unproblematic imperial and somatic framing of the island and its people that privilege the male experience and use the language of seduction. Tahiti variously 'seduces', 'captivates', 'enchants', 'beguiles', 'mesmerises', 'seduces', 'pleasures', 'dazzles' and 'obliges'; she is 'virginal', 'fragrant', 'languid' and 'scandalous' – descriptions which continually draw on and reaffirm sompatopias to merge the feminine and the exotic. Such narratives also serve to confirm colonial imperatives and the rightness of the colonial project, and the globalized tourism industry continues to represent 'new' lands such as Tahiti as fertile, sexually permissive, pleasurable, seductive and sensuous destinations, awaiting the explorers' (and travellers') touch. In promulgating such narratives, tourism is actively embracing 'the allegorical genre of colonial ethnography' which is 'a nostalgic, redemptive text that preserves a primitive culture on the brink of extinction for the historical record of its Western conquerors' (Kincheloe and McLaren, 2000, p. 326).

In tourism studies there is thus an urgent need to foreground and critically explore the relationship between tourism, (post)colonialism and globalization precisely because global tourism rides on colonialism and travel and fashion features hegemonically circulate the latter's discourses. In fact, here we can see 'the over-determined conjuncture of cultural and sexual difference, and their mutual interface: sex and race at the heart of capitalism's imperial process' (Pollock, 1992, p. 72). Crucially, of course, imagination and desire fuel place myths and such discursive formations have real consequences for contemporary Polynesian society. Internationally the continued eroticization of the Polynesian woman obscures imperialism's ongoing violent impacts (such as the South Pacific nuclear test programmes of France and the USA), and on the islands themselves, the colonial project continues to reverberate in the marginalization of women in French Polynesian society. Feminist scholars of the Pacific argue that before European contact, Polynesian women played key social, economic and political roles and that through processes of Christian proselytization, European colonial policies and capitalist social differentiation, the status of Polynesian women has deteriorated considerably (see Walker, 2005). Axiomatic to these transformations in the status of Polynesian women are the images of Polynesian women created by foreigners. Thus, Manderson and Jolly (1997) emphasize how the alluring objectification of Polynesian women underlies the politics of colonialist and masculinist spectatorship which has shaped the present-day tourist economy in the Pacific. They go so far as to argue that the continued circulation of colonial images of Polynesian women has left them speechless in local and national matters of politics and economics. Certainly, it seems as though historical perceptions of Polynesian women continue to shape the ways in which they are (or are not) integrated into contemporary economic and political spheres in French Polynesia – historical perceptions which underpin the postcolonial discourses of the South Pacific perpetuated in today's global travel industry. What further evidence do we require of the need to confront the entwinement of colonialism, scopophilia and tourism?

Acknowledgement

The authors are grateful to Jeanne van Eeden for introducing them to the work of Linda Nochlin, Lynn Nead and Griselda Pollock.

References

Anderson, K. (1996) Engendering race research: unsettling the self–other dichotomy. In: Duncan, N. (ed.) *Bodyspace: Destabilizing Geographies of Gender and Sexuality*, Routledge, London, pp. 197–211.

Augé, M. (1995) *Non-places: Introduction to the Anthropology of Supermodernity*. Verso, London.

Bade, P. (1979) *Femme Fatale: Images of Evil and Fascinating Women*. Mayflower Books, New York.

Barnes, T.J. and Duncan, J.S. (1992) *Writing Worlds: Discourse, Text and Metaphor in the Representation of Landscape*. Routledge, London.

Beckenbridge, C.A. (1989) The aesthetics and politics of colonial collecting: India at the world fairs. *Comparative Studies in Society and History* 31(2), 195–216.

Bishop, R. (2005) Freeing ourselves from neo-colonial domination in research: a Kaupapa Màori approach to creating knowledge. In: Denzin, N.K. and Lincoln, Y.S. (eds) *The Sage Handbook of Qualitative Research*, 3rd edn. Sage, Thousand Oaks, California, pp. 109–138.

Browne, P. (2001) South specific. *Conde Nast Traveller* (November) 129–139.

Brydon, A. (1998) Sensible shoes. In: Brydon, A. and Neissen, S. (eds) *Consuming Fashion: Adorning the Transnational Body*. Berg, Oxford, pp. 1–22.

Busby, G. and Klug, J. (2001) Movie-induced tourism: the challenge of measurement and other issues. *Journal of Vacation Marketing* 7(4), 316–332.

Butler, R.W. (1990) The influence of the media in shaping international tourist patterns. *Tourism Recreation Research* 15(2), 46–53.

Castree, N. (2004) David harvey. In: Hubbard, P., Kitchin, R. and Valentine, G. (eds) *Key Thinkers on Space and Place*. Sage, London, pp. 181–188.

Chipperfield, M. (2004) The real Tahiti. *Conde Nast Traveller* (November) 188–201.

Cohen, S. (2002) Sounding out the city: music and the sensuous production of place. In: Dear, M.J. and Flusty, S. (eds) *The Spaces of Postmodernity: Readings in Human Geography*. Blackwell, Oxford, pp. 262–276.

Craik, J. (1994) *The Face of Fashion*. Routledge, London.

Crick, M. (1989) Representations of international tourism in the social sciences: sun, sex, sights, savings and servility. *Annual Review of Anthropology* 18, 307–344.

Crouch, D. (ed.) (1999) *Leisure/Tourism Geographies: Practices and Geographical Knowledge*. Routledge, London.

Curry, D. (1993) Decorating the body politic. *New Formations* 19, 69–82.

d'Hauteserre, A. (2005) Maintaining the myth: Tahiti and its islands. In: Cartier, C. and Lew, A. (eds) *Geographical Perspectives on Globalization and Touristed Landscapes*. Routledge, London, pp. 193–208.

Desmond, J.C. (1999) *Staging Tourism: Bodies on Display from Waikiki to Sea World*. University of Chicago Press, Chicago, Illinois.

Dicks, B. (2003) *Culture on Display: The Production of Contemporary Visitability*. Open University Press, Berkshire, UK.

Entwistle, J. (2002) The dressed body. In: Evans, M. and Lee, E. (eds) *Real Bodies: A Sociological Introduction*. Palgrave, London, pp. 133–166.

Ewen, S. (1991) Marketing dreams: the political elements of style. In: Tomlinson, A. (ed.) *Consumption, Identity and Style*. Routledge, London, pp. 41–56.

Fanon, F. (1984) *Black Skin, White Masks*. Pluto Press, London.

Fisher, J. (2002) Tattooing the body, making culture. *Body and Society* 8(4), 91–107.

Gronow, J. (1997) *The Sociology of Taste*. Routledge, London.

Gupta, A. and Ferguson, J. (1992) Beyond culture: space, identity and the politics of difference. *Cultural Anthropology* (February) 6–23.

Hall, C.M. (1997) *Tourism in the Pacific Rim: Development, Impacts and Markets*, 2nd edn. Longman, South Melbourne, Australia.

Hall, C.M. (1998) Making the pacific: globalization, modernity and myth. In: Ringer, G.

(ed.) *Destinations: Cultural Landscapes of Tourism*. Routledge, London, pp. 140–153.

Hall, C.M. and Page, S. (eds) (1996) *Tourism in the Pacific: Issues and Cases*. International Thomson Business Press, London.

Hall, S. (1997) The spectacle of the 'Other'. In: Hall, S. (ed.) *Representation: Cultural Representation and Signifying Practice*. Sage and The Open University, London, pp. 223–290.

Henningham, S. (1992) *France and the South Pacific: A Contemporary History*. University of Hawaii Press, Honolulu, Hawaii.

Howells, R. (2003) *Visual Culture*. Polity Press, Cambridge.

Hubbard, P., Kitchin, R. and Valentine, G. (eds) (2004) *Key Thinkers on Space and Place*. Sage, London.

Hughes, P. (1998) Atoll story. *Conde Nast Traveller* (August) 87–93.

Jaworski, A. and Pritchard, P. (2005) (eds) *Discourse, Communication and Tourism*. Channel View Press, Clevedon, UK.

Jenkins, O.H. (2003) Photography and travel brochures: the circle of representation. *Tourism Geographies* 5(3), 305–328.

Johnston, L. (2001) (Other) bodies and tourism studies. *Annals of Tourism Research* 28(1), 180–201.

Jokinen, E. and Veijola, S. (1997) The disoriented tourist: the figuration of the tourist in contemporary cultural critique. In Rojek, C. and Urry, J. (eds) *Touring Cultures: Transformations of Travel and Theory*. Routledge, London, pp. 23–51.

Kahn, M. (2003) Tahiti: the ripples of a myth on the shores of the imagination. *History and Anthropology* 14(4), 307–326.

Kahn, M. (forthcoming) Postcards from Tahiti: picturing France's colonial agendas, yesterday and today. In: Morgan, N. and Robinson, M. (eds) *Cultures through the Post: Tourism and Postcards*. Channel View, Weston, Massachusetts.

Kincheloe, J.L. and McLaren, P. (2000) Rethinking critical theory and qualitative research. In: Denzin, N.K. and Lincoln, Y.S. (eds) *Handbook of Qualitative Research*, 2nd edn. Sage, Thousand Oaks, California, pp. 279–313.

Lewes, D. (2000) *Nudes from Nowhere: Utopian Sexual Landscapes*. Rowman & Littlefield, Maryland.

Mackie, V. (2000) The metropolitan gaze: travellers, bodies and spaces, intersections. Available at: www.sshe.murdoch.edu.au/intersections/issue4/vera

Manderson, L. and Jolly, M. (1997) *Sites of Desire: Economies of Pleasure*. University of Chicago Press, Chicago, Illinois.

Morgan, N. (2004) Problematising place promotion. In: Lew, A.A., Hall, C.M. and Williams, A.M. (eds) *A Companion to Tourism*. Blackwell, Oxford, pp. 173–183.

Morgan, N. and Pritchard, A. (1998) *Tourism Promotion and Power*. Wiley, Chichester, UK.

Nash, D. (1989) Tourism as a form of imperialism. In: Smith, V. (ed.) *Hosts and Guests: The Anthropology of Tourism*, 2nd edn. University of Pennsylvania Press, Philadelphia, Pennsylvania, pp. 37–52.

Nead, L. (1988) *Myths of Sexuality: Representations of Women in Victorian Britain*. Basil Blackwell, Oxford.

Neissen, S. and Brydon, A. (1998) Introduction: adorning the body. In: Brydon, A. and Neissen, S. (eds) *Consuming Fashion: Adorning the Transnational Body*. Berg, Oxford, pp. ix–xvii.

Nixon, S. (1997) Circulating culture. In: Du Gay, P. (ed.) *The Production of Culture/Cultures of Production*. Sage, London, pp. 179–234.

Nochlin, L. (1989a) Lost and found: once more the fallen woman. In: Nochlin, L. (ed.) *Women, Art, and Power and Other Essays*. Thames & Hudson, London, pp. 57–85.

Nochlin, L. (1989b) Eroticism and female imagery in nineteenth-century art. In: Nochlin, L. (ed.) *Women, Art, and Power and Other Essays*. Thames & Hudson, London, pp. 136–144.

O'Barr, W.M. (1994) *Culture and the Ad: Exploring Otherness in the World of Advertising*. Westview Press, Boulder, Colorado.

Osborne, P. (2000) *Travelling Light: Photography, Travel and Visual Culture*. Manchester University Press, Manchester, UK.

Payne, B. (1997) Beauty beyond measure. *Conde Nast Traveler* (July) 82–92.

Pink, S. (2001) *Doing Visual Ethnography: Images, Media and Representation in Research*. Sage, London.

Pollock, G. (1988) *Vision and Difference: Femininity, Feminism and the Histories of Art*. Routledge, London.

Pollock, G. (1992) *Avant-garde Gambits 1888–1893: Gender and the Colour of Art History*. Thames & Hudson, London.

Pritchard, A. and Morgan, N. (2000a) Privileging the male gaze: gendered tourism landscapes. *Annals of Tourism Research* 27(3), 884–905.

Pritchard, A. and Morgan, N. (2000b) Constructing tourism landscapes: gender, sexuality and space. *Tourism Geographies* 2(2), 115–139.

Pritchard, A. and Morgan, N. (2005) On location: (re)viewing bodies of fashion and places of desire. *Tourist Studies* 5(3), 283–302.

Pritchard, A. and Morgan, N. (2006) Hotel Babylon? Exploring hotels as liminal sites of transgression and transition. *Tourism Management* 27(5), 762–772.

Pritchard, A. and Morgan, N. (2007) *Tourism, Identity and Embodiment*. Channel View Press (in press).

Riley, R., Baker, D. and Van Doren, C.S. (1998) Movie induced tourism. *Annals of Tourism Research* 25(4), 919–935.

Ringer, G. (ed.) (1998) *Destinations: Cultural Landscapes of Tourism*. Routledge, London.

Rose, G. (1993). *Feminism and Geography: The Limits of Geographical Knowledge*. Polity Press, Cambridge.

Ryan, J. (1999) *Race and Ethnicity in Multiethnic Schools: A Critical Case Study*. Multilingual Matters, Clevedon, UK.

Shilling, C. (1993) *The Body and Social Theory*. Sage, London.

Simmel, G. (1981/[1904]) Fashion. In: Sproles, G.B. (ed.) *Perspective on Fashion*. Burgess, Minneapolis, Minnesota.

Soguk, N. (2003) Incarcerating travels: travel stories, tourist orders, and the politics of the 'Hawai'ian Paradise.' *Journal of Tourism and Cultural Change* 1(1), 29–53.

Soja, E. (1989) *Postmodern Geographies*. Verso, London.

Solomon, M.R. (1985) Preface. In: Solomon, M.R. (ed.) *The Psychology of Fashion*. Lexington, New York, pp. xi–xii.

Smith, B. (1984) *European Vision and the South Pacific*. Harper & Row, Sydney.

Sparke, M. (1996) Displacing the field in fieldwork. In: Duncan, N. (ed.) *Bodyspace: Destabilizing Geographies of Gender and Sexuality*. Routledge, London, pp. 212–233.

Staiff, R. (1999) Tourism and Western visual culture. Paper presented at the Australian tourism and hospitality education (CAUTHE) 9th National Research Conference, Adelaide, February, quoted in Jenkins (2003).

Tahite Tourisme (1996) *Tahiti and Her Islands*. Tahite Tourisme.

Terkenli, T.S. (2004) Tourism and landscape. In: Lew, A.A., Hall, C.M. and Williams, A.M. (eds) *A Companion to Tourism*. Blackwell, Oxford, pp. 339–348.

Thomas, N. (1994) *Colonialism's Culture: Anthropology, Travel and Government*. Princeton University Press, Princeton, New Jersey.

Torgovnick, M. (1990) *Gone Primitive: Savage Intellects, Modern Lives*. University of Chicago Press, Chicago, Illinois.

Turner, B.S. (1984) *The Body and Society*. Blackwell, Oxford.

Urry, J. (2002) *The Tourist Gaze*. Sage, London.

Uzzell, D. (1984) The alternative structuralist approach to the psychology of tourism marketing. *Annals of Tourism Research* 11(1), 79–99.

Veijola, S. and Jokinen, E. (1994) The body in tourism. *Theory, Culture and Society* 11, 125–151.

Walker, B. (2005) Catching the wave of capitalism in the wake of the nuclear age: mapping subsistence, development and environmental security in French Polynesia. Available at: http://www.ncgia.ucsb.edu/varenius/ppgis/papers/walker_b.html

Wang, N. (2000) *Tourism and Modernity: A Sociological Analysis.* Pergamon, London.

Wernick, A. (1991) *Promotional Culture: Advertising, Ideology and Symbolic Expression.* Sage, London.

Williamson, J. (1991) *Consuming Passions: The Dynamics of Popular Culture.* Marion Boyers, New York.

Wilson, E. (1985) *Adorned in Dreams: Fashion and Modernity.* Virago Press, London. Available at: www.tahiti-tourisme.com.au

11 Gendered Tourism Space: A South African Perspective

Jeanne van Eeden

Introduction

This chapter considers some aspects of the social production of space at the South African theme park, The Lost City (see Fig. 11.1), by focusing on how space is gendered and objectified for visual consumption. A number of visual and textual devices are used at The Lost City to gender the landscape according to established touristic images of masculinity and femininity. Although the trope of masculinity influences the iconography of The Lost City, the chapter is more concerned with how the space is feminized in terms of discursive and ideological practices such as spatial representation, gender politics, colonialism, tourism and themed entertainment. It suggests that the stereotype of an exotic, feminized Africa naturalizes distortions of history and culture precisely because feminization denotes a cultural politics whereby otherness is rendered powerless, passive and merely decorative. A basic premise is therefore that the ideological apparatus of today's 'leisure imperialism' (Morgan and Pritchard, 1998, p. 165) perpetuates the cultural construction and invention of Africa that resulted from the dual Western pillars of colonialism and capitalism. Accordingly, the politics of spectacle and desire for otherness expressed by imperialism now manifest in the contemporary entertainment economy, which creates fantasy images that position an imaginary Africa as the site of cultural appropriation and touristic consumption. The ideological underpinnings of landscapes of leisure such as The Lost City thus intersect with colonialism and the discourses of advertising and tourism, which frequently recycle romanticized, colonial-style markers in order to reinstate power relationships based on race, class and gender (see Root, 1996). Tourism images are not, of course, just imposed on countries, but are commonly generated by governments and the tourism industry to highlight local differences and to distinguish places from other tourist destinations (Gmelch, 2004, p. 18). By means of this, essentialist and clichéd images are kept in cultural circulation and frame expectations of tourism spaces such as The Lost City.

©CAB International 2007. *Tourism and Gender: Embodiment, Sensuality and Experience* (eds A. Pritchard *et al.*)

Fig. 11.1. Aerial view of The Lost City at Sun City. (From Poole, 1993, p. 32.)

In order to interrogate the manner in which space is represented at The Lost City in terms of a specific set of power relations, it is necessary to refer to a body of texts that deal with social spatialization, feminist cultural geography and tourism. Cultural criticism, which questions the capacity entertainment has to perpetuate ideological constructs, is still quite undertheorized in South Africa, and the role that spaces such as theme parks, casinos, shopping malls and cultural villages play in postcolonial, post-apartheid South Africa deserves further investigation. The Lost City has been selected for discussion because it is a prime example of a constructed landscape that was specifically designed to convey the so-called 'essence of Africa' (Hall, 1995, p. 197). This chapter thus examines the manner in which spatiality is able to reproduce social relations of power and how the feminization of Africa, formerly constituted by colonialism and now disseminated by tourism, is maintained at The Lost City.

The Lost City

The South African leisure entrepreneur, Sol Kerzner, visualized the Sun City hotel, casino and entertainment complex in 1978 (Fig. 11.2). When it opened in 1979, it was the first equivalent of Las Vegas-style entertainment in South Africa. Since Sun City was conceptualized around gambling and risqué entertainment, then illegal in South Africa, it was sited in a neighbouring homeland of apartheid South Africa,

Fig. 11.2. Aerial view of The Lost City with Sun City in the right background. (From Hawthorne, 1996, p. 32.)

Bophuthatswana. The Nationalist apartheid government had divided black people into their ethnic groups and allocated them ten separate Bantu homelands or *bantustans*, as inscribed in Act No. 68 of 1951, the infamous Bantu Authorities Act. Believing that the homelands should be allowed to develop independently of white capital, white-owned industries sprang up in the areas bordering on the homelands. In effect, this policy, while claiming to encourage the future independence of the homelands, as enacted in the 1959 Promotion of Bantu Self-Government Act, led to the homelands being politically and economically dependent on South Africa, and this neocolonialist situation was exploited by many business enterprises. Kerzner made an agreement with the Bophuthatswana government concerning the role Southern Sun Hotels would play in the development of the homeland (Wessels, 1989, p. 34). Hence, 'tourism [was] implicated in the maintenance of apartheid through its close linkages with the former bantustan system . . . [and] tourism contributed 8.6% to the GDP of the former Bophuthatswana' (*Business Day*, 11 July 1994, quoted in McKenzie, 1994, p. 27). Self-governing status was granted to seven of the homelands, including Bophuthatswana, from 1971 onwards, and full independence was given to Bophuthatswana in 1977. With the advent of the first democratic government in South Africa in 1994, the former homelands were incorporated into the nine newly designated provinces.

It is significant in terms of the social production of space that Sun City was literally established in 'another country'. This emplacement served to condone activities such as illicit sex in a site distant from the domestic sphere, thereby echoing the practices enacted during colonialism, as will be suggested later in this chapter. Journalist Andrew Donaldson (2000, p. 1) remarks that Sun City 'was seen as an anaesthetised Sodom for suburbia, a glitzy getaway for middle South Africa seeking respite from the Puritanism of Christian nationalism; a place just 90 minutes' drive from Johannesburg where they could indulge in otherwise illegal activities like gambling, topless revues and arty soft-porn movies'. The eroticized lure of Sun City was inscribed in both the marginal physical space it occupies, as well as in the activities that took place there. Shields (1991, pp. 3–5) has examined the manner in which the cultural categorization of spaces and places frequently operates according to binaries such as high/low culture. The category of 'low' culture often comprises connotations of otherness, fashioning certain places into marginal or in-between spaces because they may be, for example, 'the site of illicit or disdained social activities' (Shields, 1991, p. 3). In the course of time, a set of place-images, usually based on stereotypes and 'an imaginary geography', comes to be associated with the space and forms the set of conventions that circulate in culture (Shields, 1991, pp. 6, 60). This explains how the popular place-image of Sun City as 'Sin City' and 'the temptress in the wilderness' (Ashton, 1997, p. 3) highlighted forbidden pleasures to characterize it as the site of freer modes of behaviour. This portrayal is continued by the tourism industry, which often advertises Sun City in a comparable manner as 'Africa's adventure destination – The Wild North West. For those in search of bright lights, Las Vegas style – decadent entertainment and upmarket accommodation' (Department of Tourism, 1998, p. 12).

The Lost City theme park and Palace Hotel were added to the Sun City resort site in 1992. The American architect Gerald Allison, who had previously been involved with projects for the Walt Disney Company, was selected to realize Kerzner's vision of exotic, mythical Africa. Allison summed up his vision thus:

> The Lost City [is] a fantasy world in the heart of South Africa. The client specified a luxury hotel of unprecedented opulence and originality. The 68-acre site, in the midst of a volcanic crater 100 miles from the nearest urban center, was unremarkable and the area technologically primitive. The challenge sparked a literary blueprint: A fictional narrative of a mythical lost kingdom became the basis of design, and all public areas and guestrooms carry out this theme.
>
> (Hotels & Resorts. The Palace of The Lost City)

Allison also formulated the (in)famous 'Legend of the Lost City', which structures the thematic unity, narrative, iconography and spatialization of the site. A shortened version of the Legend recounts:

> Centuries before tall ships were ever dreamed about, long before the dawn of a western civilisation, a nomadic tribe from northern Africa set out to seek a new world, a land of peace and plenty. The tribe wandered for many years in search of such a magical place, and at last their quest was rewarded. The land they discovered to the south became the legendary valley of the sun, known today as the Valley of Waves. Not only did they bring with them a rich culture, but also architectural skills which were exceptional even by today's standards. Something special was created: from the jungle rose an amazing city with a magnificent Palace, a world richer and more splendid than any they had ever known. Then a violent earthquake struck this idyllic valley, the survivors fled, never to return and left it to be found and restored by archaeologists centuries later.
>
> (Sun International, 1997, p. 1)

It is significant that the (male) tropes of travel, archaeology and discovery are invoked in the Legend. Colonial powers instituted various regimes of hegemonic control over colonized, and hence arguably 'feminized' space. These mechanisms included the enframing of the colonized land by diverse modes of spatial domination and surveillance such as naming and mapping, and rendering the colonized land visually pleasing and picturesque according to Western aesthetic tropes. It is thus suggestive that these devices are frequently echoed in the manner in which theme park landscapes are created in contemporary society. Theme parks are stage-like spaces that are designed to be consumed visually (Urry, 1995, p. 220), and their origins in 19th-century world fairs establishes the intersections between capitalism, imperialism and a contemporary culture of display (see Weinstein, 1992). The Disney Company transformed innocuous amusement parks into highly controlled landscapes that reveal a selective attitude towards fact and inscribe ideologies such as gender codes (Zukin, 1991, pp. 221–223; Willis, 1995, pp. 2–3). Precisely because theme parks are invented environments ostensibly dedicated to whimsy, their extreme social control and potentially capitalist, racist and sexist subtexts are conveniently disguised (Soja, 1989, p. 246; Chaplin and Holding, 1998, p. 8). Not only do the textual and ideological systems of theme park entertainment and colonialism overlap, but they also intersect with the discourse of tourism, which is commonly understood as a contemporary form of colonialism. Before pursuing this line of thought, it is necessary to investigate some salient aspects of the politics of space and gender in order to demonstrate how gendered spatiality and the feminization of Africa interact at The Lost City.

Space, Power and Gender

Since the 1960s, there has been a growing interest in the constitutive power of social spatialization. Social spatialization designates the social construction of the spatial – how, in other words, places are allocated a social identity, function and place in society (Shields, 1991, pp. 31, 63). This interest led to the desire to uncover the hidden geographical texts that underpin the masculinist and phallocentric gendering of space (Soja, 1989, p. 2, 1996, p. 109). Foucault's (1993, p. 168) belief that space is 'fundamental in any exercise of power' has assumed particular importance in the analysis of the social construction of space. Lefebvre's (1991, pp. 17, 26) conviction that '([s]ocial) space is a (social) product' refers to the fact that invented spaces embody a process of signification that operates according to social practices that reflect power relations and hegemonic practices. Landscape, as a symbolical expression of society, thus uses society's cultural codes to represent class, gender and race relations that are simultaneously imposed and sustained by powerful institutions (Zukin, 1991, p. 16). This symbolic penetration by capital into space is suggestive in terms of the argument in this chapter and will be referred to again.

The 'gendered nature of space, place and landscape . . . [and] . . . gendered *leisure* space' (Aitchison, 1999, p. 24) is one of the topics that has been interrogated by (feminist) cultural geography, which is concerned with problematizing and denaturalizing discourses regarding social space and identity. Cultural geography is particularly interested in modalities of power and representational strategies that operate in landscapes (Gregory and Ley, 1988, p. 115), and also examines the role that leisure, tourism and culture play in the construction of otherness, difference and the gaze (Urry, 1995, p. 228; Aitchison, 1999, pp. 19, 31). Aitchison (2000, pp. 137, 138) has pointed out how tourism destinations are constructed as 'foreign and exotic, and the people within these landscapes as Other', and this aligns seamlessly with postcolonial feminist theory that offers a 'critique of the gendered legacy of colonialism' that is still evident in contemporary society. Both feminist cultural geography and postcolonial discourse examine the interrelated questions of race, gender, class, empire, nature, subjection and marginalization that resulted from the topographical inscriptions of imperialism and patriarchy (Soja, 1996, p. 126). This is particularly significant in South Africa because apartheid consistently located power relations in the landscape. Not only have racial and gender segregation been enacted in South African work and leisure spaces, but otherness and ethnicity have also been positioned as sites of spectacle and entertainment (Bank and Minkley, 1998, pp. 1–2, 6) since colonial times. Because Sun City is situated in an area fraught with colonial and postcolonial conflicts and contested histories that are endemic to South Africa, including the forced removal of people from the land, it automatically bears the ideological traces of colonialism.

According to Lefebvre, space becomes fetishized and is a condensation of the social relations of its production. In his explanation of the social production of space, Lefebvre (1991) identifies three methods of conceptualizing space: spatial practices (how space is perceived), representations of space (how space is conceived) and representational spaces (how space is lived). Representations of space encompass the manner in which space is designed, managed, presented and represented. Representations of space are always informed by ideologies, and manifest in the ability of a set of images to convey the identity of a place (Urry, 1995, p. 228). In this regard, Lefebvre (1991, p. 42) singles out architecture for its facility in constructing spatial identity. In terms of this chapter, this could include the way in which the image of an exotic Africa is constructed at The Lost City by means of the Legend, fantastical architecture and the resort's promotional material. Although representational spaces resonate with cultural and symbolic meanings attached to space that are embedded in the history of people, they can reflect a displaced sense of place that implicates a denial of locality, causing '[h]istory . . . [to be] experienced as nostalgia, and nature as regret' (Lefebvre, 1991, pp. 42, 51). What is important for an investigation of gendered space at The Lost City is that representational spaces can connote binaries such as masculine/feminine, which are then reflected in the representations of space (cf. Lefebvre, 1991, p. 245). Lefebvre (1991, p. 59) sums up as follows: '[I]n the spatial practice of neocapitalism . . . representations of space facilitate the manipulation of representational spaces.' Accordingly, the representations of space at The Lost City obliterate the original culture, history and identity of the terrain and irrevocably alter the meaning of the landscape by rendering it exotic and the site of (imperial) nostalgia and entertainment.

Lefebvre (1991, pp. 48, 50) uses the term 'abstract space' to designate space that dispenses with space-time specificity and endorses the discourses of technology, knowledge and power. Abstract space is the domain of the bourgeoisie and capitalism and stands in opposition to absolute space that reflects the 'bonds of consanguinity, soil and language' (Lefebvre, 1991, pp. 53, 57, 49). Capitalism is able to extend its authority by sustaining the structures that define it, leading to the commodification of public space, corporate landscapes and spaces of consumption (Soja, 1989, p. 91; Mitchell, 2000, p. 2). There are clear ideological connections between the spatial practices of capitalism, patriarchy and colonialism, which are defined by their desire to extend power; in order to achieve this, they colonize abstract space. Lefebvre (1991, p. 352) makes the point that capitalism endorses the exploitation of regions devoted to the consumption of space; leisure spaces (such as The Lost City) consequently embody the 'consumption of space, sun and sea, and of spontaneous or induced eroticism, in a great "vacationland festival"' (Lefebvre, 1991, p. 58). Lefebvre (1991, pp. 309–310) argues that the metaphorical use of the fragmented female body as a commodity for exchange value is also a product of abstract space. This fetishized body is frequently used to underscore the sexualized code of (leisure) spaces by invoking exoticism, eroticism and escapism (Fig. 11.3). An example of this can be seen in a brochure for the Emerald Casino Resort outside Vanderbiljpark in South Africa; its theme is 'Cape to Cairo'. A bare-breasted black woman in tribal beads is superimposed on a picture of a Kenyan safari lodge

Fig. 11.3. Advertisement for Sun City: 'The fun begins at Sun City'. (From Sun International, 2004.)

bathed in a golden sunset, and the text states: 'The Emerald Hotel brings visions of a time of longer, lazier, sun-filled days, with every wish or need taken care of' (Emerald Safari Resort & Casino [sa]: sp). Similarly, print advertisements for the South African liqueur Amarula Cream have featured images of black women since the 1990s. A recent advertisement, entitled 'Taste the spirit of Africa', shows a white man and a woman of colour with evocative words such as the following: 'explore the untamed plains of the African savannah . . . exotic fruit . . . aphrodisiac . . . fertility rites . . . alluring . . . seduction . . . romance' (*Femina Magazine*, November 2005, p. 107).

Lefebvre (1991, pp. 56, 384) reasons that leisure spaces are hierarchical dominated spaces that impose or valorize particular relationships between people within specific spatial contexts. He implies thereby that the rituals and gestures of leisure spaces sanction the 'genital order of the family' (Lefebvre, 1991, p. 384); hence, a normative gender code is implicitly embedded in the ideological representation of leisure space. Lefebvre (1991, pp. 310, 353) explains that the identification between leisure, sex, desire and pleasure takes place in spaces dedicated to the representation of leisure: '[I]n holiday resorts or villages, on ski slopes or sun-drenched beaches. Such leisure spaces become eroticised . . . to the illusion of festivity. Like play, Eros is at once consumer and consumed.'

Gender is recognized as one of the fundamental organizing principles of social life, and influences the social construction and representation of space through which the world is experienced. Gender relations are not consistent, but can vary according to the social spaces where they are enacted, which means that all social spaces are symbolically gendered to some extent (Barker, 2000, p. 293). The manner in which the unequal status of women has been rendered in spatial arrangements has been theorized by cultural geography's examination of gendered spaces (cf. Spain, 1992; Aitchison, 1999, pp. 24–26). Spatialized feminism focuses on the spatial articulation of power relations between the sexes, including 'the differential use, control, power and domination of space, place and landscape for social, economic [leisure] and environmental purposes' (Aitchison, 1999, p. 25). The effects of industrial capitalism's separation of work from leisure, whereby leisure was defined 'in relation to paid (male) employment' (Aitchison, 2000, p. 141) and the concomitant rise of a modernist sensibility in social spaces, have been extensively theorized. This has led to the conventional alignment between mass culture, consumption and femininity. Huyssen (1986, p. 47) contends: '[T]he political, psychological, and aesthetic discourse around the turn of the [19th] century consistently and obsessively genders mass culture and the masses as feminine, while high culture . . . clearly remains the privileged realm of male activities.' The separation of work from leisure (masculine/feminine) brought into play a range of gendered binary oppositions such as public/private, culture/nature and production/consumption (cf. Fiske, 1989, pp. 18–22; Aitchison, 1999, p. 30). The inscription of gender relations in the spatial practices of modernism, patriarchy and capitalism identified women with the spaces of domesticity, but they 'could enter and represent selected locations in the public sphere' – those of entertainment and display' (Pollock, 1988, p. 79).

Gender relations are evident in how societies arrange and manage public and private spaces, and space itself is invariably coded as female. Massey (1994, p. 183) has drawn attention to the fact that Lefebvre suggested that the spaces and cultural practices of modernity were already decisively gendered as masculine. She explains that time is habitually equated with history, progress, civilization, science, politics, reason, transcendence, order, narrative, vitality, sequential coherence and logic – in other words, so-called (male) modernist ideas. Space, on the other hand, signifies statis, reproduction, nostalgia, emotion, aesthetics, the body, immanence, chaos, neutrality, passivity, description and lack of coherence (Massey, 1994, pp. 257, 267). The dichotomies or binary oppositions such as culture/nature, based on the ideological construction A/Not-A, establish differences that privilege the dominant social group. Massey (1994, p. 257) therefore postulates that the time/space dichotomy is similar to the man/woman binary wherein the latter signifies lack or absence. This, she argues, underlies not only the social construction of gender difference, but also the power relations instituted and maintained by the processes of social spatialization.

Spaces therefore have the capacity to express gendered states of mind (Shields, 1991, p. 29); because public space is coded as masculine, it follows that feminized space is offered up to the masculine gaze for consumption. Spatial metaphors have traditionally been gendered, so that '[n]ature has been seen as characteristically female . . . [and] capital [or the explorer] "penetrates" peripheral area' (Cosgrove and Domosh, 1993, p. 30). Feminized space is subject to discovery, penetration and consumption; this characterization assumes a potent agency in colonial discourse where the African landscape was represented as a vast *tabula rasa*, uninhabited, unpossessed, virgin territory that justified capitalist expansionism and the 'heroic white [male] penetration of the Dark Continent' (Brantlinger, 1985, p. 188).[1] The actual physical impenetrability of Africa and a lack of tangible knowledge about the mysterious continent (cf. Wheeler, 1999, p. 17) led to colonial spatial metaphors regarding deepest, darkest Africa, instituting a simplistic place-image (cf. Shields, 1991, p. 47) that continues to resonate in the Western imagination.

Leisure and touristic spaces such as theme parks condone the social gaze and visual consumption. For the purposes of this chapter it is suggested that The Lost City is an example of abstract, feminized space because it is a tamed, miniaturized, contained environment that expresses the total control by culture of nature, or equally the binaries order/chaos, time/space and masculine/feminine. Timelessness and the notion of fixed essences are related to both the myth of Africa and the trope of exoticism (Root, 1996, pp. 37–38). According to Root (1996, pp. 37–38), passivity and timelessness 'characterise nearly all societies outside of the Western tradition and carry within them an assertion of the supposedly inherent dynamism [i.e. modernity and progressiveness] of European cultures'. Time became a marker of difference, and thus in the 19th century the Other was increasingly temporalized by being associated with past lifestyles. Accordingly, places such as Africa became the embodiment of Darwinian ideas of evolution, and the ideological underpinning thereof was 'to represent Europe's Other as its past' (Duncan, 1993, pp. 46–47). Tourist imagery is often founded on the ' "experience of timelessness", exotic otherness . . . [and presenting places] where time "stands still" ' (Cusack, 1998, p. 214). Timelessness, moreover, is associated with primitivism and nature (Morgan and Pritchard, 1998, p. 214), which are already coded as feminine. The spatial practice at The Lost City thus represents a space of consumption that migrates into the consumption of space. The Lost City is a simulacrum that conveys the consumption of a feminized, colonized and objectified Africa, specifically because images of exoticism knowingly '(re)construct both people and landscapes out of context' (Aitchison, 2000, p. 138). The next section elaborates on the ideological project of the invention and feminization of Africa and indicates some of the ways in which this resonates in the practices of tourism.

Colonialism, Tourism and Feminization: Inventing Africa

It is commonly stated that 'Africa' is largely a cultural construct and invention of the West that, according to Morgan and Pritchard (1998, p. 178), 'set Africa up as a foil to Europe' and consistently represented it in a specific manner. Early legends of Africa were inscribed in the western archaeology of Africa, and influenced the ways in which it was represented in literature and popular culture. Pieterse (1992, p. 24) observes that from the time of ancient Greece a split was evident in the 'image of . . . multiple Africas: the Africa of Egypt and the Nubian kingdoms . . . and a "wild", unknown Africa'. Although Africa was hardly ever a monolithic concept, colonial explorers, missionaries, travellers, archaeologists and adventure writers tended to envision it in a specific manner that served to establish it as a site of objectified fantasy. The stereotypical myth of Africa, founded on incredible tales of adventure and fear of the savage, resulted from the ideology of imperialism; the primary task of this myth was to legitimate the colonial enterprise as a civilizing mission (Stam and Spence, 1983, p. 5; Hall, 1995, p. 188). The premise that Africa had to be civilized was the product of the conventional construct of Africa as the Dark Continent that was disseminated by Victorian ideology. Travelogues such as Sir Henry Morton Stanley's (1841–1904) *Through the Dark Continent* (1878) and scientific treatises were paralleled by numerous romanticized, fictional tales of exotic worlds 'being mastered by heroic European males' (Duncan, 1993, p. 50).

The most important adventure stories that colluded in the consolidation of the myth of Africa in the late 19th and early 20th centuries included those by Henry Rider Haggard, Edgar Rice Burroughs and John Buchan. Most of these stories were formulaic elaborations of the imperial impulse, and dealt with heroic and mythic quests and exploration that were produced for an essentially male audience (Brantlinger, 1985, p. 193; Bunn, 1988, pp. 1, 7, 8). Many of these generic tales dealt with the idea of '[l]ost civilizations which have been swallowed up in the "African darkness"' (Pieterse, 1992, p. 110). Haggard's novels *King Solomon's Mines* (1885), *She* (1887) and *Allan Quatermain* (1887) encapsulated all the romantic elements that constructed and validated the myth of Africa: vast landscapes, mysterious ruins, maps, mines, hidden or lost utopian cities, volcanoes, treasure and a great white queen (cf. Bunn, 1988). These novels were popular precisely because they corroborated the cultural preconceptions of colonial audiences. The Legend of the Lost City replicates this notion of 'the legend of the lost light of civilisation in the heart of Africa' (Hall, 1995, p. 186). Indeed, the architect Gerald Allison admitted that he had been inspired by popular culture when formulating the Legend of The Lost City, and in particular by the filmic versions of Tarzan, Indiana Jones and *The African Queen* (1951) (Gates, 1998).

From at least the 12th century Europeans believed Africa to be a 'mythical land full of fantastic human and non-human creatures' (Duncan, 1993, p. 47); travellers' stories and fictional tales from the Middle Ages onwards had prepared people to expect a continent of alien and barbaric forms, savagery and primitivism (Hall, 1995, p. 186; cf. Wheeler, 1999). At the same time, many stories characterized Africa as a mysterious exotic paradise, with untold riches and lost civilizations, which were compounded in two interrelated stories concerning the Queen of Sheba and the legendary Christian, Prester John (Hall, 1995, pp. 181–182). It was the perceived exoticism of these two figures that was fascinating to Europeans (Pieterse, 1992, pp. 24–25). Prester John and the Queen of Sheba continued to intrigue explorers and writers until late in the 19th century and laid the foundation of the meta-narrative on which the Legend of The Lost City is based, in which 'the old mythology is repeated without challenge. At the heart of Africa is the Lost City of the Queen of Sheba and her fabulous diamond mines' (Hall, 1995, pp. 183, 196).

The visual lexicon of the myth of Africa includes imagery based on royalty, wealth and nature that are reflected in the representation of space at The Lost City. Up to the 17th century, travellers to Africa admired its royal courts and cities (Pieterse, 1992, p. 36), and this fascination with ancient African royalty was later incorporated in the idea of the noble savage of Enlightenment politics. The idea of Africans as noble, innocent or simple savages at one with nature was countered by the construction of them as primitive, beastly and evil, but in both images, the notion of sensuality and sexuality featured strongly (Pieterse, 1992, pp. 30, 35; Morgan and Pritchard, 1998, pp. 178–179). The representation of human presence is glossed over at The Lost City and common types that exemplify primitivism, such as the fierce warrior, witch doctor or cannibal (Pieterse, 1992, pp. 77, 79), are not invoked, possibly because of their negative connotations. Many representations of Africa are inclined to concentrate on exotic nature and specifically on animals and the romanticized myth of the African jungle (Stam and Spence, 1983; Pieterse, 1992, p. 35); depictions of people usually show so-called tribal people who are used as anonymous signifiers of the mythic notion of Africanness (Morgan and Pritchard, 1998, p. 224) (Fig. 11.4). The current touristic representation of South Africa as the home of exotic flora and fauna is therefore the culmination of a long colonial inscription. For instance, the coconut palm tree that is used to connote paradise at The Lost City is not indigenous to Africa, but was originally imported by Europeans from the Indian Ocean (Pieterse, 1992, p. 36). Similarly, the iconography of The Lost City is based on an elaborate vocabulary of real and imagined flora and fauna and the stereotypical idea of the boundless African sun that connotes sensuality, exoticism and eroticism. Once again, it can be suggested that this aestheticization of exoticism renders it purely decorative, manageable and unthreatening – hence feminized.

The myth of Africa is based on a set of power relations that has made it the preferred 'American popular-culture image of Africa' based on 'prior colonial

Fig. 11.4. Postcard of South Africa showing iconic imagery such as Table Mountain, The Lost City, a leopard and a 'typical' African child. (From 2001.)

status, local politics, national forces, and global international requirements' (Bruner, 2004, pp. 144, 145). Pieterse (1992, pp. 11, 97) makes two interrelated points: first, that the myth of Africa transformed the stereotypes of Africa into spectacle, and second, that Western fantasies of power were enacted once the dangers of Africa had been subjugated, and consequently 'Africa came more and more to resemble a vast recreational area'. Pieterse (1992, p. 67) adds that Africa was rendered by explorers and travellers as a 'stage décor', and this empty cultural space could be filled by the fantastical imaginings of Europeans. This also confirms that from an early stage, African otherness was depicted as entertainment. Hall (1995, p. 181) believes that this mythical image of Africa informed Hollywood films, novelists such as Wilbur Smith and ultimately the founding myth of The Lost City.

Rendering Africa an exotic spectacle for Western consumption went hand in hand with the process of feminization, which implies that qualities traditionally perceived to be feminine, such as passivity, irrationality and guile, were associated with prelinguistic forms of expression and so-called primitive cultures (Bunn, 1988, pp. 14, 20–23). This manner of categorizing the world conferred marginal status on difference and otherness. Aitchison (2000, p. 136) argues that 'that which is defined as Other is accorded a gender and this gender is always feminized'. Gendered discourses concerning the body, sexuality and the imagination were projected onto Africa, constituting the gendered legacy of colonialism that still exerts its influence. Orientalism and postcolonial feminist theory have pointed out that exoticism and fantasy have consistently been located in otherness by the West. Orientalism incorporated the sexualization of Others, and accordingly the feminization of Africa and the Orient (Pieterse, 1992, pp. 172, 173). Orientalism contributed to the historical construction of woman as Other, and once feminized, Africa became the object of the male gaze and subject to colonial spatial practices (Bunn, 1988, p. 12). This notion has also been applied to America by Sardar (1996) in his scrutiny of the Disney film *Pochahontas*. He observes that a tradition of visual iconography associated America with a sensual young maiden: '[T]he languor of the sexually charged figure of America was intended to suggest she was at the very least ready to be husbanded by Europe' (Sardar, 1996, p. 18). Colonial (and later tourist) representations of landscapes were founded on gendered power

relationships that structured the male gaze as active, technological, scientific, imperial and rational, whereas feminized nature and distant landscapes, the objects of
this gaze, were perceived as passive, irrational, wild, bountiful, picturesque and
seductive (Morgan and Pritchard, 1998, pp. 198–199).

This feminizing impulse was fully established in the 19th century, which witnessed the 'conjunction of aesthetics, sexuality and colonialism' (Pollock, 1992,
p. 9). Travel, and specifically the tropical journey, became the embodiment of the
Western search for difference, unfettered sexuality and the exotic Other (Pollock,
1992, p. 8; Mackie, 1998, p. 3). The conflation between travel and sexual desire
found expression in spaces where escapist fantasies could be enacted against timeless, exotic, natural settings. The body of the racially other woman signified nature,
escape from the urbanized, industrial West, and total difference – 'temporal, sexual, cultural, [and] racial' (Pollock, 1992, pp. 40, 47). According to Said (1978,
p. 190), 'the Orient was a place where one could look for sexual experience unob-
tainable in Europe', and consequently sexuality that was repressed at 'home' was
projected onto the fetishized Other (Lalvani, 1995, p. 269). Africa in particular
was positioned as the site of unrepressed sexuality and temptation for white men
(Brantlinger, 1985, pp. 194–196), based on the stereotyping of black women as
highly sexualized, willing temptresses (Geist and Nachbar, 1983, p. 164; Gilman,
1985, p. 231). This stereotyping is found at tourist destinations and theme parks
that represent exotic otherness by means of imagery that denotes 'the use and
enjoyment of other cultures, particularly of those whose representation . . . is primarily colonial, as the site for sexual fantasies and desire otherwise unavailable or
unrepresented' (Kuenz, 1995, pp. 72–73).

Contemporary sex tourism,[2] which constructs foreign women as exotic, available, submissive and desirable, has become an extension of colonial practices that
endorses unequal power relations between countries and genders (Mackie, 1998,
p. 4). As previously noted, Sun City has traditionally been known as 'Sin City', and
its detachment from 'South Africa' meant that it signified sexual freedom as the
Other of repressive puritanism and apartheid. Already in 1980, only a year after
Sun City had opened, a report found that prostitution had increased significantly in
the area (Strijdom et al., 1980). Recent findings suggest, however, that sex tourists
in South Africa are mainly South African (Smith, 2001, p. 28); although sex tourism in this case may not be dependent on international tourism and multinational
capital, it still reveals the conventional construction of desire for exotic sexual
experiences in marginal or carnival spaces.

There are many correlations between the practices and discourses of colonialism
and tourism; both deal with monolithic generalizations and stereotypical imagery
that construct other cultures according to a gaze that privileges the white, Western,
heterosexual male of modernity (Pollock, 1992, p. 61; Morgan and Pritchard, 1998,
pp. 5, 169; Bruner, 2004, pp. 127–128). Tourism institutes cultural stereotypes that
operate from the perspective of the West, and packages space and labour-free landscapes that echo a colonial attitude towards land: 'Tourists, like colonists, anticipate
territory as empty space. . . . A place where time stands still or is reversed into a
utopian space of freedom, abundance and transparency' (Cusack, 1998, p. 214).
Tourism imagery and rhetoric frequently refer to former colonial relationships and
use familiar colonial markers (Morgan and Pritchard, 1998, p. 217), fashioning an

Fig. 11.5. The Tusk Lounge in The Palace Hotel. (Photograph by author.)

imperialist nostalgia that reproduces cultural clichés, suspect histories and romantic fantasies (Rosaldo, 1989; cf. Root, 1996; Bruner, 2004, p. 133). In this regard, it is significant that the manner in which space is represented at The Lost City, and particularly in The Palace Hotel, is compellingly reminiscent of colonial times (Fig. 11.5). Moreover, Sun City has specifically targeted the French, German and British markets (*Pretoria News Business Report*, 1999, p. 9). Since many of its visitors stem from these former colonial giants, it is reasonable to suppose that they have certain expectations of reliving a lifestyle evocative of the past. But the tourist gaze in South Africa predates The Lost City by many decades; South Africa was starting to market itself in terms of exoticism and otherness from the 1920s onwards. Tourists were enticed with images of the country's natural beauty, wildlife, exotic women and so-called 'native' villages. These 'typical' villages, such as Chief Islang's kraal in Bechuanaland, were constructed from the 1920s onwards, and fulfilled tourists' needs to see something dramatic, exotic and, if possible, barbaric to Western eyes, but enframed by Western modes of civilization (see Wolf, 1991).

It is clear that tourism imagery reflects colonial relations, but because it emanates from gendered societies, it also reinforces gendered relations (Kinnaird *et al.*, 1994, pp. 2, 5; Morgan and Pritchard, 1998, p. 3). Aitchison (1999, p. 29, 2000, p. 128) asserts that the feminist analysis of tourism should comment on 'gender relations in the production and consumption of tourism activities and images' and the manner in which foreign landscapes and people are represented as the exotic Other. Enloe (1989, pp. 40–41) points out that the idea of travelling for adventure and pleasure has always been gendered, encapsulating specific ideas of what constitutes masculinity and femininity, and she believes that this informs the political agenda of the tourism industry. Since erotic freedom and escapist fantasies were conventionally located in the colonies, tourism, as the logical extension of imperialism, promised 'the Western male the fantasy of absolute power over foreign women once enjoyed by his grandfather in the colony' (Root, 1996, pp. 32, 40). Tourism is often constructed on gendered fantasies, so that women and sexualized imagery are used to portray the 'exotic' nature of a destination (Kinnaird *et al.*, 1994, p. 14). Since the tourist gaze is usually assumed to be male, touristic myths, signs, symbols and fantasies are male-oriented in their representation of the consumption of exoticism (Kinnaird *et al.*, 1994, p. 14; Mackie, 1998, p. 3). Many of the colonial metaphors of exotic, pristine, natural, virginal and desirable places are replicated in the rhetoric of tourism's othering gaze – both the physical landscape and the corporeal landscape of the woman become the sites 'upon which the explorer or the tourist can make his mark' (Aitchison, 2000, p. 138).

Tourism is conventionally predicated on masculine notions regarding adventure, leisure and the exotic, and women are conventionally used to suggest the quintessence of the exotic (Enloe, 1989, pp. 20, 28). In terms of Western gender politics, myths and fantasies that associate men with action, power, modernity and entitlement, and women with passivity, availability, nature and ownership by men, are disseminated by the tourism industry (Pollock, 1992, p. 50; Kinnaird *et al.*, 1994, p. 13). Because various discourses have linked women with the experience of the exotic, tourism destinations are sexualized or eroticized, creating feminine tourism landscapes that resonate throughout the history of travel (Morgan and Pritchard, 1998, pp. 193, 198). These landscapes frequently invoke a utopian impulse and the rhetoric of the Garden of Eden, reworked into thematic, atmospheric backdrops for the tourist gaze. The Lost City, for example, is marketed as a utopian beach paradise amidst tropical forest and exotic pools and gardens, where 'fantasy becomes reality'. Gendered tourism landscapes such as these operate on the principles of 'feminine seduction and masculine adventure', where the 'feminine landscape seductively invites the man to come and discover her treasures and (hetero-)sexual allure structures her description' (Morgan and Pritchard, 1998, pp. 199, 203). The next section applies some of these notions to an examination of the gendering of space at The Lost City.

Gendered Space at The Lost City

A metonymic association between a woman's body and the African landscape (Bunn, 1988, p. 1) generated colonialist spatial metaphors of conquest and possession of the wild African continent. Gendered colonial tropes such as discovery, naming, mapping and 'monarch-of-all-I-survey' descriptions were markers of the uncontested gaze of male presence (Pratt, 1992, pp. 30, 33, 60, 205; Bunn, 1988, pp. 11, 15), and many of these mechanisms are enacted at The Lost City. For example, The Lost City is clearly established on the notion of heroic male discovery and adventure, from the initial discovery of the Edenic space by the so-called ancient tribe to the later discovery of its ruins by the 'archaeologist and custodian . . . Kerzner . . . the creator, discoverer and interpreter of this Enchanted Ruin' (Hall, 1995, p. 181). In keeping with this mythmaking, Kerzner was identified with a romanticized Indiana Jones-type figure, and the South African press often referred to him as 'Indiana Sol of the Lost City of Bop'. Thus, not only did 'a modern explorer stumble upon the Lost City', but visitors are also urged to 'discover the hidden treasures of The Lost City' and to negotiate the 'adventure paths' and 'trails of discovery' in the Garden (Sun International, 1996).

Another example of a colonial legacy is located in a pictorial map of The Lost City (Fig. 11.6). This privileges a Western gaze and pictorial perspective, presenting a picturesque view of the empty land in the manner of monarch-of-all-I-survey promontory descriptions found in 19th-century male travel writings (Pratt, 1992, pp. 205, 213–216). The myth of an empty landscape was sanctioned by official historiography that stressed that the interior of South Africa was unpeopled until the 19th century (Coetzee, 1988, p. 177). The spatial metaphor of an 'empty country', passively awaiting colonial or touristic intervention, is also suggestively conjured up in a Sun City brochure: '[T]he olive-green and ochre slopes of the Pilanesberg mountain range in Bophuthatswana in southern Africa lay sleepy and untouched under the blazing Africa sun . . . where once only black eagles rose on the midday thermals and the shy duiker scurried through the undergrowth' (Poole, 1993, p. 3). The map of The Lost City shows two proscenium-like columns that direct the possessing gaze over the panoramic vista, which fades into a picturesque luminous distance. The map

Fig. 11.6. Pictorial map of The Lost City. (From Sun International, 1996.)

focuses on The Palace Hotel, and there are telling distortions and omissions in the representation of space that sustain the fantasy of a timeless world: close to nature, passive and the site of endless possibilities for the explorer or tourist.

There are many other examples of gendered spaces, activities, language and iconography at The Lost City. In keeping with the meta-narrative of the myth of Africa, the power structure of The Lost City is resolutely androcentric, patriarchal and regal. This is reflected in its slogan 'Africa's kingdom of pleasure', and the city was ostensibly built 'as a tribute to the King who had led [his people] to their Utopia' (Sun International, 2000). Edensor and Kothari (1994, p. 168) discuss masculinized tourism sites where 'masculine spheres of activity (war and militarism, statesmanship, exploration, scientific invention, public life)' are valorized to the virtual exclusion of female concerns, and this strategy is echoed at the representation of space at The Lost City.[3] The masculinist cosmology of The Lost City states that the North African tribe ventured 'in search of the blessed land which had appeared to their King in a vision', and they 'believed their kings and nobles descended from cloud covered mountaintops' (Sun International, 2000). Even the Royal Staircase was 'once the exclusive passageway of kings and princes' (Hawthorne, 1996, p. 14). The male figures mentioned in the lore of The Lost City include King Khumo, King Mothapi, the wise old man Modise, the engineer Kgedi, general Mosenyi and astronomers, 'ancient workers', athletes, wrestlers, evil sorcerers and a lovelorn prince 'who wished to win the heart of the girl he loved' (Sun International, 1996). The male figures engaged in typical male activities such as mining and cartography, and the astronomers assumed responsibility for choosing 'the correct times for planting, harvest, and feast days. Once when two princes claimed the throne, the astronomers decided which would be the next king' (Sun International, 1996).

Fig. 11.7. The Palace Hotel at The Lost City. (From Poole, 1993, pp. 2–3.)

The masculine coding employed in the representation of space at The Lost City includes the towers of the Palace Hotel, which are important markers of royalty and authority. According to Lefebvre (1991, p. 49), towers are symbols of the repressive arrogance that epitomizes abstract space, and the 70m high King Tower is flanked by the suitably smaller Queen Tower (Fig. 11.7). Hall (1995, p. 180) furthermore suggests that '[t]he power of the king was marked out by appropriately gendered symbols: the strength and size of the gorilla in the "Kong Gates" of the city; the hunting prowess of the leopard . . . [and] the kudu "spirit guardian", with its huge spiralled horns' (Figs 11.8–11.10). The 10m high Kong Gates fulfil an important symbolic function by signalling the containment of space and order, which is further emphasized by the strict (male) symmetry of the elephant guard on the Bridge of Time that leads to The Lost City.

The feminization of The Lost City is reflected in the creation of an exotic atmosphere, which is conveyed most clearly at the Valley of Waves, a beach

Fig. 11.8. The Kong Gates and Bridge of Time at The Lost City. (From Sun International, 2000.)

Fig. 11.9. A kudu on one of the towers of The Palace Hotel. (From Poole, 1993, p. 4.)

paradise that invokes all the clichés associated with suntanned bodies, exoticism and eroticism. The only explicit reference to women, at the wishing well in The Lost City, is the clichéd declaration that links women with romance: 'This was the centre of ancient village life, where women came to draw water and gossip. A girl accidentally dropped a coin into the well and saw the face of her husband to be in the water. Girls do the same today hoping to see the man of their dreams' (Sun International, 1996) (Fig. 11.11). The most important building at The Lost City, the Palace Hotel, is unequivocally and suggestively both feminized and eroticized:

> From her very foundations to each intricately ornate tower reaching up to the sky, The Palace of The Lost City is sumptuous and sophisticated luxury . . . by day, she shimmers under an African sun . . . by night she is the jewel of Africa, illuminating the surroundings with a warm, inviting glow . . . a million lights flood The Palace with the promise of a sultry African night.
>
> (Sun International, 2000, p. 2)

Fig. 11.10. The leopard at the Temple of Creation at The Lost City. (From Poole, 1993, p. 13.)

This type of feminine landscape seductively invites the gendered and objectifying gaze of the first world tourist and resonates with distant memories of empire, out-of-Africa adventure and uncontested possession.

It is significant that even though there are no explicit visual depictions of the ancient inhabitants of The Lost City, the binary opposites of male/female are evoked in countless ways; the Legend of The Lost City is an important constituent in this. The predominance of male signifiers, however, does not exclude female presence, but rather conjures up an elusive, mysterious feminine presence precisely because of its absence. The point is that the metonymic associations between exoticism, feminized imagery and Africa have been inscribed in popular culture for so long that they continue to resonate, although now as empty signifiers in the simulacral world of The Lost City. Aitchison (1999, p. 32) comments that '[w]hilst sex tourism frequently generates symbols of women as the "exotic other", heritage tourism often creates the "invisiblized other" where emphases upon nationhood, and industrialized or militarized landscapes draw upon a history which renders women invisible from the landscape' (see Edensor and Kothari, 1994). Both of these strategies can be identified at Sun City and The Lost City, respectively. In the former, women are explicitly positioned as the site of spectacle, display and consumption (e.g. in the extravaganzas and soft-porn films offered by the 'temptress in the wilderness'), whereas in the latter they are evoked more subtly in the gendered code of exoticism (see Root, 1996).

Fig. 11.11. The plaque at the wishing well at The Lost City. (Photograph by author.)

Conclusion

This chapter has pointed out a few aspects of the gendered legacy of colonialism at The Lost City, based on the premise that an entertainment landscape has the capacity to express, reflect and form cultural politics. As previously stated, Kerzner wanted The Lost City to convey the *essence of Africa*, and it is not coincidental that the essence of the so-called Dark Continent has consistently been perceived as feminine. The sexualization of otherness and the feminization of Africa signal asymmetrical power relations that consign Africa to the status of entertainment. By aestheticizing and eroticizing exoticism and depicting other cultures as simply decorative, Europeans implied that these cultures held no threat to colonial hegemony (Root, 1996, p. 76). The lure of gendered, exotic otherness is part of the rhetoric of tourism that recycles the politics of domination enshrined in the racialization and feminization of colonial space. This colonial connection between Africa, leisure and entertainment still structures how Africa is perceived, and indeed sells *herself* to the tourism market. The South African tourism board, Satour, wants to concentrate on cultural tourism in its marketing of South Africa because it believes that this 'allows communities to develop a sense of pride' (Begg, 1998, p. 16). But because South African cultural tourism is equated with either cultural villages[4] or township tours, both of which are fraught with problems of cultural misrepresentation, the possibility of perpetuating 'tribal' clichés seems to be inevitable.

This chapter also suggested that a theme park can be interpreted as a miniature colonial landscape, signifying the complete control of nature in a hermetic, feminized space; The Lost City is accordingly similar to a small colony that conjures up the illusion of timelessness, placelessness and of a colonial lifestyle frozen in time. The Lost City is deliberately denied spatial and temporal specificity in order to assist fantasy, and the connotations of feminized space enhance the consumption of otherness. This inscription and representation of space is not liberating because it can be read as an extension of colonial strategies of domination. Root (1996) points out that popular culture and tourism frequently disclose a nostalgia for the 'good old days of colonialism', and what concerns critics is that third world countries are becoming exotic playgrounds for Western tourists. The gendered fantasies of power and otherness that operate at The Lost City are the result of gendered tourism marketing that forges invidious associations with the myth of Africa. Shields (1991, pp. 14, 22) points out that the culturally mediated reception of how places are represented is dependent upon an entire system of social meanings; a place can only be given meaning in relation to other places and practices. The symbolic meaning and status assigned to The Lost City consequently mark it as a sign of leisure space and colonial-style, gendered dreams of power and entitled consumption that signal a problematic cultural politics of Africa.

Acknowledgement

All figures are reproduced by kind permission of Sun International.

Endnotes

1 Sex tourism emanates from the notion that first world tourists 'receive, and third world workers . . . provide personalised, and often embodied, services such as cooking, cleaning, serving . . . entertainment, and sexual services' (Mackie, 1998, p. 9).
2 Enloe (1989, p. 32) also observes that tourism images usually resort to stereotypical representations of femininity and masculinity in which men are militarized and women are represented as welcoming and available in their femininity. In a brochure for the Emerald Casino Resort referred to earlier (Emerald Safari Resort & Casino [sa]: sp), a noble black male figure is superimposed on an image of imposing architecture, extending the gendered connotations of culture, power and tradition.
3 Sun City offers a tour of the local Ledig village in their Cultural Tour (Sun International, 1999, p. 2).

References

Aitchison, C. (1999) New cultural geographies: the spatiality of leisure, gender and sexuality. *Leisure Studies* 18(1), 19–41.

Aitchison, C. (2000) Poststructural feminist theories of representing others: a response to the 'crisis' in leisure studies' discourse. *Leisure Studies* 19(3), 127–144.

Amarula Cream Advertisement (2005) *Femina Magazine*, (November) 107.

Ashton, L. (1997) The temptress in the wilderness goes legit. *Saturday Argus Out and About*, 20–21 September, 3.

Bank, A. and Minkley, G. (1998) Genealogies of space and identity in Cape Town. *Kronos. Journal of Cape History* 25. Available at: http//www.uwc.ac.za/arts/ihr/kronos/editorial.html

Barker, C. (2000) *Cultural Studies: Theory and Practice*. Sage, London.

Begg, A. (1998) 'New' Satour is a glint in Michael Farr's eye. *Pretoria News Business Report*, May 8, p. 16.

Brantlinger, P. (1985) Victorians and Africans: the genealogy of the myth of the Dark Continent. *Critical Inquiry* 12, 166–203.

Bruner, E.M. (2004) The Maasai and the Lion King: authenticity, nationalism, and globalization in African tourism. In: Gmelch, S.B. (ed.) *Tourists and Tourism: A Reader*. Waveland Press, Long Grove, Illinois, pp. 127–156.

Bunn, D. (1988) Embodying Africa: woman and romance in colonial fiction. *English in Africa* 15(1), 1–28.

Chaplin, S. and Holding, E. (eds) (1998) *Consuming Architecture*. Wiley, Chichester, UK.

Coetzee, J.M. (1988) *White Writing: On the Culture of Letters in South Africa*. Radix, Sandton, South Africa.

Cosgrove, D. and Domosh, M. (1993) Author and authority: writing the new cultural geography. In: Duncan, J. and Ley, D. (eds) *Place/Culture/Representation*. Routledge, London, pp. 25–38.

Cusack, T. (1998) Migrant travellers and touristic idylls: the paintings of Jack B Yeats and post-colonial identities. *Art History* 21(2), 201–218.

Department of Tourism and Environmental Affairs (1998) Advertising supplement on the North West Province. *Pretoria News*, 30 September, 12.

Donaldson, A. (2000) The chips are down. *Sunday Times Insight*, 30 July, 1.

Duncan, J. (1993) Sites of representation: place, time and the discourse of the Other. In: Duncan, J. and Ley, D. (eds) *Place/Culture/Representation*. Routledge, London, pp. 39–56.

Edensor, T. and Kothari, U. (1994) The masculinisation of Stirling's heritage. In: Kinnaird, V. and Hall, D. (eds) *Tourism: A Gender Analysis*. Wiley, Chichester, UK, pp. 164–187.

Enloe, C. (1989) *Bananas Beaches and Bases: Making Feminist Sense of International Politics*. University of California Press, Berkeley, California.

Fiske, J. (1989) *Reading the Popular*. Routledge, London.

Foucault, M. (1993) Space, power and knowledge. In: During, S. (ed.) *The Cultural Studies Reader*. Routledge, London, pp. 161–169.

Gates, H.L. (1998) Into Africa with Henry Louis Gates: lost cities of the South. Television programme broadcast, August 1999, on e-tv.

Geist, C.D. and Nachbar, J. (eds) (1983) *The Popular Culture Reader*, 3rd edn. Bowling Green University Popular Press, Bowling Green, Ohio.

Gilman, S.L. (1985) Black bodies, white bodies: toward an iconography of female sexuality in late nineteenth-century art, medicine, and literature. *Critical Inquiry* 12, 204–242.

Gmelch, S.B. (2004) *Tourists and Tourism: A Reader*. Waveland Press, Long Grove, Illinois.

Gregory, D. and Ley, D. (1988) Editorial: culture's geographies. *Environment and Planning D: Society and Space* 6, 115–116.

Hall, M. (1995) The legend of the Lost City, or, the man with golden balls. *Journal of Southern African Studies* 21(2), 179–199.

Hawthorne, T. (1996) *Lost City: Africa's Kingdom of Pleasure*. Struik, Cape Town, South Africa.

Hotels & Resorts. The Palace of The Lost City. Available at: http: //www.watg.com/lostcity.html

Huyssen, A. (1986) *After the Great Divide: Modernism, Mass Culture, Postmodernism*. Indiana University Press, Bloomington, Indiana.

Kinnaird, V., Kothari, U. and Hall, D. (1994) Tourism: gender perspectives. In: Kinnaird, V. and Hall, D. (eds) *Tourism: A Gender Analysis*. Wiley, Chichester, UK, pp. 1–34.

Kuenz, J. (1995) It's a small world after all. In: Klugman, K., Kuenz, J., Waldrep, S. and Willis, S. (eds) *Inside the Mouse: Work and Play at Disney World*. Duke University Press, Durham, North Carolina, pp. 54–78.

Lalvani, S. (1995) Consuming the exotic other. *Critical Studies in Mass Communication* 12(3), 263–286.

Lefebvre, H. (1991) *The Production of Space* (trans. D. Nicholson-Smith). Blackwell, Oxford.

Mackie, V. (1998) The metropolitan gaze: travellers, bodies and spaces. Available at: http//www.sshe.murdoch.edu.au/intersection/issue4.vera.html

Massey, D. (1994) *Space, Place and Gender.* Polity Press, Cambridge.

McKenzie, P. (1994) A sociological study of tourism in South Africa: a case study of Gold Reef City. MA dissertation, University of the Witwatersrand, Johannesburg, South Africa.

Mitchell, K. (2000) The culture of urban space. *Urban Geography* 21(5). Available at: http//www.vhwinston.com/ug/abstract/ad000505.pdf

Morgan, N. and Pritchard, A. (1998) *Tourism Promotion and Power: Creating Images, Creating Identities.* Wiley, Chichester, UK.

Pieterse, J.N. (1992) *White on Black: Images of Africa and Blacks in Western Popular Culture.* Yale University Press, New Haven, Connecticut.

Pollock, G. (1988) *Vision and Difference: Femininity, Feminism and the Histories of Art.* Routledge, London.

Pollock, G. (1992) *Avant-garde Gambits 1888–1893: Gender and the Colour of Art History.* Thames & Hudson, London.

Poole, M. (1993) *The Palace of the Lost City at Sun City, Republic of Bophuthatswana, Southern Africa.* Struik, Cape Town, South Africa.

Pratt, M.L. (1992) *Imperial Eyes: Travel Writing and Transculturation.* Routledge, London.

Pretoria News Business Report (1999) Foreign markets targeted for future growth. *Pretoria News Business Report,* 28 June, 9.

Root, D. (1996) *Cannibal Culture: Art, Appropriation, and the Commodification of Difference.* Westview, Boulder, Colorado.

Rosaldo, R. (1989) Imperialist nostalgia. *Representations* 26, 107–122.

Said, E.W. (1978) *Orientalism.* Routledge, London.

Sardar, Z. (1996) Walt Disney and the double victimisation of Pocahontas. *Third Text* 37, 17–26.

Shields, R. (1991) *Places on the Margin: Alternative Geographies of Modernity.* Routledge, London.

Smith, C. (2001) Sex tourism begins in South Africa. *Mail and Guardian,* 12–18 October, 28.

Soja, E.W. (1989) *Postmodern Geographies: The Reassertion of Space in Critical Social Theory.* Verso, London.

Soja, E.W. (1996) *Thirdspace: Journeys to Los Angeles and Other Real-and-Imagined Places.* Blackwell, Oxford.

Spain, D. (1992) *Gendered Spaces.* University of North Carolina Press, Chapel Hill, North Carolina.

Stam, R. and Spence, L. (1983) Colonialism, racism and representation. *Screen* 24(2), 2–20.

Strijdom, H.G., Schurink, W.J., Van der Burgh, C. *et al.* (1980) *The Effects of the Sun City Hotel Complex on the Immediate Social Environment: An Exploratory Study.* Human Sciences Research Council, Pretoria, South Africa.

Sun International (1996) *NuMaps Bird's Eye View of The Lost City.* NuMaps, Cape Town, South Africa.

Sun International (1997) Fact sheet: The Palace. Unpublished press release, May. Public Relations Department, Sun City, South Africa.

Sun International (1999) Encounters of The Lost City kind. Unpublished press release. Public Relations Department, Sun City, South Africa.

Sun International (2000) *The Lost City at Sun City.* Art Publishers, Johannesburg, South Africa.

Sun International (2004) Print advertisement. *Beeld,* June, 23, p. 16.

Urry, J. (1995) *Consuming Places.* Routledge, London.

Weinstein, R.M. (1992) Disneyland and Coney Island: reflections of the evolution of the modern amusement park. *Journal of Popular Culture* 26(1), 131–164.

Wessels, L.H. (1989) Sun City (Pilansberg Bophuthatswana) – 'n ontwikkelingsontleding in streekverband. MA dissertation, Unisa, Pretoria, South Africa.

Wheeler, R. (1999) Limited visions of Africa: geographies of savagery and civility in early eighteenth-century narratives. In: Duncan, J. and Gregory, D. (eds) *Writes of Passage: Reading Travel Writing*. Routledge, London, pp. 14–48.

Willis, S. (1995) The problem with pleasure. In: Klugman, K., Kuenz, J., Waldrep, S. and Willis, S. (eds) *Inside the Mouse: Work and Play at Disney World*. Duke University Press, Durham, North Carolina, pp. 1–11.

Wolf, J.B. (1991) A grand tour: South Africa and American tourists between the wars. *Journal of Popular Culture* 25(2), 99–116.

Zukin, S. (1991) *Landscapes of Power: From Detroit to Disney World*. University of California Press, Berkeley, California.

12 Advertisements as Tourism Space: 'Learning' Masculinity and Femininity from New Zealand Television

FABRICE DESMARAIS

Introduction

There is now an extensive literature on tourism advertising, much of it focusing on the role of advertising in promoting destinations: creating symbolic expectations for prospective tourists through textual and audio representations (see Morgan and Pritchard, 2000). In the case of New Zealand, advertising in the tourism-generating countries creates a particular New Zealand 'reality', usually based around hyperbolic visions of the landscape, the native flora and fauna (Morgan and Pritchard, 2005, 2006) or sport (Higham, 2005). The hosting of two successive America's Cup sailing events, close associations with rugby (through the world-renowned New Zealand All Blacks and the super 12 competition) and Queenstown's reputation as one of the world's most famous extreme sport destinations have all contributed to attract 'sport tourists' to New Zealand in some numbers (see Higham and Hinch, 1999). Indeed, the British Lions rugby tour attracted more than 20,000 tourists to New Zealand, generating a total GDP impact of NZ$135.2 million according to research commissioned by the Ministry of Tourism (Covec, 2005).

Despite this focus on tourism advertising, there has been no research which explores how media representations and discourses (including advertising) can work as an important tourism 'space' for visitors within destinations. This chapter argues that television advertising representations at the tourism destination can communicate particular meanings about its peoples and values which may conflict with the projected images presented in the tourists' country of origin. In other words, advertising plays a part in the brief and superficial process of acculturation tourists go through when visiting a country. In this context, tourists regularly experience the local media and the advertising it carries in places such as backpacker hostels' television rooms, pubs or in their hotel rooms. As Dru (1996, p. 1) notes:

> You check into a hotel in another country. The first thing you do when you get to your room is turn on the television. You zap for a while and inevitably come upon

a few commercials. They have a tone, a color, a flavor, somehow different from those you know. Something indefinable that makes them unlike those you're used to seeing. The reason is simple. Nothing reflects a country and an age better than its advertising. It is the very expression of the values of the times.

In view of this role of advertising, this chapter explores how gender is portrayed within the little recognized tourism space that is the domestic advertising of the 'host' tourist destination. The work presented here is part of a wider study which is concerned with analysing the ways in which long-stay tourists' visions of New Zealand are affected by the advertising messages they encounter on New Zealand television. It analyses a corpus of prime time New Zealand television commercials, focusing on commercials that use sport as a key referent. This focus was chosen because sport imagery (defined as people engaged in sporting activities and sport endorsements) is a major element of New Zealand advertising discourse and because gender differences tend to be particularly marked in sport (Scraton and Flintoff, 2002). The original idea for this study sprang from my discussions with both short- and long-stay visitors to New Zealand (particularly foreign students) who experience its local media as a leisure and entertainment activity. The comments from these visitors made it clear that advertising was a site in which tourists learn a great deal about the country visited and that advertising is especially noticed because of the entertainment value it provides. Indeed, in the self-regulated New Zealand media advertising landscape, advertising messages are very difficult to avoid because there is no limit on advertising time on television channels. Suich (1996) reported that the amount of advertising screened on New Zealand television is on average 12 minutes per hour (source: AGB MCNair). TVNZ, for example (representing channels '1' and '2'), guarantees that it imposes its own limit on advertisements of no more than 12 minutes per hour while TV3 allows up to 13.9 minutes of advertising per hour (Smith, 1996).

Using the model of random sampling advocated by many advertising studies (see Samiee and Jeong, 1994), a total of 1365 commercials were recorded from four New Zealand television channels between August 1998 and October 2005. In line with other studies, all duplicate commercials were eliminated and, as a result, 967 commercials form the study sample, of which 176 (or 18.2%) used sport imagery, making it a dominant theme in New Zealand advertising discourse. In presenting a constructionist discursive analysis (Hall, 1997) of the content of these television commercials, my study departs from the mainly quantitative empirical approach of most advertising studies. Such a cultural studies approach expressly involves thinking about advertising and culture as ideologies, so that advertising, as an institution embedded in culture, is seen to create an ideological order, placing certain topics in a position of hegemony within the advertising discourse of a country. Such a view understands advertising to be a signifying system, a symbolic classification, a language based on a system of thought privileging certain forms, meanings and definitions (Williamson, 1978). These, in turn, become part of tourists' understandings of the country they are visiting.

Having briefly introduced the study and considered the research approach it adopts, this chapter will now move on to outline the significance of sport in New Zealand and to consider the theatrical representations of gender and the gendered nature of representations evident in New Zealand advertising. I will argue that advertising messages that use the core national theme of sport are meaningful not only for local viewers but also for visitors who see the media and learn from it; thus, I map the gendered imagery in relation to the important national site of sport.

Sport and New Zealand Nationhood

Sport is an extremely important part of New Zealand culture: this is a country where almost a quarter of the television news bulletin on its main network is devoted to sports (Atkinson, 1994). It has long been a central site where national identity is constructed and maintained and this critical role of sport in the formation and maintenance of New Zealand national identity has been acknowledged by many authors from different fields (see Sinclair, 1986; Phillips, 1996; Laidlaw, 1999a,b; Patterson, 1999; Collins, 2000). Scholars such as Jobling (1991) have discussed the almost fanaticism for sport in New Zealand, whilst Nauright and Black (1996, p. 206) noted that 'in no two countries [New Zealand and South Africa] has sport in general, and rugby in particular, been a more powerful force in the construction of "national identity"'. The *New Zealand Official Yearbook*, a source of commonly held cultural beliefs, has commented that 'New Zealand is perhaps best known for the calibre of its international sportspeople' (1998, p. 285) and that '94% of New Zealanders [are] interested and/or involved in sport' so that 'the country carries an international reputation for sporting excellence that belies its size' (2004, p. 237). Such sentiments are also reflected at governmental and agency levels so that Sport and Recreation New Zealand (2002, p. 11) argues that it is 'important to our national identity that we are world-leaders in some sporting disciplines'.

Significantly, the centrality of (men's) rugby and the national men's rugby team (the All Blacks) to a sense of shared community in New Zealand is widely accepted (Sinclair, 1986; Fougere, 1989; Perry, 1994; Phillips, 1996; Hope, 2002). For over a century, New Zealand rugby has functioned to unite the nation – when the All Blacks played, the nation tuned in to listen or watch (Day, 1999). New Zealand's love affair with rugby was cemented with the first official rugby tour to England in 1905 and the success of that team has become a foundational myth of the country (Wensing, 2003). According to Hope (2002, p. 235), the team was considered to embody the developing national spirit 'of hard, uncompromising, self-reliant men who played with pride, ingenuity, and passion for their country'. New Zealand's incredible winning record over the next 75 years served to anchor rugby as the central focus of nationalism, an articulation that has endured even in the face of significant disruptions – such as the 1981 South African Springbok Rugby Tour which divided the nation (see Richards, 1999). Certainly, in New Zealand television advertising, rugby has a tremendous economic value that derives from the cultural, social, political and 'mediatic' value it has accumulated through the decades (see Phillips, 1996), so that sport and national signs are often articulated to create symbolic and cultural value around goods (Desmarais, 2003).

The Theatrical Representation of Gender

The notion of advertising as a theatrical production of gender is widely accepted (Goffman, 1979; Van Zoonen, 1994; Gunter, 1995; Simonton, 1995; Tebbel, 2000). So too is the understanding that advertisers want their messages to be easily understood by viewers and that they therefore often use stereotypical situations and characters easily identifiable by audiences of a specific cultural environment (Leiss *et al.*, 1986; Van Zoonen, 1994). As a result, the roles adopted by men and women in commercials have consistently been found to be heavily stereotyped (Thoveron, 1987; Van Zoonen, 1994; Gunter, 1995). The fact that the media in general, and advertising in particular, proposes restrictively stereotypical portrayals of gender has been confirmed by many empirical studies across a range of countries such as the USA (McArthur and Resko, 1975; Bretl and Cantor, 1988), Portugal (Neto and Pinto, 1998), the UK (Furnham and Bitar, 1993; Furnham and Skae, 1997), Italy (Furnham and Voli, 1989) and Australia (Mazzella *et al.*, 1992). Through these restrictive stereotypical portrayals, viewers 'learn' another new 'reality' about the country they are visiting: a mediated reality of gender roles and representations which help to construct the national imaginary of – in this case – New Zealand.

Engendered Sports Commercials

It is often noted that sport has long been equated with masculinity – particularly in the English-speaking world (Chandler and Nauright, 1996) and this study reveals that over two-thirds (69%) of all sports-oriented television commercials in New Zealand exclusively feature men (Table 12.1). By comparison, just 11 commercials (6%) only featured sportswomen as product endorsers or women in sporting contexts (5 of them being netball). The remaining quarter of commercials (44) featured both men and women. Such skewed figures reveal that sports-focused advertising on New Zealand television is an overwhelmingly masculine world which presents viewers with a very particular view of society. Moreover, when we interrogate the advertising at a deeper, qualitative level, it is evident that not only does women's sport figure less frequently but also the discursive formations in the commercials construct an extremely gendered image of New Zealand society.

Masculinity and sport-oriented commercials

Popular discourses have long constructed New Zealand as a man's country (Phillips, 1996) and traditional concepts of masculinity abound in its television advertising (Perry, 1994). In those examined for this study, commercials which used sport as their main theme typically highlighted masculine virility, toughness and power. Sport imagery – particularly rugby imagery – was often used in commercials to

Table 12.1. Gender of characters portrayed in sporting situations in commercials.

Commercials with females only		Commercials with males only		Commercials with both males and females		Total
n	%	*n*	%	*n*	%	*(n)*
11	6	121	69	44	25	176

transfer notions of assertiveness, hard masculinity and tough competition from the male sportsmen to the advertised products, creating brands with aggressive and masculine brand personalities (see Morgan and Pritchard, 2000).

Whilst commentators have noted that 'popular culture and sports media tend to glorify the violent use of the male body in sports' (Messner and Sabo, 1994, p. 93), the promotion of violent behaviour through the depiction of intense and brutal images of rugby matches and hyperbolic visions of the male muscled body is particularly noticeable in New Zealand. Here we are presented with an extreme form of masculinity and the commercials depict men performing impossible feats of strength (in one commercial for energy bars we see a man bench-pressing a truck) or possessing the ability to move into space like rockets. The male body is portrayed as a powerful machine that requires regular maintenance and which can be disciplined and controlled through regimentation and military training to achieve sporting or consumption goals. A typical commercial featured the sweat-shined All Blacks rugby players working out in a gymnasium. The strength and power of these men was connoted by shots of brutal rugby tackles intercut with camera close-ups of pumping thigh and bicep muscles, set to a soundtrack of audible groans and heavy metal rock music. Here, we see an excessive masculinity, where 'the macho rugby player [seems to be] a drag queen, parading excesses of machismo in the same way that the regular queen parades extremes of "femininity"' (Star, 1993, p. 65).

Any tourist to New Zealand could not fail to notice the array of marketing efforts (particularly the extensive sponsorship deals) which surround sports competitions in the country, notably rugby competitions such as the super 14, the tri-nations or recently the British Lions' tour. In addition to commercials for specific televised sports events, those companies which sponsor sports events and teams (including products such as chocolate bars and beer) also rely heavily on sport-focused advertising and images of bone-crushing rugby tackles set to heavy metal rock music are once again the standard fare. Take several commercials for a television channel: black storm clouds and thunder provided the background for fast-moving images of violent collisions, tackles, winning moves, decisive passes and skilful side-stepping from the New Zealand All Blacks rugby team. These images of match-winning glory were accompanied by heavy metal music and a deep resonant male voice-over – elements which together created an atmosphere of masculinity and power and presented these as part of a unified national discourse.

Rugby is deeply entwined with constructions of New Zealand nationhood, and the games' valorization of physical strength, courage and manliness built on mental toughness can be traced back to the 'pioneer spirit' discourses of the turn of the 19th century (Phillips, 1996). Moreover, there is a long New Zealand tradition of regarding rugby as analogous to war and of seeing rugby players as embodiments of military values (Phillips, 1996). This notion of rugby as war was echoed in one commercial, where famous rugby players from New Zealand were transformed into bombs that flew to destroy the northern hemisphere, exploiting and foregrounding the rugby rivalry between countries of the northern and southern hemispheres. This particular commercial thus emphasized conflict and combat and the role of the audience's national allegiance in the consumption of these televised rugby competitions.

Interestingly, of course, whilst New Zealand advertising campaigns in the major tourism-generating countries represent it as a welcoming and friendly country keen to play a positive role in our globalized world, its domestic advertising typically exploits geographic nationalism (see Desmarais, 2004), especially in relation to sport. This was clearly seen during the last British Lions rugby tour of New Zealand (2005), when a commercial depicting a tattooed Maori warrior facing up to a roaring lion was typical of the advertisements for the televised rugby matches. Another commercial portrayed the British people as slow-thinking and easily outwitted by their New Zealand opponents (interestingly of course, the UK is a significant tourism market for New Zealand and several thousand British tourists followed the Lions tour in New Zealand). One particular commercial characterized the archetypal British couple as David and Victoria Beckham (a famous footballer and his celebrity wife, oft-labelled Posh and Becks by the tabloid press), portraying David Beckham as the effeminate British male and Victoria as narcissistic and vain. Their portrayal was juxtaposed with images and messages in the second part of the commercial which promised that the All Blacks rugby team would demonstrate to British outsiders their superior toughness and masculinity, normalizing hyper-masculinity.

Femininity and sport-oriented commercials

The invisibility of female athletes in mass media sports coverage is well documented (e.g. Sabo and Jansen, 1992; McGregor and Melville, 1993; McGregor, 1994; Pirinen, 1997; Koivula, 1999; Eastman and Billings, 2000); indeed, Kane and Greendorfer (1994, p. 31) have commented that women in sport media are simply 'symbolically annihilated'. In addition to being under-represented in media coverage, sportswomen are also likely to find themselves stereotyped and trivialized – the subjects of gender marking (Duncan, 1990; Koivula, 1999; Weiller and Higgs, 1999) which emphasizes feminine characteristics and favours heterosexuality (Kane and Parks, 1992; Pirinen, 1997; Elueze and Jones, 1998; Koivula, 1999) and infantilization (Duncan, 1990; Daddario, 1994; Elueze and Jones, 1998). This study reveals a similar pattern in New Zealand sports-oriented television advertising. Women were hugely under-represented in these types of advertisements and when they did feature, their femininity, attractiveness and sexuality dominated the characterizations, which also endorsed their relative powerlessness compared with their male counterparts.

Thus, when they did feature female characters, most New Zealand commercials that used sport and were aimed at women emphasized female domesticity and 'cosmetic fitness', i.e. the use of sport (together with some other product) to obtain an attractive body (Coakley, 1998, p. 217). One particular commercial featured Barbara Kendall (a several-times windsurfing world and Olympic champion recognizable to both domestic and international audiences) promoting a brand of household appliances. The social environment constructed in the commercial was that of everyday domestic life and Barbara was portrayed as having responsibility for the management of this domestic world. Her comments – 'my husband loves using his […] large-capacity washing machine, and it's only $1199' – defines her as an authority on household appliances (rather than windsurfing) and addresses other women, clearly implying that the domestic world of appliances is part of the gender sphere of women.

In its key tourism markets, New Zealand is promoted as a country of extreme sports and healthy living. The discourse of New Zealand television advertising firmly links women and sport and the achievement of thin desirable bodies, and there are many commercials which suggest that the path to beauty and fitness is the consumption of healthy food. For instance, the internationally famous Silver Ferns (the New Zealand women's netball team) player Bernice Mene, in a commercial for a brand of frozen food, was valorized not for her sports performances (as her male counterparts were) but as a role model promoting cosmetic fitness and 'acceptable' eating behaviour to other women. In this commercial aimed at women, the ideal female body was clearly seen to be slender and fit – the product of considerable bodily maintenance. Thus, Bernice's father (a famous sportsperson himself) is heard in the advertisement telephoning her to check whether his 'little girl [was] looking after herself': a patriarchal voice reinforcing the division between father and daughter, supervisor and supervised, responsible and irresponsible, as well as framing the female champion as requiring guidance. However, this patriarchal voice appears not only to interrogate Bernice but also to ask the commercial's women viewers whether they too are looking after their bodies and whether they are good models of cosmetic fitness.

In this context, it was also interesting to note that many of the New Zealand television commercials that depicted women in sporting situations or that advertised women's sports equipment used a male voice-over. Thus, one commercial for netball shoes aimed at women used a male rugby player as an endorser. These were not the only ways in which signifiers of femininity or female worlds contrasted with signifiers of masculinity or masculine worlds; it was also evident in the soundtracks used in sports commercials. For example, commercials for a sponsor of the New Zealand women's netball team used a light and youthful music score that contrasted totally with the heavy metal music in commercials featuring male rugby characters. Such a finding echoes Feder-Kane's (2000, p. 207) analysis of women's figure skating in which he comments: '[T]he narrative surrounding the women's competition [figure skating] is sickly sweet in its presentation of the competitors' femininity.'

In common with television advertising elsewhere, New Zealand commercials reproduce a very particular view of graceful femininity and those which took sport as their theme reflect stereotypical signifiers of femininity such as grace and elegance. Femininity in sports is usually constructed in opposition to masculinity (Guttmann, 1996) and those sports constructed as 'appropriate' for women reflect Victorian ideals of femininity (Snyder and Spreitzer, 1983), so that those that involve attempts to physically overcome opponents by body contact are not generally regarded as acceptable for women. Such constructions of femininity can be seen in one commercial for a brand of cars in which a woman ice skater was portrayed dancing to Ravel's Bolero in front of Milford Sound (a famous New Zealand tourism landmark). Here we can see the grace of the woman skater, her moves connoting style, elegance and refinement, transferring to the 'stunning style and design' of the new car models.

Other commercials not only articulated stereotypical constructions of gender, but also clearly entwined gender with the national mythology of New Zealand – operating as a 'lesson' to tourists about New Zealanders' values and cultural expectations. Thus, one commercial for a local airline, which featured a customer addressing the viewer and then having a short conversation with a female member of the cabin crew at a check-in counter, draws upon stereotypical representations of New Zealand femininity:

> MAN: What kinds of people make such an airline? Take that young woman there, dynamic, intelligent, focused, encouraged to make her own decisions. Judging by her aura of competency, you'd say she was from a rural background. Probably several brothers, no sisters, a bit of a tomboy, the usual resentment at not being able to play rugby, although she did have a pony, her parents still own the land and their fondest wish is to see her married.
>
> MAN: Brothers?
>
> WOMAN: Only child.
>
> MAN: Sport?
>
> WOMAN: Touch rugby.
>
> MAN: But you did have a pony?
>
> WOMAN: Allergic.
>
> MAN: Err no surprises there then . . .

It is irrelevant that the man's preconceived ideas were wrong, the point we should note here is the way this commercial clearly defined the subject positions of New Zealand women to the outside world. This commercial in fact can be seen as part of a discourse that contributes to fixing New Zealand gender idiosyncrasies through social participation in sport and life in the country. The commercial presents viewers with a model of the rural New Zealand family and reinforces which physical activities country girls are expected to participate in: she is portrayed as enjoying typical female sporting pursuits such as riding and as aspiring to participate in 'male' activities such as rugby. Once again, rugby is seen as a game which men play and women 'support'. Indeed, numerous commercials depict women as rugby spectators. Typically, in one such commercial, a female champion netball player was seen eating her meal while watching an All Blacks rugby game, and therefore supporting male sport.

Conclusion

As I noted at the start of this chapter, while advertising campaigns in the tourists' country of origin work to construct one New Zealand 'reality' (usually based around images of spectacular scenery and awe-inspiring landscapes), the domestic advertising which they are exposed to once they reach the destination communicates a very different view of its people and values. Moreover, television advertising works as an important tourism space for people visiting a country not simply because of its pervasiveness and entertainment appeal. It is also regarded as a more credible 'version' of the reality of the destination, precisely because tourists see it as an authentic part of the everyday life of New Zealanders: this must be the reality of life in New Zealand because it is part of the mundane, not some advertising campaign for the country paid for by its tourism organization. In other words, such advertising plays a key role as an agent of cultural pedagogy in the process of acculturation tourists go through when visiting a country. Yet, advertising research in tourism studies has neglected this important element in the formation of tourists' images of host destinations.

As we have seen here, sport is an extremely important part of New Zealand culture and has played a significant role in creating and shaping the mythologies of New Zealand nationhood. It is also a dominant theme in New Zealand advertising discourse. In this chapter I have mapped how engendered portrayals in New Zealand sports-oriented television advertising construct a particular view of that country's culture and national values and suggested that this 'instructs' tourists in their understanding of New Zealand life. The analysis of the 1365 commercials taped during the study period (August 1998 to October 2005) clearly reveals that signifiers of femininity or female worlds contrasted totally with signifiers of masculinity or masculine worlds. Women were routinely portrayed as having a strong relationship to the domestic context and to 'feminine values and interests' such as health and beauty, whilst at the same time lending emotional and collective support to male sportspeople (especially rugby players). On the other hand, embodiments of hyper-masculinity built on physical and mental toughness were commonly depicted (again usually centred around rugby or using rugby players as role models). Certainly, there is no doubt that the ideologies invested in advertising media privilege particular forms, meanings and identities over others and such restrictive and stereotypical portrayals of women and men 'teach' visitors a particular version of 'reality' about the country they are visiting and are part of the wider tourism experience at the destination, forming part of the tourist's ideas about everyday New Zealand life. It seems that there is much potential for research which explores the extent to which such national and cultural imageries impact on the preconceived ideas tourists have of a destination and whether these 'naive' images are challenged or confirmed through the tourists' actual exposure to the domestic media of the destination.

References

Atkinson, J. (1994) Structures of television news. In: Ballard, P. (ed.) *Power and Responsibility*. Broadcasting standards Authority, Wellington, pp. 43–74.

Bretl, D. and Cantor, J. (1988) The portrayal of men and women in US television commercials: a recent content analysis and trends over 15 years. *Sex Roles* 18(9/10), 595–609.

Chandler, T.J.L. and Nauright, J. (1996) Introduction: rugby, manhood and identity. In: Nauright, J. and Chandler, T.J.L.

(eds) *Making Men: Rugby and Masculine Identity*. Franck Cass, London, pp. 1–12.

Coakley, J.J. (1998) *Sport in Society: Issues and Controversies*. Irwin/McGraw-Hill, Boston, Massachusetts.

Collins, C. (ed.) (2000) *Sport in New Zealand Society*. Dunmore Press, Palmerston North, New Zealand.

Covec (2005) The economic impact of the 2005 DHL Lions Series on New Zealand. Available at: http://www.covec.co.nz/pdf/lions_eia.pdf

Daddario, G. (1994) Chilly scenes of the 1992 winter games: the mass media and the marginalization of female athletes. *Sociology of Sport Journal* 11(3), 275–288.

Day, P. (1999) Sport, the media and New Zealand. In: Patterson, B. (ed.) *Sport, Society and Culture in New Zealand.* Stout Research Centre, Wellington, New Zealand, pp. 93–102.

Desmarais, F. (2003) *The Discourse of New Zealand and French Television Advertising: A Comparative Approach.* Thesis. The University of Waikato, Hamilton, New Zealand.

Desmarais, F. (2004) Advertising differences: professional communicators, positioning strategies and national cultures. *Australian Journal of Communication* 31(3), 93–110.

Dru, J.M. (1996) *Disruption: Overturning Conventions and Shaking Up the Marketplace.* Wiley, New York.

Duncan, M.C. (1990) Sport photographs and sexual difference: images of women and men in the 1994 and 1988 Olympic Games. *Sociology of Sport Journal* 7(1), 22–43.

Eastman, S.T. and Billings, A.C. (2000) Sportcasting and sports reporting. *Journal of Sports and Social Issues* 24(2), 192–213.

Elueze, R. and Jones, R.L. (1998) A quest for equality: a gender comparison of the BBC's TV coverage of the 1995 world athletic championships. *Women in Sport and Physical Activity Journal* 7(1), 45–67.

Feder-Kane, A.M. (2000) 'A radiant smile from the lovely lady': overdetermined femininity in 'ladies' figure skating. In: Birell, S. and McDonald, M.G. (eds) *Reading Sport: Critical Essays on Power and Representation.* Northeastern University Press, Boston, Massachusetts, pp. 206–233.

Fougere, G. (1989) Sport culture and identity: the case of rugby football. In: Novitz, D. and Willmott, B. (eds) *Culture and Identity in New Zealand.* GP Books, Christchurch, New Zealand, pp. 110–122.

Furnham, A. and Bitar, N. (1993) The stereotyped portrayal of men and women in British television advertisements. *Sex Roles* 29(3/4), 297–310.

Furnham, A. and Skae, E. (1997) Portrayals of men and women in British television advertisements. *European Psychologist* 2, 44–51.

Furnham, A. and Voli, V. (1989) Gender stereotypes in Italian television advertisements. *Journal of Broadcasting and Electronic Media* 33, 175–185.

Goffman, E. (1979) *Gender Advertisements.* Harvard University Press, Cambridge, Massachusetts.

Gunter, B. (1995) *Television and Gender Representation.* John Libby, London.

Guttmann, A. (1996) *The Erotic in Sports.* Columbia University Press, New York.

Hall, S. (1997) The work of representation. In: Hall, S. (ed.) *Representation: Cultural Representations and Signifying Practices.* Sage, London, pp. 13–74.

Higham, J.E.S. (ed.) (2005) *SportTourism Destinations: Issues, Opportunities and Analysis.* Elsevier Butterworth-Heinemann, Oxford.

Higham, J.E.S. and Hinch, T.D. (1999) The development of super 12 and its implications for tourism: the case of the Otago highlanders. Industry report submitted to Otago Rugby Football Union, Southland Rugby Union, North Otago Rugby Union, Dunedin City Council Economic Development Unit, Tourism Dunedin, Waitaki District Council, Invercargill City Council, Southland Economic Development Unit. Available at: http://www.business.otago.ac.nz/tourism/research/electronicpubs/super12/index.html

Hope, W. (2002) Whose all blacks? *Media, Culture and Society* 24(2), 235–253.

Jobling, I.F. (1991) Sport and the state: the case of Australia and New Zealand. In: Landry, F., Landry, M. and Yerles, M. (eds) *Sport: The Third Millenium/le troisième millénaire.* Proceedings of the International Symposium, Quebec, Canada, 21–25 May 1990. Les presses de l'Université Laval, Sainte-Foy, Canada, pp. 251–259.

Kane, M.J. and Greendorfer, S.L. (1994) The media's role in accommodating and resisting stereotyped images of women in sport. In: Creedon, P.J. (ed.) *Women, Media, and Sport: Challenging Gender Values*. Sage, Thousand Oaks, California, pp. 28–44.

Kane, M.J. and Parks, J.B. (1992) The social construction of gender difference and hierarchy in sport journalism: few new twists on very old themes. *Women in Sport and Physical activity Journal* 1(1), 49–83.

Koivula, N. (1999) Gender stereotyping in televised media sport coverage. *Sex Roles* 41(7/8), 589–604.

Laidlaw, C. (1999a) *Rights of passage*. Hodder Moa Beckett, Auckland, New Zealand.

Laidlaw, C. (1999b) Sport and national identity: race relations, business, professionalism. In: Patterson, B. (ed.) *Sport, Society and Culture in New Zealand*. Stout Research Centre, Wellington, New Zealand, pp. 11–18.

Leiss, W., Kline, S. and Jhally, S. (1986) *Social Communication in Advertising: Persons, Products, and Images of Well-being*. Methuen, New York.

Mazzella, C., Durkin, K., Cerini, E. and Buralli, P. (1992) Sex role stereotyping in Australian television advertisements. *Sex Roles* 26(7/8), 243–259.

McArthur, L.Z. and Resko, B.G. (1975) The portrayal of men and women in American television commercials. *Journal of Social Psychology* 97, 209–220.

McGregor, J. (1994) Media sport. In: Trenberth, L. and Collins, C. (eds) *Sport Management in New Zealand: An Introduction*. Dunmore Press, Palmerston North, New Zealand, pp. 115–129.

McGregor, J. and Melville, P. (1993) The invisible face of women's sport in the New Zealand Press. *Metro (Film, Television, Radio, Multimedia)* 96, 35–39.

Messner, M.A. and Sabo, D.F. (1994) *Sex, Violence and Power in Sports: Rethinking Masculinity*. Crossing Press, Freedom, California.

Morgan, N.J. and Pritchard, A. (2000) *Advertising in Tourism and Leisure*. Butterworth-Heinemann, Oxford.

Morgan, N. and Pritchard, A. (2005) (PR)omoting place: the role of PR in build-ing New Zealand's destination brand relationships. *Journal of Hospitality and Leisure Marketing* 12(1/2), 157–176.

Morgan, N. and Pritchard, A. (2006) Promoting niche tourism destination brands: case studies of New Zealand and Wales. *Journal of Promotion Management* 12(1), 17–33.

Nauright, J. and Black, D. (1996) Hitting them where it hurts: Springbok-all black rugby, masculine national identity and counter-hegemonic struggle, 1959–1992. In: Nauright, J. and Chandler, T.J.L. (eds) *Making Men: Rugby and Masculine Identity*. Franck Cass, London, pp. 205–226.

Neto, F. and Pinto, I. (1998) Gender stereotypes in Portuguese television advertisements. *Sex Roles* 39(1/2), 153–164.

New Zealand Official Yearbook (1998) 101st edn, Statistics New Zealand. GP Publications, Wellington, New Zealand.

New Zealand Official Yearbook (2004) 104th edn, Statistics New Zealand. David Bateman, Wellington, New Zealand.

Patterson, B. (ed.) (1999) *Sport, Society and Culture in New Zealand*. Stout Research Centre, Wellington, New Zealand.

Perry, N. (1994) *The Dominion of Signs: Television, Advertising and Other New Zealand Fictions*. Auckland University Press, Auckland, New Zealand.

Phillips, J. (1996) *A Man's Country?* Penguin Books, Auckland, New Zealand.

Pirinen, R.M. (1997) The construction of women's positions is sport: a textual analysis of articles on female athletes in Finnish women's magazines. *Sociology of Sport Journal* 14, 290–301.

Richards, T. (1999) *Dancing on our Bones: New Zealand, South Africa, Rugby and Racism*. Bridget Williams Books, Wellington, New Zealand.

Sabo, D. and Jansen, S. (1992) Images of men in sports media. In: Craig, S. (ed.) *Men, Masculinity and the Media*. Sage, Newbury Park, California, pp. 169–184.

Samiee, S. and Jeong, I. (1994) Cross-cultural research in advertising: an assessment of methodologies. *Journal of the Academy of Marketing Science* 22(3), 205–217.

Scraton, S. and Flintoff, A. (eds) (2002) *Gender and Sport: A Reader*. Routledge, London.

Simonton, A.J. (1995) Women for sale. In: Lont, C.M. (ed.) *Women and Media: Content, Careers, Criticism*. Wadsworth Publishing Company, Belmont, California, pp. 143–164.

Sinclair, K. (1986) *A Destiny Apart: New Zealand's Search for National Identity*. Allen & Unwin, Wellington, New Zealand.

Smith, P. (1996) Shooting the paymaster. In: Smith, P. (ed.) *Revolution in the Air*. Longman, Auckland, New Zealand, pp. 151–164.

Snyder, E. and Spreitzer, E. (1983) *Social Aspects of Sport*, 2nd edn. Prentice-Hall, Englewood Cliffs, New Jersey.

Sport and Recreation New Zealand (2002) *Our Vision, Our Direction*. Sport and Recreation New Zealand, Wellington, New Zealand.

Star, L. (1993) Macho and his brothers: passion and resistance in sports discourse. *Sites* 26(Autumn), 54–78.

Suich, M. (1996) *Benchmarking Public Broadcasters: How TVNZ Compares with Other State-owned Broadcasters in Australia, Britain and Canada*. TVNZ, Auckland, New Zealand.

Tebbel, C. (2000) *The Body Snatchers: How the Media Shapes Women*. Finch Publishing, Sydney, Australia.

Thoveron, G. (1987) *How Women Are Represented in Television Programmes in the EEC; Part 1: Images of Women in News, Advertising, Series, and Serials*. Commission of the European Communities, Brussels, Belgium.

Van Zoonen, L. (1994) *Feminist Media Studies*. Sage, London.

Weiller, K.H. and Higgs, C.T. (1999) Television coverage of professional golf: a focus on gender. *Women in Sport and Physical Activity Journal* 8(1), 83–100.

Wensing, E. (2003) New Zealand national identity in print media representations of 2002 Commonwealth Games. Unpublished MA Thesis. University of Waikato, Hamilton, New Zealand.

Williamson, J. (1978) *Decoding Advertisements: Ideology and Meaning in Advertising*. Marion Boyars, London.

13 Gender Posed: The People Behind the Postcards

GREG RINGER

Introduction

[handwritten margin note: o remedy for all disease or ills, originalness]

As the world's largest service industry, tourism is increasingly perceived by proponents as a socio-economic panacea for indigenous communities. A central tenet of this argument presumes that tourism can help ensure environmental conservation and, simultaneously, both employ and empower women and ethnic minorities. Yet, the selling of local people and their practices as tourist 'attractions' too often transfigures the social history and culturally constructed landscapes of the destination by mediating the formation of identities long defined through gender, behaviour and belief. This chapter therefore highlights the evolving roles of women and men in the globalization of tourism, as they decipher and interpret their history and 'place' as visitors and denizens of locations increasingly (re)defined by the images and discourse of travel marketing. More specifically, it examines the interplay between gender and tourism by drawing attention to: (i) the manner in which our spatial and cognitive experiences as hosts and visitors – and the resultant choice of destinations and leisure activities for either enjoyment or employment – are shaped by cultural constructions, perceptual images and social practices of gender and sexuality, including prescribed clothing and physical appearances, ritualized behaviour and notions of work and equity; and (ii) venues where tourism, as an industry and a socio-economic sphere of human activity, might engender positive change at the local and international levels in existing social, environmental and financial conditions. The following research is intended to encourage both critical – and creative – appreciation and further discussion on the direction and discourse of tourism development and marketing in the magnification and marginalization of cultural traditions and local heritage.

Tourism and Gender Intersects

The nexus of tourism and gender lies, in part, in the human constructions of the destination, both architectural and emotive, and the quality and context of peoples' encounters with the attraction (Fig. 13.1). A major employer of women and ethnic minorities, the experience, identity and meaning of travel in many communities have long been defined by the nature of the recreational act, including whether an individual engages as a user of the resource or activity, an employee, or the cultural or sexual object. Equally decisive are the ideologies, images and material transactions of tourism, with traditional practices, artefacts and attire once historically prescribed by gender and sexualized behaviour, now reinforced in value by tourism or, conversely, demeaned through commercial trade, entertainment and sex tourism (Opperman, 1998; Ringer, 1998; Aitchison *et al.*, 2000; Ryan and Hall, 2001; Mansvelt, 2005).

Stylized images of women are a frequent icon of the human geography of the tourist destination in the media and travel literature, where they represent a superficial morphology of the land and the 'motherly' attention given to family, community and guests. Contrarily, such stereotypes are also employed to portray and typify female tourists as 'wild girls gone bad', in search of romantic trysts with 'exotic' male companions (Fig. 13.2). Even on the Internet, many women's web sites highlight the tips they provide those female travellers who seek 'love on the road'. Advisers share information about cosmetics and 'must have' clothing for dates, and enthusiastically encourage their readers to be 'gutsy' when travelling, as more women engage in casual sexual encounters in foreign destinations – e.g. 43% of the female visitors to Jamaica recently reported having sex with someone they met while on vacation, a

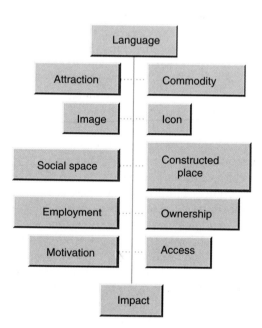

Fig. 13.1. Gender and tourism intersects.

```
┌─────────────────────────────────────────┐
│  1. Vulnerable                            │
│  2. No tech skills                        │
│  3. Older women uninterested in travel    │
│  4. Social 'escape' primary motive        │
│  5. Detail-oriented                       │
│  6. Caregiver                             │
│  7. Sex and safety symbols                │
│  8. All women are heterosexual            │
└─────────────────────────────────────────┘
```

Fig. 13.2. Stereotypes of women travellers. (From Student Survey (*n* = 246), University of Oregon, May 2005.)

number approaching the 69% of male visitors who had similar interpersonal and intercultural contacts (Coleman and Crang, 2002; Lew *et al.*, 2004).

The roles of many indigenous women are further conflicted by their dual service as consumer and as cultural broker and 'producer' of the tourist 'product', and by political and socio-economic policies that determine landownership, worker mobility and gender equality. In countries and communities around the world, disputes continue over the appropriate sexual roles and social 'place' of women (and by default, men) in the cultural landscape of the tourist destination, as well as the questionable imposition of a 'tourist culture' on the community, with women as the cultural attraction. These disagreements are typically manifested in the lack of control afforded to women over personal and community decisions; the limited access of women to funding and jobs as tour providers and travel operators; and the variegated assessments offered by both sexes of tourism's impacts on themselves and the destination. While the intensity and outcome may differ by locality, the critical issues they share involve lifestyle choices of marriage and motherhood, one's place of residency (rural/urban) and family status (income or assets), as well as professional constraints, including sexual discrimination and violence against women and girls, and educational and occupational disparities (Ringer, 1998; Apostolopoulos and Gayle, 2002; Swain and Momsen, 2002; Gmelch, 2004; Ghodsee, 2005).

Less well documented is the nature of our sexual expressions in travel, including ways in which gender guides our view of the destination, its accommodations and activities, and our interactions with local inhabitants. This omission is compounded by a tendency in some surveys to treat women and men, and the communities in which they reside, as homogeneous in thought and action. Yet, membership in any community shifts with individual agendas and the issue under debate, necessitating greater awareness of the multiple ways in which people conceive their surrounding environments, and the emotional and economic values and functions attached to each (Momsen and Kinnaird, 1993; Hawkins, 1994; Barry, 1995; Cohen, 1996; Howe *et al.*, 1997; Opperman, 1998; Hemmati, 1999). There is a crucial need, therefore, to move beyond descriptive studies of gender and travel in order to better understand social processes and the sexually demarcated space of local places. To do so successfully will require a panoptic vision informed by direct observation and verifiable information provided by both male and female participants engaged in the leisure activity. Although highly subjective, and perhaps more emotive and qualitative than empirically quantitative, such data is invaluable in that it is informed by personal experience. As such, even a modicum of understanding of the commonalities and differences – however subtle the aggregation – may help us to meaningfully bridge the current gaps that impede women and men as equal participants in the long-term success of many tourist attractions and destinations.

Tourism presents considerable potential to satisfy local desires for sustainable income generation and poverty elimination, and to provide meaningful, informed interactions for cultural sharing and networking. Achievement of these possibilities could help to equalize the uneven political, economic and social roles that now define many women and men through travel, and thereby enable more people to directly participate in, and benefit from, the informative and profitable outcomes of community-supported recreation, education and conservation. At the same time, though recent critiques of gender in leisure studies focus on tourists and the travel industry as agents of social change, several critical themes remain underappreciated, including the commercialization of local sites, people and cultures for visitor activities; the marginalization of 'host' communities, including the commodification and subjugation of women and children as tourist attractions, as well as the production and privatization of tourist landscapes and services. As a result, the meaning and value of daily practices and social behaviour that define a group of people and their places are casually removed from the planning matrix with a rhetorical razor that effectively disempowers community authority and disenfranchises residents (Sinclair, 1997; Ringer, 1998, 2004; Sharpley and Telfer, 2002; Swain and Momsen, 2002).

To better understand the apparent paradox which tourism presents its destinations, this chapter provides an analysis that applies cognitive mapping techniques to graphically elucidate the structure, identity and meaning of the destination for tourists and local people alike, as their shared 'attractions' become further embedded in the global tourism economy. Using Geographic Information Systems (GIS) to adjust the resolution and scale, environmental perceptions were gathered from visitors and residents of select rural destinations in North America and the Pacific, as the inhabitants transition from barter-based economies and natural resource extraction to sustainable tourism attraction. These composite maps were then overlaid atop physiographic and demographic data of each 'host' community. This allowed community planners and leaders to visualize the patterns and consequences of recreation and tourism over time as visitation grows. Such images – through the social and recreational activities and gendered roles which they reflect – can suggest probable challenges and outcomes for socially, ecologically and economically sustainable tourism at the local and regional level.

The mapping component also provided important details about the zones of visitor – resident interaction and associated behaviour, and helped to identify areas deemed to be either ecologically or aesthetically significant or culturally 'sacred'. In this manner, the cognitive maps articulate tourism's function as both agent and process in the creation and cognizance of social identity, needs and expectations for all participants, and suggest critical pathways for its implementation and success in the destination community. By further exploring how people see and act within their immediate environs, it may be possible to learn even more about the human construction and communication of tourist 'attractions', including the manner by which the tourist 'product' becomes feminine or masculine in its marketing and reproduction of kinship systems in society as a whole (Hall, 1969; Gould and White, 1986; Magi, 1989; Momsen and Kinnaird, 1993; Kinnaird and Hall, 1994; King, 1996; Kempadoo, 1999; Pizam and Mansfeld, 1999; Mansvelt, 2005).

Experience Assessment

Visitor choices regarding preferred activities are influenced by a number of factors. Among the most decisive are the geographic location of a destination and its relative ease of access, and the natural and social conditions of the site, including ecological and ethnic diversity, and the perceived 'attractiveness' of the available options for entertainment and recreation. Equally pivotal is the presumed 'authenticity' of indigenous practices and history, a perception shaped by the level and character of interaction between visitors and residents, the expectations and realizations of both in promoting tourism, and individual responses formed by gender, ethnicity, education and other demographic factors. Our preferences for certain leisure activities, and the use of the recreational spaces which surround them, reflect a broad range of personal views, visions and values that are both socially and sexually constructed from ritualized systems of belief and practice. Gendered through individual acts of creation, presentation and consumption, the choices we make as tourists reflect our personal motivations for travel and reveal much about their connection to specific destinations, the experiences we seek upon arrival and the steps we take to actively manage and minimize our impacts. Organized, summarized and localized through patterns of communal behaviour and our recollections of the spatial environment, they further reveal 'a tourist landscape both physically and emotionally bounded by features that may simultaneously reassure, identify, satisfy, or disquiet the viewer' (Gould and White, 1986, p. 47; see also Hall, 1969; Aitchison *et al.*, 2000; Reynolds, 2004).

The natural and cultural environments of a destination are the means by which it achieves international recognition and attracts tourists. However, the distinctive, socially constructed landscape of local people, and the knowledge contained therein, is too frequently obscured by the industry-constructed image of the tourist environment and, with it, the stories of the human community, nature and the history of both. These metaphors of situation and function are crucial, though, in articulating the relationships that people establish with one another and the local environment, and in highlighting distinctive social values that form the basis of community narratives and institutional practices, and have historically served to moderate social and political change and tension (Redclift and Sinclair, 1991; Hall, 1993; Harvey *et al.*, 1995; Pizam and Mansfeld, 1999; Enloe, 2000).

By establishing the sentiment evoked by specific recreational activities, mental maps thus provide a palimpsest of the recreational landscape and its social history, reflecting a topology of experience that is both defined and distorted by our encounters with tourism at the local level, and by our own sexual identity. They also distinguish the space of the visitor from the inhabited place of local people, and thus draw further attention to the challenges faced by women and minorities in society overall, the influence of traditional power structures (including patriarchy) and sexually prescribed tasks and behaviour, the availability of capable facilitators both inside and outside the community, and the degree of local support for long-term goals (Richter, 1998). As such, they enable us to better assess the experiential meanings of varied tourist activities for various users over time, including age- and gender-related interests and impacts specific to the destination and its recreational attractions and facilities. Understanding these cognitive perceptions may allow us to proactively anticipate and manage the transitory and often spontaneous nature of the tourist visit itself by correlating expected and observed visitor behaviour with the images presented in travel brochures, on the Internet and in the media. Such a holistic assessment will hopefully broaden our understanding of the extent to which tourism shapes the experience of travel, as defined by the gender, language, perceptions, motivations, expectations and identities of both visitors and their 'hosts'.

Wrangell-St Elias National Park and Preserve, Alaska

Research undertaken between 1989 and 2004 in the twin Alaska 'ghost' towns of Kennicott and McCarthy proposed a new direction in tourism studies, one that recognizes a socially defined landscape often overlooked in the traditional literature of tourism, leisure and hospitality. Through the values and meanings ascribed by visitors, residents and the tourism industry – including those socially constructed and those taken for granted – communities become tourist destinations, interpreted and defined within a larger cultural and physiographic network. Abandoned in 1938, Kennicott and McCarthy were 'rediscovered' in 1989 by outdoor recreationists, and the mountains and national park that once shielded them now beckon to ever-increasing numbers of tourists. Since 1989, the number of short-term visitors alone has increased by nearly 1000%, augmented by a swelling number of seasonal residents and small service providers, and the situation shows no signs of abating in the near future. Instead, by 2020, the US National Park Service Regional Office in Alaska estimates that recreational visits to the park and preserve will exceed 152,200 persons a year (or more than triple the total recorded in 2005). Because of the tourism growth, and the disproportionate number who now opt to stay in the two towns, rather than camp in designated wilderness areas as was the norm through the early 1990s, friction is growing among residents who struggle to cope with the demand. Although the intensity of the conflict is relatively new to these communities, whose members have long prided themselves on their ability to govern by consensus, it is certainly not rare in other Alaskan towns and villages, where tourism and outdoor recreation-oriented retail trades and services now constitute the dominant element of the regional economy.

Anxious to ascertain the extent to which changing expectations were affecting individual perceptions and behaviour, the research project was initiated:

(i) to collect demographic and cognitive data as a baseline for documenting future change; and (ii) to encourage a proactive, community tourism plan by giving form to the experiential landscapes of those who come to Kennicott–McCarthy. First, the study sought to use cognitive mapping techniques to determine how people perceived the two towns and the multiple landscapes that envelope them: physical, social and historic. Second, it tried to define what place experiences were reflected in the mapped images of the different groups who used the area, including the functional or emotional quality served by different landscape features, and what they suggested for natural and recreational resource managers who sought to control the visitor experience and conserve the environment upon which it depended. The desire was to ascertain whether environmental perception might assist park planners to cope with the increased tourism, while simultaneously preserving opportunities for community development and the rural lifestyle and identity that characterizes the Alaskan 'Bush'. Although the qualitative nature of cognitive mapping presents some difficulty for those who prefer the statistical 'accuracy' of quantitative measurements, such maps excel in making obvious the emotional significance that residents and visitors attach to communities like Kennicott–McCarthy.

For the exercise, participants in the assessment were asked to draw maps of the immediate area, pinpointing sites where they recreated or socialized, without reference to base maps and/or geographic references. This step minimized subjective biases and predetermined responses that might result from symbolic suggestions of omission or inclusion. The use of freehand maps also encouraged participants to depict a wider range of activities over a broader area, rather than the constricted responses so often produced when topographic positions and elevations are specified (Gould and White, 1986; Magi, 1989; Momsen and Kinnaird, 1993; King, 1996; Ringer, 1996, 1997; Coleman and Crang, 2002). Select groups of residents and non-residents were evenly divided in gender and closely matched in age, though residents tend to be younger on average. Both groups were also predominantly well-educated, though residents possessed a disproportionately greater number of graduate degrees. This unexpected finding astonished those tourists who presume that local people are illiterate because of their rural subsistence lifestyles.

Nearly half of the visitors (40.7%) obtained their information and motivation for the trip from the personal recommendations of friends and family, and only secondarily from travel sources (35.2%) or the US National Park Service (6.5%). This contradicts the assertions of some local people who hold the Park Service most responsible for the tourism growth, though certainly the park itself serves as an attraction. Both residents and tourists recognize similar landscape features, though visitors are less knowledgeable about features beyond the immediate environs of the towns or their accommodations. As a result, they most frequently described the park in terms of the scenery surrounding the old mining buildings, and the recreational opportunities afforded by the glacier and mountains nearby (Fig. 13.3a). Residents, in contrast, rely on the physiographic landscape to establish both implicit and explicit territorial boundaries. For them, the allure of the park lies as much in the social relationships that govern their viably functioning mining community as it does in the aesthetic and historic qualities that entice

Fig. 13.3a. Cognitive map of non-residents (short- and long-term visitors) to Kennicott and McCarthy, Wrangell-St Elias National Park, Alaska.

visitors (Fig. 13.3b). Collectively, the results depict a postmodern environment delineated by the behaviour of tourists and residents alike, reflecting an eclectic framework of ideas, experiences and expectations derived both anecdotally and directly, with the evidence laid out in the historically contingent, socially constructed character of the emergent destination. In this manner, the collection of 'place' images more fully illuminates the critical role that tourism development plays in shaping the morphology of Kennicott and McCarthy as travel destinations, through the influx of new ideas and changing patterns of social behaviour.

Kosrae, Federated States of Micronesia

Cognitive mapping techniques were also employed to examine the qualitative effects of tourism on the Micronesian island of Kosrae, now in transition from a patriarchal, subsistence-based society to a world destination for marine tourism. Approximately 1.5 million visitors travel to the Pacific islands each year, most jour-

Fig. 13.3b. Cognitive map of residents of Kennicott and McCarthy, Wrangell-St Elias National Park, Alaska.

neying to Guam or the Republic of Belau, where the tourist infrastructure is highly developed and there are established airlinks with Japan and Australia. However, Kosrae has slowly gained some popularity, and now ranks third in total arrivals in the Federated States of Micronesia (FSM), with nearly 3000 visitors a year. Although this number might appear insignificant compared with other destinations in the East Asia–Pacific region, the impact is disproportionately higher because of the island's topography and the relative isolation and traditional nature of Kosraean culture (PATA, 1992; Hall, 1993; Lockhart *et al.*, 1993; Apostolopoulos *et al.*, 2001; Apostolopoulos and Gayle, 2002; Ringer, 2004). The abundance of visitor-subsidized attractions in the Pacific is clear evidence of tourism's significant financial contribution to the regional economy. Yet, its role in diminishing the meaning of local practices and places as tourist venues also demands attention. In fact, the continued emphasis on tourism's economic benefits diverts attention from 'possibly the biggest issue tourism [faces] . . . and its most serious restraint . . . its potentially damaging impact on the people and places visited' (PATA, 1992, p. 3). However profitable the monetary gain for Kosraean government and businessowners, it is the support and hospitality of the island residents which will ultimately determine tourism's survival and success (Ringer, 1992).

Research and anecdotal evidence provided by Kosraean residents stress tourism's influence in everyday life, mediating the formation of local identities and cultural patterns of behaviour and communication through the parameters of its development. At the same time, these socially constructed geographies and expectations are frequently marginalized in the plans and aspirations of visitors and developers. Many Kosraeans believe that the growing popularity of tourism, regionally and worldwide, is solid proof of its potential to spur local development. However, less than 10% of the population had ever ventured off the island until the late 1990s, and the international media remains the primary source for many islanders to assess tourism's probable impacts. As a result, there is no apparent community consensus over tourism, and some village leaders are opposed to the undesirable social effects they associate with the tourism industry in other Pacific island destinations. Nevertheless, tourism has tremendous potential to become a viable industry on Kosrae as the state seeks economic independence from the USA. The challenge, therefore, for residents and industry leaders alike, is to identify activities that attract tourists interested in the natural and human environments of Kosrae, minimize their social impacts and ensure that tourism directly benefits community residents.

Community roles on Kosrae have traditionally been defined by family affiliation, villages of residency and gender. Men work primarily in woodworking and subsistence agriculture, while women engage in weaving, fishing or catch mangrove crabs for local use or purchase by visitors. Like many Pacific islanders, older Kosraeans have also retained the aptitude to traverse long distances on land and water with only cognitive imagery, rather than formal maps. This knowledge of spatial perception is also evident in their stories and architecture, and the way in which information of distance and location is woven into their daily lives. Determined to preserve this cultural framework while promoting expanded tourism, the Kosrae State Division of Tourism initiated a comprehensive, community-based assessment. One component of the project entailed a limited study in 1998 involving cognitive perception of residents and visitors regarding their activities and attitudes about ecotourism on Kosrae. Respondents to the cognitive mapping exercise were asked to depict and label the physical landscape according to its perceived function (path, landmark, activity centre, neighbourhood or community, and boundary or edge, whether physical or perceptual).

Upon completion, a composite map of the multiple images was used to designate selected community sites for special management and protection. The synthesized maps were also employed to distinguish the behaviour of residents, who exhibited greater appreciation of the natural history and environments of Kosrae, from those of visitors, whose maps reflected a narrower range of place experiences, and an emphasis on tourism facilities and physical landmarks. Notable demographic differences of age, gender and village of residency further distinguished the representations of Kosraeans. While the total number of participants was statistically insignificant (less than 1% of the island's population and visitor population was surveyed), it was deemed sufficient to establish a baseline to monitor future change as tourism evolves on the island.

Perhaps unsurprisingly, the dominant images of tourists are the natural features depicted in travel publications, indicating that most come to see Kosrae's scenic marine environment and mountainous interior. Rare are indicators of the island beyond the hotels, restaurants or dive shops, and absent from most of the visitors' maps are the five villages in which Kosraeans dwell. On the maps of residents, however, is more detailed information regarding the human landscape. Populated by individual homesteads and family names, the fields and groves of the men, and the canals and fishing sites of women, every village is identified through symbols of human history and gendered practice. Extending beyond the visitor periphery, the diversity of cultural landscapes included evidence of social organization by gender in the depictions of older Kosraean adults, whose images reflected their separate work spheres and knowledge (Fig. 13.4a). This gender difference is, however, missing from the maps of younger Kosraeans, whether male or female. Instead, Kosraeans under age 40 of both sexes share a greater awareness of the island as a whole than do their elders, due in part to jobs in the tourism industry which enable them to traverse the island and become better acquainted with its ecology (Fig. 13.4b).

Such data, however subjective, should therefore prove useful to tourism planners and developers, who may consider communities and tourists to be homogeneous, when in reality both categories are widely heterogeneous and frequently hold dissimilar notions of tourism as an appropriate tool of economic development. The variety in perceptions and experiences of place further underscore the critical role that tourism plays in shaping the human mosaic of travel destinations. The cultural construction of the tourist destination, which is as much a process of 'place creation' as it is of community revival, represents a direct link between expectation and realization filtered through local beliefs and behaviours that produce widely varied outcomes. A failure to consider these variations fully from the perspective of

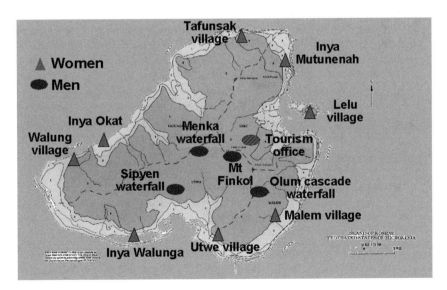

Fig. 13.4a. Cognitive map of the social activity centres of women and men over age 40 on Kosrae, Federated States of Micronesia.

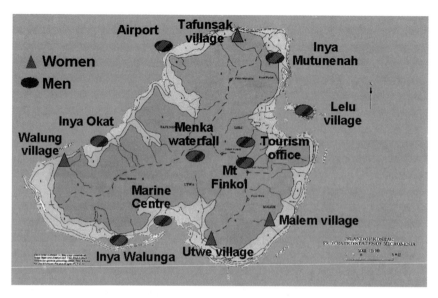

Fig. 13.4b. Cognitive map of the social activity centres of women and men under age 40 on Kosrae, Federated States of Micronesia.

different users (visitor/resident, male/female, adult/youth) may thus seriously hinder efforts to understand tourism's long-term impacts on the broader community.

Conclusion

Part of tourism's appeal is the opportunity it provides both visitors and residents to immerse themselves in another place and persona, and to engage other people and cultures directly. In search of cultural immersion and environmental education, tourism may however lead to the marketing of culture and the pursuit of the exotic, rather than an affirmation of local culture. The situation is further aggravated by the lack of experience and expertise in many communities in reconciling the sometimes opposing goals of economic growth with cultural and ecological preservation. As a result, a central issue for many tourism proponents and opponents is the long-term consequences of gradually replacing a social landscape that has evolved through time, *in situ*, with one that caters primarily to visitors' stereotypes while at the same time trying to conserve finite resources and increase awareness among young residents of their own cultural history and gender identity.

While destinations worldwide welcome the ever-increasing numbers of domestic and international tourists, there is corresponding awareness of tourism's paradox: in fostering economic growth, tourism may *also* threaten – directly and indirectly – the cultural environment that sustains local people and constitutes their identity. Many of the social and behavioural transformations associated with tourism development and other modernization processes are readily apparent to the casual visitor, including the preference for imported food, clothing, music and movies. Yet, only a position of social intimacy reveals the inhabited, socially constructed form beneath the distractions of the tourists, a seemingly intangible structure around which women and men learn to communicate, play, motivate and navigate. Although admittedly highly personalized and localized, the contours of this behavioural landscape may be as influential in determining the effectiveness of sustainable tourism and community planning processes as the presence of more scientifically established 'facts'.

If tourism is to prove successful, careful thought must be given to the ability and willingness of local community leaders to evaluate and absorb the potential communal and social costs that tourism development will entail. A successful resolution requires the implementation and acceptance of appropriate management policies that provide clear, long-term benefits to both tourist and resident, and create positive links between recreational interests, nature and cultural conservation, and visitor education and destination choice. These, in turn, require a development model carefully attuned and responsive to the perceptions and expectations of the people of the destination. The expansion of tourism around the globe affords women and men both opportunities and challenges, as they negotiate new gender roles and identities in a social landscape still defined in many countries by patriarchal rule and sexually restrictive practices. Whether defined as sex, companionship, romance or an interactive cultural experience with someone outside the community, the nature and context of social interaction and empowerment through travel are rapidly evolving. The consequences of such change may include more economic power for women, as well as greater expectations for future profitability and employability through education and a greater diversity of occupational choices. At the same time, the 'unbalancing' of traditional marital roles may lead women to devote less time to child-rearing and housework and other social changes.

Tourism may also further perpetuate the 'male' practices of prostitution by capitalizing on the limited opportunities afforded local men for economic prestige and power. As tourists, women possess greater power in defining and controlling their own relationships with indigenous men, with an increase in emotional conflicts for men as they experience a loss of economic control, and a sense of manipulation of both local women and men for personal gain. The end result is a reproduction and reinforcement of racial and cultural superiority and domination over the 'hosts' of the destination. Consequently, there is a need to explore alternative ways in which tourism, as an industry and a recreational activity, can strengthen the potential for change in current conditions, particularly in terms of facilitating proactive collaboration between community residents and tourists, and in the selection of marketing images and media venues. In addition, there is a need to defend women from complaints that the creation of tourism jobs further reinforces inauthentic practices and beliefs, and the loss of traditional family lifestyles through social and political change.

The key, perhaps, is to take specific steps to maintain or revive authentic cultural practices and art, to educate visitors about prostitution and other inappropriate social impacts and to minimize sexual misunderstandings between tourists and residents. It is here that cognitive maps may prove useful, for they make visible 'our place in the world [and the manners by which we define and] orient ourselves' (King, 1996, p. 40). Any map is, admittedly, an imperfect portrayal of a world both chaotic and complex. Consequently, there are undeniable weaknesses with this methodology, including a reliance on data that are distorted by personal experience, miscommunication and generalized observations, and limited by time and ethnocentrism. However, such images do provide a tangible evidence of the multiple 'places' experienced by tourists and inhabited by residents as they negotiate the destination. This functional overview of the tourist landscape graphically reflects the activities and contact zones in which residents and non-residents directly engage, providing meaningful indicators of change in the past and of possible trends in visitor interests and resident (dis)satisfaction in the future. Also apparent are more abstract networks delineated by kinship and gendered roles in society. Through such visual and emotive insights, perceptual maps provide much-needed access to local processes and relationships organized by function and form. They also help dispel the persistent notion that indigenous communities are always relatively homogeneous. Instead, the highly personalized and fragmented nature of the mental maps submitted by local residents and visitors to the destinations described in this text demonstrate the variability and subjectivity of place attachment and gender identity. While the images are certainly generalized and superficial in their presentation of what is real, they are critically influential in creating a common sense of community and identity.

Continued analysis of such maps would therefore enable community planners and managers to visualize and interpret variations in the meaning and structure of social symbols and territory, and thereby better understand and sensitively anticipate problems of development before they arise or take hold. Through the insertion of individual perceptions of visitors and residents in the process, graphic evidence of existing social behaviour, community identities and associated landscape values is displayed for consideration by decision makers, and provides a baseline against which future cognitive and tangible modifications can be documented. By enabling community leaders and planners to see the destination as its users currently do, such insights would substantially improve our understanding of the gender segregation and impacts reflected in the discourse, function and communication of local identity. Greater appreciation of the qualitative and emotional effects of tourism may also facilitate the development of facilities and activities that support local efforts to improve health care and access to technology and financial credit for women, and enhance the dignity of women by equalizing work disparities and dispelling the common view of women as 'cheap' labour. Only in such a manner will we succeed in fostering travel that is ecologically sustainable and socially empowering in recreation settings worldwide.

Acknowledgements

I wish to express appreciation for the financial support provided by the Center for the Study of Women in Society at the University of Oregon in undertaking some of the research presented in this paper. I also wish to thank the women and men of Micronesia and Alaska for their willingness to participate in my studies of the experiential landscapes of tourism in their communities, and especially to Teresa Weaver for her continued support and understanding.

References

Aitchison, C., MacLeod, N. and Shaw, S. (2000) *Leisure and Tourism Landscapes: Social and Cultural Geographies*. Routledge, London.

Apostolopoulos, Y. and Gayle, D. (eds) (2002) *Island Tourism and Sustainable Development: Caribbean, Pacific, and Mediterranean Experiences*. Praeger Publishers, Westport, Connecticut.

Apostolopoulos, Y., Sonmez, S. and Timothy, D. (eds) (2001) *Women as Producers and Consumers of Tourism in Developing Regions*. Praeger Publishers, Westport, Connecticut.

Barry, K. (1995) *The Prostitution of Sexuality*. New York University Press, New York.

Cohen, E. (1996) *Thai Tourism: Hill Tribes, Islands, and Open-ended Prostitution*. Studies in Contemporary Thailand, No. 4, White Lotus, Bangkok.

Coleman, S. and Crang, M. (eds) (2002) *Tourism: Between Place and Performance*. Berghahn Books, London.

Enloe, C. (2000) *Bananas, Beaches and Bases: Making Feminist Sense of International Politics*. University of California Press, Berkeley, California.

Ghodsee, K. (2005) *The Red Riviera: Gender, Tourism, and Postsocialism on the Black Sea*. Duke University Press, Durham, North Carolina.

Gmelch, S. (2004) *Tourists and Tourism: A Reader*. Waveland Press, Long Grove, Illinois.

Gould, P. and White, R. (1986) *Mental Maps*, 2nd edn. Allen & Unwin, Boston, Massachusetts.

Hall, C.M. (1993) *Tourism in the Pacific: Development, Impacts and Markets*. Longman Cheshire, Melbourne.

Hall, E.T. (1969) *The Hidden Dimension*. Doubleday, Garden City, New Jersey.

Harvey, M., Hunt, J. and Harris, J.R. (1995) Gender and community tourism dependence level. *Annals of Tourism Research* 22, 349–368.

Hawkins, D.E. (1994) Ecotourism: opportunities for developing countries. In: Theobald, W. (ed.) *Global Tourism: The Next Decade*. Butterworth-Heinemann, London, pp. 261–273.

Hemmati, M. (ed.) (1999) *Gender and Tourism: Women's Employment and Participation in Tourism*. UN Environment and Development Forum, UK Committee, London.

Howe, J., McMahon, E. and Propst, L. (1997) *Balancing Nature and Commerce in Gateway Communities*. Island Press, Washington, DC.

Kempadoo, K. (ed.) (1999) *Sun, Sex, and Gold: Tourism and Sex in the Caribbean*. Rowman & Littlefield, Lanham, Maryland.

King, G. (1996) *Mapping Reality: An Exploration of Cultural Cartographies*. Macmillan, London.

Kinnaird, V. and Hall, D. (eds) (1994) *Tourism: A Gender Analysis*. Wiley, Chichester, UK.

Lew, A., Hall, C.M. and Williams, A. (eds) (2004) *A Companion to Tourism*. Blackwell, Oxford.

Lockhart, D.G., Drakakis-Smith, D. and Schembri, J. (eds) (1993) *The Development Process in Small Island States*. Routledge, London.

Magi, L.M. (1989) Cognition of recreation resources through photographic images. *South African Geographical Journal* 71, 67–73.

Mansvelt, J. (2005) *Geographies of Consumption*. Sage, London.

Momsen, J.H. and Kinnaird, V. (eds) (1993) *Different Places, Different Voices: Gender and Development in Africa, Asia, and Latin America*. Routledge, London.

Opperman, M. (ed.) (1998) *Sex Tourism and Prostitution: Aspects of Leisure, Recreation and Work*. Cognizant Communication, Elmsford, New York.

PATA (Pacific Asia Travel Organization) (1992) *PATA Conference Daily*. PATA, Hong Kong.

Pizam, A. and Mansfeld, Y. (eds) (1999) *Consumer Behavior in Travel and Tourism*. Haworth Hospitality Press, New York.

Redclift, N. and Sinclair, M. (eds) (1991) *Working Women: International Perspectives on Labour and Gender Ideology*. Routledge, London.

Reynolds, N. (2004) *Geographies of Writing: Inhabiting Places and Encountering Difference*. Southern Illinois University Press, Carbondale, Illinois.

Richter, L. (1998) Exploring the political role of gender in tourism research. In: Theobald, W. (ed.) *Global Tourism: The Next Decade*, 2nd edn. Butterworth-Heinemann, Oxford, pp. 391–404.

Ringer, G. (1992) *Nature-based Attractions Development Project: Assessment and Management Plan*. Kosrae State Divison of Tourism, Tofol, Federated States of Micronesia.

Ringer, G. (1996) Wilderness images of tourism and community. *Annals of Tourism Research* 23(4), 950–953.

Ringer, G. (1997) Beyond the boundaries: social place in a protected space. *GeoJournal* 41(3), 223–232.

Ringer, G. (ed.) (1998) *Destinations: Cultural Landscapes of Tourism*. Routledge, London.

Ringer, G. (2004) Geographies of tourism and place in Micronesia: the 'sleeping lady' awakes. *The Journal of Pacific Studies* 26 (1–2), 131–150.

Ryan, C. and Hall, C.M. (2001) *Sex Tourism: Marginal People and Liminalities*. Routledge, London.

Sharpley, R. and Telfer, D. (eds) (2002) *Tourism and Development: Concepts and Issues*. Channel View Publications, Clevedon, UK.

Sinclair, M.T. (ed.) (1997) *Gender, Work and Tourism*. Routledge, London.

Swain, M. and Momsen, J. (eds) (2002) *Gender/Tourism/Fun(?)*. Cognizant Communication, Elmsford, New York.

14 Travelling Beyond the Boundaries of Constraint: Women, Travel and Empowerment

CANDICE HARRIS AND ERICA WILSON

Introduction

In the academic field of tourism, much of the literature on gender, women and tourism has focused on the experiences and representations of women as *producers* of tourism, or as 'gendered hosts' (Gibson, 2001). Women are studied with regard to their roles as tourism and hospitality employees (Abbott Cone, 1995; Wilkinson and Pratiwi, 1995; Cukier *et al.*, 1996), as providers of sex tourism (Oppermann, 1999; Ryan, 2000) and as objects of desire in tourist imagery (Enloe, 1989; Morgan and Pritchard, 1998). More than a decade ago, Kinnaird and Hall (1994) called for the analysis of 'gendered tourists', stressing that the assumptions behind people's leisure and motivation travel need to be challenged and reconsidered. They argue that motivations to travel are gendered, as they are constructed out of the social realities and contexts of the men and women who participate in tourism. The different ways in which female *and* male travellers are viewed by their societies is important, because the expectations of involvement in tourism are mediated by several stakeholders and are always grounded in gendered perspectives.

The study of the behaviour and experiences of women as tourists is still in its incipient stages compared to other fields of study (e.g. geography, cultural studies and feminist social sciences). Indeed, it was only in the late 1970s and early 1980s that women specifically become the subject of academic tourism research (Smith, 1979), but a growing body of literature of the 'female travel experience' attests to the unique needs, motivations and constraints that face women who travel. Advancing our understanding of the women as *consumers* of travel, or as 'gendered tourists' (Gibson, 2001), is vital given estimates that today, women represent around half of both the pleasure and business travel markets, respectively (Westwood *et al.*, 2000; Pennington-Gray and Kerstetter, 2001; Rach, 2001; Harris, 2002). Women are also now more prominent on the backpacker circuit, with demographic results in empirical studies by Kain and King (2004) and Newlands (2004) showing that females tend to be more highly represented in the backpacker market. Some recent estimates suggest that in the first years of the new millennium, half of all business travellers will be female (Popcorn and Marigold, 2000). Such trends have seen hotels, airlines and other tourism ventures finding ways to tap the potential of this 'new' market of corporate travellers (Westwood, 1997; Harris, 2002; Harris and Ateljevic, 2003).

From the above, it is clear that the study of female tourists is potentially an area ripe for academic inquiry. Indeed, Timothy (2001) states that research into female tourists' desires, motivations and experiences are in 'desperate need of additional examination' (p. 242). Furthermore, there is a need to tell women's stories of travel and tourism in their own voices and words (Norris and Wall, 1994; Swain, 1995; Gibson and Jordan, 1998; Small, 1999). To the present authors' knowledge, there are no empirical studies available comparing women's experiences of business and pleasure travel. The main reason for this, no doubt, is that there exists a staunch polarization in the literature between 'business' and 'pleasure' travel. Tourism has been traditionally identified as a leisure pursuit, and academic research on the topic largely investigates tourist behaviour as leisure-oriented and as occurring during spare time. Business travel, in contrast, is viewed as travel to facilitate people working away from their normal place of employment for a short period of time (Davidson, 1996). The traditional polarization of business and pleasure travel is underpinned by the 'work/leisure dichotomy'. As Uriely (2001, p. 1) points out, 'tourism and work are usually perceived as two contradicting fields of human activity'. As such, leisure has been posited as dichotomous to work. Examples of this type of thought are reflected in the following excerpts from the tourism motivation literature:

> Travel liberates us from obligations . . . from the regulations which oppress us in everyday life . . . travel is *double free time*: it frees people from work and from home.
> (Krippendorf, 1997, p. 42, italics added)

> Tourism is a 'modern ritual' in which the populace *gets away from it all*, the 'it all' being ordinary workaday, mundane life, particularly work, which includes the workplace, homework, and housework.
> (Graburn, 1983, p. 11, italics added)

From a gendered perspective, however, holiday leisure cannot always be described as an escape or as a simple polarity to work. Studies have shown that for many women, the continuation of domestic and familial care is still expected, even on vacation (Wearing, 1990; Bella, 1992; Deem, 1996, 1999). The notion of escape becomes even more problematic in the context of travel for business, where businesswomen travellers often feel compelled, through e-mails, phone calls and other means, to continue their domestic care for partners, children and home even while away for work (Harris, 2002; Hewlett, 2002). As such, in both business and pleasure travel, the chance for true escape from the confines of home and domestic responsibility may be more limited for women.

While recognizing the valid and important impact of gendered and societal constraints on women's lives and travel experiences, this chapter specifically explores the ways in which business and solo independent travel can act as a site of empowerment and resistance for women. Previous studies of women's participation in leisure and tourism have focused on the constraints and challenges that women face when trying to seek access to, or participate in, leisure and tourism activities (e.g. Little, 2000; Wilson and Little, 2005). In this chapter, we make an effort to move beyond boundaries and call attention to the positive benefits that women can find through travel. Using the pooled results of two separate qualitative studies into women's experiences of independent travel – one on Australian women's solo pleasure travel and the other on New Zealand women's business travel – the benefits of travel, and the opportunities for empowerment and resistance that such travel may afford are explored.

Travelling Beyond Boundaries: Women, Independent Travel and Empowerment

Traditional Western gender distinctions have promoted the image of travellers as being men (Leontidou, 1994). Travellers in the 18th and 19th centuries were often labelled as 'adventurers' and 'explorers', and such labels are still generally attributed to men (Little and Wilson, 2005). These labels were thoroughly masculinized, as masculinity and global exploration have been as tightly woven together as masculinity and soldiering (Enloe, 1989). In many societies, women travellers have historically battled societal restrictions and tarnished reputations as a result of their choice to travel – or to dare to write about their travels (Apostolopoulos and Sonmez, 2001; Wilson, 2004). However, while independent itineraries were tied up with male connotations of bravery and exploration, women did negotiate to find ways to travel, and to travel independently. In fact, by the mid-1800s, the growing numbers of independent women travellers could be referred to as a notable 'trend' (Pemble, 1987). The 19th-century reign of England's Queen Victoria in particular has been heralded as the golden age of travel, and this golden age enveloped women travellers as well (Robinson, 1994). The Victorian travellers of this age were said to be privileged women, the oft-sheltered daughters of well-educated and highly regarded families (Clarke, 1988). No longer were they travelling merely as accompanists to their husbands, however; these Victorian women were travelling independently and alone.

Women who travelled independently during these times challenged ideological assumptions, representing an attempt to break the boundaries of convention and traditional feminine restraints (though they may not have consciously recognized or acknowledged that they were doing so) (Robinson, 1990). While guidebooks and anthologies on or for women travellers tend to provide either historical accounts of grand journeys (e.g. Hamalian, 1981; Robinson, 1990) or tips on how to travel safely and successfully overcome the myriad of constraints associated with female travel (White, 1989; Swan and Laufer, 1998), a more recent body of literature has emerged with emphasis on the empowering and beneficial aspects of travel for the contemporary, independent woman (Bond and Michael, 1999; Steinbach, 2000; Bond, 2001).

Constraints, defined as factors that inhibit one's ability to participate in desired leisure activities, have informed much of the leisure literature over the last two decades (Jackson and Scott, 1999). Many studies of women's leisure have adopted a constraints framework, with findings suggesting that women tend to be more highly and uniquely constrained in their ability to access, and fully enjoy, their leisure pursuits (Henderson, 1991; Jackson and Henderson, 1995; Little, 2000). A similar constraints focus has been found in the work on women as tourism consumers. A common constraint discussed revolves around issues of fear and safety, implying that women's experiences are often limited by having to keep to safe routes, and thus reducing opportunities to venture further beyond (Jordan and Gibson, 2000; Carr, 2001; Wilson and Little, 2005). Another form of constraint revolves around gendered notions of social and cultural acceptability, whereby 'her' behaviour is moderated to keep within the bounds of social and cultural norms of the host destination, as well as her own perceptions of appropriate female behaviour (Gibson and Jordan, 1998; Wilson and Little, 2003). Specific to business travel, women find that holding multitudinous roles, the presence of prevalent ideological structures around female behaviour and traditional dichotomies such as work – home culminate to present tensions and challenges for their participation in business travel (Harris, 2002). Many of the constraints in business travel that Harris found in her doctoral study come from the women's experiences of balancing a contemporary role in business with a portfolio of traditional ones around the home, their social life and of being female.

In the last decade or so, there has been a notable shift in the literature away from constraints, to a discussion of *negotiation* (Jackson *et al.*, 1993). Several authors now speak of individuals' active power in their ability to negotiate through their constraints. In this sense, constraints can no longer be viewed merely as blanket 'barriers' or insurmountable 'boundaries'. In fact, as many authors now concur, leisure can occur 'despite constraint' (Kay and Jackson, 1991). More relevantly, research is showing that women in particular are increasingly refusing (whether consciously or unconsciously) to be bound by their constraints, and finding ways to negotiate and resist (Henderson and Bialeschki, 1993; Shaw, 1994; Little, 2002; Wilson and Little, 2003).

This new focus on negotiation does not mean that constraints do not still offer a necessary and useful lens for viewing and understanding women's leisure. Rather, as researchers we must refrain from examining *only* constraints, as doing so runs the risk of telling only half of the story of human experiences of leisure and tourism (Samdahl and Jekubovich, 1997; Raymore, 2002). Wearing and Wearing (1988) offered the analogy of 'squashed ants' to describe the preoccupation of researchers who emphasize negative constraints when studying women's experience of leisure. Such an emphasis may lead to the literature becoming dominated by a 'woman as passive victim' discourse, rather than positing women as active, empowered agents, capable of taking action to overcome challenges and enjoy life to its fullest. Indeed, constraints do act as boundaries affecting people's choices, opportunities and actions, but perhaps such boundaries are necessary. As Shogan (2002) argues, people need rules and boundaries to set structure in their lives; without such structure we would not possess the motivation and desire needed to overcome life's challenges. In turn, overcoming constraints and limitations can lead to feelings of achievement and an increased feeling of power.

Feminist researchers have become increasingly interested in leisure as a site of empowerment for women (see Freysinger and Flannery, 1992; Henderson *et al.*,

1996; Green, 1998; Ashton-Schaeffer *et al.*, 2001; Shaw, 2001). Empowerment can be defined as

> an interactive process through which people experience personal and social change, enabling them to take action to achieve influence over the organizations and institutions which affect their lives and the communities in which they live.
>
> (Whitmore, cited in Hutchison and McGill, 1992, p. 134)

Independent forms of travel have been recognized by some authors as vehicles for women to feel empowered and to take control of their lives (Hall and Kinnaird, 1994; Butler, 1995; Pesman, 1996; Kinnaird and Hall, 2000). MacKinnon (1997) has described pleasure travel, particularly that taken overseas and by oneself, as a means to greater independence for women. Similarly, Riley (1988) found that women used long-term independent travel as a way to increase feelings of independence and self-control. Gibson and Jordan (1998), in their comparative study of American and British solo female travellers, showed that solo travel provided a sense of freedom, empowerment, and enhanced feelings of confidence, whilst Elsrud's (1998) study of Swedish female backpackers found that independent forms of travel provided women with a feeling of freedom and control of their own time at travel destinations. Likewise, The South Australian Tourism Commission (1996), in their detailed study of women who travel, found that the major benefit of travel was an enhanced feeling of psychological well-being. Furthermore, Pennington-Gray and Kerstetter (2001) examined the benefits that university-educated women sought from their pleasure travel experiences. One of the most important benefits from travel included having an opportunity to educate themselves through an increased knowledge of different places. Such findings suggest that independent pleasure travel for women offers a unique and important method for increasing women's sense of self, confidence and empowerment.

Leisure has been described as a 'heterotopia', or 'an area for women's resistance to dominant discourses which keep them in passive and subordinate positions in society' (Wearing, 1994, p. 9). A 'heterotopia' is a space where women can resist, rather than submit to, male hegemonies and patriarchal systems of domination. The very idea of negotiation, as an active act or strategy to overcome constraints, is a form of resistance in which women become active, self-enabling participants in life rather than victims of an oppressive, patriarchal society (Green, 1998). Certain types of travel, such as independent travel abroad, are also now being discussed as heterotopias, or spaces of potential resistance for women (Wearing and Wearing, 1996; Warner-Smith, 2000). For young women growing up in the 1950s and 1960s in Australia and New Zealand, when women's roles were discussed in terms of their contribution to home and raising children, independent travel allowed women the opportunity to transgress and resist gendered ideologies of what was 'feminine', and to escape conventional norms about women's roles and responsibilities (Butler, 1995; Ghose, 1998). In essence, independent forms of travel may provide 'a space which permitted the rewriting of the script of what it [is] to be a woman' (Warner-Smith, 2000, p. 44).

As stated previously, this chapter makes a deliberate effort to move beyond a focus on women's boundaries and constraints to call attention to travel as a platform for empowerment. Women's business and pleasure travel experiences create opportunities for them to gain empowerment in themselves; power that is also reflected to others. Travel means venturing into new spaces, away from familiar people and contexts, thus providing opportunities for women to resist constraining ideas, beliefs and norms of 'appropriate' behaviour. Moving the focus from (but still incorporating and acknowledging) constraints, to view women's travel through the fresh lenses of empowerment and resistance, means that women can be seen as active participants who make their own choices and actions, rather than as passive victims of circumstance and constraint.

Research Design and Methodology

The results that follow in this chapter present a joint analysis from two studies of how women experience travel, and find a sense of empowerment, in the contexts of leisure and business. An interpretive, qualitative and feminist approach to research methodology was favoured in both studies in an attempt to understand the meaning of women's solo tourist experiences. The first study (Wilson, 2004) relied upon semi-structured, in-depth interviews with 40 Australian women, which asked about their past experiences of overseas independent pleasure travel. The other study (Harris, 2002) employed six focus groups with New Zealand women business travellers. Both studies were designed to cover a broad array of questions related to women's backgrounds and travel experiences, including life histories; travel history and experience; travel preparation techniques; travel motivations; constraints and challenges; negotiation strategies and outcomes or benefits associated with their travel.

Each study adopted a grounded, unfolding approach to data analysis, largely rejecting positivistic axioms of drawing a priori samples in advance of data collection (Glaser and Strauss, 1967; Lincoln and Guba, 1985). An interpretive, qualitative and feminist approach to research methodology was favoured in an attempt to understand the meaning of women's travel experiences. Analysis of themes in both the solo and the business travel studies found some interesting similarities around women's own construction of their lives and travel experiences, enabling concepualization of contributes to a description of the concept of empowerment.

Our position as 'insiders' in research on women's travel

In alignment with an interpretive feminist perspective, as authors of this chapter we consider our experiences and personal involvement with the research topic as assets to the design and operation of our studies. We recognize that our personal world views, social class level, educational experience and travel histories impact on what we study, how we study it, and the way in which our 'findings' are written and presented as discourse. As Bates (1999, p. 17) states: 'We all have some form of built-in gender bias and that presents a Catch-22. Even though we may feel we are being objective and looking only at the facts, the very facts we see may be influenced . . .' Being an insider rather than a 'distant authority', however, has advantages in understanding women's lives and travel experiences, and it has helped us in the identification of issues and interpretation of themes. As an 'insider' the 'researcher will acquire an in-depth knowledge of the tourism phenomena or experience that is grounded in the empirical world – a world where there are multiple realities rather than one "truth" to explain tourism phenomena' (Jennings, 2001, p. 40). According to Harding (1991), reflexivity in research should be viewed not as a 'problem', as it is in traditional positivitist approaches, to a 'resource' that adds depth and richness to our understanding of the social world. As the present authors' respective reflections help to demonstrate, we felt our positions as 'insiders' was a strength of the research design, helping to build relationships with the women with whom we engaged during the years of the research process:

> I consider myself an insider in this study; with the ability to empathise with and get close to participants. My professional roles have required me to travel for business purposes, giving me first-hand experience as a female business traveller. I have also held management roles, requiring me to manage business travel budgets and business travel arrangements for staff. Stories told to me by my mother from her experiences as an air hostess during the 1960s in New Zealand have also given me some insight into gender relations in historical tourism production structures. During my research I found myself constantly analysing the stories told to me in relation to my own experiences. The participants provided me with opportunities to empathise with them, as well as opening my eyes to new issues for consideration and representation. A particular strength of the research design is that it enabled me to work with a community that displays many aspects of sameness to me.
>
> (Candice, researcher on businesswomen's travel study)

> It would have been nearly impossible for me to try to understand and interpret what these forty women were saying and meaning without having some first hand knowledge of the constraints that they faced. This solo travel 'knowledge' removed some of the distance between us as relative strangers who, in most cases, had not met prior to the interview. Many women naturally expected me to speak about my own experiences of life and of travel within the interview experience. I felt that if I was to ask these women to talk about themselves and their personal lives, and to take the time to do so out of their very busy lives, then it was only fitting to reciprocate with my own stories and experiences. Like a normal conversation between two people, in which personal details and opinions are often not divulged until trust is established, many of the women opened up in interviews, after knowing that I also had shared similar experiences. In this way, common ground was established, and I was seen as more of an insider of equal stance rather than as a distant authority or outsider. This can be seen in the words of one woman during her interview, who noted:

> I've probably never ever talked to anyone in this much detail, because I'm a great believer in never talking about something to someone unless they can share somewhat in that experience, because it gets very boring for them. . . . But the fact that you have been to different places means you've actually experienced it – you've been alone. (*Jo, solo woman traveller*)
>
> (Erica, researcher on solo women's travel study)

Themes of Empowerment

Using a method of 'constant comparison' to analyse the women's stories from both studies (Glaser and Strauss, 1967), key quotes or sections from interviews and focus groups were continually compared and contrasted against other similar quotes or sections, allowing for the development of two overarching themes which help to describe women's empowerment through travel: (i) personal development and increased confidence; and (ii) the indulgence of room to move and time for self. These two themes, discussed below, are reflective of the tourist experience overall, and meld elements of motivation, benefit, and outcome – all contributing to a sense of empowerment.

First, it is important to note that both the business and pleasure women travellers faced a number of constraints on their travels, thus these challenges and restrictions cannot be ignored. For instance, the independent pleasure travellers reported barriers such as fear for personal safety, self-doubt, others' perceptions and harassment, among others. The women business travellers spoke of stress, loneliness, concern for home, guilt for leaving their families, and the pressures of competing in the often male-dominated industries in which they worked. While it was important to understand how these constraints impacted on the women's respective travel experiences, it is not the purpose of this chapter to report on these challenges in any detail. The aim, as outlined earlier in this chapter, was to move beyond constraints to tell the stories of how women transcended their limitations and achieved benefits. There was clear evidence of a strong and positive desire on the part of both samples of women to actively negotiate their constraints. Pushing their personal, social and practical boundaries, the women we spoke to – whether business or pleasure travel was their goal – reported strikingly similar benefits, the main ones being increased confidence, freedom from responsibility and improved social skills.

Personal development and increased confidence

Both researchers were told stories of overcoming fear and self-doubt to embark on travel. As one woman noted, her travels involved continually 'pushing beyond my fear barriers' (Anita, solo traveller). Transcending their fears of travel resulted in increased confidence and self-growth for many of the pleasure travellers. 'Travel has made me feel more confident within myself and made me feel strong' (Kate, solo traveller). 'Travel provides me with opportunities to grow personally through overcoming obstacles and meeting challenge' (Hillary, solo traveller). This increased strength and confidence transferred into everyday life, as one woman found upon returning to her career after a long stint travelling alone:

> I came back and I really pushed to get change for my career path. I was very pushy, which wasn't me, and insisted that I be given an opportunity to try something else, and I got what I wanted. . . . I got into an environment where I was speaking in front of people on a regular basis, training, giving presentations to leadership teams and quite senior people in the bank. For a shy, nervous person this was big stuff. . . . I couldn't imagine myself doing what I did before I'd gone away – just the level of confidence was not there to try. (Sue, solo traveller)

Similar comments were made by a young traveller in her mid-twenties. 'Before I went travelling, I was timid about some things. I wouldn't say what I really thought. . . . I think a lot of women don't know how to say no, whereas I just outrightly go "no!". . . . So it's taught me to say yes and no very clearly' (Jo, solo traveller). For the businesswomen travellers, work trips were regarded as a valued resource because of the opportunities and status that they enabled. Being allowed to travel to act as a representative of their host organization was clearly a factor that increased the women's confidence. 'I feel important being sent to represent my organisation' (April, business traveller). The respect that several women gained from friends, family and colleagues by undertaking travel and negotiating new challenges contributed greatly to building their personal and professional confidence.

Both sets of women also discussed the social benefits of travel, such as meeting other people (especially if they travelled alone), learning how to relate to others, and establishing friendships. 'I've made lots of new friends, that's been the best thing – the friendships I've made' (Amy, solo traveller). 'I'd always thought of myself as a loner, but realised I was way more social and outgoing than I'd thought' (Kate, solo traveller). For some of the female pleasure travellers, having to meet and interact with new people helped to develop confidence in themselves and their social abilities. Interacting with people in new contexts and cultures was not something they had done frequently in their lives:

> If you're on your own you meet people a lot easier . . . you sort of get a lot more confidence and you think oh well, I'm here by myself, I've gotta get up off my arse and go and meet people. (Mandy, solo traveller)

> I learnt how to be alone and enjoy solitude. (Hillary, solo traveller)

Several of the business travellers also spoke of enjoying the social interaction and networking opportunities that work trips could provide. As one woman noted, 'I far prefer to do business with people I have met in person as knowing people personally makes it much easier to meet my objectives' (Amanda, business traveller). Likewise, a young, single businesswoman found that business trips actually improved her ability to meet like-minded peers in her own industry. 'I like to go away, to do more interesting jobs, meet more people and network' (Melinda, business traveller). The importance of building personal relationships with business stakeholders was recognized by all the business women travellers, hence emphasizing the value and empowerment that can come through face-to-face interaction.

The indulgence of room to move and time for self

Another theme of empowerment was connected to finding a sense of freedom and liberation through both business and solo travel. For many women, this sense of liberation was a result of being freed from responsibility and care for significant others, such as family, children, friends and work colleagues. 'The benefits are freedom, freedom, freedom. . . . Travel gives me freedom to do what I want and not have to worry about others' (Anita, solo traveller). Travel provided a space for indulging in one's own free time.

> You don't have to be anything. Just be yourself – totally – complete freedom to do whatever. You find yourself – you get a lot of confidence. (Dana, solo traveller)

> It's being responsible for my own decisions. Travelling with somebody would not have been the same, because I think you make plans and consult with somebody else and you have to compromise. (Anna, solo traveller)

Despite feeling stressed and fatigued, the business women travellers also found that work trips provided a space where women could achieve some escape from the multitudinous roles and domestic responsibilities they held at home. Business trips away from home allowed some women an 'indulgent' chance to experience leisure time that was just their own, without obligations to family and children. Hotel rooms were seen as a particular haven for escape, freedom and 'quiet time'. 'When I'm on my own then I get room service, change into my pyjamas, hop into bed early, and maybe have a bath. . . . It's nice and is a good thing about travelling for work. There's just no one there – it's indulgence time, it's a treat' (Georgia, business traveller). Other business travellers expressed similar sentiments. 'I like to get into my pyjamas about 6 pm, then watch the news in my bed. It is a big treat for me to park up in front of the telly from that time onwards' (Petra, business traveller). 'It is nice to have quiet time to think your own thoughts and not have to speak to anyone, once you are in a hotel room' (Victoria, business traveller).

Some businesswomen travellers commented that short, overnight work trips provided a much-needed break from the everyday continuity of their significant relationships. 'I actually like being on my own, as I don't have that much time alone. It is a dedicated night on your own, which is nice as you can do your own thing' (Madeline, business traveller). 'It is quite nice to have a break away for one night from my partner. Quiet time' (Kate, business traveller). The break away from partners and other life stakeholders was desired by many of the participants; however, it was also time away that required negotiation and often was 'accepted' if the time was not for an extensive period. Not having to prepare food was also viewed as a form of escape by some participants, particularly from responsibility for domestic duties in the home. 'I love being on an airplane – it is really exciting. I can't think of anything better than sitting in a seat for 12 hours and having someone bring my meals and other things' (Liz, business traveller). 'You can completely think about yourself continually. Put your dishes outside' (Nicole, business traveller). It was a treat for food to be prepared, served and cleaned away. 'You can order in food, having people to cook you a meal' (Sophie, business traveller). 'The food appears, just like magic!' (Justine, business traveller).

Conclusion

This chapter has demonstrated that both independent business and solo travel provide women in Australia and New Zealand with opportunities to push the boundaries of constraint, and to find sources of inspiration, empowerment and self-development. Constraints were evidenced through women asking questions such as: Where is it safe for me to go? Should I leave my family? Is it appropriate to travel alone as a woman in that country? Despite these constraints, however, it was also found that women found ways to negotiate through these questions so they could access travel and reap the benefits that travel allows. Analysis of the women's words in both the solo travel and business travel studies showed that similar themes of empowerment emerged. These themes revolved around increased confidence experienced from negotiating constraints, freedom from everyday domestic and familial responsibilities, and improved social skills from interacting with people in new and different contexts. These results support previous research on women's leisure and tourism behaviour, which suggest that independent, solo forms of travel generate feelings of independence, freedom, self-reliance and confidence (Wearing, 1990; Shaw, 1994; Butler, 1995; Gibson and Jordan, 1998). The findings also provide weight for the concept that humans act through individual choice and reason (or 'agency'), rather than as passive acceptors of societal norms and structures (Shaw, 1994; Little, 2002).

Viewing women's travel experiences through the lenses of empowerment and resistance is a shift from the predominant focus on constraint. Solo independent travel, in particular, emphasized a woman's need to learn to cope on her own, a necessity for her well-being and development of her identity. As one solo traveller found, she was keen to encourage other women also to find empowerment and a sense of self through travel. 'I want to encourage people and I want to encourage them the permission to have a dream . . . my travels overseas have been empowering to me, and I want to share that and show others how they can' (Dot, solo traveller). Business travel also provided empowerment for women, as it was an activity associated with success, status and importance. The women business travellers cited several benefits, including increased visibility both internally and externally, opportunities to see new places, and chances for social interaction with new and different people. These women discussed how travel enabled them to establish connections and gain diverse experiences, which empowered them as successful and confident players in their own organizations and in the global business arena. Almost all of them recognized the importance of business travel for facilitating performance thus providing several personal and career benefits.

A surprising, but pleasant, gain from our research on women's travel is the impact it has had on our own lives and empowerment as women and as academic researchers. When designing the research we each hoped that the women would feel comfortable in participating, giving us the data that initially we desired. It is fair to say though that our actual research encounters rewarded us (and we hope the women who participated) in a myriad of positive ways. We have both often discussed how privileged we feel having the richness of the women's lives and stories shared with us. While some stories were funny, several touching, others alarming, many inspirational, all were indeed rich, detailing not just their travel experiences, but also rich tapestries of their wider lives. The conversations with the women were personally a very enjoyable part of the research process for us. We could relate to stories told and share experiences with the women we spoke with. Reciprocally, the cumulative appreciation gained from speaking with the women, and in turn reflecting on our own travel experiences, facilitated understanding and rapport: primary goals of a feminist, interpretive approach to research (Reinharz, 1992; Ateljevic *et al.*, 2005). Our shared enjoyment and learning from the research can be shown with reflexive excerpts from the authors' respective theses:

> I can identify with many of the realities women face, having travelled to attend meetings and conferences. I also recognise many of the benefits of meeting stakeholders, industry peers and fellow researchers for my own career and for my organisation. Visiting new regions and countries is also a particular personal highlight of business travel. In contrast to the benefits exposed, I also have first hand experience of many of the stressors that participants associate with business travel. The experiences of longer days worked, and blurring of the work/leisure dichotomy, resulting in increased feelings of fatigue are appreciated. The challenges in balancing personal and professional life with the need to consider well being are also something I have encountered. Gaining further experience as an ethnographer and traveller in the field was enjoyable and gave me a heightened awareness of my own experiences as a business traveller, and of the portrayals and norms of business travel in New Zealand. Still today I often think about the women's stories and how they continue to have resonance with the trips I make.
>
> (Candice)

During the years of writing this thesis, I took a number of small solo trips related to both work and pleasure. While travelling, I always brought with me the voices and words of the women I had interviewed. Their experiences were with me at all times, offering help and insight as I negotiated my own constraints as a solo woman traveller. Returning from these trips, I was able to consider and re-assess what the women had said in interviews, and this lent a fresh insight into analysis of the data. I have also found that listening to these forty women's stories of constraint and negotiation have enabled me to find ways to negotiate my own personal and professional challenges. By putting these stories into perspective through consideration of the gendered and feminist literature, I have been able to achieve a greater understanding of the challenges women confront on an everyday basis in all aspects of society. Listening to the women's stories and trying to understand them through the gendered and feminist literature has irrevocably altered my life and way of looking at the world. From this point onwards, my outlook on the world and society will always include a consideration of gender. This gendered lens now colours how I see myself in relation to others, how I act and write professionally and how I deal with my own personal relationships. My own personal and professional growth during the five-year period of writing this thesis has been immense. While studying other women's journeys, I found that I myself had also embarked on a solo journey of sorts – a journey of self-discovery which saw me question my views about the world, how I related to people and what I thought was important in the pursuit of academic knowledge.

(Erica)

In conclusion, this chapter has aimed to shift the lens from constraints to viewing the positive aspects of empowerment and agency which can be experienced by women through travel. The goal, however, was not to dismiss the very real and evident constraints that women face in their everyday contexts and travel lives. The authors wish to encourage, in any analysis of constraints, an inclusion of concepts such as empowerment and resistance, to demonstrate women's agency and individual choice in the context of constraining societal and gendered norms. While constraints can be negotiated over the short term, the benefits women experience through increased confidence and improved social skills can be life-changing and long term. These benefits appear to remain with women after the itineraries, photos and souvenirs are packed away and such benefits are transferable and portable to other arenas of everyday life, both at home and work. While the two studies' contexts (business and solo travel) are different, their respective results reveal striking similarities in terms of the benefits women received, such as empowerment, increased self-confidence, freedom from responsibility and improved social skills. Such findings help to build a picture of women travel consumers as active and empowered agents, resisting rather than succumbing to their reported constraints.

References

Abbott Cone, C. (1995) Crafting selves: the lives of two Mayan women. *Annals of Tourism Research* 22(2), 314–327.

Apostolopoulos, Y. and Sonmez, S. (2001) Working producers, leisured consumers: women's experiences in developing regions. In: Apostolopoulos, Y., Sonmez, S. and Dallen, J.T. (eds) *Women as Producers and Consumers of Tourism in Developing Regions*. Praeger, Westport, Connecticut, pp. 3–17.

Ashton-Schaeffer, C., Gibson, H., Holt, M. and Willming, C. (2001) Women's resistance and empowerment through wheelchair sport. *World Leisure* 43(4), 11–21.

Ateljevic, I., Harris, C., Wilson, E. and Leo Collins, F. (2005) Getting 'entangled': reflexivity and the 'critical turn' in tourism studies. *Tourism Recreation Research* 30(2), 9–21.

Bates, D. (1999) Moderator's gender can influence a focus group. *Marketing News* 33(5), 17–19.

Bella, L. (1992) *The Christmas Imperative: Leisure, Family, and Women's Work*. Fernwood Publishing, Halifax, Nova Scotia.

Bond, M. (2001) *Gutsy Women: More Travel Tips and Wisdom for the Road*. Travelers' Tales, San Francisco, California.

Bond, M. and Michael, P. (eds) (1999) *A Woman's Passion for Travel*. Travelers' Tales, San Francisco, California.

Butler, K.L. (1995) Independence for Western women through tourism. *Annals of Tourism Research* 22(2), 487–489.

Carr, N. (2001) An exploratory study of gendered differences in young tourists' perception of danger within London. *Tourism Management* 22, 565–570.

Clarke, I.F. (1988) Wandering women: the right connections. *Tourism Management* 9(1), 78–82.

Cukier, J., Norris, J. and Wall, G. (1996) The involvement of women in the tourism industry of Bali, Indonesia. *The Journal of Development Studies* 33(2), 248–270.

Davidson, P. (1996) The holiday and work experiences of women with young children. *Leisure Studies* 15(2), 89–103.

Deem, R. (1996) No time for a rest? An exploration of women's work, engendered leisure and holidays. *Time and Society* 5(1), 5–25.

Deem, R. (1999) How do we get out of the ghetto? Strategies for research on gender and leisure for the twenty-first century. *Leisure Studies* 18(3), 161–177.

Elsrud, T. (1998) Time creation in travelling: the taking and making of time among women backpackers. *Time and Society* 7(2), 309–334.

Enloe, C. (1989) *Bananas, Beaches and Bases*. Pandora, London.

Freysinger, V.J. and Flannery, D. (1992) Women's leisure: affiliation, self-determination, empowerment and resistance? *Society & Leisure* 15(1), 303–322.

Ghose, I. (1998) *Women Travellers in Colonial India: The Power of the Female Gaze*. Oxford University Press, Delhi, India.

Gibson, H. (2001) Gender in tourism: theoretical perspectives. In: Apostolopoulos, Y., Sonmez, S. and Dallen, J.T. (eds) *Women as Producers and Consumers of Tourism in Developing Regions*. Praeger, Westport, Connecticut, pp. 3–17.

Gibson, H. and Jordan, F. (1998) Shirley Valentine Lives! The Experiences of Solo Women Travellers. Paper presented at the Fifth Congress of the World Leisure and Recreation Association, 26–30 October, Sao Paulo, Brazil.

Glaser, B.G. and Strauss, A.L. (1967) *The Discovery of Grounded Theory: Strategies for Qualitative Research*. Aldine, Chicago, Illinois.

Graburn, N.H.H. (1983) The anthropology of tourism. *Annals of Tourism Research* 10(1), 9–33.

Green, E. (1998) 'Women doing friendship': an analysis of women's leisure as a site of identity construction, empowerment and resistance. *Leisure Studies* 17(3), 171–185.

Hall, D. and Kinnaird, V. (1994) A note on women travellers. In: Kinnaird, V. and Hall, D. (eds) *Tourism: A Gender Analysis*. Wiley, Chichester, UK, pp. 188–209.

Hamalian, L. (1981) *Ladies on the Loose: Women Travellers of the 18th and 19th Centuries*. Dodd, Mead, New York.

Harding, S. (1991) *Whose Science? Whose Knowledge? Thinking from Women's Lives*. Cornell University Press, Ithaca, New York.

Harris, C. (2002) Women and power: a study of New Zealand women business travellers. Unpublished PhD thesis, Victoria University of Wellington, New Zealand.

Harris, C. and Ateljevic, I. (2003) Perpetuating the male gaze as the norm: challenges for 'her' participation in business travel. *Tourism Recreation Research* 28(2), 21–30.

Henderson, K.A. (1991) The contribution of feminism to an understanding of leisure constraints. *Journal of Leisure Research* 23(4), 363–377.

Henderson, K.A. and Bialeschki, M.D. (1993) Negotiating constraints to women's physical recreation. *Society & Leisure* 16(2), 389–412.

Henderson, K., Bialeschki, M.D., Shaw, S. and Freysinger, V. (1996) *Both Gains and Gaps: Feminist Perspectives on Women's Leisure*. Venture, State College, Pennsylvania.

Hewlett, S.A. (2002) Executive women and the myth of having it all. *Harvard Business Review* 80(4), 5–11.

Hutchison, P. and McGill, J. (1992) *Leisure, Integration and Community*. Ontario Leisurability Publications, Concord, California.

Jackson, E.L. and Henderson, K.A. (1995) Gender-based analysis of leisure constraints. *Leisure Sciences* 17(1), 31–51.

Jackson, E.L. and Scott, D. (1999) Constraints to leisure. In: Jackson, E.L. and Burton, T.L. (eds) *Leisure Studies: Prospects for the Twenty-first Century*. Venture, State College, Pennsylvania, pp. 299–321.

Jackson, E.L., Crawford, D.W. and Godbey, G. (1993) Negotiation of leisure constraints. *Leisure Sciences* 15(1), 1–11.

Jennings, G. (2001) *Tourism Research*. Wiley, Milton, Queensland.

Jordan, F. and Gibson, H. (2000) Whose space is this anyway? The experiences of solo women travellers. Paper presented at the Annual Conference of the Institute of British Geographers, 4–7 January, Brighton, UK.

Kain, D. and King, B. (2004) Destination-based product selections by international backpackers in Australia. In: Richards, G. and Wilson, J. (eds) *The Global Nomad: Backpacker Travel in Theory and Practice*. Channel View, Clevedon, UK, pp. 196–216.

Kay, T. and Jackson, G. (1991) Leisure despite constraint: the impact of leisure constraints on leisure participation. *Journal of Leisure Research* 23(4), 301–313.

Kinnaird, V. and Hall, D. (1994) *Tourism: A Gender Analysis*. Wiley, Chichester, UK.

Kinnaird, V. and Hall, D. (2000) Theorizing gender in tourism research. *Tourism Recreation Research* 25, 71–84.

Krippendorf, J. (1997) The motives of the mobile leisureman: travel between norm, promise and hope. In: France, L. (ed.) *The Earthscan Reader in Sustainable Tourism*. Earthscan, London, pp. 38–53.

Leontidou, L. (1994) Gender dimensions of tourism in Greece: employment, sub-cultures and restructuring. In: Kinnaird, V. and Hall, D. (eds) *Tourism: A Gender Analysis*. Wiley, Chichester, UK, pp. 74–105.

Lincoln, Y.S. and Guba, E.G. (1985) *Naturalistic Inquiry*. Sage, Newbury Park, California.

Little, D.E. (2000) Negotiating adventure recreation: how women can access satisfying adventure experiences throughout their lives. *Society & Leisure* 23(1), 171–195.

Little, D.E. (2002) Women and adventure recreation: reconstructing leisure constraints and adventure experiences to negotiate continuing participation. *Journal of Leisure Research* 34(2), 157–177.

Little, D.E. and Wilson, E. (2005) Adventure and the gender gap: acknowledging diversity of experience. *Society & Leisure* 28(1), 185–208.

MacKinnon, A. (1997) *Love and Freedom: Professional Women and the Reshaping of Personal Life*. Cambridge University Press, Cambridge.

Morgan, N. and Pritchard, A. (1998) *Tourism, Promotion and Power: Creating Images, Creating Identities*. Wiley, Chichester, UK.

Newlands, K. (2004) Setting out on the road less travelled: a study of backpacker travel in New Zealand. In: Richards, G. and Wilson, J. (eds) *The Global Nomad: Backpacker Travel in Theory and Practice*. Channel View, Clevedon, UK, pp. 217–236.

Norris, J. and Wall, G. (1994) Gender and tourism. *Progress in Tourism, Recreation and Hospitality Management* 6, 57–78.

Oppermann, M. (1999) Sex tourism. *Annals of Tourism Research* 26(2), 251–266.

Pemble, J. (1987) *The Mediterranean Passion: Victorians and Edwardians in the South*. Oxford University Press, Oxford.

Pennington-Gray, L.A. and Kerstetter, D.A. (2001) What do university-educated women want from their pleasure travel experiences? *Journal of Travel Research* 40(1), 49–56.

Pesman, R. (1996) *Duty Free: Australian Women Abroad*. Oxford University, Melbourne.

Popcorn, F. and Marigold, L. (2000) *EVEolution: The Eight Truths of Marketing to Women*. Hyperion, New York.

Rach, L. (2001) *The Changing Nature of Female Business Travelers: A Review of the Findings of a Study Conducted by New York University and Wyndham Hotels and Resorts*. New York University, New York.

Raymore, L.A. (2002) Facilitators to leisure. *Journal of Leisure Research* 34(1), 37–51.

Reinharz, S. (1992) *Feminist Methods in Social Research*. Oxford University Press, New York.

Riley, P.J. (1988) Road culture of international long-term budget travelers. *Annals of Tourism Research* 15, 313–328.

Robinson, J. (1990) *Wayward Women: A Guide to Women Travellers*. Oxford University Press, Oxford.

Robinson, J. (1994) *Unsuitable for Ladies: An Anthology of Women Travellers*. Oxford University Press, Oxford.

Ryan, C. (2000) Sex tourism: paradigms of confusion? In: Clift, S. and Carter, S. (eds) *Tourism and Sex: Culture, Commerce and Coercion*. Pinter, London, pp. 23–40.

Samdahl, D.M. and Jekubovich, N.J. (1997) A critique of leisure constraints: comparative analyses and understandings. *Journal of Leisure Research* 29(4), 430–453.

Shaw, S.M. (1994) Gender, leisure, and constraint: towards a framework for the analysis of women's leisure. *Journal of Leisure Research* 26(1), 8–22.

Shaw, S.M. (2001) Conceptualizing resistance: women's leisure as political practice. *Journal of Leisure Research* 33(2), 186–201.

Shogan, D. (2002) Characterizing constraints of leisure: a Foucaultian analysis of leisure constraints. *Leisure Studies* 21(1), 27–38.

Small, J. (1999) Memory-work: a method for researching women's tourist experiences. *Tourism Management* 20(1), 25–35.

Smith, V.L. (1979) Women: the taste-makers in tourism. *Annals of Tourism Research* 6, 49–60.

South Australian Tourism Commission (1996) *Women and Travel: South Australian Holiday Patterns of Adelaide Women*. South Australian Tourism Commission, Adelaide.

Steinbach, A. (2000) *Without Reservations: The Travels of an Independent Woman*. Bantam Books, Sydney.

Swain, M.B. (1995) Gender in tourism. *Annals of Tourism Research* 22(2), 247–266.

Swan, S. and Laufer, P. (1998) *Safety and Security for Women Who Travel*. Travelers' Tales, San Francisco, California.

Timothy, D.J. (2001) Gender relations in tourism: revisiting patriarchy and underdevelopment. In: Apostolopoulos, Y., Sonmez, S. and Dallen, J.T. (eds) *Women as Producers and Consumers of Tourism in Developing Regions*. Praeger, Westport, Connecticut, pp. 235–248.

Uriely, N. (2001) 'Travelling workers' and 'working tourists': variations across the interaction between work and tourism. *International Journal of Tourism Research* 3(1), 1–8.

Warner-Smith, P. (2000) Travel, young women and 'The Weekly', 1956–1968. *Annals of Leisure Research* 3, 33–46.

Wearing, B. (1990) Beyond the ideology of motherhood: leisure as resistance. *Australian and New Zealand Journal of Sociology* 26(1), 36–58.

Wearing, B.M. (1994) The pain and pleasure of gendered leisure. *World Leisure and Recreation* 36(3), 4–10.

Wearing, B. and Wearing, S. (1988) 'All in a day's leisure': gender and the concept of leisure. *Leisure Studies* 7(2), 111–123.

Wearing, B. and Wearing, S. (1996) Refocussing the tourist experience: the flâneur and the choraster. *Leisure Studies* 15(4), 229–243.

Westwood, S. (1997) A missed marketing opportunity? Is the airline industry catering for the needs of today's business woman? Unpublished undergraduate dissertation, University of Wales Institute, Cardiff, UK.

Westwood, S., Pritchard, A. and Morgan, N.J. (2000) Gender-blind marketing: businesswomen's perceptions of airline services. *Tourism Management* 21, 353–362.

White, M. (1989) *Going Solo: The Essential Guide for Solo Women Travellers*. Greenhouse, Elwood, Victoria, Australia.

Wilkinson, P.F. and Pratiwi, W. (1995) Gender and tourism in an Indonesian village. *Annals of Tourism Research* 22(2), 283–299.

Wilson, E. (2004) A journey of her own? The impact of constraints on women's solo travel. Unpublished PhD dissertation, Griffith University, Australia.

Wilson, E. and Little, D.E. (2003) 'It'd take a lot to stop me!': How women negotiate the constraints of solo travel. In: Griffin, T. and Harris, R. (eds) *Current Research, Future Strategies: Bridging Uncertainty – Proceedings of the 9th Annual Asia Pacific Tourism Association Conference*. University of Technology, Sydney, Australia, pp. 834–845.

Wilson, E. and Little, D.E. (2005) A 'relative escape'? The impact of constraints on women who travel solo. *Tourism Review International* 9, 155–175.

15 An Israeli Lesbian's Travel Experience: A Heterosexual Man's Interpretation of Her Diary

Yaniv Poria

Introduction

In recent decades a significant body of literature has emerged which discusses the experiences of gays and lesbians (Russell, 2001), particularly in geography (e.g. Weightman, 1980, 1981; Bell, 1991; Binnie and Valentine, 1999), social anthropology (e.g. Kates and Belk, 2001), health sciences (e.g. Hinchliff et al., 2005) and psychology (e.g. Goldfried, 2001). This has resulted in the emergence of the interdisciplinary field of gay and lesbian studies, evidenced by numerous undergraduate courses and journals such as *Gay and Lesbian Psychology*, *Journal of Homosexuality* and *Journal of Gay and Lesbian Studies*. In this interdisciplinary work, studies commonly centre on issues linked with marginalization, identity and the social exclusion of gays and lesbians by heterosexual society and its effects on gays' and lesbians' lives.

Tourism studies have mainly emphasized the importance of tourism and leisure in the expression of gay and lesbian identities (e.g. Hughes, 1997; Aitchison, 1999; Clift and Forrest, 1999a,b; Pritchard and Morgan, 1999). In much of this work, the focus has commonly been on experience of spaces which are not the usual places of residence. These studies conclude that the tourist experience provides gays and lesbians with the opportunity of feeling existential authenticity, providing an outlet from the heterosexual norms of society. The existence of gay and lesbian travel agencies, advertising campaigns and specialized guidebooks, as well as concerted marketing efforts by destinations perceived to be 'gay-friendly', indicate that the gay and lesbian community is 'on the map as a unique market segment' (Russel, 2001). Yet, despite recognition that tourism is important to gays and lesbians (Clift and Forrest, 1999a,b), there is still much to be done on the subject, particularly as Pritchard (2004) notes, since the existing research is overwhelmingly focused on the experiences of gays and often ignores lesbian voices and experiences (some notable exceptions include the empirical studies conducted in some of the UK's gay- and lesbian-friendly cities by Bialeschki and Pearce, 1997; Pritchard et al., 2002).

When researching a relatively sensitive topic it is often necessary to build up an increasingly comprehensive picture through a series of small-scale studies, each extending the insights gained from previous work. Puar (2002) and Visser (2003) challenge studies conducted at 'gay landscapes' in North America and the UK, which commonly results in findings that represent only certain segments of the gay and lesbian population and particularly privileges the voices of gays living in cities with a highly developed gay scene. This study aims to address this gap and explores a lesbian's tourist experience in the context of Israel. Through a comparison of her experience in different spaces – the spaces where she commonly lives (her home and open spaces near her house) and those spaces in which she is involved in tourist activity (in different contexts of her life) – the chapter explores issues of concealing (individual) sexual identity, behaviour in certain spaces and perceptions of spaces.

This chapter therefore presents an examination of an Israeli lesbian's travel experience based on analysis of her published diary. Comparison of her experience and attitudes towards various spaces (particularly her apartment, the neighbouring open spaces and those locations she visits as a tourist) suggests that her perception of spaces as being 'free from people she knows' allows her and her partner to benefit from anonymity, to live a lesbian lifestyle and to benefit from a sense of existential authenticity. It emerges that the only space in which she experiences these feelings of self-expression is in the accommodation she uses during her tourist trips. The chapter therefore highlights her need for anonymity and its importance in the construction of her lesbian identity as a result of the prevailing social norms of Israeli society. Thus, I argue that Israeli culture and its social norms play a key role in understanding such tourist experiences and their associated meanings and conclude with a discussion of the implications of using 'real' diaries as a source of information.

Tourism, Lesbians and Gays

Lesbians and gays are often subject to social disapproval, prejudice and discrimination in contemporary societies (Bell, 1991). This can result in feelings of insecurity and isolation when interacting with other social groups, in harassment, and even in physical violence (Weightman, 1980; Knopp, 1990). This may explain why attempts to conceal sexual identity, known as 'non-disclosure', 'stigma management' or 'survival strategies', are common among gays and lesbians (Carragher and Rivers, 2002). In light of these circumstances, it could be assumed here that individual sexual orientation may have an effect on a person's experience of space, and specifically on her travel experience and the meanings she attaches to different spaces. Gays and lesbians who are open about their sexuality can suffer from social stigma and social risks, including violence (Weightman, 1980; Lewis and Ross, 1995; Kirby and Hay, 1997), whilst those who do not reveal their sexuality may be in a constant internal struggle, even acting as heterosexuals in their own homes (Kirby and Hay, 1997). For both groups, the tourist experience – as a place and period of time in which they are far from their normal place of residence (Hughes, 1997; Pritchard et al., 2000) – presents a potential opportunity to be 'themselves'.

Such notions are rooted in research that suggests that tourism (specifically the distance of tourists from their usual environments) allows individuals to shed the norms that control their daily routines (Turner and Ash, 1975; Shields, 1992). This feeling of existential authenticity exists when tourists may feel that they can be themselves and express themselves more freely than in their daily lives (Wang, 1999; Uriely, 2005) and may explain the importance assigned to tourism by and for the gay and lesbian communities.

As I outlined above there is a growing interest in gay and lesbian tourism research. These can be discussed under five main themes (see Poria, 2006): studies that highlight the sociodemographic characteristics of the gay and lesbian population; studies exploring the motivation for tourist activities; a group of studies exploring the commodification of sexual orientation in tourist spaces; research examining discrimination towards gays and lesbians (mainly in the hospitality industry); health research on HIV and gays' travel patterns. Yet surprisingly, over a decade since the first tourism studies of gays, research attention has not yet focused on understanding lesbians' tourist experiences. As in other research disciplines, the lesbian population still receives only limited attention from tourism scholars (Hughes, 1997; Clift and Forrest, 1999b; Pritchard *et al.*, 2002). Moreover, the data that are collected for many studies often come from residents or tourists in cities with a highly developed gay scene (e.g. Brighton and Manchester in the UK or San Francisco in the USA), which results in a skewed view of gay and lesbian travel experiences. In addition, very little attention has yet been paid to specific sites of the tourist experience (such as hotel rooms). Such gaps in our understanding of gay and lesbian tourism experiences and perceptions of tourist sites and spaces highlight the need for further research, particularly work which broadens our knowledge in a range of geographic contexts.

Gays and Lesbians in Israel

There is little published research on gays and lesbians in Israeli society (Kama, 2000) and that which has been done can be divided into two groups: studies dealing with the place of gays and lesbians in society and studies dealing with gay and lesbian tourist-related activities. The first group of studies is typified by that of Kuntsman (2003) who addresses the radicalization and ethnicization of Russian lesbian immigrants in Israel. She illustrates how lesbian immigrants mark spaces as homophobic, asexual, liberal or queer and suggests that Israel is a more liberal country than Russia in terms of its attitudes to sexuality. The second group of studies focus on tourism-related activities. For example, Poria and Taylor (2001) examined gay and lesbian online travel purchasing behaviour and suggested that (unlike in countries such as the UK) one of the main reasons that Israeli gays and lesbians use the Internet is that they are afraid that the travel agency staff might know them personally.

Specifically, Poria and Taylor argue that in Israel gays and lesbians worry that their sexuality might be revealed due to the 'small country syndrome' where 'everyone knows everyone else'. Two further studies (Poria and Oppewal, 2003; Poria, 2006) endorse this suggestion revealing that gays and lesbians often prefer to stay at hotels where there is less chance they will be recognized by other hotel guests. Moreover, the Poria and Oppewal (2003) study of gay and lesbian cyber communities contends that given the 'invasiveness' of Israeli society, gays and lesbians attempt to choose a hotel with cooperative staff who will not reveal their sexual identity in public. Common to all these studies is the suggestion that gays are more afraid to reveal their sexuality in public than lesbians, that local culture plays an important role in the understanding of gay and lesbian experiences, and that both gays and lesbians consider their private homes to be the ultimate spaces where they can safely reveal their sexual identities.

Using a Diary to Understand a Lesbian's Experiences in Israel

This study makes use of an underused research resource in tourism studies – a published diary. Diary accounts have been commonly used in tourism to investigate the links between duration of travel, travel patterns (e.g. decision making while travelling, number of travel companions) and spending patterns (e.g. Thornton *et al.*, 1997; Vogt and Andereck, 2003); occasionally, they have been used in tourism studies focusing on heritage and nature-based tourism (e.g. Markwell, 1997; Laws, 1998). A published diary has several characteristics which differentiate it from such diary accounts. In the present study, the diary was not written at a researcher's request, but is commercially published and publicly available. Furthermore, in this diary, the travel experience is not the key focus of the account, but forms only part of the individual's everyday lived experiences. Such diaries are known in academic discourse as public unsolicited personal documents (Gibson, 1995; Hodder, 1998) and they have already been recognized as rich sources of information in areas such as sociology and anthropology and are especially popular in feminist research (Cotterill and Letherby, 1993; Romanucci-Ross, 2001).

Important to this current study are the attributes of diary accounts as sources of information which minimize researcher influence and involvement (except as an interpreter of their meaning). In addition, such diaries can be particularly self-revealing and honest (Breakwell and Wood, 1995; Miller, 2000) and thus shed light on individuals' emotions and their private thoughts and interpretations (Wilkins, 1993). Of course, there are some criticisms of the use of diaries in social science research as a diary can only refer to a particular individual and as such, is 'subjective' in nature. The diary examined in this chapter is entitled *To Kiss You in a Field of Daisies* (2000) and was written by architect and photographer, Aviva Evron (hereinafter referred to as the author/diarist/writer). The diary is written in Hebrew and published by Yedioth Ahronot, a popular mainstream publisher with no specific ideological philosophy. The diary uses two writing styles. The first is general descriptions of the diarist's actions, commonly referring to undefined time periods, whilst the second is detailed descriptions of activities which took place on a certain date. The diarist, in a short interview with me, confirmed that the book represents her public diary and can be freely described and analysed.

The diary covers the period from September 1992 to June 1994 and describes a period in the author's life from the moment she renews an acquaintance with someone she knew previously until the point they decided to live together and raise children as a lesbian couple. In general, the diary describes the development of the relationship between the author and her lover, who are both women in their thirties. It includes the development of their friendship, their efforts to conceal the nature of their relationship, and their reasons for not wanting it to become public. The writer and her partner live in the Tel Aviv area, a city with many beaches and parks which is often characterized as gay- and lesbian-friendly, possessing a rich cultural scene and many meeting places for the homosexual community (Cassels, 2000; Hoffman, 2005).

In assembling the analysis and discussion of the diary I first subjected it to thematic content analysis to illuminate underlying themes (Smith, 1995), specifically focusing on the writer's discussion of the different spaces in the city. Then, in line with interpretative phenomenology analysis, careful consideration was given to the symbolic meaning attached to objects and events to which the diarist refers. This was considered appropriate as it provided a framework through which the writer's experience could be examined. In addition, links between the themes I identified (e.g. the spaces to which the writer refers) and situational factors (e.g. the status of the diarist's relationships with her partner and her companions on visits to those spaces) were investigated. The analysis was not guided by any specific prior hypotheses, but rather allowed key themes to emerge from the data. It aimed at clarifying such topics as the reasons for moving from one space to another, the meanings assigned with moving to another space, whether the diarist related to her companion in that space, her companion on the visit, etc. It was assumed that analysing these topics, particularly the comparison of the experience in different spaces, would provide insight into a lesbian's tourist experience. The translation of quotations was checked by an Israeli proficient in Hebrew and English.

The Diarist, Her Lover and Israel

The analysis centred around three spaces: the writer and her friends' apartments, open spaces (the parks and beach) near her home, and spaces the writer 'inhabited' as a tourist. The diarist assigns two attributes to Israel which are important in understanding her tourist experience. First, Israel is referred to as a country 'where everyone knows everyone' and it is clear from her diary that when she is in public spaces with her lover, the writer is afraid that someone might recognize them. Second, the diarist, and to a greater extent, her lover, believe that lesbianism in Israel may lead to social stigma, and be a possible threat to certain elements of their lives. Thus, the diarist's lover, a child psychologist, is particularly concerned with losing clientele and possibly being viewed as less professional by her colleagues. The following quotation taken from dialogues between the writer and her partner highlights this issue:

> My mother would die if she knew. [. . .] My sister would excommunicate me, she'd distance her children from me to avoid my sick influence. My friends would distance themselves [. . .] the neighbours would point at me, turn their heads after me in the street with a knowing smile on their lips, or I'd see them in clouds of concern about the loss of value of their apartments . . . I'm sure they'll fire me [. . .] my boss won't

take the risk of employing me, and rightly. Surely, parents won't agree to bring their kids for counselling with a psychologist like that. Everyone will run away. I'm sure it'll ruin my career. I'm convinced. (p. 23)

The diarist also highlights norms of behaviour which are important to understanding her daily activities as well as her tourist experience. One such example is the freedom to visit a friend without prior notice. This is illustrated later as being important to the understanding of the writer's perceptions of certain spaces. In addition, two significant issues should be noted with respect to the writer and her lover. First, the diarist has considered herself lesbian ('I always preferred the wrong sex', p. 28) since childhood, whilst her lover, in contrast, argues that she wants to live with a man in a 'normal' family and does not see herself as lesbian. She claims that until the current relationship with the diarist, she had never fallen in love or been sexually aroused by a woman. Second, the diarist suggests that she and her partner are not familiar with the lesbian scene either inside or outside of Israel and do not know other lesbian couples. At the beginning of their relationship, they perceived lesbians as 'strange manly women':

We'd only heard about lesbians, we didn't know any, but we knew they're different, masculine women who hadn't found a man, so they live with women. We had nothing in common with them. We knew we were alone in the world. (p. 26)

Looking for a private sphere: home, neighbourhood and hotel rooms

The home is described in the diary as a space where the writer and her partner are free to live together as a lesbian couple. The diary includes descriptions of regular mundane activities such as eating, watching television and making love (which the diarist suggests can only happen in their own homes). Their home is perceived as a space for activities that cannot be performed in public view (unlike heterosexuals), because they would be identified as lesbians. For example, they dance together at home. It is very important to highlight that the diarist and her partner are constantly afraid of being recognized as lesbians, even in their own home and thus they take several steps in order to prevent this, such as leaving home separately early in the morning to avoid being seen, taking their shoes off when climbing the stairs, and unlocking the door quietly. When at home, they are afraid of the sound of the elevator, fearing that it may bring an unexpected visitor (common in Israel), who might discover their relationship.

The couple also make frequent visits to the public open spaces near the author's home, including several parks and beaches. These visits are classified by the diarist according to who is accompanying her: no one; other companions such as a 'blind date' and social companions; and her partner. When visiting these places on her own, the diarist refers to them as somewhere she can relax and feel free from others and makes no reference to her lesbianism. She visits these places when she feels pressured and in need of isolation from others; her commentaries refer to the natural scenery and to the peace and quiet there which relaxes her.

The following example illustrates the diarist's experience of open spaces. Through her visit to a local beach (which she described as being a tourist in her own city), we can understand the meaning she assigns to her experiences there. During one visit she met a man she did not know, and they discussed very personal issues. He told her about his divorce and she spoke frankly about her relationship with her lover, which at that moment was at a critical stage. It is interesting to note that in this environment (located very close to her home), she argued that she felt like a tourist and felt safe enough to share her sexuality with a stranger (the two did not ask for each other's names) – both 'exposed' themselves but retained their anonymities:

> Wednesday afternoon – I went to mess around in the sea, find peace. I wandered around like a tourist, no car, no bags, no camera – great. A man sat next to me on rocks of the marina wave breaker and started a conversation. He told me he's going through a painful divorce, and I told him in the openness between strangers that I'm finishing a romance with a woman, and it's hard for me. [. . .] We parted even without knowing each other's names. (p. 150)

At other times, the diarist visits such open spaces in the company of friends and acquaintances rather than her lover. On these occasions, the open space is described by the writer as one in which she feels relatively safe and at ease. When the author is accompanied by her lover, however, they show physical affection in a way that reveals the nature of their lesbian relationship and consider these open spaces as places in which they are isolated from a heterosexual environment, even though they are aware that they are in a public place. This is a description of a visit to the park next to their home:

> We sat on the green, cold rug overlooking the pools of water that reflect the trees and palms, and glittering street lights. I knew we were very close to the busy Tayasim Road [a famous road in Israel] and to hundreds of living rooms where people sit in the pale television light watching the world's bad news: and here, on the grass, under the old rubber tree, none of that exists. Everything is quiet, cut off, you and me. I put my arm around your shoulder. 'Are you crazy, in a public place?' you warned me. Stop it, nobody cares. Besides, what public place? Feel this place . . . (p. 86)

On other occasions when the diarist and her partner visit open spaces, the same pattern emerges. Although aware that the space is public, they act as if they were in a semi-protected space, where they do not have to hide their relationship. In this context, it is interesting to compare this behaviour with that of the diarist when she purchased a book on homosexual love in a mainstream bookstore: although the simple act of buying such a book does not indicate sexual orientation she did not buy the book at her usual bookstore and indeed checked several times to ensure there was nobody present who knew her. This contrasts sharply with her perception of the anonymity of the open spaces.

The diary also describes several tourist trips the diarist takes with her partner in Israel and these descriptions can be divided into those of spaces inside and outside the hotel room. In fact, the diary begins with a tourism trip the writer describes a vacation she took with her partner and some friends in the city of Eilat, a popular resort in the south of Israel. She refers to the vacation generally as 'a chance to escape' and interestingly, they stay in a different hotel from their friends. Here, their hotel room serves as the ultimate space in which they feel completely isolated and free to be a lesbian couple. The diarist specifically describes the room during the vacation as 'an escape to a protected environment [. . .]. When we escaped back to the air-conditioned room that was just ours, all the fears and concerns vanished' (p. 19). In a similar fashion, when on a tourist trip in the north of Israel, the diarist again describes this as a period of freedom from the daily routine and from social norms. Once again, the vacation accommodation allows the couple to be themselves and it is described as a space where the writer can avoid the 'hysteria of her normal life'; it provides her with the opportunity to feel safe and protected and as such she can do and feel things which she cannot even in her own home.

Reflecting on a Lesbian Israeli's Diary

Aviva Evron's diary descriptions suggest that when she is a tourist (especially when she is in a hotel room) she feels free of social pressures and can experience her lesbian relationship in a way she cannot at other times and in other places. Echoing Hughes' (1997, p. 3) suggestion that tourism helps to 'facilitate(s) the construction of a homosexual identity', travel affirms and constructs the writer's lesbian relationship by providing an escape from those heterosexual spaces in which the diarist and her partner cannot show physical affection (Valentine, 1996). Interestingly, some studies (Pritchard et al., 2000, 2002) found that many gays and lesbians want to be among people like themselves whilst on vacation (especially those who are open about their sexuality and who live in cities with well-developed gay and lesbian scenes); in this case, the diarist showed almost no interest in meeting other lesbians (who may be able to recognize her).

In terms of Aviva Evron's feelings of being 'herself', it is useful to consider the concept of authenticity, which is central to tourism studies and to the understanding of tourist behaviour (Reisinger and Steiner, 2006). Understanding of the term has shifted from the objective to a constructivist perspective, which highlights the role of the individual in the construction of attributes associated with the object or presentation displayed (Uriely, 2005). Wang (1999) identified two kinds of authenticity: the authenticity of toured objects and existential authenticity. Specifically, he highlights the latter as relevant in understanding tourist experiences which are not based on the authenticity of the object (Reisinger and Steiner, 2006). Wang argues that 'people feel they themselves are much more authentic and more freely self-expressed than in everyday life, not because they find the tour objects are authentic but simply because they are engaging in nonordinary activities, free from the constraints of the daily life' (1999, p. 3). It is argued that when she is a tourist, the diarist is involved in an existential authentic experience, she feels more herself in a hotel room than in her own house.

Clearly, for this woman, the tourist experience is important to her construction of her lesbian relationship. However, in contrast to most studies in which the participants had already revealed their sexuality and identified themselves as lesbians, it is important to remember that she was a woman who (at the time) had not 'come out'. For her, the idea of the home as a shelter from everyday heterosexualized society has less relevance and as a result of social practices and conventions in Israel (where friends arrive unannounced) she does not feel safe as a lesbian even in her own apartment; clearly such is the deeply embedded power of the hetero-normative gaze that it even permeates individuals' homes. Interestingly, this is similar to the situations of gays during their military service (Kaplan and Ben-Ari, 2000), where the army offered them a safer environment than their own homes.

As I discussed above, the tourism studies and human/cultural geography literature emphasize that gay- and lesbian-friendly areas provide a safe environment for these people to be themselves, as well as the opportunity to socialize with like-minded individuals (Rushbrook, 2002). This has been seen to be particularly important during the coming-out process (Ivy, 2001) and thus Weightman (1980) suggests that gay bars have the attributes of a private place as a result of the secrecy they provide. She highlights the importance of this space in the self-identification process, whilst Pritchard *et al.* (2002) highlight the importance of these spaces for their sense of community. In Aviva Evron's case, however, areas popular with gays and lesbians did not provide a safe environment for her since she was worried about being seen and recognized (in such a tight-knit community) and were less relevant as she was in a long-term relationship.

This indicates the influence of culturally specific contexts (in this case Israel) on gay and lesbian behaviour. It is clear that the invasiveness of Israeli society means that the diarist feels unsafe and constantly struggles to conceal her sexuality, even in her own (and her partner's) home. Only when she is away in a hotel room can she be truly free to be herself. Nowhere is the importance of the individual subjective sense of freedom during a tourist experience more obvious (Moore *et al.*, 1995; Uriely, 2005) and endorses the theoretical framework suggested by Poria *et al.* (2003) for the understanding of tourism, in which the individual's perception of time as 'free' is important to a person's tourist experience. In this study, these researchers argue that a person may feel like a tourist even when he or she is located close to home, or distant from home but away for less than 24 hours. They specifically emphasize the individual's perception of the time frame as 'free' as important for understanding tourist experience. For Aviva Evron, feeling and acting as a tourist in the open spaces close to her home or in her hotel room conveys a liberating sense of freedom, allowing her to break free from the hetero-normative gaze.

As well as establishing the importance of particular cultural contexts, this chapter's discussion of the diary also reveals other potential lines of enquiry for tourism studies generally and for gay and lesbian tourism studies in particular. Issues of security and spatial awareness in crowds have been virtually ignored in tourism research and it may be that the presence of certain groups of people is relevant in understanding the tourist experience of lesbians. Poria (2006), for example, suggested that gays' behaviour is influenced by the presence of children in a hotel, preventing them from open displays of affection. In Aviva Evron's case, the presence of others, or more accurately, the presence of others who might recognize her, prevents her from public displays of affection. Yet, whilst she was afraid of recognition, there is no sense in the diary that either she or her partner feared physical violence – something similar to other studies (Harper and Schneider, 2003).

In conclusion, therefore, this discussion of an Israeli lesbian's diary has revealed some interesting insights and raised a number of issues surrounding the role of culturally specific practices on lesbians' behaviours. Aviva Evron's experiences as an Israeli are different to those of some of the lesbians whose voices have previously been heard in tourism studies. Basing this study on her diary has allowed the researcher to study her behaviour in a natural setting (Phillimore and Goodson, 2004), but of course, the representativeness of the findings cannot be gauged, and, from a tourist studies' perspective, travel was not the main focus of the diary. Yet the most fundamental methodological issue here is that the study is an Israeli heterosexual man's interpretation of the diarist's experience.

I cannot deny that my own interpretation may have influenced my understanding of Aviva Evron's actions and feelings. But based on my experience working with gay and lesbian participants and researchers, being an 'outsider' has certain advantages. An 'outsider' researcher (in this case, part of the majority group) who builds trust (and works) with her or his research participants may highlight what may be considered trivial and unimportant to those belonging to the group, thus providing a deeper understanding of behaviour and its meanings. I would argue that those who are not part of the social group at the core of any study have the ability to bridge the 'gap' between majority and minority groups, bringing insights to different audiences. The key concern in such a project (as in any social science study) is to endeavour to build relationships with those with whom we co-create tourism knowledge based on respect, empathy and reciprocity.

References

Aitchison, M.C. (1999) New cultural geographies: the spatiality of leisure, gender and sexuality. *Leisure Studies* 18, 19–39.

Bell, D.J. (1991) Insignificant other: lesbian and gay geographies. *Area* 23(4), 323–329.

Bialeschki, M.D. and Pearce, K.D. (1997) 'I don't want a lifestyle – I want a life': the effect of role negotiations on the leisure of lesbian mothers. *Journal of Leisure Research* 29(1), 113–131.

Binnie, J. and Valentine, G. (1999) Geographies of sexuality – a review of progress. *Progress in Human Geography* 23(2), 175–187.

Breakwell, G.M. and Wood, P. (1995) Diary techniques. In: Breakwell, G.M., Hammond, S. and Fife-Schaw, C. (eds) *Research Methods in Psychology*. Sage, London, pp. 293–301.

Carragher, D.J. and Rivers, I. (2002) Trying to hide: a cross-national study of growing up for non-identified gay and bisexual male youth. *Journal of Clinical Child Psychology and Psychiatry* 7(3), 463–480.

Cassels, P. (2000) Israel is making great strides on gay issues. Available at: http://baywindows.com/news/2000/03/02/LocalNews/Israel.Is.Making.G

Clift, S. and Forrest, S. (1999a) Factors associated with gay men's sexual orientation and risk of holiday. *Aids Care* 11(3), 281–295.

Clift, S. and Forrest, S. (1999b) Gay men and tourism: destinations and holiday motivations. *Tourism Management* 20, 615–625.

Cotterill, P. and Letherby, G. (1993) Weaving stories: personal autobiographies in feminist research. *Sociology* 27(1), 67–79.

Evron, A. (2000) *To Kiss You in a Field of Daisies*. Yedioth Ahronoth, Tel Aviv (in Hebrew).

Gibson, V. (1995) An analysis of the use of diaries as a data collection method. *Nurse Researcher* 3(1), 66–73.

Goldfried, M.R. (2001) Integrating gay, lesbian, and bisexual issues into mainstream psychology. *American Psychologist* 56(11), 977–988.

Harper, G.W. and Schneider, M. (2003) Oppression and discrimination among lesbian, gay, bisexual, and transgender people and communities: a challenge for community psychology. *American Journal of Community Psychology* 31(3/4), 243–252.

Hinchliff, S., Gott, M. and Galena, E. (2005) 'I daresay I might find it embarrassing': general practitioners' perspectives on discussing sexual health issues with lesbian and gay patients. *Health & Social Care in the Community* 13(4), 345–353.

Hodder, I. (1998) The interpretation of documents and material culture. In: Denzin, N.K. and Lincoln, Y.S. (eds) *Collecting and Interpreting Qualitative Materials.* Sage, Thousand Oaks, California, pp. 110–129.

Hoffman, W. (2005) Gay life in Israel. Available at: http//www.planetout.com/travel/article. html?key=109&sernum=3280

Hughes, H. (1997) Holidays and homosexual identity. *Tourism Management* 18, 3–7.

Ivy, R.L. (2001) Geographical variation in alternative tourism and recreation establishment. *Tourism Geographies* 3(3), 338–355.

Kama, A. (2000) From terra incognita to terra firma: the logbook of the voyage of gay men's community into the Israeli Public sphere. *Journal of Homosexuality* 38(4), 133–162.

Kaplan, D. and Ben-Ari, E. (2000) Brothers and others in arms. *Journal of Contemporary Ethnography* 29(4), 396–432.

Kates, S.M. and Belk, R.W. (2001) The meaning of lesbian and gay pride day. *Journal of Contemporary Ethnography* 30(4), 392–429.

Kirby, S. and Hay, I. (1997) (Hetero) sexing space: gay men and 'straight' space in Adelaide, South Australia. *Professional Geographer* 49(3), 295–305.

Knopp, L. (1990) Social consequences of homosexuality. *Social Geography*, May, 20–25.

Kuntsman, A. (2003) Double homecoming: sexuality, ethnicity, and place in immigration stories of Russian lesbians in Israel. *Women's Studies International Forum* 26(4), 299–311.

Laws, E. (1998) Conceptualizing visitor satisfaction management in heritage settings: an exploratory blueprinting analysis of Leeds Castle, Kent. *Tourism Management* 19(6), 545–554.

Lewis, L.A. and Ross, M.W. (1995) The gay dance party culture in Sydney: a qualitative analysis. *Journal of Homosexuality* 29(1), 41–69.

Markwell, K.W. (1997) Dimensions of photography in a nature-based tour. *Annals of Tourism Research* 24(1), 131–155.

Miller, T. (2000) Shifting layers of professional, lay and personal narratives: longitudinal childbirth research. In: Ribbens, J. and Edwards, R. (eds) *Feminist Dilemmas in Qualitative Research: Public Knowledge and Private Lives.* Sage, London, pp. 58–71.

Moore, K., Cushman, G. and Simmons, D. (1995) Behavioral conceptualization of tourism and leisure. *Annals of Tourism Research* 22(1), 67–85.

Phillimore, J. and Goodson, L. (2004) Progress in qualitative research in tourism: epistemology, ontology, and methodology. In: Philliomore, J. and Goodson, L. (eds) *Qualitative Research in Tourism: Ontologies, Epistemologies and Methodologies.* Routledge, London, pp. 137–155.

Poria, Y. (2006) Assessing gay men and lesbian women's hotel experiences: an exploratory study of sexual orientation in the travel industry. *Journal of Travel Research* 44(3), 327–334.

Poria, Y. and Oppewal, H. (2003) A new medium for data collection: online news discussions. *International Journal of Contemporary Hospitality Management* 4(5), 232–236.

Poria, Y. and Taylor, A. (2001) 'I am not afraid to be gay when I am on the net': minimising social risk for lesbian and gay consumers when using the Internet. *Journal of Travel and Tourism Marketing* 11(2/3), 127–142.

Poria, Y., Butler, R. and Airey, D. (2003) Revisiting Mieczkowsi's conceptualization of tourism. *Tourism Geographies* 5(1), 26–38.

Pritchard, A. (2004) Gender and sexuality in tourism research. In: Lew, A., Hall, C.M. and Williams, A. (eds) *A Companion to Tourism*. Blackwell, Oxford, pp. 316–326.

Pritchard, A. and Morgan, N.J. (1999) The gay consumer: a meaningful market segment? *Journal of Targeting, Measurement and Analysis for Marketing* 6(1), 9–20.

Pritchard, A., Morgan, N.J., Sedgley, D., Khan, E. and Jenkins, A. (2000) Sexuality and holiday choices: conversation with gay and lesbian tourists. *Leisure Studies* 19, 267–282.

Pritchard, A., Morgan, N. and Sedgley, D. (2002) In search of lesbian space? The experience of Manchester's Gay Village. *Leisure Studies* 21, 105–123.

Puar, J. (2002) A translational feminist critique of queer tourism. *Antipode* 34(5), 935–946.

Reisinger, Y. and Steiner, C.J. (2006) Reconceptualizing object authenticity. *Annals of Tourism Research* 33(1), 65–86.

Romanucci-Ross, L. (2001) Celebrants and the celebrity: biography as trope. *American Anthropologist* 103(4), 1174–1178.

Rushbrook, D. (2002) Cities, queer space, and the cosmopolitan tourists. *A Journal of Lesbian and Gay Studies* 8(1&2), 183–206.

Russell, L.I. (2001) Geographical variation in alternative tourism and recreation establishments. *Tourism Geographies* 3(3), 338–355.

Shields, R. (1992) Places on the margins: alternative geographies on modernity. Sage, London.

Smith, J.A. (1995) Semi-structured interviewing and qualitative analysis. In: Smith, J.A. Harr'e, R. and van Langenhove, L. (eds) *Rethinking Methods in Psychology*. Sage, London, pp. 9–26.

Thornton, P.R., Shaw, G. and Williams, A.M. (1997) Tourist group holiday decision making and behaviour: the influence of children. *Tourism Management* 18(5), 287–297.

Turner, L. and Ash, J. (1975) *The Golden Hordes: International Tourism and Leisure Periphery*. Constable, London.

Uriely, N. (2005) The tourist experience: conceptual developments. *Annals of Tourism Research* 32(1), 199–216.

Valentine, G. (1996) (Re)negotiating the heterosexual street, bodyspace. In: Duncan, N. (ed.) *Destablizing Geographies of Gender and Sexuality*. Routledge, London, pp. 146–155.

Visser, G. (2003) Gay men, tourism and urban spaces: reflections on Africa's 'gay capital'. *Tourism Geographies* 5(2), 168–189.

Vogt, C.A. and Andereck, K.L. (2003) Destination perceptions across a vacation. *Journal of Travel Research* 41, 348–354.

Wang, N. (1999) Rethinking authenticity in tourism experience. *Annals of Tourism Research* 26(2), 349–370.

Weightman, B.A. (1980) Gay bars as private places. *Landscape* 24, 9–16.

Weightman, B.A. (1981) Commentary: towards a geography of the gay community. *Journal of Cultural Geography* 1, 106–112.

Wilkins, R. (1993) Taking it personally: a note on emotion and autobiography. *Sociology* 27(1), 93–100.

16 Embodying Everyday Masculinities in Heritage Tourism(s)

DAN KNOX AND KEVIN HANNAM

Introduction

Tourism studies have historically suffered from an inadequate politics of identity and an underdeveloped theorization of gender roles and identities. This chapter sets out to propose some possible ways in which the conceptualization of tourism as an unremarkable part of everyday life can begin to address these shortcomings. We suggest that a performative understanding of the playing out of gender can be allied to a vision of serious leisure, the reflexive production of biography and the practices of everyday life. To this end, the chapter traces out the sets of practices that effect the creation of masculine subjects and objects in two tourist settings. It is argued that embodied performances in heritage tourist settings help to concretize and stabilize certain male identities. The Highland Games of Scotland and Viking heritage tourism in Scandinavia form the empirical case-study material from which conceptual insights are drawn and further research agendas proposed.

Within the discourses of the social sciences, tourism tends to be figured as something remarkable or unusual in itself. Tourism research is primarily concerned with the spectacular and the 'Other' and any turn to the everyday is seen as remarkable in itself. This ignores a number of social scientific traditions of engagement with the quotidian and bypasses the opportunities presented to us by such attention to the mundane. If we accept that the distinction between the holiday and the everyday is unsustainable, one of the very real dangers for any kind of tourist studies (whether critical or otherwise) is that it becomes irrelevant or trivial. If critical tourism studies must operate at the margins of a number of more mainstream academic disciplines, theories and approaches that negate the possibility of a focus on tourism as in any sense logical or interesting is unlikely to prove to be a path to respectability. Nevertheless, a committed critical turn necessitates an engagement with the very kinds of non-representational theories that enable us either to resituate tourism as a marginal concern or to place tourism at the very centre of social and cultural lives (see Franklin, 2003). As optimistic critical tourism academics, we need to grasp the potential for a sustained focus on tourist behaviour to offer explanations that both precede and follow tourist activity and have far wider implications for social research. In short, a genuinely critical tourist studies places tourist studies at the very core of the concerns of the contemporary social sciences, facilitating and necessitating interactions with geographers, sociologists, anthropologists, economists, historians and those working in other fields.

Examples of work in the social sciences that demonstrates a concern with the quotidian might offer us some guidance in situating tourism within wider and deeper flows of human action. Much anthropological work, particularly that in the ethnographic tradition, has been avowedly interested in the everyday knowledges and practices of peoples as well as politically committed to the poly-vocal 'thick description' (Geertz, 1983) of, and engagement with, those everyday practices. Even where these works have not been preoccupied with the spectacle of dramatic ritual, they have often been about the everyday lives of groups of people spectacularly different to anthropologists, ethnographers and their audiences. These everyday practices are objectified as the social actors are spectacularly Othered. The critical social sciences, however, do offer us a rich ethnographic tradition of engagement with Western societies and tourism studies itself continues to move in a qualitative direction. What, though, do we mean by *everyday life*?

Everyday Masculinities

One way of conceiving of everyday, potentially unremarkable, practice is as an unremarkable banality. The notion of the banal expresses all of the flow of everyday and commonplace activities and occurrences that are neither highly dramatic nor unusual. In problematizing the everyday, it has to be remembered that, despite their very banality, such knowledges do not pre-exist their, often unnoticed, enactment. Gender undoubtedly falls into the range of social markers that are recreated and regulated through day-by-day practice. Tourism provides a number of opportunities for the continuation of the everyday practices of home, but also for transgressions, the trying out of new or different gender roles and relationships. Equally importantly, however, tourist events and behaviours provide a context within which representations of gender can be consumed through observation either of public events or simply the practices of other holidaymakers. Popular and academic narratives of tourism as escape to a liminal zone are clear that boundaries and identities can be experimented with, temporarily moved or elided during the tourist encounter.

Both staged and 'organic' patterns of behaviour while on holiday perform some work in representing, creating and performing gender roles and identities that are either specific to hosts or guests, or constitute an additional liminal identity. Gender attributes vary between cultures and between contexts and the notion of liminality captures an understanding that tourists, while potentially escaping the strictures, norms and conventions of home, do not ordinarily fully participate in the corresponding norms of behaviour of their host culture. Gender roles are particularly fluid and dynamic on vacation because of the potential to escape all moral censure or policing, and the behaviours expected of males and females can vary. In the contexts considered here, male tourists are presented with the opportunity for the acceleration of the rate of the signification of masculinity, rather than being enabled to present themselves in more feminine ways or, indeed, being presented with more subordinate visions of the male. Gender roles and identities are closely connected and co-dependent on each other. For the purposes of this chapter gender identities involve both positive processes of personal self-identification and external ascription of gender roles, while gender role refers to the whole complex of personality attributes, relationship expectations, sexual behaviours and domestic behaviours that attach to masculinities and femininities. Masculinities and femininities are frequently constructed and defined in opposition to one another and as such to talk of one without the other is nonsensical (Shurmer-Smith and Hannam, 1994). Connell (1987, p. 183) noted: ' "Hegemonic masculinity" is always constructed in relation to various subordinated masculinities as well as in relation to women. The interplay between different forms of masculinity is an important part of how a patriarchal social order works.'

Mainstream understandings of consumption in a tourist or leisure setting have much to offer us in an analysis of gender that is inherently related to everyday life. While notions of gazing on difference or seeking out the authentic may be marginal to this particular enterprise, the ideas surrounding cultural capital and serious leisure can provide us with a theoretical foothold. Stebbins' (1992) serious leisure thesis and ideas concerning the consumption of the familiar (Prentice and Andersen, 2003) suggest that tourist consumption and behaviour should not be separated out from more general life experiences and everyday practice. Performing particular kinds of masculinity is a process of the accumulation of cultural capital in that it impacts on esteem within a particular community or social grouping. Additionally, serious leisure is about the processes of identity creation and an extension of general leisure patterns indulged in at home, such that the holiday becomes not so much a break in activity as a short period of increased activity. Tourist behaviour is seen by Stebbins (1992) to be a 'career-like' pursuit in that it is lifelong and is about the collecting of experiences as well as, more importantly, being about the (re)performance of identity and the construction of a biography. Thus, in our account of relations between masculinity and tourist practice, tourism becomes a personal, biographical and reflexive project or enterprise that is related to consumptive choices both at home and away. These processes are as crucial to mass tourists as to the reflexive, middle-class 'cultural' tourists that cultural tourism studies has tended to concern itself with.

We should bear in mind also Bourdieu's (1977) notion of habitus as an internalized relationship to social structures and knowledge in reflecting that the construction and display of gender roles and identities is not necessarily a conscious process. He suggests that particular patterns and conventions of behaviour within certain 'fields' are internalized, such that social life is almost self-regulating. This chapter, then, is about the reproduction, through embodied practice and representation, of sociocultural structures such as tourist practices, tourist spaces and the gender order. We explore these practices in two related contexts: the Highland Games of Scotland and Viking heritage events in Scandinavia.

Highland Games

The Highland Games events of Scotland have evolved into a public spectacle that involves the display of national identities to both domestic and overseas tourists. Tightly tied in with manifestations of Scottishness at such festivals, however, are the production and consumption of idealized visions of gender. The visions of masculinity and femininity invoked on the Highland Games field go hand in hand with the broader understandings of the Scottish nation of which they constitute an important part and which provides the banal backdrop for such spectacular displays of Scottishness. Knox (2004) has written about the emergence of a compliant, deferential and youthful model of femininity from Highland dancing competitions, and how this is regulated through the rule-making institutions that surround the practice of dancing itself. Highland dancing is predominantly a female pursuit, and competitions ordinarily feature only pre-teenage and teenage individuals. It is, however, interesting to note that, historically, Highland dancing in its codified and ritualized form was practised almost exclusively by males, and males in military service in particular. In the 19th century, the Highland Regiments of the British Army used Highland dancing as a form of physical fitness training, believing that the rigours of the dances, and the discipline required to correctly perform them, would promote strength and dexterity. Again, this illustrates the concurrent emergence of visions of nationality and gender identity, as well as reflecting the strength of a martial vision of Scottish history (Knox, 2006).

Contemporary Highland dancing competitions, regulated worldwide by the Scottish Official Board of Highland Dancing, feature only limited opportunities for male participation. The dances in their official form have become so skewed towards female participation that masculine roles exist largely as an adjunct to female-led dances. For example, males are required as partners in some dances, but, where insufficient numbers of male dancers are available, as is almost invariably the case, females will partner each other. The second opportunity for male intervention in Highland Games dance competitions is in the Scottish version of the Irish Jig. The dance represents an Irish washerwoman in a raging bad temper at her errant, drunken husband. It is widely held that this comic version of the Jig is intended to be a humorous pastiche of Irish dancing that pokes fun both at the Irish and their dance traditions, but it could also be argued that it represents something about gender roles and relations between the genders. The ritualized and embodied practice of dancing as public spectacle creates and sustains apprehensions of gender, but is primarily of interest in the displays of femininity it shapes. Of more direct interest to this analysis of masculinity are the heavy events competitions.

The primary representation of gender and embodiment of Scottishness that can be witnessed at a Highland Games or Gathering is the heavy events competition. Bag-piping, dancing and light athletics are all minor attractions as compared to the antics of the athletes that compete in the heavy events at Highland Games and Gatherings. Arguably the greatest spectacle at the games, and without a doubt that attracting the largest number of spectators, the heavy events are a very important part of what defines a Highland Games and an important signifier of the Scottishness of such meetings. A Highland Games heavy event competition today consists of five or more events in which all entrants must compete to be scored in the overall competition, although prizes are awarded for and records set in each individual event. All of the events are throwing events designed to demonstrate raw masculine strength and require a mastery of technique as well as no small measure of ability. It goes almost without saying, of course, that, as professional athletes, heavy eventers are highly trained and dedicated men (or sometimes, rarely, women) – it is certainly no longer the case that people can simply turn up and throw with no prior experience. Games do, however, remain open in that people wishing to participate can still usually enter the competitions on the field on the day of the meeting, assuming they are appropriately attired. Judges reserve the right to disqualify or not allow the participation of any person they feel cannot meet the necessary standard or who cannot compete in a controlled and safe way without, for example, launching a caber into the throng of spectators lining the arena. Only professional athletes registered with the Scottish Games Association (SGA) can compete in the major professional competitions that attract prize monies – although amateur competitions are open to SGA athletes.

The SGA was formed in 1946 to rationalize and standardize the many localized, varying and idiosyncratic sets of rules that were then in use at games across Scotland (Jarvie, 1995; SGA, 2000). The SGA acts as the governing body of the professional games in Scotland as well as playing a role in the recording, notification and maintenance of world records in the heavy events. It is no longer, if ever it truly were, the case that local men meet up on holidays and high days to throw logs, stones and improvised weights around in a test of their competing masculinities. The heavy events, like the Highland Dancing, do not escape discourse or discursively expressed and communicated rules. While the actual acts required in adhering to rules may be physical, it remains the case that the rationale and existence of those rules is communicated linguistically – even though they may be internalized and operating at a level of practical-consciousness for individual, experienced competitors.

In examining the cultural history of the Highland Games and particularly the heavy events, a key character we must discuss is that of Donald Dinnie (Allan, 2000; Webster and Dinnie, 2000). Nobody, either previous to or since, has achieved the levels of local, national and international recognition and celebrity that Dinnie did. Interestingly, the link between heavy events and strongmen has recently been re-established with the expansion of the Aberdeen Highland Games to 2 days (as of 2001) to enable the inclusion of the World's Strongest Man tournament. Aberdeen City Council felt that the accommodation of such a prestigious international event would swell attendance at, and raise the profile of, their municipal Highland Games.

The heavy athletes at the games in the north-east of Scotland are a small and, with regular visits to regional games, recognizable group of men. We can see the emergence and playing out of some stereotypes of Highland masculinity and identity in that the heavy events are traditionally competed by men (and dancing largely left to women in recent times). The displays of strength required of the heavy athletes and the apparently ancient origins of some of the events hint at the mythical Highland past of fearless and immensely physically powerful Clan warriors taking time out to demonstrate their prowess. In the same way that the Highland dancing is about the public and ritualized display of femininity, the 'heavies' are about the performance of a particularly physical masculinity. Thus, these two very different types of performances ensure that an imagined Highland Scotland is populated entirely by big strong men and beautiful, objectified women.

These men spend large periods of time every day strength training in preparation for the heavy events and conditioning their bodies for maximum performance. Athletes take part in between two and three games per week at the height of the summer games season. Having trained, with reference to the rules (both official and unofficial) of technique, all that remains is for the athletes to put their kilts on and enter the arena. Individual games require that 'all male competitors must appear in Highland dress' (Aberdeen Highland Games, 1999; Stonehaven Highland Games, 1999). What we are concerned to show here is that the regulation and control of the body of one person can communicate meanings to others and that some of those meanings are about the nation. Now, while it may not seem that important precisely how a caber is tossed by a man in a kilt, our contention would be that the precise technique matters as it enables us to say something about the performative chains of causation that enable particular things to be cited as well as shedding light on the act of citation. Thus, the way the athlete tosses the caber is a direct result of the instruction he has received in doing so and is additionally, indirectly, crucial as a perlocutionary effect in the representation of national visions of gender that take place at the Highland Games. SGA rules in Scotland, and NASGA (North American Scottish Games Athletics) rules in North America, precisely govern the conditions under which a caber might be tossed and how this might be done. Thus, the context of the heavies is strictly controlled and limited, and every bodily movement measured and observed as the athletes perform their throws. Arguably, simply saying that Scotland or Highland Scotland is signified and constructed when men in kilts throw logs around would be a good place to start but would hardly, in itself, constitute a thoughtful and useful analysis. Key in all of this is the display of masculinity and, relatedly, militarism. One of the clearest examples of the military imagery that prevails at Highland Gatherings is the March of the Lonach Men in full Highland dress and carrying weaponry. While the primary cultural manifestations may be national in character, there are substantial gender elements in performance of dance and athletic events at Highland Games meetings. These gender elements re-establish ready-made and relatively fixed visions of idealized Scottish national masculinities that have implications on the field and beyond in terms not only of national identities, but also of gender roles and identities. If we turn now to Viking events we can see similar everyday masculinities and femininities being performed, again with an accelerated signification.

Viking Heritage Tourism

Viking themed tourism and leisure has grown since the 1970s mainly in Scandinavia, but also elsewhere in Western and Eastern Europe. New Viking themed museums have been established, and older museums have shifted their emphasis towards more Viking period material. The current Viking themed tourism and leisure industry is now quite extensive being based upon various museums, heritage centres, theme parks, village reconstructions and seasonal festivals, trading fairs or markets supplemented by the activities of Viking re-enactment or 'living history' societies. Interest in Viking themed tourism and leisure has led to a very full calendar of festivals and events that can attract up to 15,000 visitors daily. The active membership of the groups or societies that form the basis of any Viking festival may reach several hundreds but active membership is relatively small and more commonly in the order of 10 or 20 (Hannam and Halewood, 2006).

This research is based upon a series of semi-structured interviews with key tourism personnel and Viking re-enactment personnel, tourism literature from both bureaux and hobby groups and participant observation conducted at Viking festivals at a number of key sites in Norway, Sweden, Denmark, Germany, the UK and Poland over the last 6 years. However, it is beyond the scope of this chapter to examine the full geographical scope and organizational depth of Viking themed festivals in Europe (see Hannam and Halewood, 2006).

On average over 50 Viking festivals take place each year of varying sizes and duration. Most last 3 or 4 days and consist of approximately 200 transnational participants and around 3000 visitors per day. Most are in rural locations, however, a few take place in fairly large cities such as Stockholm or York and have a very different atmosphere. Most Viking festivals are built upon or around an existing tourist attraction such as an archaeological site, a museum or a heritage centre. Indeed, many Viking festivals use their location to confer added authenticity and thus symbolic value.

In general, the participants at Viking festivals are costumed as of the Viking period and sell goods which replicate, to a greater or lesser degree, styles, patterns, materials and techniques of the Viking period. Re-enactment activities vary from building replica houses and boats through to cooking or mock fighting and acting in public shows. Some people represent warriors, some craftsmen and others are in various kinds of trade. The central feature of most Viking festivals are the 'craft fairs' or 'folk markets'. The market, itself, is usually accompanied by a play, combat displays, horse-riding displays, and/or craft demonstrations. Most Viking festivals, and particularly those in Scandinavia, take place often in a rural and historically pertinent setting. For example, a Viking festival in Sweden promotes itself as: a 'performance with beautiful costumes, racy stories, many laughs but also seriousness' (Viking Heritage, 2002). As we shall see the organizers of most festivals are highly concerned with the degree of authenticity that they convey; most participants are men who are involved in combat displays – embodied masculine displays of strength and skill.

The attraction of the Viking historical period for both tourists and participants is perhaps twofold. First, we have the Anglo-American stereotypical representation of Viking heritage. This is of seafaring, sexist and bloodthirsty men raping and pillaging. This depiction has been widely propagated by the mass media in various films starring legendary actors such as Kirk Douglas, books and popular literature (e.g. the long running cartoon strip *Hagar the Horrible* in a national newspaper in the UK). Indeed, as recently as August 1999 the classic Hollywood image of the Vikings was shown to be still current with the release of the film *The 13th Warrior* directed by John McTiernan and starring Antonio Banderas. The Vikings in this film were subsequently described in *The Times* as following 'a simple but classic recipe: big men with big swords under a big sky' (30 August 1999, p. 40).

Second, and in contrast to the Anglo-American representation, in Scandinavia the image of Vikings in popular culture finds fewer references to war and warriors. Here the Viking representation is very much concerned with the people who abroad were known as pirates, but at home lived in a well-ordered sustainable society. Viking themed tourism and leisure in Scandinavia has largely attempted to give greater credence to the latter representation (Halewood and Hannam, 2001). However, although the producers of Viking themed tourism and leisure are often trying to put forward a more balanced picture, it is still the more bloodthirsty image that initially inspires both tourists and participants to visit sites and engage in performing Viking masculinity.

It is through the actual social experience of the festivals themselves then that Viking themed gender roles and identities are performed, actualized and maintained in particular through consumptive hedonism. The festival at Åland in Iceland is described thus:

> Here you can smell the atmosphere of the Viking age and take part in old Viking traditions. . . . As during the Viking Age, you can trade among other things, salt, fish, meat and skin. At the market you can also buy crafts of metal, wood, wool and other nature materials. The making of many of the crafts are demonstrated and you get an opportunity to try yourself. The market invites you to listen to medieval music, song, tales and to watch dance, small dramas, etc. There are games and plays which are fun for both adults and children and you can eat, drink and enjoy yourself.
>
> (Viking Heritage, 2002)

Tourists are specifically excluded from the night-time events when the male participants, who have during the day competed and performed in the combat displays, drink alcohol to excess and assert their masculinity in bawdy revelry.

Ideas concerning authenticity are utilized as part of the construction and expression of gendered Viking identities by participants. This 'authenticity' is, however, emphatically staged. MacCannell's (1992) notion of 'staged authenticity' refers to the contrived presentation of sites/sights as if they are authentic. He argues that the tourist is in search of the real as everyday life is saturated with artifice:

> The rhetoric of tourism is full of manifestations of the importance of the authenticity of the relationships between tourists and what they see: this is a *typical* native house; this is the *very* place the leader fell; this is the *actual* pen used to sign the law; this is the *original* manuscript; this is an *authentic* Tlingit fish club; this is a *real* piece of the *true* Crown of Thorns.
>
> (emphasis in the original, MacCannell, 1976, p. 14)

The Viking promotional literature is awash with similar references to the 'real' as authentic. For example, at Borre in Norway it is claimed that you can meet Vikings

> that carry on a trade of high quality just like the *real* Vikings did during their time. For instance: Iron extraction and working, wood working like making wooden vessels, etc. You might also see comb-, bead- and bow-manufacturing, dressing of fur skins, dressmaking, the shoemaker's workshop, weaving and so on. You will also experience Vikings, fully dressed for battle, exercise a struggle 'upon life or death' on the battle field. . . . During the market a contest of archery with *real* longbows will be going on and at this arena visitors will have the opportunity to test that noble skill of archery.
>
> (our emphasis, Viking Heritage, 2002)

What we find then is a claim to having performed as a Viking in the festivals is also a claim for a more *authentic* masculinity or femininity, harking back to a mythologized Viking past when gender roles and identities were more clearly defined and demarcated – men were men and women were women. For example, archery and weaving signify specific everyday activities that are linked to ascribed gender roles that would not normally be tolerated in 21st-century Norway. Although Viking festivals may appear to be transgressive, liminal spaces, in fact they codify fairly conservative gender roles and identities as participants enact everyday practices.

Conclusions

This chapter has demonstrated how gender is an everyday concern and experience, and needs to be reperformed everyday. Further research on tourism-based representations of gender needs to further explore the ways in which masculinities are (re)created in the everyday practices of men as well as the clear relationships between home/everyday and away/holiday that potentially problematize a focus on tourism as such. However, we contend that tourism, both domestic and international, should be examined as a lifelong series of events, moments and encounters that heighten gender signification and are thus particularly important in the shaping and regulating of gender roles and identities whether constructed through personal embodied practice or through exposure to representations. The symbolic content of representations is internalized as knowledge that later shapes the production of gender performance and thus must be considered alongside material practice despite theoretical shifts away from the politics of representation. Indeed, in the examples explored above, there is a clear relationship between the discursive and the non-discursive in the way in which texts of various kinds impact on physical behaviours and display, and vice versa, in a recursive loop of meaning and practice. Thus the experience of tourism is particularly formative in terms of self-identity because it is a punctuation mark within the more regular flow of domestic, everyday life. Visits to other places and interactions with other cultures always remain a notable departure but from the perspective of exploring these masculinities it seems that the state of liminality primarily offers a non-transgressive opportunity to be extremely the same.

References

Aberdeen Highland Games (1999) *Souvenir Programme*. Privately published.

Allan, C. (2000) Introduction. In: Webster, D.P. and Dinnie, G. (eds) *Donald Dinnie: The First Sporting Superstar*. Ardo Publishing, Ellon, UK.

Bourdieu, P. (1977) *Outline of a Theory of Practice*. Cambridge University Press, Cambridge.

Connell, R. (1987) *Gender and Power*. Polity Press, Cambridge.

Franklin, A. (2003) *Tourism: An Introduction*. Sage, London.

Geertz, C. (1983) *Local Knowledge: Further Essays in Interpretive Anthropology*. Basic Books, New York.

Halewood, C. and Hannam, K. (2001) Viking veritage tourism: authenticity and commodification. *Annals of Tourism Research* 28(3), 565–580.

Hannam, K. and Halewood, C. (2006) European viking themed festivals: an expression of identity. *Journal of Heritage Tourism*, forthcoming, 1, 17–31.

Jarvie, G. (1995) *Highland Games: The Making of the Myth*. Edinburgh University Press, Edinburgh.

Knox, D. (2004) The Highland society of the spectacle: regulating bodies and figuring the national heritage at the Highland Games. In: Aitchison, C. and Pussard, H. (eds) *Leisure, Space and Visual Culture: Practices and Meanings*. LSA, London, pp. 99–115.

Knox, D. (2006) The sacralized landscapes of Glencoe: from massacre to mass tourism, and back again. *International Journal of Tourism Research*, forthcoming, 8, 185–197.

MacCannell, D. (1976) *The Tourist*. Macmillan, London.

MacCannell, D. (1992) *Empty Meeting Grounds*. Routledge, London.

Prentice, R. and Andersen, V. (2003) Festival as creative destination. *Annals of Tourism Research* 30, 7–30.

Scottish Games Association (2000) *Highland Games: Handbook*. Privately published, Edinburgh, UK.

Shurmer-Smith, P. and Hannam, K. (1994) *Worlds of Desire, Realms of Power: A Cultural Geography*. Arnold, London.

Stebbins, R. (1992) *Amateurs, Professionals, and Serious Leisure*. McGill-Queen's University Press, London.

Stonehaven Highland Games (1999) Commemorative Programme. Privately published.

Viking Heritage (2002) *Viking Events*. Gotland University College, Visby, Sweden. Available at: http://viking.hgo.se (accessed 3 February 2006).

Webster, D.P. and Dinnie, G. (2000) *Donald Dinnie: The First Sporting Superstar*. Ardo Publishing, Ellon, UK.

17 In Search of Lesbian Space? The Experience of Manchester's Gay Village

ANNETTE PRITCHARD, NIGEL MORGAN AND DIANE SEDGLEY

Introduction

It has been contended for some time that patriarchy infuses the sociocultural relationships that characterize the phenomenon known as tourism (Enloe, 1989, p. 20), but despite the established tradition of gender studies in the leisure literature (see Aitchison, 2000 for a review), women's experiences continue to remain on the margins of tourism studies (Morgan and Pritchard, 1999, p. 3). This is perhaps not surprising given that the social science research collective, dominated as it is by a traditional research perspective 'grounded in, derived from, based on and reinforcing the experience, perceptions and beliefs of men' (DuBois, 1983, p. 106), has long relegated women to the private as opposed to the public domain. Moreover, a positivist, industry-oriented perspective, has itself dominated the tourism research tradition. This, together with tourism's reluctance to engage with critical research perspectives, has resulted in the development of a narrow gender research agenda that has largely focused on the economic and sexual relations that characterize the industry (Pritchard and Morgan, 2000a,b). By contrast, leisure researchers have established the importance of gender as a shaper of leisure experiences (see Aitchison, 1999; Coalter, 2000) and have explored how human status characteristics such as class (Deem, 1986; Wimbush and Talbot, 1988), race and ethnicity (Raval, 1989), sexuality (Valentine, 1993) and disability (Henderson *et al.*, 1995) combine to create points of empowerment or oppression in women's leisure worlds.

By contrast, tourism studies is only beginning to engage with research that suggests that tourism experiences are constrained by social norms (Jordan, 1998, p. 72) and, as a result, there is a small but growing body of tourism work which explores the social experiences of the gay and lesbian community (see Hughes, 2000; Pritchard *et al.*, 2000a). Extant research in this area has examined a range of issues. These include: the relationship between holidays and homosexual identity (Hughes, 1997, 1998, 2000); the sexual behaviour of gay men in tourism spaces (Forrest and Clift, 1998); the touristification of gay spaces (Pritchard *et al.*, 1998);

motivations of gay and lesbian tourists (Clift and Forrest, 1999; Pritchard *et al.*, 2000b). Significantly, with some exceptions (e.g. Pitts, 1999; Skeggs, 1999; Pritchard *et al.*, 2000a), much of this work has focused on the experiences and activities of gay men. As a result, the experiences of lesbians have been marginalized, despite the fact that the gay and lesbian community is clearly 'a heterogeneous, culturally diverse group of men and women who, despite their common bonds, have diverse identities' (Greene, 1997, p. xi). These identities are also gendered and reflect 'the huge power differential based on gender between lesbians and gay men' (Beeghley, 1996, p. 135). As Chouinard and Grant (1996, p. 178) point out, it is difficult to discuss 'lesbians and gay men in the same breath . . . [as] human experience is gendered . . . [and] common experiences cannot be presumed'. Notions of a homogeneous *gay* community and *gay* spaces therefore potentially obscure gay men's oppression of lesbians whilst reinforcing notions of a patriarchal society in which the male experience subsumes the female and becomes regarded as some gender-neutral 'norm'.

Whilst this chapter seeks to shed more light on the social processes that shape gay and lesbian leisure space, it specifically examines the experiences of lesbians. In doing so, it seeks to contribute to the putative body of tourism research that is focusing on gendered and sexualized leisure. It should be noted that many of the issues concerning space and sexuality which are articulated have also been explored in a major research project funded by the Economic and Social Research Council (entitled 'Violence, Sexuality and Space') which explored the use of space by three different groups: gay men, lesbians and heterosexual women (see Skeggs, 1999). This chapter's primary contribution to gender tourism research, however, is to provide further support for the conceptualization of leisure processes and spaces as both heterosexist and androcentric (Valentine, 1996; Morgan and Pritchard, 1998; Aitchison, 1999; Pritchard *et al.*, 2000a). Its principal focus is an analysis of the relationship between gay men and lesbians; in particular, the ways in which gay male presence, power and control dominates gay space and threatens lesbian space. It examines the impact of gender on lesbians' use of public (and in particular, gay) leisure space, in their relationships and negotiations with gay men and in their encounters with heterosexuals of both genders. The chapter thus begins by briefly discussing the sociocultural construction of gay space and the powerful dynamics that underpin its emotional geography. It then discusses the study's methodological approach before presenting and discussing the findings of the research conducted with lesbians in Manchester's Gay Village – one of the first and most successful gay quarters in the UK. The chapter concludes by outlining the limitations of the study and suggests a number of avenues for future research.

The 'Policing' of Public Space

Cultural geographers, amongst others, have established that space and place are complex concepts – cultural constructions that are subject to change and negotiation (e.g. Shields, 1991; Shurmer-Smith and Hannam, 1994). Space thus emerges as a 'difficult, uneasy' concept in which:

> [P]laces do not exist in a sense other than culturally, and as a result they appear and disappear, change in size and character . . . according to the way in which people construct them. Places then have no objective reality, only intersubjective ones.
>
> (Shurmer-Smith and Hannam, 1994, p. 13)

Moreover, not only are all places constructed intersubjectively, they also inherently 'express . . . social divisions' and, as a result, any examinations of space must also explore its 'emotional geography' (Shields, 1991, p. 6). In addition, such explorations must also confront the powerful psychological and ideological meanings of space, described by Olwig (1993, p. 312) as 'the stuff of poetry more than science'.

As sociocultural constructions then, leisure spaces are continually subject to confrontations as 'power, identity, meaning and behaviour are constructed, negotiated and renegotiated according to socio-cultural dynamics' (Aitchison and Reeves, 1998, p. 51). City spaces, for example, are negotiated spaces where decisions are made about group visibility, recognition and legitimacy (Keith, 1995; Zukin, 1995, 1996). As with all negotiations, however, some groups are more powerful than others and thus more 'entitled' to claim and dominate both physical and social spaces. Thus, work has demonstrated how space is racialized (Segal, 1990; Anderson, 1996; Cohen, 1997), gendered (Valentine, 1989; Rose, 1993; Pritchard and Morgan, 2000a,b) and heterosexualized (Valentine, 1996). However, as Aitchison (1999, p. 19) points out: 'Whilst the concepts of *spatialized feminism* and *gendered space* have been well documented in geography, this is less true in relation to leisure studies.' As she continues, only recently have leisure (and to an even lesser extent, tourism) researchers begun to 'acknowledge that the synergy between gender relations and spatial relations is a major contributor to leisure relations.' The challenge for leisure studies is, in Scraton and Watson's (1998, p. 123) words, to investigate '. . . the complexities of space . . . as a site for the maintenance and reproduction of complex power relations'. This chapter contends that the gendering and heterosexualization of leisure spaces is part of a much wider discursive framework grounded in complex, multidimensional cultural, social and historical systems. Utilizing this framework of power for its analysis, this chapter focuses on the ways in which space (in this case leisure sites) can be seen as socioculturally constructed.

Valentine (1996, p. 146) has discussed how public spaces are essentially heterosexual places: '[T]he street . . . is not an asexual place. Rather, it is commonly assumed to be "naturally" or "authentically" heterosexual.' It is a space where heterosexuals can publicly express their identities through intimacy, such as holding hands or kissing, whereas gay men and lesbians are often made to feel uncomfortable or unsafe when displaying such behaviour (Stanko and Curry, 1997; Taylor and Jamieson, 1997). As space is constantly contested, however, the heterosexual nature of the street is by no means fixed; rather it is subject to continual challenge. Myslik (1996, p. 157), for instance, has discussed the development of spaces that 'have come to be identified in and outside the gay community as gay spaces'. These are places which enable not only open displays of intimacy and affection but also provide access to a variety of gay- and lesbian-friendly services and facilities, including shops and bars. Such places include New York, San Francisco and Miami Beach in the USA, Sydney in Australia, Amsterdam, Ibiza, Mykonos and

Gran Canaria in Europe and Manchester, Brighton and London in the UK (see Holcomb and Luongo 1996; Hughes, 1997).

Gay and Lesbian Space

Gay and lesbian spaces are empowering places, providing men and women with a sense of community and territory. As such, they are 'sites of cultural resistance with enormous symbolic meaning' (Myslik, 1996, p. 167). Such places are also subject to heterosexual attack, either via abuse or by encroachment leading to the dilution and erosion of gay and lesbian spaces and identities (Valentine, 1996; Pritchard *et al.*, 2000b). Such is the impact of the latter that opinion in some gay and lesbian places (such as Manchester's Gay Village, our case study here) is split over whether they should retain their gay and lesbian identities or whether they should become 'just' another city centre attraction for heterosexual visitors (Pritchard *et al.*, 2000a). Significantly, it is the commercial sector that has driven the evolution of Manchester's Gay Village, dictating the formation of a 'market place in which queer people are now seen as cultural consumers, just another tribe amidst and like all other cultural consumers' (Whittle, 1994, p. 37).

The development of Manchester's Gay Village has been well documented with several articles concentrating on the degaying process that has occurred as the area has become more attractive to heterosexual visitors (see Pritchard *et al.*, 2000a). However, these studies have tended to concentrate on how the development of the Village and the degaying process has affected gay men and little attention has been given to the role of lesbians within the Village or to the significance, role and meaning of the Village to them. Since public spaces are not merely heterosexual places but are also male places, gender is critical to the construction of space and indeed, spaces and places are 'both shaped by, and a shaper of, gender in a gender-space dialectic' (Aitchison and Reeves, 1998, p. 51). It is undoubtedly true that the issue of women's use of public leisure space is one which deserves much more examination because marginalization is configured in diverse and complex ways – sexuality, gender, race and social class combine to create layers of oppression (Pritchard and Morgan, 2000a). Such oppression is not deliberately orchestrated, as masculinism, for instance, 'is not understood as a conscious conspiracy' but rather 'a complex series of . . . discursive positions, relations and practices' (Rose, 1993, p. 10). Instead:

> Discourses intersect, so that certain identities are constituted as more powerful and more valuable than others; thus, in the dominant culture of the West now, a white bourgeois heterosexual man is valued over a black working class lesbian woman.
>
> (Rose, 1993, p. 6)

Thus, the experiences of lesbians in tourism spaces such as Manchester – as women *and* lesbians – are at least doubly marginalized in the tourism literature, as they are in life.

The problems of developing female spaces must therefore be seen in the context of a society where public space has been traditionally characterized as male space – as Valentine (1989) has contended, women's use of space is constructed by patriarchal discourses. A body of work has now developed which explores the practices that encourage women to restrict themselves to designated, supposedly safe spaces (Butler, 1990; Gardner, 1995; Valentine, 1996; Stanko and Curry, 1997) and how the architectural construction of space is highly gendered (Booth *et al.*, 1996). In such ways, 'most women learn that they do not belong in many public spaces, that many spaces are not for them' (Skeggs, 1999, p. 222). Various explanations have been put forward to explain the lack of lesbian places in Manchester's Gay Village (as elsewhere). Some authors have pointed to the fact that, unlike most lesbians, gay men 'have a greater volume of, and access to, different forms of legitimate capital which can be spatialized' (Skeggs, 1999, p. 216). Others have suggested that women, unlike men, lack 'territorial aspirations' and place more importance on relationships (Cassells, 1993). Alternatively, the invisibility of women within Manchester's Gay Village could also be explained by the nature of the area in which the Village is located – formerly an isolated, derelict warehouse district that many women might have found intimidating. It may thus have taken time for women to feel confident in a recently gentrified area which now has open-fronted, attractive bars and a 24-hour culture patronized by the gay community.

Rothenberg (1995, p. 168) has suggested that 'a specifically gay female entertainment spot is unlikely to establish itself . . . unless there is already a protective gay male population in the area' – the very epitome of patriarchy. In addition, Skeggs (1999, p. 225) has described the Village as a safe place in which: 'Male gay space offers security, it is a space where women (whatever their sexuality) are safe from the constant male gaze present in heterosexual space; it is a space away from constant evaluation and judgement.' Such contentions suggest that gay space facilitates women's use of public space because, not only is gay male space protective, but it is a place where women are not exposed to an objectifying and sexualizing male gaze. Significantly, heterosexual women benefit as much from this space as lesbians. As Skeggs (1999, p. 225) noted, heterosexual women are attempting to use the Manchester Village in order to distance themselves from heterosexual men, 'the male gaze' and the 'unremittingly heterosexual masculine culture that comprises cities at night'. However, Skeggs (1999, p. 226) also suggests that

> the presence of straight women in predominantly male gay space makes lesbians feel uncomfortable. They did not feel physically threatened by straight women but felt that the space, which was always precariously associated with lesbians, was no longer theirs to occupy.

This chapter therefore attempts to examine lesbians' experiences in, and uses of, gay space using the Manchester Village as a case study. In particular, it discusses the impact and significance of the Village's only lesbian bar – *Vanilla*. It will also attempt to address questions relating to women's use of public leisure space, lesbians' relationships and negotiations with gay men as well as their encounters with heterosexual men and women in gay spaces.

Study approach

Since the study required an exploration of the complexity of lesbians' experiences of the social world, a qualitative research strategy was adopted. Unfortunately, such research approaches have tended to be overlooked in favour of quantitative approaches in both leisure studies (Scott and Godbey, 1990) and, to an even greater extent, in the field of tourism (Cohen, 1988). Indeed, at the beginning of the third millennium, 'much tourism scholarship . . . reflects this bias in favour of rigorous, quantitative and scientific methods' (Walle, 1997, p. 524), whilst qualitative research techniques continue to suffer from a credibility gap. The quantitative techniques so favoured, however, are particularly unsuitable to research that relates to the subjective, to notions of meaning and feelings – enquiries which are of relatively little concern to positivist approaches and research agendas.

Informal in-depth interviews were used to explore women's experiences of the Village and their interactions with other Village users, both before and after the opening of *Vanilla*. Of particular interest was the participants' perceptions of the impact and significance of *Vanilla*'s opening. In-depth interviews were the preferred research method as they facilitated both an understanding of the interviewees' perspectives and the meanings that the interviewees attached to those situations and social contexts that were important to them (Finn *et al.*, 2000). Interviews also expose the interpretative practices through which the participants construct their version of the social world (Potter and Mulkay, 1985). The research strategy adopted here recognized that 'social researchers do not just apply a set of neutral techniques to the issues which they investigate. Research is part of a dynamic, reflexive, engagement with social and cultural worlds' (Seale, 1998, p. 2). Significantly, as Bailey (1996, p. 72) notes, 'the informal interview is reciprocal – both the researcher and the member in the setting engage in the dialogue'. As a result, interviews offer the opportunity to achieve 'more authentic' and 'less exploitative' accounts of experience than other research techniques (Seale, 1998, p. 205).

As with all research techniques, there was concern over the number of interviews that should be undertaken. Pidgeon and Henwood (1997) have noted how sampling considerations are interconnected with data collection. Given the challenges of researching the potentially sensitive issue of sexuality, this study recruited participants by a process of 'snowballing' (Ryan, 1995, p. 103) – using initial and subsequent participants to suggest others who fell within the sample frame, in this case lesbians who worked in or frequented venues in Manchester's Gay Village. This snowballing technique was particularly suitable, given that it was impossible to estimate the base population from which a sample could be drawn in advance. In terms of the extent of data collection, there are no definitive guidelines as to the number of interviews which should be conducted, although it is suggested that qualitative research should be continually reviewed as the research is being conducted – when further insights are not forthcoming, then the fieldwork should cease (Churchill, 1995). This philosophy guided the approach here and ten in-depth interviews were conducted with lesbians (including an interview with the owner of *Vanilla*, the Village's only lesbian bar): all the respondents were white and aged between 20 and 40.

Making sense of qualitative data is a difficult process and one which is complicated by a scenario in which 'there are few rules to guide your analysis and writing and to help you gain analytic insights into the contours of everyday life in the setting' (Bailey, 1996, p. 89). In this study, each of the ten interviews were taped and then transcribed, documenting the data so that those not involved in the research can follow the chain of enquiry (Yin, 1989). In terms of the interpretation of qualitative data, Ryan (1995) suggests that four tests should be applied to affirm reliability: credibility; transferability; dependability; and conformability. As Mason (1996) notes, given the non-standardization of many methods for generating qualitative data, a researcher will be unable to perform 'simple' reliability tests. In this study, each co-author independently reviewed the transcripts and then agreement was sought on the patterns that emerged (Bailey, 1996). A further significant (although frequently overlooked) analytical stage in a study of this kind is the writing up of the research. This provided a further opportunity to review the research material and its significance. As Richardson (1994, pp. 516–517) suggests, writing is not merely something that is done at the end of the research process:

> Although we usually think about writing as a mode of 'telling' about the social world, writing is not just a mopping-up activity at the end of a research project. Writing is also a way of 'knowing' – a method of discovery and analysis.

In search of lesbian space?

A number of themes emerged from the interviews, particularly centring on the heterosexist and the androcentric nature of space in the Gay Village. Given that all the interviews were conducted with lesbians, it is not unexpected that it is their concerns that figure largely and their relationships with heterosexual men and women and with gay men that dominate the discussion. Having said this, the interviewees clearly perceived a number of tensions between the Village's lesbian community and its gay male clientele, in addition to feeling distinctly threatened by the often aggressive, sexualizing behaviour of heterosexual male leisure consumers in the Village.

The Village: homosexual space is male space

The female research participants were very aware that to all intents and purposes Manchester's Gay Village had been essentially male space prior to the establishment of *Vanilla*. Opened in December 1998 as a 'contemporary women's bar', it is the only female-only venue within the Village (and is, in fact, the first 7-day-week lesbian venue in the UK). Until the advent of *Vanilla*, the provision for women in the Village was confined to the occasional lesbian night in one of the bars or clubs within the Village. Interestingly, the lack of provision for women had been justified by a variety of reasons, including the non-profitability and non-sustainability of women-only venues or events. As one participant commented: 'for years everyone said, it won't work, it will never make money, you'll never sustain it, you can only sustain a women's night once a week.' These perceptions were given credence at the time despite the popularity of women-only nights that were often oversubscribed. As one woman put it:

> When Fussy Pussy was on, this place was heaving, I had people queuing up to get in, it was like, where do they all come from? I was absolutely amazed how many came out because it's a women-only night, no men allowed; they all came out of the woodwork; it was amazing.

The lack of a permanent, regular, defined and recognized lesbian space, however, meant that lesbians tended, as one put it, 'to stay at home thinking that they've not really got a place to go'. As a result, the Village has been a predominantly male space (Skeggs, 1999). Although, despite the lack of a female venue within the Village, lesbians had been regular users of the Village before *Vanilla* opened, using the existing gay bars and participating in gay and lesbian events such as the Mardi Gras. Having said this, the participants thought that these bars did not really cater for women. In fact, they were frequenting male bars and venues, which, not surprisingly did not satisfy their needs: 'they were full of gay men . . . it's mainly men to look at, it's a bit boring really'. This was in direct contrast with the diverse range of venues catering for men in the Village, provision that appeared to reflect how the Village was described (both by regular Village users and 'onlookers') as an essentially male 'gay' space. As one of the interviewees said:

> The men have got their fetish nights, they've got all their hell fire and fist nights, they've got their seedy bars their nice cruisy bars, dance bars, they've got everything they want. Because it's always been known as the Gay Village, they've got all the variety there. They've always got something to pick from. We have one women's bar.

Many of the women interviewed in this study had long wanted to participate in the Village's social scene and had wanted female-only venues. Indeed, many noted that since it has been open the success of *Vanilla* reveals just how much such a venue had been needed. As one noted:

> The assumption [before *Vanilla* opened] was that either women didn't have the money or the women who did have the money didn't come out in the Village. It wouldn't be sustained, you wouldn't get the custom throughout the week and you'd only get it at weekends. That was the assumption. No one was prepared to take the risk . . . . None of the big brewers did.

The invisibility of lesbians in Manchester's Gay Village seems to confirm the strength of 'heteropatriarchy, that is . . . a process of sociosexual power relations which reflects and reproduces male dominance' (Valentine, 1993, p. 396). The large commercial operators failed to recognize that the homosexual community is divided along gendered lines and that women's needs differ from those of gay men – whose male norms are seen to be society's norms. As one commented:

> I think people are waking up to the fact that we [lesbians] do have an identity other than the gay-man identity within the Village. We do need to be catered for, there is a market out there for us and we are willing to participate in it.

As the owner of *Vanilla* was keen to stress, the absence of lesbian venues should not be interpreted as being the result of a lack of demand:

> If you know anything about the women's scene, which we obviously do, then you're aware that there's also a lot of professional women out there that [sic] want their own space . . . I've worked on the gay scene for a long time, worked in the café/bar restaurant scene for the last 12 years and I'm a gay woman myself, and I'm sick of not being catered for.

Participants suggested that this scenario was not merely restricted to Manchester's Gay Village but was repeated in 'the gay scene' across the country: 'After Mardi Gras last year I think a lot of people have realized that there is a women's-only bar in Manchester because there isn't one in Birmingham.' As a result, *Vanilla* is attracting business from across the UK: '[H]uge numbers come from outside

Manchester – Scotland, Sheffield, Leeds every weekend. . . . . People come a long way to come here.'

Lesbians, heterosexual men and heterosexual women

Gay and lesbian space is uneasy space, contested and threatened and lesbians' uneasy relationship with the Village has been complicated by the 'degaying' of the quarter (Pritchard *et al.*, 1998). As the area has become more attractive to heterosexuals, lesbians (like many gay men) have become increasingly alienated from their own space, which they originally claimed and in which their sexuality can be affirmed. Whilst heterosexual consumers had always made use of the Village, in the past this usage had been limited in terms of its volume and frequency. Now however:

> they come out to the Village much more often . . . probably over the last five years it's changed particularly with the last three Mardi Gras, it's hard to decide whether this year's or last year's was the worst, full of *scallie* people who just don't want to be here, not straight people who want to come down and be nice about it and respect the gay venues and have a good time, they were just coming down to treat it as a gay theme park, hurl abuse at people. In fact, . . . a lot of straight people who really like the Village and respect it . . . said they'd never come to Mardi Gras because it's so straight and so scary that they hate it.

Some participants were even less keen on 'straight' people using the Village, although they were conscious that mixed use was sometimes acceptable, as one woman commented:

> I don't particularly like it; my feeling is that they should go to their own pubs, especially in Manchester. I work with a lot of straight people in Manchester and they'll talk about going out to the Village on a Saturday night and they've got the whole city open to them, this is our space. But where do you draw the line? If I was going out with some heterosexual friends and some gay friends, I would take them down to the Village, but I do object to heterosexual couples coming to watch.

What lesbians in this study resented was 'when we can go to their pubs then fine, they can [come here] I don't see why we should have integration in ours first'. For example, one respondent described incidences where gay women (and perhaps also men) were being discriminated against in favour of heterosexuals:

> The thing that annoys me is queuing up in bars like Via Fossa and Paradise when they say you're not gay and then proceed to let in a girl in a bridal gown on her hen night with a group of obviously straight girls. You feel like saying, now hang on get your policy right, this is a gay venue, why are you letting in big groups of obviously straight girls and lads? You can't expect them to get it right every time as not everybody looks gay or looks straight, but sometimes you just look at these bars and think the policy has gone to pot here. There is something very wrong with your door policy.

Women also spoke of how the degaying process resulted in the Village becoming a threatening environment, a place where they were often targeted now because of their sexuality, as one respondent commented:

> There were a number of occasions when we were walking down Canal Street and we got abuse from straight people. We'd feel unsafe walking there because there would

be loads of men with bottles in their hands just waiting for something to happen. It created the environment where you didn't want to be in the Village anymore. In fact, I took six months out from the Village after that.

The degaying of the Village has meant that lesbians have been made to feel uncomfortable about their sexuality in the Village. In particular, the presence of 'straight' men has meant they have had experience of becoming the objects of persistent male sexual advances. As one participant complained:

> The thing that annoys me is being approached by straight lads who won't take no for an answer. You're in the Village, sitting at a table with a group of friends and a group of straight guys come over saying 'Can I buy you a drink?' We say 'you're wasting your time', they say, 'oh no, we're just buying you a drink' and we say 'we've heard all the lines, go away'.

Many of the lesbians interviewed in this study found the presence of 'straight' men in the Village increasingly problematic:

> I don't like it because of the way they look at you and the way they treat the transsexuals and transvestites because they just stare and take the mickey out of them – it's their territory so why should they do it? We don't do it to them.

In many ways, those who define themselves as lesbians, bisexual, transsexual or queer have become the object of the 'gaze' as the Village has become subject to heterosexual encroachment. As one lesbian said:

> I was standing outside the door on Saturday night and there was a really fabulous drag queen walking down the street with a couple of gay male friends and this group of eight straight people went up to them, laughing at them and then got out a camera, wanting their picture taken with them, it was like being at a freak show. I come here because I enjoy it here and feel safe here and I don't want to have to go out there and have photos taken of my friends because they look freakish to other people.

Lesbians' relationships with straight women were less problematic, although not free of tension. Most participants seemed to feel that this was 'alright' or 'okay', feeling that 'a lot of them come in because they don't feel threatened because a gay man's not going to go at them'. 'Straight' women were felt to be much less of a 'problem' than 'straight' men who are 'the ones who cause problems'. As one lesbian said:

> [a]s long as the women don't give us grief and respect the space. We've got nowhere else to go. I don't want to segregate but you do want a sanctuary, it's a very straight world.

Having said this, several lesbians commented how 'straight' women did not tend to visit lesbian venues because they disliked women-only places: 'I know a lot of my straight friends feel more comfortable at a mixed venue. If you say women only, its "arrgh".' Another participant felt that 'straight women feel more threatened in a woman-only environment'; whilst another pointed out that, there is 'the assumption that you're there to meet somebody at a women-only venue'.

Lesbians and gay men in the Village
Significantly, the research highlighted a number of problems that lesbians had experienced with the Village's gay male users. Gay men's attitudes and behaviours towards

lesbians were identified on several occasions as the predominant source of women's tensions in the Gay Village. In many respects, the attitudes of gay men towards gay women were perceived as more threatening and offensive than those of 'straight' men. Gay men were felt to exhibit the same patriarchal attitudes to lesbians as 'straight' men, reinforcing the notion that 'public space has been traditionally characterized as male space' (Pritchard *et al.*, 2000a, p. 16). Significantly, many lesbians felt that their relationships with gay men in the Village were difficult and that the men were not particularly supportive of the lesbians' presence in what they regarded as 'their' Village. Whilst the women wanted to be 'made to feel as welcome in the men's scene', unfortunately this was not the case; as one woman commented:

> Gay men, especially the older ones, are quite intimidating. They're not very welcoming towards the women. The younger ones, who've just come out, are a bit standoffish. Places like the New Union are fine because everybody mixes and it's easy going, but places like Manto and The Rembrandt, which are male-dominated, can be very intimidating.

Another lesbian described how gay men were off-putting and pretentious when lesbians occupied 'their space' – 'the way they carried themselves, the way they acted, very camp when they don't need to be'. Many comments highlighted an underlying competitiveness that is symptomatic of territorial challenges: 'They [gay men] look at you. They look you up and down and puff their cheeks out as if to say, "God, not another one" . . . especially if you look better than them. They don't like being beaten on things like that.'

Lesbian space as 'sanctuary'

In a climate where some bars are full of gay men who 'never really want to integrate with the women [but]. . . generally prefer to have their own space' it is perhaps not surprising that, prior to the opening of *Vanilla*, lesbians had little real claim to, or stake in, the Village, and 'never received a friendly response from them'. As the first women-only space in the Village, *Vanilla* has since taken on an increasingly important role for women, becoming a safe, lesbian sanctuary; a place where women can escape the pressures they face outside, even in the rest of the Village. As one woman commented:

> Women can come in here on their own and sit at the bar and chat, whereas there is quite a strong male domination to most of the other bars. A woman can come into this bar and sit on her own and it's probably more comfortable for her to do that here than anywhere else. We do get a lot of women who come in here after work, read the paper, chill out and sit at the bar and chat. They wouldn't feel as comfortable doing that anywhere else.

The importance of such a 'sanctuary' in the Village should not be underestimated, particularly in a scenario where:

> If you go out to mixed venues and you're not very comfortable and not very confident, it can be very scary. This is a safe, friendly environment to come into. Also, if you're new on the scene, you know you can come in here and it's going to be all right.

As another woman pointed out:

> I know I can come in here on my own and I will know the bar staff and at least one other member of the clientele. It's nice to come in here, have a quiet cup of coffee

or a beer and be in familiar surroundings. I could go somewhere else in the Village and it may be very male-orientated or it may be a straight or a mixed crowd and I wouldn't feel at ease. This place is everything you want it to be.

In claiming this space, the women feel that, not only have they created a safe haven for themselves where they can escape the prejudices experienced elsewhere in the Village, but ironically they have also created what they feel is now one of the most gay spaces in the Village: 'That's what's good about *Vanilla*. . . . On the whole, this place is more gay than any of the other places in the Village because it's not as appealing.' As a result:

> There's no reason to come in here unless you're lesbian. Straight girls are not interested so therefore the straight men don't come in. The gay men only come in with their friends. You have more of a guarantee when you come in here that you're going to have more of a gay night than anywhere else.

One woman particularly liked the fact that that *Vanilla* had led to a reversal of power, where men are now only allowed in on their terms. They have to be with a woman and numbers are limited:

> I talked before about the male domination. . . . *Vanilla* is my space and if men want to come in they have to be accompanied by women. It's a complete turnaround and it's no hassle in here, just easygoing.

The significance of a defined lesbian space should not be underestimated. *Vanilla* operates not only as a meeting place for women – 'I've been out of the scene for a long time. It's wonderful, since *Vanilla* opened, I'm seeing women and meeting up with women that I've not seen in years' – it also appears to be taking on an important and extended role in these women's lives. It is not simply a place to drink and escape the pressures existing in the rest of the Village, but it is developing into a centre through which sports, holidays, excursions and nights out are arranged. These extended support functions seem to emanate from the isolation of lesbians in society as a whole. As one of *Vanilla*'s users described her experiences:

> I play football. I'm a student at University and used to play for their team but it was homophobic. Now *Vanilla* has a team. We play football and there's no prejudice. Also, there is a softball team starting fairly soon . . . the possibilities are endless. If we make a suggestion, it is listened to and taken seriously.

Another commented:

> We've arranged quite a lot of social events . . . which are women-orientated. If you go out with your male friends, whether they're straight or gay, there's always something missing. They're looking for something different. It's nice mixing with people that are the same as you.

However, there is a limit to *Vanilla*'s ability to accommodate increasing expectations. The more popular it has become, the more varied are the demands. The challenge will be to continue to satisfy its clientele and also maintain the interest and support of such a diverse single interest group. This is a difficult task for one venue that started as a café bar, without other lesbian spaces:

> You see the same faces all the time, it's not incestuous but if you stay in the same place for long enough, what do you expect. . . . Perhaps if there was more than

one bar, you'd get different people going in them but, because it's the only one, everybody flocks here. It would be nice to have a change.

Conclusions

This small-scale research study has focused on the difficult and complex interactions that characterize lesbians' relationships with other groups of tourism and leisure consumers in Manchester's Gay Village. The case study has highlighted how space is indeed a contested and uneasy concept, characterized by intersubjective relationships and social divisions. It has also revealed how sexuality and gender combine to constrain women's consumption of public leisure space, suggesting that not only is gender critical to the construction of space, what Aitchison and Reeves (1998) have termed the 'gender-space dialectic', so too is sexuality. Previous discussions therefore, which have tended to subsume gender within their explorations of gay communities and gay spaces, have perhaps unwittingly reinforced notions of a patriarchal society and obscured gay men's oppression of lesbians (Beeghley, 1996).

Gay and lesbian spaces have emotional and psychological importance as empowering places in a 'straight' world. However, in the case of Manchester's Gay Village, this space did not appear to empower lesbians because of the patriarchic power dialectics characterizing the sociocultural construction of that space. The women interviewed in this study do have territorial ambitions in the Village – their own space is important to them, it confirms their place in the Village and it supports the development of social networks for lesbians in a hostile, hetero-patriarchic world. Lesbian space is an exceptionally difficult space to claim, however, since the more powerful and more established gay male community in that area does not particularly welcome women. Lesbians' relationships with gay men thus emerge as often difficult and uneasy; fraught by tension frequently derived from lesbians and gay men's competitive use of a limited space. The women thought that gay men exhibited patriarchal attitudes towards the Village's public space, which they saw as essentially male space and thus tended to be wary of territorial challenges from lesbians. Yet, without the existence of those gay communities, in a hetero-patriarchic world, it seems unlikely that lesbians would have gained even this tenuous foothold.

The rare phenomenon of lesbian space allows women to exercise an unusual degree of control over what has to date been a male dominated environment. The lesbian club, *Vanilla*, in essence, provides a sanctuary for women from what is not only a very hetero-patriarchic, but also a homo-patriarchic world. Ironically, this lesbian space is considered by the women who have claimed it to be the 'most' gay space in the Village since 'straight' consumers have no interest in the club and gay men only enter it on the women's terms. It remains to be seen, however, if such lesbian venues become subject to the same heterosexual encroachment and subsequent degaying as their more established gay male counterparts.

Whilst gay men and lesbians have claimed this area of Manchester as gay space, they are not its only users and this study has highlighted a number of interesting issues regarding the degaying of gay spaces. Just as the heterosexual nature of public spaces is subject to continual challenge (Duncan, 1996), sometimes leading to the creation of gay and lesbian spaces, so too are those gay and lesbian spaces the subject of a growing heterosexual challenge (Oliver Wilson, 1999). The research in this study suggests that lesbians (in the same way as gay men) have become increasingly alienated from their spaces and places by what could be termed 'a heterosexual invasion' of the Village. This invasion has many consequences and engenders a variety of responses from the women – ranging from annoyance and objection to more open hostility. In particular, the women feel constrained and intimidated by the increasing presence of 'straight' men in an environment that they felt belonged to them and this was considered to be threatening the 'sanctity' of the Village, making it a less safe space for women. Significantly, it has led to the objectification of those who define themselves as lesbian, bisexual, transsexual or queer, all of whom have become subject to 'straight' attention, ridicule and threat, as they become the focus of the heterosexual gaze.

This research, whilst based on a small number of in-depth interviews, has highlighted a number of issues that would benefit from greater exploration and examination – most obviously in relation to the experience of lesbians in public leisure spaces. Future research, however, also needs to focus on the impacts of gender and sexuality on women's and men's use and perceptions of leisure and tourism spaces. The role and influence of heterosexuality deserves a much wider exploration than hitherto and sexuality needs to be investigated as a shaper of both heterosexual and homosexual tourism behaviour. Similarly, the influence of gender and sexuality on the construction of public leisure space would benefit from further explorations of the relationships between gay men and lesbians. Certainly, there is scope for further work on lesbians' relationships with space and this study suggests that patriarchal notions have perhaps, until now, influenced the terms of the discussion. Of itself, this is perhaps not surprising, given DuBois' (1983) contention that social science research has tended to be characterized and reinforced by the male experience. However, as increasingly mature fields of social science enquiry, both tourism and leisure studies must more openly embrace alternative epistemologies if greater insights into the sociocultural phenomena known as 'tourism' and 'leisure' are to be gained.

Acknowledgement

This chapter first appeared as Pritchard, A., Morgan, N. and Sedgley, D. (2002) 'In search of lesbian space: the experience of Manchester's Gay Village', *Leisure Studies* 21(2): 105–124 (http://www.tandf.co.uk/journals). The authors are grateful to Taylor & Francis Ltd for their kind permission to reproduce it here.

References

Aitchison, C. (1999) New cultural geographies: the spatiality of leisure, gender and sexuality. *Leisure Studies* 18, 19–39.

Aitchison, C. (2000) Poststructural feminist theories of representing others: a response to the 'crisis' in leisure studies' discourse. *Leisure Studies* 19, 127–144.

Aitchison, C. and Reeves, C. (1998) Gendered (bed)spaces: the culture and commerce of women only tourism. In: Aitchison, C. and Jordan, F. (eds) *Gender, Space and Identity. Leisure, Culture and Commerce.* Leisure Studies Association, Brighton, UK, pp. 47–68.

Anderson, K. (1996) Engendering race research: unsettling the self-other dichotomy. In: Duncan, N. (ed.) *Bodyspace: Destabilizing Geographies of Gender and Sexuality.* Routledge, London, pp. 197–211.

Bailey, C. (1996) *A Guide to Field Research.* Pine Forge Press, Thousand Oaks, California.

Beeghley, L. (1996) *What Does Your Wife Do? Gender and the Transformation of Family Life.* Westview Press, Oxford.

Booth, C., Darke, J. and Yeandle, S. (1996) (eds) *Changing Places: Women's Lives in the City.* Paul Chapman Publishing, London.

Butler, J. (1990) *Gender Trouble: Feminism and the Subversion of Identity.* Routledge, London.

Cassells, F. (1993) quoted in Rothenberg, T. (1995) Lesbians creating urban social space. In: Bell, D. and Valentine, G. (eds) *Mapping Desire: Geographies of Sexualities.* Routledge, London.

Chouinard, V. and Grant, A. (1996) On being not even anywhere near the project: putting ourselves in the picture. In: Duncan, N. (ed.) *Bodyspace: Destabilizing Geographies of Gender and Sexuality.* Routledge, London, pp. 170–196.

Churchill, G.A. (1995) *Marketing Research: Methodological Foundations.* The Dryden Press, Orlando, Florida.

Clift, S. and Forrest, S. (1999) Gay men and tourism: destinations and holiday motivations. *Tourism Management* 20, 615–625.

Coalter, F. (2000) Public and commercial leisure provision: active citizens and passive consumers? *Leisure Studies* 19(3), 163–182.

Cohen, E. (1988) Traditions in the qualitative sociology of tourism. *Annals of Tourism Research* 15(1), 29–45.

Cohen, P. (1997) Out of the melting pot into the fire next time: imagining the East End as city, body, text. In: Westwood, S. and Williams,

J. (eds) *Imagining Cities: Scripts, Signs, Memory.* Routledge, London, pp. 73–86.

Deem, R. (1986) *All Work and No Play? The Sociology of Women's Leisure.* Open University Press, Milton Keynes, UK.

DuBois, B. (1983) Passionate scholarship: notes on values, knowing and method in feminist social science. In: Bowles, G. and Duelli Klein, R. (eds) *Theories of Women's Studies.* Routledge & Kegan Paul, London.

Duncan, N. (1996) Sexuality in public and private spaces. In: Duncan, N. (ed.) *Bodyspace: Destabilizing Geographies of Gender and Sexuality.* Routledge, London, pp. 127–145.

Enloe, C. (1989) *Bananas, Beaches and Bases: Making Feminist Sense of International Politics.* Pandora, London.

Finn, M., Elliott-White, M. and Walton, M. (2000) *Research Methods for Leisure and Tourism.* Butterworth Heinnemann, Oxford.

Forrest, S. and Clift, S. (1998) Gay tourist space and sexual behaviour. In: Aitchison, C. and Jordan, F. (eds) *Gender, Space and Identity.* Leisure Studies Association, Brighton, UK, pp. 163–176.

Gardner, C.B. (1995) *Passing By: Gender and Public Harassment.* University of California Press, Berkeley, California.

Greene, B. (1997) (ed.) *Ethnic and Cultural Diversity Among Lesbians and Gay Men: Psychological Perspectives on Lesbian and Gay Issues,* Vol. 3. Sage, Thousand Oaks, California.

Henderson, K., Bedini, L., Hecht, L. and Schuler, R. (1995) Women with physical disabilities and the negotiation of leisure constraints. *Leisure Studies* 14, 17–31.

Holcomb, B. and Luongo, M. (1996) Gay tourism in the United States. *The Annals of Tourism Research* 23, 711–713.

Hughes, H. (1997) Holidays and homosexual identity. *Tourism Management* 18(4), 3–7.

Hughes, H. (1998) Sexuality, tourism and space: the case of gay visitors to Amsterdam. In: Tyler, D., Robertson, M. and Guerrier, Y. (eds) *Managing Tourism in Cities: Policy, Process and Practice.* Wiley, Chichester, UK, pp. 163–178.

Hughes, H. (2000) Holidays and homosexuals: a constrained choice? In: Robinson, M., Long, P., Evans, N., Sharpley, R. and Swarbrooke, J. (eds) *Reflections on International Tourism: Expressions of Culture, Identity and Meaning in Tourism.* Business Education Publishers, Sunderland, UK, pp. 221–230.

Jordan, F. (1998) Shirley Valentine: where are you? In: Aitchison, C. and Jordan, F. (eds) *Gender, Space and Identity. Leisure, Culture and Commerce.* Leisure Studies Association, Brighton, UK, pp. 69–88.

Keith, M. (1995) Ethnic entrepreneurs and street rebels: looking inside the inner city. In: Pile, S. and Thrift, N. (eds) *Mapping the Subject: Geographies of Cultural Transformation.* Routledge, London, pp. 355–370.

Mason, J. (1996) *Qualitative Researching.* Sage, London.

Morgan, N.J. and Pritchard, A. (1998) *Tourism Promotion and Power: Creating Images, Creating Identities.* Wiley, Chichester, UK.

Morgan, N.J. and Pritchard, A. (1999) *Politics and Power at the Seaside: The Development of Devon's Resorts during the Twentieth Century.* University of Exeter Press, Exeter, UK.

Myslik, W.D. (1996) Renegotiating the social/ sexual identities of place: gay communities as safe havens or sites of resistance. In: Duncan, N. (ed.) *Bodyspace. Destabilizing Geographies of Gender and Sexuality.* Routledge, London, pp. 156–169.

Oliver Wilson, C. (1999) Chasing pink dollars. *Time,* 12 July, 30–31.

Olwig, K. (1993) A sexual cosmology: nation and landscape at the conceptual interstices of nature and culture; or what does landscape really mean? In: Bender, B. (ed.) *Landscape. Politics and Perspectives.* Berg Publishers, Oxford, pp. 307–343.

Pidgeon, N. and Henwood, K. (1997) Grounded theory: practical implementation. In: Richardson, J.T.E. (ed.) *Handbook of Qualitative Research Methods for Psychology and the Social Sciences.* BPS Books, Leicester, UK, pp. 86–101.

Pitts, B.G. (1999) Sports tourism and niche markets: identification and analysis of the growing lesbian and gay sports tourism industry. *Journal of Vacation Marketing* 5(1), 31–50.

Potter, N. and Mulkay, M. (1985) 'Scientists' interview talk: interviews as a technique for revealing participants' interpretative practices. In: Brenner, M. *et al.* (eds) *The Research Interview: Uses and Approaches.* Academic Press, quoted in Seale, C. (1998) *Researching Society and Culture.* Sage, London, p. 212.

Pritchard, A. and Morgan, N.J. (2000a) Constructing tourism landscapes: gender, sexuality and space. *Tourism Geographies* 2(2), 115–139.

Pritchard, A. and Morgan, N.J. (2000b) Privileging the male gaze: gendered tourism landscapes. *Annals of Tourism Research* 27(3), 884–905.

Pritchard, A., Morgan, N.J., Sedgley, D. and Jenkins, A. (1998) Reaching out to the gay tourist: opportunities and threats in an emerging market segment. *Tourism Management* 19(3), 273–282.

Pritchard, A., Morgan, N.J. and Sedgley, D. (2000a) Exploring issues of space and sexuality in Manchester's Gay Village. In: Robinson, M., Long, P., Evans, N., Sharpley, R. and Swarbrooke, J. (eds) *Reflections on International Tourism. Expressions of Culture, Identity and Meaning in Tourism.* Business Education Publishers, Sunderland, UK, pp. 225–238.

Pritchard, A., Morgan, N.J., Sedgley, D., Khan, E. and Jenkins, A. (2000b) Sexuality and holiday choices: conversations with gay and lesbian tourists. *Leisure Studies* 19(2), 267–282.

Raval, S. (1989) Gender, leisure and sport: a case study of young people of South Asian descent – a response. *Leisure Studies* 8, 237–240.

Richardson, L. (1994) Writing: a method of inquiry. In: Denzin, N.K. and Lincoln, Y.S. (eds) *Handbook of Qualitative Research.* Sage, Thousand Oaks, California, pp. 516–529.

Rose, G. (1993) *Feminism and Geography. The Limits of Geographical Knowledge.* Polity Press, Cambridge.

Rothenberg, T. (1995) 'And she told two friends.' Lesbians creating urban social space. In:

Bell, D. and Valentine, G. (eds) *Mapping Desire: Geographies of Sexualities.* Routledge, London, pp. 164–169.

Ryan, C. (1995) *Researching Tourist Satisfactions – Issues, Concepts and Problems.* Routledge, London.

Scott, D. and Godbey, G.C. (1990) Re-orienting leisure research: the case for qualitative methods. *Society and Leisure* 13(1), 189–205.

Scraton, S. and Watson, B. (1998) Gendered cities: women and public leisure space in the 'postmodern city'. *Leisure Studies* 17, 123–137.

Seale, C. (ed.) (1998) *Researching Society and Culture.* Sage, London.

Segal, L. (1990) *Slow Motion: Changing Masculinities, Changing Men.* Virago, London.

Shields, R. (1991) *Places on the Margin: Alternative Geographies of Modernity.* Routledge, London.

Shurmer-Smith, P. and Hannam, K. (1994) *Worlds of Desire, Realms of Power: A Cultural Geography.* Arnold, London.

Skeggs, B. (1999) Matter out of place: visibility and sexualities in leisure spaces. *Leisure Studies* 18, 213–232.

Stanko, B. and Curry, P. (1997) Homophobic violence and the self 'at risk': interrogating the boundaries. *Social and Legal Studies* 6(4), 513–532.

Taylor, I. and Jamieson, R. (1997) 'Proper little mesters': nostalgia and protest masculinity in de-industrialised Sheffield. In: Westwood, S. and Williams, J. (eds) *Imagining Cities: Scripts, Signs, Memory.* Routledge, London, pp. 152–178.

Valentine, G. (1989) The geography of women's fear. *Area* 21, 385–390.

Valentine, G. (1993) Hetero(sexing) space: lesbian perceptions and experiences of everyday spaces. *Society and Space* 11, 395–413.

Valentine, G. (1996) (Re)negotiating the heterosexual street. In: Duncan, N. (ed.) *Bodyspace: Destabilizing Geographies of Gender and Sexuality.* Routledge, London, pp. 146–155.

Walle, A.H. (1997) Quantitative versus qualitative tourism research. *Annals of Tourism Research* 24(3), 524–536.

Whittle, S. (1994) Consuming differences: The collaboration of the gay body with the cultural state. In: Whittle, S. (ed.) *The Margins of the City–Gay Men's Urban Lives.* Arena Press, Hampshire.

Wimbush, E. and Talbot, M. (eds) (1988) *Relative Freedoms: Women and Leisure.* Open University Press, Milton Keynes, UK.

Yin, R.K. (1989) *Case Study Research: Design and Methods.* Sage, London.

Zukin, S. (1995) *The Culture of Cities.* Blackwell, Oxford.

Zukin, S. (1996) Space and symbols in an age of decline. In: King, A.D. (ed.) *Re-Presenting the City: Ethnicity, Capital and Culture in the 21st-Century Metropolis.* Macmillan, Basingstoke, UK, pp. 43–59.

18 (Un)veiling Women's Employment in the Egyptian Travel Business

NASHWA SAMIR EL-SHERIF IBRAHIM, ANNETTE PRITCHARD AND ELERI JONES

Introduction

A sizeable literature has developed over the last two decades (e.g. Brownell, 1993; Biaz and Umbreit, 1994; Fulford and Herrick, 1994; Kinnaird and Hall, 1994; Crafts and Thompson, 1995; Sinclair, 1997; Oppermann, 1999; Woods and Viehland, 2000; Knutson and Schmidgall, 2001; Bird and Lynch, 2002), which has deepened our understanding of the nature and extent of women's employment in the tourism industry around the globe – from Europe (Iverson and Sparrowe, 1999; Doherty and Manfredi, 2001) and the Americas (Kempadoo, 2001; Roehl and Swerdlow, 2001) to Asia (Ng and Pine, 2003). However, much of this work is overwhelmingly dominated by the Eurocentric approaches, practices and epistemologies which continue to shape and govern tourism scholarship (Pritchard, 2006). So far, very little research has explored women's tourism employment in Islamic societies where all aspects of life are guided by different value sets and world views. It is our contention here that interpretations of tourism and gender employment issues which are grounded in Western cultures and philosophies cannot simply be transferred to an Islamic context. Instead, more inclusive and diverse approaches are required so that we can develop alternative ways of understanding gendered employment contexts which take account of the values and philosophies of Islamic societies. To this end, this chapter (written by one Egyptian and two British female academics) focuses on the relationship between the wearing of Islamic dress (veiling) and women's employment in the Egyptian travel sector.

In Western societies the issue of veiling has become increasingly prominent in media discourses and debates over its appropriateness in certain contexts are ongoing in countries such as the UK and the Netherlands, whilst France has recently enacted legislation to ban the wearing of all religious symbols in schools. This chapter focuses on the issue of veiling in the Egyptian employment context, particularly in travel agencies where veiling has also become a topic of debate. It begins by providing a brief history of the veil and an overview of its significance in Islamic societies. Our attention then shifts to explore the role of women in the Egyptian labour force in general and in the tourism sector in particular. We then discuss the impact of veiling on women's employment opportunities and career development prospects in the Egyptian travel industry. The chapter is based on the first author's doctoral thesis and uses both primary and secondary data sources: the former being a set of interviews conducted with travel agency managers, travel consultants and staff and students in the Faculty of Tourism and Hotel Management at Cairo's Helwan University.

The Veil and Islam

Veils are articles of clothing that cover some or all of the head or face. They are worn almost exclusively by women (although there are some exceptions, as in the case of the Tuareg tribes of western Africa) and have different functions and various styles. For centuries women have worn veils for different purposes such as when in mourning, at wedding ceremonies, and to hide their identities when engaged in clandestine activities; more pragmatically, veils are sometimes worn to protect the complexion from sun and wind damage or to keep dust out of the face and of course, they are also used for religious purposes in the Christian, Mormon and Islamic faiths. The practice of veiling predates Islam by many centuries. In the Near East, Assyrian kings introduced the veil and the seclusion of women and beyond the Near East, the practice of hiding one's face and living in seclusion appeared in classical Greece, in the Byzantine Christian world, in Persia and in India among upper class women (Skidmore College, undated).

According to the rules of Islam, Muslim women are required to cover their entire bodies – except for the hands and the faces – and not to reveal their adornment except to their husbands, fathers, husbands' fathers, sons, husbands' sons, brothers, brothers' sons, sisters' sons, sisters in Islam, female slaves, old male servants and small children (The Noble Qur'an 24:31). In addition, the Noble Qur'an 33:56 also states:

> O Prophet! Tell your wives and your daughters and the women of the believers to draw their cloaks all over their bodies. That will be better, that they should be known (as free respectable women) so as not to be annoyed. And Allah is Ever Oft-Forgiving, Most Merciful.

It should be noted, however that (according to the Noble Qur'an 2:256) there is no compulsion over dress codes in the Islamic religion and that each person is free to choose whether or not to be religious, what religion to follow and how observant to be in that religion (Al-Muhajabah, undated).

As Islam reached other lands, regional practices, including the seclusion of women and the covering of their faces, were adopted by the early Muslims. Yet it was only in the second Islamic century that the veil became commonplace and until around the 10th century, only a small proportion of urban women were veiled and secluded while rural and nomadic women were not. In the Middle Ages numerous laws were developed which placed women at a greater disadvantage than previously; for instance, under the Mamluk rule in Egypt (1261–1517) decrees were issued which urged strictness in veiling and argued against the right of women to participate in public life. Sociocultural changes in the second half of the 19th century however, challenged these views and pioneer reformers and philosophers such as Refaaa Al Tahtawi were key promoters of both women's education and employment. After his return from his educational mission in France, Refaaa Al Tahtawi published a book entitled *Takhlis al-Ibriz fi Takhlis Paris* (The Manners and Customs of Parisians) in which he compared the conditions of French women to those of Egyptian women and advocated raising the female marriage age to enable them to benefit from education. In 1872, Al Tahtawi published *Al-Murshid al-Amin fi Ta'lim al-Banat wal-Banin* (The Honest Guide to the Education of Girls and Boys) in which he called for equality of educational opportunities and advocated women's right to work; as such he was the first modern Egyptian to call for equality of educational and cultural opportunities (Elsaddah and Abu-Ghazi, 2003).

Other Egyptian pioneer reform advocates included Fathi Zaghlul, Sa'd Zaghlul, Ibrahim al-Muweilhi, Jamal al-Din al-Afghani, Adib Ishaq and Mohamed Abdou, all of whom challenged the misleading concepts that deprived Egyptian women of their natural rights to acquire knowledge and to participate in public life. Such efforts were followed by those of Qasim Amin, who called for the liberation of Egyptian women and their right to education. In support of his view that the improvement of women's educational status would lead to the improvement and development of the whole of Egyptian society, Qasim Amin published *Tahrir al-Mar'a* (The Emancipation of Women) in 1899 and *Al-Mar'a al-Gadida* (The New Woman) in 1900. His ideas reflected those who closely linked the emancipation of women and the rejection of veiling to national movements for independence but at the time, both books provoked harsh criticism and Qasim Amin was attacked for being Westernized, and accused of heresy and atheism. Nevertheless, a group of writers and contemporary thinkers supported his attempt to liberate women from the hard cultural and social boundaries surrounding them (Elsaddah and Abu-Ghazi, 2003). For this group, changing the roles of women in society was central to attempts to convince the colonial powers that their subject nations were ready to govern themselves and women were encouraged to be symbols of the new state and of social progress.

To this end, male leaders of nationalist movements encouraged women to join them and to appear more freely in public, which some women gradually did. In 1910, a young Turkish woman attracted attention by daring to be photographed. At about the same time, educated women in Turkey began to leave the house unveiled, but still wearing hijab. The most dramatic public unveiling was undertaken by the Huda Shaarawi (chair of the Egyptian Feminist Union) who uncovered her face in front of the crowds upon her arrival from the International Feminist Conference held in Rome in 1923 – a revolutionary act in the history of Egyptian women. Following suit were Ibtihaj Kaddura in Lebanon, Adila Abd al-Qudir al-Jazairi in Syria and much later Habibah Manshari in Tunis (Elsaddah and Abu-Ghazi, 2003).

Here it should be stressed that for many Muslim women it was not the wearing of the veil that was the issue, but that the veil symbolized the relegation of women to a secluded world that prevented their participation in public life. However, as the 20th century progressed, a revival of veiling and the reintroduction of more modest dress reasserted itself in many Islamic societies for a number of reasons. In areas where Islam was resisted and believers felt threatened (like Indonesia and the Philippines) conservative dress became a symbol of cultural resistance and a mechanism to assert Islamic identity. Similarly, during militant struggles for independence, such as those against the French in Algeria or the British in Egypt, some women purposely kept the veil in defiance of Western styles and values. In various national and religious quarters, therefore, the veil rather than signifying inferiority came to symbolize the uniqueness and superiority of Islam. To this day it remains a contested cultural practice and the subject of much debate amongst women's groups over its use. For some women wishing to pursue professional and public social lives, veiling allows them freer movement outside the confines of the home and in leaving their homes members of this upwardly mobile group are actively defining new roles for themselves, rather than defending traditional ones. For other women, veiling is a rather more problematic practice and for them raises questions of personal freedom.

Islam has not prescribed a particular dress style for Muslim women as long as such styles do not contradict with the principals of dressing modestly (Baig, undated). However, seven conditions for Muslim women's dress have been identified: clothing must cover the entire body so that only the hands and face may remain visible (according to some jurisprudence Islamic schools); the material must not be so thin that one can see through it; the clothing must hang loose so that the shape and form of the body is not apparent; female clothing must not resemble the male's clothing; the design of clothing must not resemble the clothing of the non-believing women; the design must not consist of bold designs which attract attention; clothing should not be worn for the sole purpose of gaining reputation or increasing one's status in society (Baig, undated; Islamic Boutique, undated; Syed, undated; Syed, 2001).

In the contemporary language of Egypt, three common styles of veiling can be identified: Hijab (a variety of styles in which Muslim women use scarves or large pieces of cloth to cover their hair, neck and sometimes shoulders leaving the entire' face open); Khimar (a semi-circular form of headscarf requiring no pins or fasteners with an opening for the face, worn usually to bust level or longer); Niquab (a large robe that covers the entire body, including the head and face). The Niqab has two common forms: the *half niqab* (a simple length of fabric with elastic or ties worn around the head) and the *full* or *gulf style niqab* (a total face cover – many of which have a second more sheer cover that is worn to cover the eyes (Seattle Times Company, 2001; Skidmore College, undated; Syed, 2001). Whilst Muslim women are not compelled to wear Islamic dress by law in Egypt (as in some countries like Saudi Arabia and Iran) an increase in the number of veiled women in recent years is very noticeable and these vary widely from simple kerchiefs and elaborate headscarves to full face-and-body coverings.

Women and the Egyptian Labour Force

The Egyptian labour force is estimated to include approximately 20 million people (CAPMAS, 2003). About two million (10%) of people are unemployed and women

are much more likely to experience unemployment than their male counterparts
– around a quarter compared to 5%. The National Council for Women (NCW)
have been very active in researching and producing policy documents on women
in the Egyptian labour market and their research (NCW, 2001) has highlighted
how women's employment has historically been influenced by the phases of Egypt's
economic development. At the beginning of the 19th century Egypt's largely rural
economy provided major employment opportunities for women in both the agricultural and manufacturing sectors. The textile industry in particular employed a
high percentage of women workers to the point where they became the core of the
female industrial workforce. At the same time women maintained a major role in
the agricultural sector and they continued to take on heavy duties related to the
sector, including irrigation and planting, as well as engaging in rural commerce
(NCW, 2001).

Then, the July 1952 revolution sparked radical socio-economic and political
changes in Egypt. The laws and constitution of the revolution asserted the principle
of complete equality of rights and duties between men and women; they also underlined women's commitment to motherhood and childhood. Legislation establishing
the rights of women working in government agencies and the public and private
sectors were seen to be the major factors that drove women to join the workforce at
a rapid rate. In addition, labour migration to other countries throughout the 20th
century has created vacancies in the labour force that have given women further
economic opportunities, whilst at the same time, many women found themselves
to be the sole heads of the household – thus forcing them to join the workforce.
Currently, women can be found working throughout the various sectors of both the
formal and informal economy. The degree of women's participation varies from
one sector to another, though it is generally low, especially in the formal private
sector. In general, government agencies are women's main employers, with women
representing a third of all government employees, although future opportunities for
women's employment are predicted to be greater in the private sector (El-Hamaky,
2001).

At a professional level, Egyptian women form 83% of nurses, 56% of social
and welfare specialists, 48% of secretaries, 40% of teachers, 39% of clerks, 38% of
accountants, 35% of university teaching staff, 31% of doctors and 10% of engin-
eers (NCW, 2000; CAPMAS, 2003). Women also account for almost a quarter of
professors (NCW, 2000b), a proportion which bears favourable comparison with
the figures in many Western countries. However, women's representation in management in Egypt is generally low. According to the 1996 census, women occupied
about 12% of the senior managerial positions with about 25%, 10% and 6% held
in the government, public and business, and private sectors, respectively. In middle
management, women held 31% of the positions in the government while no statistics were available for the public or private sectors (NCW, 2000). In terms of a
sectoral distribution, women accounted for almost half of health and social welfare
employees, just over a third of education, under a fifth of agricultural and fisheries,
over a tenth of industry and mining and (of most interest to us in this chapter) 14%
of tourism employees (CAPMAS, 2003).

Despite the many improvements in the socio-economic and political position
of women since Egyptian independence, many challenges remain including: the

ongoing lower levels of women's employment; their concentration in the low-productivity sectors; women's rights; discrimination and empowerment in social, civil and political society (Radwan, 2001). Illiteracy remains a significant problem for women in Egypt, particularly in rural areas where almost twice as many women (63%) as men (36%) are illiterate (CAPMAS, 2003). Such a high female illiteracy rate is a major obstacle to women's participation in economic activities and consequently drastically affects their involvement in different aspects of Egyptian life. The Egyptian government is actively addressing this problem through various legislative and educational initiatives including compulsory free schooling which aims to eradicate illiteracy completely by the year 2007 (in this they are supported by the NCW). The fight against illiteracy is evidence of a wider educational renaissance in modern Egypt and equality of opportunity and educational upgrading are high government priorities, attracting enormous annual resources. Government education is free from pre-primary school through to university and postgraduate education. In the fiscal year 2004/2005, the estimated budget for education was 25.8 billion Egyptian pounds (equivalent to approximately US$4.2 billion) representing about 15% of the total government annual budget (Al-Ahram, 2004). Moreover, about 1.5 million students (54% males and 46% females) were enrolled in Egyptian universities at the start of the 21st century (NCW, 2002).

Women in the Egyptian Travel Business

There is very little statistical information available for women's employment in the Egyptian tourism sector. In 2003 the tourism industry accounted for around 2% of the total Egyptian workforce or some 337,000 persons. Of these, 290,000 (86%) were male and 47,000 (14%) were female (CAPMAS, 2003). There are no recent official statistics for female employment in private sector tourism establishments in Egypt – the only data being the results of a survey conducted in 1991 by the Egyptian Ministry of Tourism in collaboration with the Central Agency for Public Mobilisation and Statistics and published in 1993 (CAPMAS, 1993). This study showed that approximately four-fifths of employees were male and that women were particularly evident in departments such as reservations (56%), marketing and sales (38%) and information technology (38%). Women dominated in secretarial jobs, where they formed almost 90% of the workforce. Women's representation in senior management was relatively low at around 13%, as was their representation in middle management, where the highest proportions were in sales (17%) and public relations (15%).

Unfortunately, no official efforts have been made to update this survey conducted in the early 1990s. The most recent research on women's employment in Egyptian travel agencies and the factors influencing their career development (conducted for the first author's doctoral thesis, Ibrahim, 2004) indicated that women represent a quarter of the workforce in travel agencies (occupying 21% of private and 30% of public sector posts). On average, women occupy a third of managerial positions in the public agencies and a quarter in the private ones, where they hold 26% and 20% of the middle and senior management positions respectively. Women thus continue to dominate secretarial work, whilst men dominate the accounting, tourism, sales and marketing, and operational and ground handling departments, especially any areas which require outdoor and night-work (see Table 18.1). The overall picture is that women remain under-represented at senior managerial level in Egyptian travel agencies, although there are many more opportunities at middle management level.

Women's employment experiences

There are a number of social and cultural practices which influence women's employment in the Egyptian travel industry, some of which are common to the vast majority of women and others which are of particular concern to women who choose to veil themselves. The findings of the study reported here indicated that women's career development in Egyptian travel agencies is influenced by three groups of closely interrelated overlapping and interacting personal, organizational and societal factors. Personal factors can be divided into family-related and individual-related, whilst five family-related factors can be identified (parents' attitudes towards unmarried daughters, husbands' attitudes towards wives' careers, dual career demands, work/family conflicts and career interruptions) as well as two individual related factors (work motivation and career choices). Organizational factors are: initial staffing decisions, promotion decisions, family-friendly arrangements, training opportunities, informal systems of career development and equal opportunity (EO) policies. Societal factors are: religious doctrine, social mores, gender stereotypes, legislation, government programmes and social change.

In this section, we will try to use the voices of the research participants wherever possible to highlight the impact of such cultural practices on women's employment opportunities. Whilst it is undoubtedly true that all societies are patriarchal to a greater or lesser degree, patriarchal structures which dominate Oriental societies (Abu Zaid, 2000) have particular social consequences for women and mean that in conventional social practice women are under the control and guidance of male guardians. As a result, certain work practices which are common in the travel industry pose real problems for the vast majority of Egyptian women. Practices such as 'delays after the regular working day, travelling away from home on business trips or dealing with people whom I don't know' (in the words of one female tourism student) were identified by research participants as unacceptable

Table 18.1. Male and female employment in public and private travel agencies by department. (From Ibrahim, 2004.)

Department	Men (%)	Women (%)	Total employees
Secretarial jobs	17	83	18
Ticketing	49	51	176
Admin and Personnel	63	37	485
Accounting	69	31	532
Tourism	79	21	632
Sales and Marketing	81	19	206
Transportation	99	1	961

work policies for the majority of Egyptian women. As another female student commented: 'No Egyptian husband accepts that his wife returns home late at night, travels away from home for business purposes or establishes business relationships with other men unless he fully understands the nature of the business she is involved in.' Interviewees and focus group participants also agreed that family-related factors have a noticeable impact on women's career development in the Egyptian travel business; as one male sales manager commented: 'familial circumstances affect women's opportunities for career development. They might be forced to [have] career interruptions. The result is that women cannot compete with their male or unmarried female counterparts.' Such family-related factors may frustrate women and hinder their career development, as in many cases, they are obliged to prioritize family considerations over work commitments (this is particularly the case as in Islamic societies the home and family are seen to be core to women's social roles). One female employer explained: 'I can understand the problem of working women. They are trapped between familial obligations and work responsibilities. This situation hinders them from building careers. They often prioritize the family to work.' Similarly, a male travel consultant noted that 'women are overloaded with familial burdens in addition to their work obligations while men have nothing to think about except work'.

Such social and cultural practices represent real challenges for women and make it difficult to promote work-based equality, regardless of the legislation enacted. Thus, for many women in the Egyptian travel industry, government and public sector employment offers many advantages over the private sector precisely because it offers 'more suitable work circumstances . . . [the] workload is less and working hours are also less. There are plenty of official holidays and opportunities for . . . unpaid leave for childcare reasons . . . there is no restriction for employing veiled women and no obligation to wear special, socially unacceptable agency uniforms' (female senior travel specialist).

Veiled Women in the Egyptian Travel Business

Inequality of opportunity is multifaceted and now we would like to focus on the experience of veiled women in the Egyptian travel industry for it appears that many of these women are doubly disadvantaged in tourism employment by comparison to their male counterparts and to women who do not wear the veil. As we discussed above, for some women the veil offers an enhanced degree of social, economic and professional freedom and indeed, observation, personal experience and previous research (Ibrahim, 2004), suggest that veiling in Egypt is by no means an obstacle for women's involvement in the many different professions. In the Egyptian travel business, however, many employers refuse to employ veiled women, although the reasons for this are rarely articulated and therefore difficult to establish. There are signs that tourism employers in Egypt are more willing to employ veiled women in their enterprises than previously; however, such willingness varies from one tourism sector to another, from one activity to another within the same sector and finally from one employer to another. Certainly, employers are less likely to employ veiled women in departments which involve direct contact with clients, although they may be employed in areas with such departments that do not have direct contact with clients on condition that employers themselves are willing to recruit veiled women in their enterprises.

Nevertheless, it should be noted that even when veiled women are employed in the travel business sector, only those who wear the hijab are accepted while those who wear the khimar or niqaab are totally rejected. One male travel consultant commented how in his experience, 'many travel agencies refuse to employ veiled women'. Another male participant suggested that 'some travel agencies do not employ veiled women at all'. At the same time, research participants commented how veiling could interfere with agency corporate dress codes. As a female tourism academic commented: 'There are many red lines against employing veiled women in the Egyptian travel agencies.' As a consequence, there was widespread recognition amongst travel agency managers and future employees (the tourism university students) that 'veiled women may have very limited job opportunities in the Egyptian travel agencies'. Although a number of interviewees suggested that some employers are less rigid in employing veiled women, there was a consensus that employers resisted the employment of veiled women in jobs that involved direct contact with clients, especially at the counter and in sales positions, although veiled women might be considered for employment in back office work activities – as the following comments suggest: 'Some travel agencies refuse to employ veiled women especially at the counter and in sales. However, veiled women may have better opportunities in the departments that do not have direct contact with clients.'

The issue of veiling has become increasingly prominent in Egyptian society in part because of the recent upsurge in women's adoption of more traditional Islamic dress codes. This increase in popularity has coincided with an increased concern amongst women that those who choose to wear the veil may be discriminated against in the travel sector. Some interviewees and university student focus group participants strongly criticized the anti-veiling discrimination evident in recruiting for job vacancies in the Egyptian travel agencies explaining that efficiency and good performance at work has nothing to do with veiling. One female student asked: 'What is the relationship between the veil and women's performance at work? . . . I cannot understand this very strange discrimination.' Whilst there was recognition that 'wearing or not wearing the veil will never affect the efficiency of the woman or change her capacity to do the job' (male tourism consultant), concomitant to this was the recognition that women were being prevented from pursuing career opportunities simply because they are veiled. A female tourism student stressed this saying: 'This phenomenon is ridiculous. How come that females seeking jobs in the Egyptian travel agencies are not given equal job opportunities only because they are veiled?' Similarly, a female accountant commented on the same phenomenon saying: 'Many women lose good job opportunities in the travel business just because they are veiled.' A male counter supervisor added: 'The tendency to reject employing veiled women decreases the opportunities open to them in the Egyptian travel job market.'

Although at present the role and status of veiled women in the Egyptian travel industry seems rather precarious and problematic, there does appear to be increasing support for the suggestion that future travel trends, particularly the growth in religious tourism in the Gulf States, could lead to more opportunities, as one female tourism academic noted: 'Religious tourism seems to be very encouraging for veiled women. Incoming tourism from the Arabian Gulf region also has plenty of room for veiled female employees . . . all of the women tourists coming from this area definitely prefer to deal with women employees rather than men. . . . Currently there is a great interest in tourism development all over the Arab nations and the Arab women must take their place in it. [The] veil cannot be a barrier for the participation of women in the development of the Arab tourism.'

Conclusion

This chapter has explored women's employment experiences in Egyptian travel agencies. We began by arguing that it was inappropriate to merely transfer Western conceptual frameworks to Islamic contexts and as we have discussed, women's experiences are highly complex and multifaceted and rooted in Egyptian social, cultural and political life. The research reported here and in the wider study it is drawn from (Ibrahim, 2004) suggests that personal, organizational and societal factors play key roles in shaping the career development opportunities available to women. Whilst at a general level these are similar to those experienced by women in all societies, their manifestation and influence dramatically varies in Islamic contexts such as that reported here. A range of positive forces are contributing to an improving experience for female employees in Egypt such as: increased public awareness of women's issues; governmental support for equal opportunities legislation; increased emphasis on the rights of working women; advocacy work by organizations such as the NCW; and supportive familial relationships (particularly with husbands). These are not unique to women working in the travel industry but reflect wider changes in Egyptian society. Counterbalancing these positive initiatives are some strong and embedded forces which also combine to constrain and directly disadvantage women's career opportunities in the travel industry. Of particular significance here are the prevailing cultural traditions, customs and social mores; the antisocial work conditions which structure travel industry employment; traditional stereotyped staffing roles; the practice of veiling; and the very real personal dilemmas posed by work/family balance.

Here we have provided a very brief and selective overview of the experience of women in the Egyptian travel industry. Much more work needs to be undertaken in the wider Islamic world to build a body of knowledge which complements the work on women's employment in tourism which is grounded in the Western social science tradition. The growth in postgraduate opportunities in countries such as Egypt offers the potential to enhance and diversify the academic collective working in this field, providing rich opportunities for intercultural insights, understandings and exchanges. This is a conversation which is only just beginning but it is one which must be pursued with vigour and mutual respect for different traditions and world views if we are to move towards more complex understandings in tourism scholarship. Such complex understandings also directly challenge Eurocentric tourism imaginaries and praxis as they require the development of polythetic comparisons in our conceptualizations of tourism and in the underpinning research praxis (Pritchard and Morgan, 2007). These dialogues – between researchers and those with whom we co-create tourism knowledge – can help us all to build more inclusive and diverse ways of understanding based on reflexivity, equality, empowerment and self-determination.

References

(Those marked with an asterisk (*) have been translated from Arabic.)

Abou Zeid, A. (2000) Positive feminine values in the cultural heritage. *Proceedings of the First Conference for Arab Women Summit, 18–20, November 2000. Research and Studies* 3, 5–22.

*Al-Ahram (2004) Proposed government budget for the fiscal year 2004/2005. *Al-Ahram Newspaper*, 128(42888), 1, 9 May.

Al-Muhajabah (2001) On veiling. Available at: www.muhajabah.com/onveiling.html

Biag, K. (2007) The Islamic Dress Code. Available at: www.albalagh.net/food_for_thought/dress.shtml

Biaz, P. and Umbreit, T. (1994) Women in hospitality management: an exploratory study of major and occupation choice variables. *Hospitality and Tourism Educator* 6(4), 7.

Bird, E. and Lynch, P. (2002) Gender and employment flexibility within hotel front offices. *Service Industries Journal* 22(3), 99–116.

Brownell, J. (1993) Addressing career challenges faced by women in the hospitality management. *Hospitality and Tourism Educator* 5(4), 11.

*CAPMAS (1993) *A Study of Employment in the Tourism Sector*, Vol. 4: *Travel Agencies*. Central Agency for Public Mobilisation and Statistics, April 1993, Nasr City, Cairo.

*CAPMAS (2003) *Statistical Year Book of A.R.E.* Central Agency for Public Mobilisation and Statistics, Nasr City, Cairo.

Crafts, D. and Thompson, L. (1995) Career advancement obstacles for women in the food service industry. *Journal of College and University Food Service* 2(3), 5–14.

Doherty, L. and Manfredi, S. (2001) Women's employment in Italian and UK hotels. *International Journal of Hospitality Management* 20(1), 61–76.

*El-Hamaky, Y. (2001) Egyptian women in the formal labour market. *Proceedings of the Third Forum, Woman and Labour Market: Formal and Informal Sectors, 8 July 2001.* NCW Publications, Cairo, No. 5, 47–58.

*Elsaddah, H. and Abu-Ghazi, E. (2003) *Significant Moments in the History of Egyptian Women*, Vol. 1, 2nd edn. National Council for Women, Committee for Culture and Media, Dar Al-Kutub Al-Misriah, Cairo.

Fulford, M. and Herrick, A. (1994) Women and work in hospitality: fair notice for the nineties. *Hospitality and Tourism Educator* 6(4), 25.

Ibrahim, N. (2004) Women's employment in Egyptian travel agencies and factors influencing their career development. Welsh School of Hospitality, Tourism and Leisure Management, University of Wales Institute Cardiff, UK.

Islamic Boutique (2006) Islamic dress code. Available at: http://www.islamicboutique.com/dresscode.asp

Iverson, K. and Sparrowe, R. (1999) Cracks in the glass ceiling? An empirical study of gender differences in income in the hospitality industry in the UK. *Journal of Hospitality and Tourism Research* 23(1), 4.

Kempadoo, K. (2001) Freelancers, temporary wives and beach-boys: researching sex work in the Caribbean. *Feminist Review* 67(1), 39–62.

Kinnaird, V. and Hall, D. (eds) (1994) *Tourism: A Gender Analysis*. Wiley, Chichester, UK.

Knutson, B. and Schmidgall, R. (2001) Challenges and opportunities for women achieving success in hospitality financial management. *Journal of Hospitality and Tourism Education* 13(3 & 4), 45.

*NCW (2000) *The Renaissance of Egypt, Women, Citizenship and Development: First Conference of the National Council for Women.* March 2000. NCW Publications, Cairo.

NCW (2001) Egyptian women in the labour market. *National Council for Women Newsletter* 6(July–August 2001), 5.

NCW (2002) *Egyptian Women in Figures*. NCW Publications, Cairo.

Ng, C. and Pine, R. (2003) Women and men in hotel management in Hong Kong: perceptions of gender and career development issues. *International Journal of Hospitality Management* 22(1), 85–102.

Oppermann, M. (1999), Sex tourism. *Annals of Tourism Research* 26(2), 251–266.

Pritchard, A. (2006) Editorial: leisure voices: getting engaged in dialogues, entanglements and conversations. *Leisure Studies* 25(4), 373–377.

Pritchard, A. and Morgan, N. (2007) De-centring tourism's intellectual universe, or traversing the dialogue between change and tradition. In: Ateljevic, I., Pritchard, A. and Morgan, N. (eds) *The Critical Turn in Tourism Studies: Innovative Methodologies*. Elsevier, Oxford, pp. 11–28.

*Radwan, S. (2001) Egyptian woman in the labour market: a future view. *Proceedings of the Third Forum, Woman and Labour Market: Formal and Informal Sectors, 8 July 2001*. NCW Publications, Cairo, No. 5, pp. 71–86.

*Rizk, S. (2001) Problems facing woman in the informal sector and the suggested policies to overcome them. *Proceedings of the Third Forum: Women and Labour Market, Formal and Informal Sectors, 8 July 2001*.

NCW Publications, Cairo, No. 5, pp. 59–70.

Roehl, W. and Swerdlow, S. (2001) Sex differences in hotel employee training in the western United States. *Pacific Tourism Review* 5(3 & 4), 143.

Seattle Times Company (2001) Interpreting veils. Available at: http://seattletimes. nwsource.com/news/nation-world/crisis/ theregion/veils.html

Sinclair, M. (ed.) (1997) *Gender, Work and Tourism*. Routledge, London.

Skidmore College (2003) The veil and veiling. Available at: http://www.skidmore.edu/ academics/arthistory/ah369/finalveil.html

Syed, I. (2001) Women in Islam: Hijab. irfiweb. org; available at: www.islamfortoday.com/ syed01.html

Syed, S. (2007) Seven conditions for women's dress in Islam: how a Muslim meets the requirements of Islamic modesty in dress and sets out their Quranic background. Available at: http://www.islamfortoday. com/7conditions.html

The Noble Qur'an, English Translation of the meanings and commentary (1417 after Higra.) Madinah Munawwarah, Saudi Arabia: King Fahd Complex for Printing of the Holy Qur'an.

Woods, R. and Viehland, D. (2000) Women in hotel management: gradual progress, uncertain prospects. *Cornell Hotel and Restaurant Administration Quarterly*, 41(5), 51–54.

19 Gender and Tourism Development: A Case Study of the Cappadoccia Region of Turkey

SERMIN ELMAS

Introduction

During the 1970s, tourism development emerged as an important focus of research and particular emphasis was placed on cross-cultural studies of tourism development and on analysis of inbound tourism's impact on third world countries. At the same time, women's employment also became a 'hot' topic within feminist discourse with many scholars arguing that paid work performed outside the home increases women's economic independence and emancipates them from their marginalization in the domestic domain as reproducers, nurturers and subsistence producers. Thus, development analysts argued that the integration of women into the tourism industry promoted female employment opportunities, developed their work-based skills and fostered 'modern' attitudes. Yet, 30 years later, the question of whether working in tourism does indeed give economic and personal independence to women remains moot. Indeed, many recent studies have clearly demonstrated that from England (Hennesy, 1994) to Greece (Leontidou, 1994), Mexico and the Philippines (Chant, 1997), Bali (Long and Kindon, 1997), Northern Cyprus (Scott, 1997) and beyond, tourism employment actually reinforces existing gender relations and perpetuates inequalities between women and men. Following such studies, this chapter will discuss the nature of women's work in tourism-related services in the Nevşehir–Ürgüp–Avanos triangle in the Cappadoccia region of central Turkey. It attempts to contribute to the growing body of gender analysis within tourism studies by examining the conditions of women's work outside the home (e.g. in hotels, restaurants and handicraft-producing workplaces) and within the home (e.g. in pensions and in handicraft production), as well as analysing the segregation of work between sexes from a gender perspective. In particular it will examine: the conditions of women's participation in social production; their motivations for work; work satisfaction; the various ways in which women are controlled and supervised; their relations with trade unions; and the mechanisms through which existing forms of gender subordination are reproduced in tourism-related organizations, as well as in the women's private lives.

The chapter reports an extensive study conducted during 1997 and 1998 in the Cappadoccia region, where at the time, there were 91 hotels and pensions, 44 restaurants, 22 travel agencies and 35 touristic handicraft-producing and trading facilities. Since the smaller hotels, city restaurants and travel agencies do not employ women in significant numbers, they were excluded from the study. This meant that the study sample comprised: one first-class motel (the only one in the region); six three-, four- and five-star hotels (from a possible 14); and four pensions (from the 14 in the region). Three of the larger touristic handicraft establishments (which both produced and sold carpets, souvenir onyx products and pottery) were also chosen as they employed relatively high numbers of women compared to other establishments. The sample was completed by two tourist restaurants (from the region's seven), which are registered by the municipalities and four domestic establishments which specialized in handicraft production. In total observations, unstructured interviews and questionnaires were conducted with 80 women working in the selected establishments, whilst 15 managers and owners (all of whom were male) were also interviewed.

The Development of Tourism and Women's Employment in the Cappadoccia Region

Like other developing countries in the 1980s, Turkey embraced tourism as an important means of implementing the export-led growth strategy recommended by the International Monetary Fund and the World Bank. As a result, in 1982 the Grand National Assembly passed the Tourism Encouragement Law which identified a range of natural, historic and sociocultural criteria necessary for designated touristic areas. Although priority was given to Turkey's coastal regions such as the Mediterranean, Aegean and Marmara, Cappadoccia was also included in this scheme. Thus, the Cappadoccia region has experienced mass tourism development since the early 1980s, primarily initiated by the Turkish government's political and economy strategies (Tosun, 1998). Cappadoccia itself forms a rough triangle, which starts about 169 miles south-east of Ankara and is located between Nevşehir, Kayseri and Niğde. As in many other regions in the country, agriculture dominates the economic sector and whilst small-scale production industries, trade and transportation are important, tourism is the second most significant industry in the region. The regions' main tourist sights are set within a small triangle between Nevşehir, Ürgüp and Avanos and besides its natural and historical attractions it is home to many cultural activities such as handicraft productions.

As a region where women's work is largely unpaid agricultural activity, Cappadoccia provides an interesting case study in which to analyse the impact of paid tourism employment opportunities on women's lives. Women are concentrated predominantly in agriculture and in sub-branches of manufacturing such as carpet-weaving; but since the 1980s, they have also been in demand as employees in hotels, restaurants and in services – a pattern which mirrors women's employment in Turkey generally. Women who left the agriculture sector are now mostly employed in the service sector (Ecevit, 1986) and the percentage of the total female labour force employed in the service sector rose from 14.3% in 1990 to 28.8%

in 2000 (State Institute of Statistics, 2000). Since the tourism industry is seasonal, intensively competitive and labour-intensive and because of the marginal characteristics of women's labour in Turkey (Ecevit, 1992) women's labour is in extensive demand. Whilst the absence of sufficient regional and national statistics makes any estimate of the number of women employed in tourism difficult, we know that in the mid-1990s, women comprised 19% of employees in accommodation operations, 7% in restaurants and 36% in travel agencies (Ministry of Tourism, 1993).

These figures are significantly out of line with those in developed countries where females outnumber males in the tourism sector (Hennesy, 1994; Purcell, 1997; Sinclair, 1997), but these official statistics are endorsed by the findings of the study reported here; for instance, in the five-star hotel that opened in Nevşehir in 1989 women constitute only 14.3% of the total workforce of 160 employees. In the four-star hotels in the study, female employees constitute 18.9% of the 273-strong workforce, whilst in the three-star hotel 6 out of 13 employees are female. In addition to the hotels, a first class motel, which is owned by Tourism Bank, was also studied. This motel has been rented and been in operation since 1983 and women constituted only 16.12% of the employees. In the two selected restaurants (which are licensed by the municipalities and privately run throughout the year), women make up 10% of the total staff. Even in the large carpet-weaving enterprise (which are largely made by female workers), only one-third of the total employees are women. These low levels of female employment in tourism-related businesses – even in Ürgüp which is an initiative tourist area – may well be the result less of economic rationality per se, than the familial ideology prevalent in Turkey.

The Proper Place of Women: Familial Ideology and Economic Rationality

In Islamic societies, the status of women has often been discussed in relation to women's roles, to cultural restrictions such as honour and shame which impact upon women's freedom and in relation to the 'private world of women' and the 'public world of men' (Kağitçibaşi, 1982). Honour, which may refer to a man's reputation in the community as determined by the chastity of the women in his family, is very important and associated largely with women's sexuality (Tucker, 1997). In Turkey, as in other Islamic societies, the familial ideology assigns women to the private domain of home – women are wives and mothers who should be guarded by their husbands, fathers and brothers who are the breadwinners and familial guardians. Thus girls' education (especially higher education) and the degree of their participation in the workforce are determined to a large degree by the permission and control of men, whilst sons are of greater value than daughters and are given priority in accessing resources and education (Göğüş-Tan, 2000). However, the urbanization of Turkey which has accelerated since the 1970s and the hardships which emerged there in the 1980s challenged existing familial ideology and most women in the country have started to work because of economic necessity (Ansal, 1995; Eraydin, 1999). The Cappadoccian women were no exception, although women there were involved in agricultural and weaving activities long before the 1980s as their home-made products were sold and distributed by their fathers (when the women were single) or their husbands (when they were married).

As the tourism industry developed and employment outside the home became widespread, women became the best candidates for employment in hotels and especially in the large carpet-weaving enterprises operated by tourism entrepreneurs from outside the region. Women from low-class urban families and rural areas soon began working there as paid labourers doing what they used to do at home. But these organizations created environments where both sexes worked side by side, although customs governing male and female work practices – in particular women's confinement to certain activities – remained extremely powerful. Men, not only as parents and husbands, but also as employers tried to allocate women 'appropriate' places. Of course, 'appropriateness' according to employers implies different things in different workplaces. Managers of the bigger hotels prefer to recruit women in departments like reception, food and beverage services and housekeeping. These duties are felt to be compatible with women's 'nature' since they are considered to be more patient than men when confronting customer problems. In food and beverage services, they are seen to be more attractive than men and to create a pleasant image of the hotel or restaurant in the eyes of customers. Finally, in the housekeeping department, women are preferred to men since they are familiar with the tasks they do at the hotel. This last point is also evident in the large carpet-weaving enterprise and in both the pottery and the onyx processing workshops. On the other hand – in the eyes of managers – as women's productivity is less than that of men in physically demanding tasks and as they are thought to be more defenceless when confronting problems, it is not considered to be appropriate to employ them as cooks, night officials, security staff and waiters. Thus, 'appropriateness', according to employers, implied two things: first, a male job is not appropriate for women because women *could not* undertake it due to their physical weaknesses; second, it is not appropriate (such as in night services) because women *must not* perform it due to moral reasons.

As a result of the values and beliefs characteristic of Turkish society, many of the women in this study were not able to ask why they worked in a specific situation, although they do know why they work outside their houses. Except for a minority of women who were educated and employed in relatively high organizational levels and those who were developing their craft skills in workplaces with the intention of operating their own businesses in the future, for 86% of the women there was no other reason for taking a job outside the home other than economic necessity. It is also evident that, aside from their desire to remain in the private domain and focus on their responsibilities as wives and mothers, over 90% of female seasonal workers working in hotels and restaurants would work as full-time year-round employees. In other words, if their employers offered them work all year, each year, they would not leave their workplaces as they would not need to look for alternative employment at the end of the season – clearly the duration of their employment in the same establishment depends not on them but on the demands of their employers. For women who work seasonally and are only employed for approximately 6 months the most important question is: Will I be employed when the new season starts? Although there is a legal requirement for Turkish businesses to re-employ previous staff the following season (Koray, 1999), seasonal female hotel workers in the study indicated that their continued employment in the same establishments depends on their employers' discretion. For those who had not been so re-employed, whilst some had found alternative employment in other hotels, 38% remained unemployed and dependent on their husbands or families and 17% had turned to informal employment such as making lace to sell to tourists.

As other studies undertaken in Turkey indicate (e.g. Ecevit, 1991), in larger-scale (as opposed to family-run) businesses, economic considerations are the primary determinant in structuring the nature of women's participation in the workforce and female staff turnover is more related to their insecure working conditions than to their individual characteristics. In this study, almost all of the women working seasonally in hotels wanted permanent employment and its associated benefits of social security and retirement payment. They were denied this as a result of a number of factors including the insecurity of the tourism labour market, a lack of investment in the sector and the limited employment capacity of tourism businesses as a result of the industry's seasonality. All of these – in combination with the familial ideology which assigns women to the private domain of home – force women into the informal tourism sector and drives down the wages paid to them by the larger tourism operators. This picture contrasts sharply with the situation in the family-based handicraft-producing organizations and pensions, where all the women performed unpaid work which they described as 'helping' their husbands. As married women they considered that they should be alongside their husbands in times of prosperity and hardship and perceived their labour not as work which should be remunerated but as 'help' for the benefit of their families – done as one of the requirements of marriage.

Gender-based Work Segregation and the Division of Labour

The study identified gender-based horizontal and vertical segregation in all the larger-scale tourism-related businesses in the region. Typically, in the hotels, women were concentrated in the housekeeping department as unskilled cleaners, whilst the more educated ones were employed in the front office as receptionists. In contrast, men typically worked as skilled or semi-skilled workers in food production, maintenance and repair services and security, whilst the food and beverage department was exclusively the domain of women. In the restaurants, local women tended to work as unskilled cleaners, whilst the men were employed as cooks and waiters alongside waitresses who were usually young and single tourism students from other regions of Turkey. In the carpet-weaving enterprise, of the 75 female employees over 86% worked in the production department, whilst most (95%) of the 125 male staff worked in the marketing department with a small number of female secretaries. In the small pottery and onyx processing workshops, the men were the master craftsmen who transformed the raw material into products, whilst the women were responsible for the product decoration and painting and for the retail sale operations.

Such gender-based horizontal segregation is typical of much tourism employment worldwide, as is the vertical gender-based segregation which also characterizes these organizations in the Cappadoccia. This study shows that women were not employed in the higher levels of the businesses and that it is men who hold the responsible positions in the hotels, restaurants, large carpet-weaving establishments and workshops as managers and owner-managers. Even in the hotel housekeeping departments – where the female employees were concentrated – only one woman occupied a management position. In all the other hotels in the study, the highest positions women occupied were housekeeping supervisors or in front-office and reception jobs. Even in the large carpet-weaving establishment (where women predominate), only five women were supervisors and instructors, whilst a male manager supervised these skilled supervisors as well as the other semi-skilled female weavers.

It emerges from the study that the allocation of men and women to particular jobs in the larger tourism-related businesses is done on the basis of attributing certain characteristics to both the jobs and each gender. Typically, men were found to occupy positions as managers, owners, salespersons and technical staff – all jobs which are valued within the organizations. In contrast, women's jobs were typically categorized as unskilled, easy and unimportant since according to managers – and even the women themselves – they perform jobs which are similar to their unpaid domestic work. In this respect, the tourism industry mirrors the general position of Turkish women who work in labour-intensive industries; thus in Turkey, following textiles, those industries which have the highest concentration of female workers are tobacco, food, garments and chemical. Just as in tourism, all these sectors are seen to be 'most suited to women as they are an extension of the work women do at home' (Ecevit, 1986, p. 123). Likewise, cleaning and serving food in hotels and restaurants are commonly defined as women's work and are seen as extensions of women's domestic tasks and responsibilities. Even though female cleaners have skills and do require training, these occupations are not classified as skilled because they are identified with women, whilst at the same time, the association of women with unskilled jobs further devalues women's work. Interestingly, when tasks such as cooking – which are among the primary domestic duties of women – are performed in hotels and restaurants by men, they are taken seriously and classified as skilled jobs. In such ways are the male and female labour forces differentially valued, classified and rewarded in the larger tourism businesses.

In the family-based small organizations (such as pensions and dwellings where bibelots are produced for sale to tourists), there was a division of labour between spouses in the production process and a detailed examination of the four pensions sampled in the study reveals that whilst two were run by both paid-workers and unpaid family members, the other two operated on the unpaid labour of wives. The first pension, operated by a husband and wife couple in Avanos, has six rooms with 16 beds. Both spouses are retired teachers and they divide their labour so that the husband deals with the pension's management, booking, accounting and servicing, whilst his wife is responsible for the cooking, cleaning and shopping with the unpaid help of a 14-year-old boy from a poor, rural family who works throughout the tourism season (from April until early September or October) in return for which the couple pay his school expenses. The second pension is larger – with 12 rooms and 45 beds and relies on a wife who works as an unpaid family worker responsible for the cooking, whilst two women are employed seasonally to undertake the cleaning.

The third pension – with ten rooms and 30 bed capacity – operates in Avanos with two paid seasonal female cleaners and the owner's wife and two sons as unpaid family workers. While the owner's wife prepares the meals, the two sons (aged 18 and 23), regarded as its future operators, deal with service activities and assist their father who manages their pocket money in return of their help in the pension. Finally, the fourth pension – this time in Ürgüp – has eight rooms with 20 beds and is operated by a husband and wife, together with their two sons and two daughters-in-law. Here again, there is a clear division of labour based on gender, with men dealing with the managerial, service and technical affairs, whilst the three women cooked and cleaned. Such a gendered division of labour was also apparent in the four small bibelot-producing workshops investigated in the study. Located in the producers' homes, these were operated by husband-and-wife couples and while the husbands bought the raw materials from dealers, bargained with traders and produced the raw bibelots, painting them and arranging them for retail was the responsibility of their wives.

It seems as though, just like the larger tourism-related businesses, the region's family-run businesses also reinforce traditional gender-based divisions of labour so that men take responsibility for the management of the business and any external negotiations whilst women contribute their unpaid domestic labour. Although it emerges that whilst women are under the control of their husbands, young men are also under the control of their fathers; young men's rewards for working in these family-run establishments are very different from their mothers' or wives'. In pensions, most of the day-to-day work is carried out by women, including tasks such as cooking and serving meals, cleaning rooms, providing tea or coffee during the day, doing the laundry and shopping for food whilst the men engage in activities such as negotiating room prices and for those services provided by the female household members. However, whilst the women work as unpaid family workers, the owners' sons – whose pocket money was managed by their fathers – clearly regarded themselves as future owners of these establishments. In contrast, as Scott (1997) has argued elsewhere, women's rewards for working in their own family-run accommodation businesses are merely an increase in domestic work, longer working hours and a decline in opportunities for social interaction with their neighbours and kin. Clearly, in these family establishments, the overlapping roles and responsibilities of work and family are closely tied to traditional expectations and responsibilities associated with gender roles and the continuing position of men as providers and of women as homemakers (despite their obvious contributions to the success of the businesses) reinforce the myths of separate worlds.

Women, Social Control, Capitalism and Patriarchy

One of the key characteristics of tourism is that it is a highly labour-intensive industry and thus one of the main ways in which employers can increase their profits is to reduce labour costs by lowering wages. Taken in combination with the fact that Turkey is a society where women's social status is determined mainly by customs, traditions and religion, this means that women's main role as homemakers and men's roles as breadwinners are often used by employers to justify paying women lower wages relative to men (Ecevit, 1991). In other words, although many working women are the sole wage earners in their families, their low wage levels are justified by their assumed dependence on men who are supposed to support them. In this study, it was found that except in the state-owned first-class motel and the five-star hotel (which had collective bargaining through trade unions) staff wage levels in the accommodation sector were set by the establishments' managers and were open to their subjective judgements. In the craft workshops the female weavers' wages were determined by the price and the number of the knots they tied each day for the carpets. This piecework payment (instead of a weekly or monthly wage) is justified by the employers on the basis that it produces a harder working and thus more productive workforce.

Traditionally workers would look to trade or employee unions to uphold their interests, but the hospitality industry has a low rate of unionization across the world (Hennesy, 1994; Sinclair, 1997). This is principally a result of the high numbers of part-time and seasonal workers in the sector, both of which are traditionally difficult to unionize and organize. Such workers are often denied the same employment rights enjoyed by full-time staff and they may consider it less worthwhile to join a union for a limited period of time (Urry, 1990). In addition, a number of studies have shown that in Turkey, although women are concentrated in certain manufacturing industries such as weaving, food processing and metallurgical industries and in service industries, especially education, banking, accommodation and entertainment (Toksöz, 1998), they are less unionized than men, only constituting 9% of all Turkish trade union members (Ecevit, 2000).

As was mentioned above, the only workers in this study who were trade union members worked in the five-star hotel and the state-owned first class motel. In the five-star hotel 84% of the male (137) and 61% of the female staff (23) were trade union members, although none of the seasonal workers was unionized. In the state-owned first class motel all personnel – whether full-time or seasonal – were trade union members. However, although all the female employees were trade union members none of the women interviewed in this study participated in union activities. This lack of participation was the result of three factors – the women's familial obligations, the negative attitudes of their managers and their own lack of commitment to the trade union. Most of the women believed that trade unions are not interested in any of their problems, with the exception of wage regulations, a finding which endorses other studies of female trade union membership patterns in Turkey (Eser, 1997; Koray, 1999). Such studies suggest that the trade unions are insensitive towards female employees' problems and in particular, fail to support them their struggles against sex segregation, for a fairer distribution of jobs, for more childcare facilities and for work-based training (Ecevit, 1991). This insensitivity towards women's problems make trade unions unattractive for even young single women who might otherwise be prepared to become active union members.

Taken as a whole therefore, a number of key issues emerge from the study. First, across the board women's wages are depressed relative to their male counterparts; second, women who work in larger organizations in the tourism sector generally have better working conditions as they operate under the aegis of labour legislation; third, in labour-intensive sectors such as tourism and the related craft establishments, wages account for a significant proportion of production costs and the control of wages is seen as central to increased productivity and work quality; and finally, that 'gender identity is [also] crucial' (Ecevit, 1991, p. 68) in determining horizontal and vertical labour divisions with the tourism and tourism-related sector. As we have seen, even in those departments and businesses where women form the majority of the workforce, most supervisors and line managers are men, who are seen to exhibit attributes and characteristics (such as aggression) which are considered appropriate for management responsibilities.

A further dimension to the position of women employees in tourism-related businesses in Turkey is their 'invisibility'. By this I mean that, in establishments like hotels where recruitment depends on informal relations, the owners or managers practise 'control' over their female employees by rendering them invisible, particularly to the external world. In Turkey, there is considerable social control over a woman's sexuality since this control is seen as not belonging to the woman herself. Thus many individuals see themselves as directly responsible for policing women's sexual behaviour, including not only parents and brothers, but also relatives and neighbours who actively scrutinize adolescent girls' behaviour (Kandiyoti, 1997). This is translated into the tourism context so that, many male accommodation operators not only strictly control their wives' and daughters' interactions with customers but also monitor the behaviour of single Turkish female guests staying in their pensions: whilst a Turkish man may rent a room for one or more nights with his foreign girlfriend, a single Turkish woman could not do the same and would even have to observe a curfew set by the pension owner for returning to the room at night.

Tucker (1997, p. 113), in her study in Göreme – a district of the Cappadoccia region – argues that 'tourists never have contact with Turkish women and the interaction with tourists is strictly the domain of men'. Whilst this is true in many instances, it should also be pointed out that young (and often attractive) Turkish women are also favoured for some jobs such as hotel receptionists which require intensive interactions with both local and foreign men. However, in such circumstances, both the employers themselves and the women's male co-workers consider that they have a key role in reinforcing the women's sexual identity and policing their sexual conduct. In the small enterprises in the study, especially in the accommodation and restaurant businesses, employers exercised strict control over their female staff. Moreover, whilst young local waiters worked alongside women in restaurants, these were not local waitresses but young, single tourism students from outside the region who were working to gain experience and to earn money for their school expenses. The hotel managers explained that the lack of local women working as waitresses in their restaurants was due to the attitude of their families. Despite living in hardship, they did not allow their daughters to work as waitresses as they thought that a mixed gender workplace would inevitably lead to sexual and emotional liaisons between staff. Other restaurant managers also suggested that the customer interactions necessary for waiting on tables were unsuitable for women as such service situations had connotations attached to the role of a hostess and were thus perceived to be associated with prostitution. Given these perceptions it is not surprising that women do not tend to work in restaurants in Turkey. Moreover, such attitudes also illustrate the complex relationship between sexuality, the construction of women's position in society and workplace practices and interactions.

It is also interesting that opposition to the employment of women as waitresses comes not only from their families and employers but also from their male co-workers. Several of the waitresses interviewed in this study said that they had experienced hostility from male colleagues as a result of the competition caused by tipping. Such competition between the waiters and waitresses is also overlain and complicated by the existing patriarchal ideology.

The Private Lives of Working Women

Whilst this study has so far focused on workplace practices, such an exploration would not be complete without a discussion of family dynamics since the interdependence of work and family is closely tied to expectations and responsibilities associated with gender roles. Thus, as we have seen, the traditional view of men as providers and of women as homemakers reinforces the myth of separate worlds. The study found that the division of labour among family members in the region follows traditional arrangements. Thus, the women shoulder the major burden for running the household: 80% of married women stated that their husbands did not share responsibility for any household chores other than paying the bills. This was true even in the households of women who worked at higher levels in organizations and in pensions where the wives' labour was crucial to the businesses' operation: clearly, a woman's entry into the workforce does nothing to alter her domestic burdens and responsibilities. Perhaps the most important domestic responsibility for working women, however, is childcare. In this study, over 80% of working women had children over pre-school age, whilst a further 17% had children under 6 years and thus needed their relatives' support as there are no childcare facilities in the women's workplaces. However, with the help of female relatives and neighbours, childcare does not seem a very salient issue for working women, although of course, child-rearing necessarily disrupts their participation in the labour market. Moreover, as earlier studies (Abadan-Unat, 1982; Duben, 1982) have noted, solving the childcare problem in this manner also reinforces the informal sector support systems, strengthens traditional family patterns and the gender-based division of labour.

Interestingly, many of the women in the study commented that employed wives had more familial power than full-time homemakers, not only in terms of financial decision making (see Vaydanoff, 1987), but also in decisions concerning women's employment, their physical mobility, their children, purchasing decisions and decisions concerning invitations for relatives, friends and others. However, notwithstanding this, the study also found that women still have less power relative to men. Whilst the men did not always share in some decisions which are traditionally considered the women's domain (such as hosting visitors), they continue to dominate in making important decisions over matters such as women's employment, physical mobility, children's education and marriages, expenditure on furniture and on other larger items. Thus, whilst the opportunities created by tourism development in the region has increased the number of women in the workforce and a growing number of families have come to rely on the contributions of working women to maintain an adequate living standard, many of the single women could not spend their salaries freely and almost all of the salaried working women contributed to a family budget, only reserving a small proportion of their wages for themselves. Significantly, much of these women's salaries help to pay for their families' cars, trucks and houses – all of which are registered to their husbands due to their commitment to the popularly held belief that everything in married life is held in common.

One of the key benefits of working outside the home, however, for the women springs from the social aspects of their work environment and the self-confidence, friendship and sense of belonging which this provides. In contrast those who work at home who spoke of their feelings of isolation, almost all the women working outside the home pointed out that their work environments provide opportunities for social interaction and that their status as wage-earners (whatever their wage levels) had a positive impact on their perceptions of self and their outlook on the world. While most of the women commented that they did not enjoy their working conditions, they did attach social and psychological value to their working lives and derive considerable work satisfaction. Thus, this study endorses the findings of Özgen and Ufuk (1998, p. 286) who have commented that 'social relationships within the workforce are one of the most important factors regarding work satisfaction of women'. It seems, therefore, that whilst women's traditional familial roles remain strong, many of those in this study derived significant self-confidence from working outside the home, many saying that it reduced their sense of isolation and some commenting that their status as contributory or even sole wage-earners in the family enabled them to respond to their husbands' domestic violence.

Conclusion

This study has explored the changing patterns of women's employment in Cappadoccia as a result of the expansion of the region's tourism industry since the 1980s. Although such employment has been seen to offer significant benefits to women's lives, it also emerges that the structure and characteristics of tourism in the region, together with the continuation of traditional gendered roles, denies women access to the labour market on the same terms as men. The larger commercial tourism employers tend to allocate women jobs based on their gender-ascribed characteristics and supposed personality traits. Such patriarchal control dictates that men are much more likely to be employed as managers, owners and sales or technical staff and their jobs are considered more valuable to the running of the organization. Likewise within family-run organizations, if jobs can be arbitrarily described as skilled or unskilled, difficult or easy and important or unimportant, it is always the women's jobs which are categorized as unskilled, easy and unimportant since they tend to replicate their domestic duties. At the same time, whilst educational level is a determinant of the type of jobs available to women, they tend to be recruited into those areas where there are less advancement opportunities. Women are ghettoized into departments which utilize their traditional domestic skills and thus employers can justify not offering training programmes and thereby further reduce their training costs. Moreover, the study suggests that increased opportunities to work as paid employees outside the home (often below the minimum wage level and without any job security) has also done little to fundamentally alter the domestic power balance. Women are not decision makers in important familial issues, they are not property-owners, their mobility remains strictly controlled by their husbands and they have little time or money to spend on leisure activities. What working outside the home (instead of working as unpaid workers in family-run businesses) does offer many women, however, is as paid social interaction with other women and a considerable amount of self-esteem. Thus, whilst paid employment in the tourism sector has increased the burden of the 'double shift', the separation of family life and workplace has also brought psychological and social benefits to these women in the Cappadoccia region, as elsewhere in Turkey.

References

Abadan-Unat, N. (1982) Social change and Turkish women. In: Abadan-Unat, N. (ed.) *Women in Turkish Society*. E.S. Brill, Leiden, The Netherlands.

Ansal, H. (1995) Çalışma Hayatında Cinsiyetçilik ve 1980lerde Türk Sanayiinde Ücretli Kadın Emeğinin Değişen Konumu. *Toplum ve Bilim*. 66, Bahar, 17–66.

Chant, S. (1997) Gender and tourism employment in mexico and the Philippines. In: Sinclair, M.T. (ed.) *Gender, Work and Tourism*. Routledge, London.

Duben, A. (1982) The significance of family and kinship in urban Turkey. In: Kağıtçıbaşı, Ç. (ed.) *Sex Roles, Family and Community in Turkey*. Indiana University, Turkish Studies 3.

Ecevit, Y. (1986) An analysis of the concentration of women wage workers in Turkish manufacturing industries. *Women, Family and Social Change in Turkey*. UNESCO, Bangkok.

Ecevit, Y. (1991) Shop floor control: the ideological construction of Turkish women factory workers'. In: Redclift, N. and Sinclair, M.T. (eds) *Working Women: International Perspectives on Labor and Gender Ideology*. Routledge, London.

Ecevit, Y. (1992) Türkiye'de Kadın İşgücünün Marjinalliği. *Bülten Dergisi*. Türk Demokrasi Vakfı Yayın Organı, Nisan, Sayı:11, 15–34.

Ecevit, Y. (2000) Çalışma Yaşamında Kadın Emeğinin Kullanımı ve Kadın Erkek Eşitliği. *Kadın-Erkek Eşitliğine Doğru Yürüyüş: Eğitim, Çalışma Yaşamı ve Siyaset*. TÜSİAD-T/2000-12/290, İstanbul, Türkiye.

Eraydin, A. (1999) *Yeni Üretim Süreçleri ve Kadın Emeği*. T.C. Baş bakanlık Kadının Statüsü re Sorunları Genel Müdürlüğü, Ankara, Türkiye.

Eser, Ş. (1997) *Part-time Çalışmanın Türkiye'de Kadın İstihdamına Etkisi*. T.C. Başbakanlık Aile Araştırma Kurumu Yayınları, Ankara, Türkiye.

Göğüş-Tan, M. (2000) Eğitimde Kadın-Erkek Eşitliği ve Türkiye Gerçeği. *Kadın-Erkek Eşitliğine Doğru Yürüyüş: Eğitim, Çalışma Yaşamı ve Siyaset*. TÜSİAD-T/2000-12/290, İstanbul, Türkiye.

Hennesy, S. (1994) Female employment in south-west England. In: Kinnaird, V. and Hall, D. (eds) *Tourism: A Gender Analysis*. Wiley, Chichester, UK.

Kağıtçıbaşı, Ç. (1982) Sex roles, value of children and fertility in Turkey. In: Kağıtçıbaşı, Ç. (ed.) *Sex Roles, Family and Community in Turkey*. Indiana University, Turkish Studies 3.

Kandiyoti, D. (1997) *Cariyeler, Bacılar, Yurttaşlar*. Metis Kadın Araştırmaları Yayınları, İstanbul, Türkiye.

Koray, M. (1999) *Gıda İşkolunda Çalışan Kadınların Koşulları ve Geleceği*. T.C. Başbakanlık Kadın Statüsü ve Sorunları Genel Müdürlüğü, Ankara, Türkiye.

Leontidou, L. (1994) Gender dimensions of tourism in Greece: employment, subcultures and restructuring. In: Kinnaird, V. and Hall, D. (eds) *Tourism: A Gender Analysis*. Wiley, Chichester, UK.

Long, H.V. and Kindon, S.L. (1997) Gender and tourism development in Balinese villages. In: Sinclair, M.T. (ed.) *Gender, Work and Tourism*. Routledge, London.

Ministry of Tourism (1993) *Manpower Survey of the Hotel and Tourism Industry*, Ministry of Tourism/ILO, Turkey, Ankara.

Özgen, Ö. and Ufuk, H. (1998) Kadınların Evde Gerçekleştirdikleri Girişimcilik Faaliyetlerinin Aile Yaşamına Etkisi. In: Çitçi, O. (ed.) *20. Yüzyılın Sonunda Kadınlar ve Gelecek*. TODAIE, Ankara, Türkiye.

Purcell, K. (1997) Women's employment in UK tourism: gender roles and labor markets. In: Sinclair, M.T. (ed.) *Gender, Work and Tourism*. Routledge, London.

Scott, J. (1997) Chances and choices: women in Northern Cyprus. In: Sinclair, M.T. (ed.) *Gender, Work and Tourism*. Routledge, London.

Sinclair, M.T. (1997) Issues and theories of gender and work in tourism. In: Sinclair, M.T. (ed.) *Gender, Work and Tourism*. Routledge, London.

State Institute of Statistics (2000) *Household Labor Survey: Turkey*, Ankara, State Institute of Statistics.

Toksöz, G. (1998) Türkiye'de Sendikal Kadın Kimliği. In: Çitçi, O. (ed.) *20. Yüzyılın Sonunda Kadınlar ve Gelecek*. TODAIE, Ankara, Türkiye.

Tosun, C. (1998) Local Community Participation in the Tourism Development Process: The Case of Ürgüp in Turkey. Unpublished PhD thesis. The Scottish Hotel School. University of Strathclyde, UK.

Tucker, H. (1997) The ideal village: interactions through tourism in central Anatolia. In: Abram, S., Waldren, J. and Macleod, D.V.L. (eds) *Tourists and Tourism: Identifying with People and Places*. Beng, Oxford.

Urry, J. (1990) *The Tourist Gaze: Leisure and Travel in Contemporary Societies*. Sage, London.

Vaydanoff, P. (1987) *Work and Family Life*. Sage, Beverly Hills, California.

Index